The Es

Selected Writings & Speeches

The Essential Douglass

Selected Writings & Speeches

Edited, with an Introduction, by

Nicholas Buccola

Hackett Publishing Company, Inc.
Indianapolis/Cambridge

23 22 21 20   2 3 4 5 6 7

For further information, please address
   Hackett Publishing Company, Inc.
   P.O. Box 44937
   Indianapolis, Indiana 46244-0937

   www.hackettpublishing.com

Cover design by Deborah Wilkes
Interior design by Elizabeth L. Wilson
Composition by Aptara, Inc.

Library of Congress Cataloging-in-Publication Data
Names: Douglass, Frederick, 1818-1895. | Buccola, Nicholas, editor.
Title: Frederick Douglass : the essential Douglass : selected writings &
   speeches / edited, with an introduction, by Nicholas Buccola.
Description: Indianapolis : Hackett Publishing Company, 2016. |
   Includes bibliographical references and index.
Identifiers: LCCN 2015035371 | ISBN 9781624664533 (pbk.) |
   ISBN 9781624664540 (cloth)
Subjects: LCSH: Douglass, Frederick, 1818–1895. | African American
   abolitionists—Biography. | Slaves—United States—Biography. |
   Antislavery movements—United States—History—19th century. | African
   Americans—History—Sources. | African American orators. | Speeches,
   addresses, etc., American—African American authors.
Classification: LCC E449.D75 A25 2016 | DDC 973.8092—dc23
LC record available at http://lccn.loc.gov/2015035371

Contents

PART III. DOUGLASS REFLECTS ON THE IMPENDING CRISIS

PART IV. DOUGLASS ON SECESSION AND CIVIL WAR

PART V. REFLECTIONS OF AN "OLD WATCHMAN ON THE WALLS OF LIBERTY": DOUGLASS AFTER THE CIVIL WAR

Acknowledgments

The preparation of this volume has been a labor of love, but much of the labor has been tedious. I would not have been able to complete this project without the work of many others. First, I must express my gratitude for the work done by previous editors of Douglass' writings and speeches. Beginning in the 1950s, the historian Philip S. Foner began publishing a series of volumes of Douglass' writings and speeches under the title *The Life and Writings of Frederick Douglass*.[1] The five volumes of *Life and Writings* were published over the course of twenty-five years, with the first volume coming out in 1950 and the last volume coming out in 1975. Foner's collection has long been out of print, but it played a vital role in getting Douglass' writings into the hands of many scholars and students over several decades. Beginning in 1979, Yale University Press began publishing the first heavily annotated, scholarly edition of Douglass' speeches under the title *The Frederick Douglass Papers: Series One—Speeches, Debates, and Interviews*, with the historian John W. Blassingame serving as series editor.[2] From 1979 to 1992, Yale published five volumes in *Series One* and these papers remain the go-to source for Douglass scholars. Four of the five volumes in *Series One* of the *Douglass Papers*, though, are also out of print.[3] The work of Blassingame and his colleagues, though, has been instrumental in preserving Douglass' body of work and in clarifying when and where he said and did the many things he said and did over his nearly six decades in public life.

Without the work of these scholars, it would have been next to impossible to produce a book like *The Essential Douglass*. Even with the wonderful foundation established by these scholars, the creation of this volume was tremendously challenging. This was, though, a challenge that needed to be met. Frederick Douglass was one of the most important figures of the nineteenth century, and we were driven by the conviction that his essential writings ought to be made available in an edition that is reasonable in size and price.[4] With

---

1. Philip S. Foner, ed., *The Life and Writings of Frederick Douglass*, 5 Vols. (New York: International Publishers, 1950).
2. John W. Blassingame, ed., *The Frederick Douglass Papers—Series One: Speeches, Debates, and Interviews* (New Haven: Yale University Press, 1979–1992).
3. It is, indeed, next to impossible for even university libraries to acquire copies of *Series One* (with the exception of Volume 4, which is available for purchase for well over 100 dollars). The *Douglass Papers* project continues to publish scholarly editions of Douglass' writings, with *Series Two* focused on his autobiographical writings and *Series Three* focused on his letters.
4. In 1999, Yuval Taylor did a great service by bringing some of Foner's work back into print

Douglass' essential writings dispersed in his three autobiographies and untold numbers of speeches, letters, and essays published in nineteenth-century newspapers and tucked away in archives, the creation of the book you hold in your hands required many, many hours and many eyes to check and recheck the accuracy of selections. My professional home is on the wonderful campus of Linfield College, which is an idyllic residential college nestled in the heart of Oregon's Willamette Valley. As a liberal arts college professor, I am blessed with many things, but a small army of graduate student collaborators is not one of them. Instead, I have the opportunity to collaborate with outstanding undergraduates on my research endeavors, and a number of these collaborators did invaluable work on this project. Maggie Hawkins, Caleb Snodgrass, Michael O'Neil, and Erin Bonzer put in many hours tracking down the selections in the volume and getting them into a form that could be easily edited. Hannah Roberts took the lead in this part of the project, and the fact that she had the organizational skills to do all that she did on this project during her freshman year is simply amazing. Jillaine Cook brought her considerable skills as a historian to bear on the footnotes and the introduction to the volume. Finally, among the student collaborators, I must single out Ellie Forness for special attention. Ellie participated in the early stages of this project, then made her way to Washington, DC, for a semester away from campus. Upon her return, she resumed work on the project and took on the tremendous challenge of tying up remaining editorial loose ends, and, in a process neither of us will miss, she worked with me to check all of the selections for accuracy against scans of the original nineteenth-century texts and newspapers. This was among the most arduous phases of the project, but we believe it was well worth it.

I am also indebted to many of my colleagues. Dawn Nowacki, Patrick Cottrell, and Dimitri Kelly are all one could possibly want in departmental colleagues. Susan Barnes Whyte, Barbara Valentine, and Rich Schmidt in Linfield's Nicholson Library provided crucial assistance that enabled us to track down the original sources we needed for this project. Susan McWilliams, Jack Turner, and several anonymous reviewers provided valuable input on this collection. I am especially grateful to Jack for pushing me to devote plenty of attention to Douglass' post-Civil War writings, which are all too often neglected. Lunch with David Blight at the Southern Festival of Books rekindled my enthusiasm for Douglass and got me thinking again about the need for a collection of his essential writings. Peter C. Myers knows more about Frederick Douglass than just about anyone in the world, and I have been lucky enough to have him

---

through the publication of an abridged version of the *Life and Writings* under the title, *Frederick Douglass: Selected Speeches and Writings*. Taylor's collection, though nearly eight hundred pages long, is missing several of Douglass' most important writings and speeches, and it is nearly 40 dollars.

read and comment on both my Douglass monograph, *The Political Thought of Frederick Douglass*, and this collection. A typical "reader report" (in my experience, at least) is about two pages. When I have been fortunate enough to have Pete as a reader, he has produced reader reports more to the tune of a dozen pages (single spaced!). This may say something about the quality of my drafts that Pete has been asked to review, but it also says something about his exceptional seriousness and generosity as a scholar. Pete's comments are always wise and constructive, and my work on Douglass has been vastly improved by his insights. The volume you hold in your hands is far better than it would have been had it not spent some time on Pete's desk.

Deborah Wilkes of Hackett Publishing Company has been incredibly supportive, enthusiastic, and patient. I am very grateful to her and to Hackett for making this book a reality.

I am also indebted to my mom, Kathy, and my dad, Tony, for providing me with so much love and inspiration. My wife, Emily, and my daughter, Luna, remind me every day how lucky I am. I am grateful to the rest of my family and my friends for their encouragement and support over the years I was working on this project.

Nicholas Buccola
Linfield College
August 14, 2015

A Note on Texts

I have tried to stay faithful to the titles of the selections as they appeared when they were originally published. In the instances when they were published with general titles like "Remarks of Frederick Douglass," I have added the topic in brackets (e.g., "Remarks of Frederick Douglass [on the Emancipation Proclamation]"). Readers familiar with *The Life and Writings of Frederick Douglass* and *The Frederick Douglass Papers* should note that both Philip S. Foner and John W. Blassingame occasionally changed or created titles in their collections of Douglass' writings. When a selection has been previously published with multiple titles, I have tried to make note of this so as to avoid confusion for readers. Most of the selections appear in their entirety. When a selection was edited for length, cuts are noted with ellipses. Because this collection is intended for classroom use and for lay readers of American history, I have tried to keep the notes minimal. At the beginning of each selection, the reader will find a footnote with a very brief introduction to the selection. Throughout each selection, brief notes were added to identify various individuals, quotations, and events that would, in my judgment and the judgment of reviewers of this collection, be helpful to the reader.

Finally, a word must be said about the selection process. In order to keep this volume to a reasonable length that would be suitable for classroom use, we have had to make some painful choices. With a writer as versatile and skilled as Douglass, it is a difficult task to separate the "essential" from the "inessential." I have tried, though, to make cuts in a way that minimizes repetition and provides the reader with a good sense of Douglass' thinking on a variety of topics during all of the eras of his nearly six decades in public life. One cannot help but wince at the thought of some of the selections (e.g., his speech on *The Civil Rights Cases*) left on the editing room floor, but such editorial sins will be forgiven by the gods of letters if the reader is inspired by this volume to seek more Douglass to read beyond what is contained here.

Time Line of the Life of Frederick Douglass

1818   Born "Frederick Augustus Washington Bailey" in Tuckahoe, Maryland

1818–1826   Lives on various plantations in rural Maryland

1826–1833   Lives in Baltimore, Maryland (with relatives of his owner, Thomas Auld)

1833   Sent back to live with Thomas Auld in rural Maryland

1834–1835   Sent by Thomas Auld to work on the farm of Edward Covey

1836   Sent back to live in Baltimore, Maryland; "hired out" to work in shipyard

1838   Escapes from slavery in conspiracy with Anna Murray (a free black woman he met in 1837); changes name to "Frederick Douglass"

1838–1841   Marries Anna Murray; settles in New Bedford, Massachusetts; begins family and begins working in shipyard

1841–1845   Meets William Lloyd Garrison, editor of *The Liberator*; invited by Garrison to become an agent of the Massachusetts Anti-Slavery Society; travels the country lecturing against slavery

1845–1847   Publishes *Narrative of the Life of Frederick Douglass, An American Slave, Written by Himself*; travels through England, Ireland, and Scotland on lecture tour; British abolitionists raise funds to purchase Douglass' freedom from Thomas Auld in 1846

1847–1851   Returns to the United States and begins process of relocating family to Rochester, New York; begins publishing his own anti-slavery newspaper, *The North Star*; continues to lecture in favor of abolition and other progressive causes

1851   Changes name of newspaper to *Frederick Douglass' Paper*

1852–1858   Continues work as writer, orator, and newspaper editor; publishes second autobiography, *My Bondage and My Freedom*, in 1855; begins publication of *Douglass' Monthly*

1859–1860   Implicated in John Brown's raid on federal arsenal at Harpers Ferry; flees to Canada to avoid arrest; embarks on lecture tour of United Kingdom

1861–1862   Writes and speaks in favor of the Union cause in the Civil War; criticizes Lincoln administration's rhetoric and policy

1863   Celebrates the Emancipation Proclamation as turning point in the meaning of the war; meets with President Abraham Lincoln at the White House to discuss the treatment of black soldiers

1864   Meets with President Lincoln again to discuss war strategy and possible role in Union war effort; endorses Lincoln's reelection

1865–1869   Continues work as writer and orator in order to promote the cause of Reconstruction and equal civil rights

1870   Moves to Washington, DC, and begins work editing a weekly newspaper called *The New Era* (later changed to *The New National Era*)

1871   Accepts appointment offered by President Ulysses S. Grant to be on commission investigating the annexation of Santo Domingo

1872–1876   Continues work as writer, editor, and orator; campaigns vigorously for Republican candidates around the country

1877   President Rutherford B. Hayes appoints Douglass to be US marshal for the District of Columbia

1881   Publishes third autobiography, *The Life and Times of Frederick Douglass*; appointed by President James Garfield to be recorder of deeds for the District of Columbia

1882   Wife, Anna Murray, passes away on August 4

1884   Marries Helen Pitts

1884–1889   Travels widely in the United States and abroad; continues speaking, campaigning for Republican candidates; appointed by President Benjamin Harrison to serve as minister resident and consul general to Haiti

1889–1895   Continues to write and speak on behalf of progressive causes; meets many who will rise to positions of leadership in next generation (e.g., Ida Wells and Booker T. Washington)

1895   On February 20, addresses meeting of the National Council of Women in Washington, DC, in the morning, returns home, and dies of natural causes

Introduction

Frederick Douglass was born into slavery as Frederick Augustus Washington Bailey in Tuckahoe, Maryland in February 1818. The first twenty years of his life consisted of "many different forms of the slave experience."[1] While still a child on the plantation of Colonel Edward Lloyd, Douglass witnessed the physical and psychological cruelty at the heart of the institution of slavery. Some examples of the horrific scenes he observed are provided in this volume in his reflections on his "Gradual Initiation to the Mysteries of Slavery" (Selection 1). Later in his childhood, while living in the home of Hugh Auld in Baltimore, he experienced the relative freedom of a "city slave" and occasional humanity on the part of his masters. One especially important occasion of humane treatment is depicted in "Life in Baltimore" (Selection 2), in which Douglass describes the experience of learning to read under the tutelage of Miss Sophia Auld. In "The Last Flogging" (Selection 3), we are provided with Douglass' harrowing and moving account of his life on the farm of the infamous "slave breaker" Edward Covey. Not only does this selection provide us with a profoundly disturbing sense of the physical and existential horrors made possible by the slave system, but, perhaps more importantly, Douglass gives an extraordinarily powerful account of how his resistance to Covey led him to some conclusions about the nature of liberation. At the age of twenty, Douglass (in conspiracy with Anna Murray, a free black woman who would become his wife) escaped from slavery and began to forge a new life and a new identity for himself. Frederick *Bailey*, the slave from Maryland's Eastern Shore, was no more; in his place, Frederick *Douglass* was born.

With his new name and his new wife, Douglass settled in New Bedford, Massachusetts in 1838, where he found work as a laborer. By the time of Douglass' escape, the institution of slavery had existed in North America for nearly two hundred years, and it had grown substantially since the founding of the republic. According to one estimate, "Between 1790 and 1830 the number of slaves in [the United States] increased from approximately 694,280 to roughly 2,000,000, despite federal law that prohibited the importation of African slaves."[2] The growth of slavery in the United States was not, though, without its discontents. During his first few years of freedom, Douglass immersed himself in the writings being produced by the burgeoning movement to abolish slavery. The most prominent voice in this movement was that of William Lloyd

---

1. William S. McFeely, *Frederick Douglass* (New York: W.W. Norton, 1991), 5.
2. C. Bradley Thompson, *Antislavery Political Writings* (Armonk, NY: M.E. Sharpe, 2004), xiii.

Garrison, an activist in Boston who since 1831 had been promoting the cause of abolition in his newspaper, *The Liberator*. In his writings, Garrison espoused a doctrine of "immediate, unconditional, and uncompensated emancipation."[3] In 1841, William C. Coffin, a New Bedford bookkeeper and abolitionist, encouraged Douglass to attend meetings of the Massachusetts Anti-Slavery Society, first in New Bedford and then on the island of Nantucket. At the meeting of the group on the island of Nantucket, Coffin called on Douglass to speak to those assembled about his experiences as a slave. Douglass was prepared for this opportunity. With the acquisition of basic readings skills as a young child as his foundation (described in "Life in Baltimore," Selection 2), Douglass began a lifelong process of self-education. At the age of twelve, he was able to purchase a copy of *The Columbian Orator*, a collection of great speeches that was originally published in 1797.[4] The *Orator* became the young Douglass' constant companion. According to biographer William S. McFeely, "Laboriously, studiously, at first, then fluently, melodically, [Douglass] recited great speeches."[5] On that fateful day on Nantucket in 1841, all of this practice would pay off. When Douglass was called upon to speak to those gathered, the career of one the great orators in American history was launched. Garrison and many of his close associates were there that day, and they were sufficiently impressed to invite Douglass to become an agent of the Massachusetts Anti-Slavery Society. It did not take long for Douglass to emerge as one of the leading spokesmen for this growing movement.

In addition to speaking on behalf of the cause of abolition during the first few years of his public life, Douglass began writing his first autobiography, *Narrative of the Life of Frederick Douglass, an American Slave, Written by Himself*. In 1845, Douglass' *Narrative* was published in Boston, with a preface by Garrison and a prefatory "Letter" by another leading abolitionist, Wendell Phillips. The book has become widely appreciated as a seminal contribution not only to the antislavery tradition but also to the American literary canon. In the *Narrative* as well as his revised and updated autobiographies, *My Bondage and My Freedom* (1855) and *The Life and Times of Frederick Douglass* (1881), he provides vivid and moving accounts of the experiences of slaves and what he called the "moral atmosphere" of slavery.

Soon after the publication of the *Narrative*, Douglass embarked on a lecture tour of the United Kingdom. During this tour, a group of abolitionists raised funds for the purpose of purchasing Douglass' freedom from Mr. Thomas Auld, who still held a legal claim to Douglass as his property. By the end of 1846, for

3. Jonathan D. Glickstein, "William Lloyd Garrison," in *A Companion to American Thought*, ed. Richard Wightman Fox and James T. Kloppenberg (Cambridge: Blackwell, 1995), 264.
4. McFeely, *Frederick Douglass*, 34.
5. Ibid., 34–35.

the sum of $711.66, Douglass' legal freedom was secured.[6] The moral acceptability of this transaction proved to be controversial among the abolitionists, and Douglass took to the pages of *The Liberator* to defend it in an open letter to Henry C. Wright, a vocal critic of compensated emancipation (see Selection 4).

In the late 1840s, Douglass also used the format of the open letter to defend the "morality" of another "transaction": his decision to escape from slavery in the first place. In his now-famous "Letter to My Old Master" (Selection 5), he offers a profound and compelling defense of the idea that each individual is the rightful owner of his or her own body and that there was, therefore, "no wrong" done when he decided to make his "faculties . . . useful to their rightful owner."

These open letters were written during a time of great transition for the country as a whole and for Douglass as an individual. As many Americans migrated westward and questions were raised about the status of slavery in the territories, Douglass was undertaking a migration of his own. While on his lecture tour of Great Britain, several activists pledged financial support for him to start his own abolitionist newspaper.[7] When he returned to the United States in 1847, he began the process of moving from Massachusetts to Rochester, New York, where he would start publishing *The North Star* (which would eventually be renamed *Frederick Douglass' Paper* and then *Douglass' Monthly*). The physical migration from Massachusetts to New York was accompanied by an intellectual migration away from Garrison and his circle of supporters.

With his name moving to the masthead of his own newspaper, Douglass felt it was incumbent upon him to engage in deep and sustained reflection on the morality, politics, strategies, and tactics of abolitionism. Douglass refined his understanding of the proper role of government, and, in perhaps the most important shift in his thinking, his attitude toward the Constitution began to change. Garrison believed that the US Constitution was proslavery and that it was therefore morally unacceptable to participate in the political institutions it authorized. Garrison took this view a step further by embracing the idea of "non-resistance," a doctrine that rejected all use of force and held that "no human government" could be sufficiently righteous to command authority.[8] In New York, Douglass came into closer association with a group of "political abolitionists" (such as Gerrit Smith and William Goodell) who rejected Garrison's proslavery reading of the Constitution and his embrace of non-resistance. While I do not think there is substantial evidence to show Douglass

---

6. McFeely, *Frederick Douglass*, 144–45.
7. Ibid., 147.
8. For more on Garrison's views, see Glickstein, "William Lloyd Garrison," 264.

ever accepted the doctrine of non-resistance, he had considered himself to be a proponent of Garrison's interpretation of the Constitution.

In "The Constitution and Slavery" (Selection 6), we find Douglass defending this view against the antislavery interpretation of the Constitution offered by Smith, Goodell, and others. After much study, thought, and debate, Douglass announced a "Change of Opinion" on the Constitution (Selection 7), holding slavery to be a "system of lawless violence" that "never was lawful, and never can be made so." In "Is Civil Government Right?" (Selection 8), Douglass offered a concise critique of the doctrine of non-resistance (in this case, as articulated by Henry C. Wright). In the place of the pacifist, no-government philosophy of Garrison and Wright, Douglass positioned himself within the great tradition of natural rights thinking (most prominently articulated by the English philosopher John Locke and most famously proclaimed in the American Declaration of Independence). According to this doctrine, all human beings are born with natural rights and the proper role of civil government is to protect those rights. While Garrison, Wright, and others were justified in condemning governments that violated natural rights or permitted the violation of those rights, they were wrong, Douglass argued, to condemn all government. "Righteous" government might be possible, he concluded, if the state played the proper role of protecting the rights of all human beings within its jurisdiction. Such protection, he reminded his pacifist friends, would sometimes require the use of force.

Douglass believed that the natural rights philosophy he defended was expressed admirably in the founding documents of the republic, especially the Declaration of Independence and the preamble to the Constitution. The realities of life in the American republic, though, fell far short of the ideals expressed in these documents. The truths that were asserted to be "self-evident" in 1776 were nowhere to be found in the morally murky legislation of this period. A prime example is the so-called Compromise of 1850, which had been heralded by political leaders such as Henry Clay and Stephen A. Douglas as a great solution to the slavery question. The Compromise allowed the admission of California to the Union as a free state, permitted the territorial legislatures of Utah and New Mexico to legalize slavery, and included a "fugitive slave law" that would bolster the federal (and therefore Northern) role in apprehending fugitive slaves and returning them to their owners in the South.[9]

Douglass utilized his voice and his pen to offer stinging critiques of the corrupt moral and political culture that could produce legislation such as the Compromise of 1850. In 1852, Douglass gave what will forever be known as his best speech and one of the greatest orations ever given in American history.

---

9. For more on the Compromise of 1850 and the Fugitive Slave Law, see John M. Murrin, et al. *Liberty, Equality, Power* (Boston: Cengage, 2008), 349–50.

The Rochester Ladies Anti-Slavery Society invited Douglass to deliver a speech to mark "The Celebration of the National Anniversary." When Douglass arrived at Corinthian Hall in Rochester on July 5, 1852 to deliver his Independence Day oration (Selection 9, which is now known as "What to the Slave Is the Fourth of July?"), it is estimated that almost six hundred people were present. I will let this remarkable address "speak" for itself, but a word must be said on its significance in Douglass' trajectory as a thinker and reformer. In "What to the Slave," we find Douglass playing the role of Old Testament prophet denouncing the hypocrisies of American life while at the same time anchoring himself—and his arguments—in an ardent commitment to American founding principles. It is this combination of biting critique and deep devotion that make this speech such a profound meditation on the nature of patriotism.

Even the limited selection of Douglass' other writings and speeches from this period that are included in this volume reveal his depth and versatility as a thinker and advocate. In "The Fugitive Slave Law" (Selection 10) and "Is It Right and Wise to Kill a Kidnapper?" (Selection 11), we find Douglass defending the righteousness of the use of force in defense of liberty. The only way to make the fugitive slave law a "dead letter," he said in his speech on the subject in 1852, "is to make half a dozen or more dead kidnappers." And in "Claims of the Negro Ethnologically Considered" (Selection 12), we find a remarkable stylistic and substantive contrast to the jeremiad style of "What to the Slave." While in the latter speech, Douglass mocks the idea that the humanity of the slave "remains to be argued," in "Claims of the Negro," he takes up the challenge of offering a rational, empirical demonstration of black humanity. Reading "What to the Slave" alongside "Claims of the Negro" reveals Douglass' philosophical and rhetorical dynamism.

Part III of this volume, "Douglass Reflects on the Impending Crisis," provides the reader with a sense of his responses to the personalities, ideas, and events that dominated the politics of the mid to late 1850s. In 1854, the aforementioned Senator Stephen A. Douglas of Illinois championed a law that effectively repealed the Compromise of 1820, which "admitted Missouri as a slave slate but had banned slavery from the rest of the [Louisiana] Purchase north of 36°30′" and divided the "area in question into two territories: Kansas west of Missouri and Nebraska west of Iowa and Minnesota."[10] Senator Douglas argued that the question of whether or not slavery would be allowed in these territories should be determined by the doctrine of "popular sovereignty." If a majority of the people in Kansas wanted slavery, he argued, they ought to have it. Senator Douglas' Kansas-Nebraska Act and the doctrine of popular sovereignty at its foundation provoked a great deal of consternation for a wide spectrum of Americans opposed to slavery, ranging from moderate Whigs like

10. Ibid., 314.

the Illinois lawyer and politician Abraham Lincoln (whose disdain for the act lit a fire of political ambition that would fuel his journey to the presidency a few years later) to the radical abolitionist John Brown, who made his way to Kansas to participate in the "guerilla war" between proslavery and antislavery forces in the territory.

Somewhere in between Lincoln and Brown, we find Frederick Douglass, who in 1854 traveled to Illinois to offer a damning critique of the Kansas-Nebraska Act, the doctrine of popular sovereignty, and the man he jokingly referred to as his "namesake": Senator Stephen A. Douglas (Selection 13). This speech provides us with a powerful example of how Douglass applied his philosophy of natural rights to the controversies of his time. The doctrine of popular sovereignty, he argued, amounted to little more than a defense of "might makes right" under the guise of "democracy." True democracy, Douglass concluded, is rooted in a commitment to human equality, and such a commitment cannot be squared with any doctrine that would permit the deprivation of natural rights.

During this period of American history, the political party system was undergoing a tremendous transformation. It is beyond my scope to examine this transformation in detail here, but there are a couple of developments worth noting. The Democratic Party was dominated by Southerners and Northern moderates like Stephen A. Douglas, and the Whig Party, the long-time principal rival of the Democrats, was on the decline, while new parties—such as the anti-Immigrant American Party (also known as the Know Nothings), the antislavery Liberty Party, and the Free Soil Party (which was opposed to the extension of slavery into the western territories)—were on the rise.

In the mid-1850s, elements from many of these minor parties began to coalesce under the banner of the new Republican Party. The Republican Party presented a bit of a quandary to radical political abolitionists like Douglass. Most Republicans failed tests of moral and ideological purity on the slavery question, but they seemed to represent the best hope for resisting the growing "slave power." The number of slaves in the United States had nearly doubled since 1830 and there was a growing belief that the "slave power" was tightening its grip on all branches of the federal government. In "What Is My Duty as an Anti-Slavery Voter?" (Selection 14) and "Fremont and Dayton" (Selection 15), the internal struggle Douglas experienced in response to the rise of the Republican Party is palpable. What is the radical reformer supposed to do when faced with imperfect electoral options? These essays reveal the evolution of Douglass' thinking in response to this enduring question.

In 1857, the Supreme Court of the United States made its most bold foray into the debate over slavery in the case *Dred Scott v. Sandford.* The roots of the case were to be found in a legal claim brought by a slave, Dred Scott, who asserted his freedom based on the fact that his owner had taken him from slave territory to free territory. In his inaugural address, delivered just two days before the decision was announced, President James Buchanan "had assured the nation" that the decision "would 'speedily and finally' settle the issue of slavery" in the territories.[11] Historian Xi Wang has provided the following summary of the judgment in this complicated case:

> First, Dred Scott, the slave from St. Louis, Missouri, who had initiated the suit for freedom for himself and his family some eleven years earlier, would continue to remain the property of his alleged owner, John F.A. Sandford. Second, no person of African descent, whether being free or in bondage, could ever be considered a citizen of the United States. Third, the Missouri Compromise of 1820, a federal law that had prohibited slavery from the unorganized territories of the Louisiana Purchase (1803), was unconstitutional because the right to own slave property was guaranteed by the Constitution.[12]

In his speech on "The Dred Scott Decision" (Selection 16), Douglass went beyond merely critiquing the legal reasoning of the court. In addition, he utilized this speech to offer a biting critique of Garrison's call for "no union with slaveholders."[13] In an 1854 speech called "No Compromise with Slavery," Garrison justified his call for the North to secede from the South by saying, "In itself, Slavery has no resources and no strength. Isolated and alone, it could not stand an hour; and, therefore, further aggression and conquest would be impossible."[14] For Garrison, disunion would be the fulfillment of moral duty on the part of the abolitionists; for Douglass, it amounted to a complete abdication of moral responsibility.

The issue of whether or not it was morally acceptable to use force in pursuit of liberation had long preoccupied Douglass. Unlike some of his pacifist colleagues in the abolitionist movement, he seems to have always been committed to the idea that violence can be made righteous if the cause is just. We can trace this view from Douglass' reflections on his fight with Covey (Selection 3) through his justification of civil government (Selection 8) to his explicit endorsement of the use of force in resistance to the fugitive slave law (Selections 10 and 11). Douglass had, furthermore, always been quick to point out that the use of force in opposition to slavery must be understood as self-defense.

---

11. Xi Wang, "The *Dred Scott* Case," in *Race on Trial*, ed. Annette Gordon-Reed (New York: Oxford University Press, 2002), 26.
12. Ibid.
13. See William Lloyd Garrison, "No Compromise with Slavery," in *Against Slavery*, ed. Mason Lowance (New York: Penguin, 2000), 130.
14. Ibid.

After all, he reminded his readers and his audiences, slavery was a system of "lawless violence" and "war begins where reason ends."[15]

In Douglass' mind the "war" over slavery in the United States began as soon as the first slave was brought to the country's shores. New fronts in this war, though, had emerged in the 1850s. In 1856, Congressman Preston Brooks of South Carolina perpetrated a brutal assault on the antislavery senator Charles Sumner of Massachusetts on the floor of the United States Senate.[16] Proslavery and antislavery settlers battled over the fate of the institution in "Bleeding Kansas." As noted above, a radical abolitionist named John Brown had participated in the guerilla warfare there and had become something of a celebrity within the abolitionist movement. Brown developed a close relationship with Douglass and tried (unsuccessfully) to recruit Douglass to participate in his ill-fated raid on the federal arsenal at Harpers Ferry, Virginia.[17] Historian John Stauffer describes the raid in this way:

> On Sunday evening, October 16, 1859, Brown and twenty-one men—sixteen whites and five blacks—invaded the federal arsenal at Harpers Ferry, Virginia. . . . Their plan was to gain control of the arsenal, distribute the cache of weapons to the large population of slaves and free blacks in the area, whom Brown expected to be ready and waiting for him, and incite an insurrection that would spread through the South and result in black freedom.[18]

Things did not go as Brown had planned and on the morning of Tuesday, October 18, the US Marines (led by Robert E. Lee and J. E. B. Stuart) captured Brown and his men. Brown would eventually be executed.[19] Although Douglass did not believe Brown's raid was wise, he did think Brown was worthy of moral defense and praise. In an open letter to the radical journalist and Brown supporter James Redpath (Selection 17), Douglass praises Brown's "principles" and "spotless integrity" and he confesses to having "little hope" that the abolition of slavery would be achieved by "peaceful means." In "The Prospect in the Future" (Selection 18), a short essay published soon after he wrote the letter to Redpath, Douglass elaborates on why he thought the time

---

15. Frederick Douglass, "Reconstruction," in *The Atlantic Monthly*, December 1866.

16. For more on the beating of Sumner, see David Herbert Donald, *Charles Sumner and the Coming of the Civil War* (New York: Knopf, 1960), 266–68.

17. For more on Brown and Douglass, see John Stauffer, *The Black Hearts of Men* (Cambridge: Harvard University Press, 2002). For more information about Brown's attempt to recruit Douglass, see 248–49.

18. Ibid., 237.

19. Douglass himself was implicated as a conspirator in the raid and the governor of Virginia (Henry Wise) attempted to have Douglass arrested. See Stauffer, *Black Hearts of Men*, 249–50.

for "reason and morality" had ended and the time for "courage . . . in defense of liberty" had begun.

And then the war came. In Part IV of this volume, the reader will find several examples of Douglass' reflections on the "Dissolution of the American Union" (Selection 19) and the outbreak of the Civil War. The theme of moral clarity is especially prominent in the selections included from 1862 and 1863 (Selections 20, 21, 22, 23, and 24). In response to the moderation of President Abraham Lincoln, Douglass played the role of radical critic. Where, Douglass asked, is the "moral feeling" in Lincoln's cold and calculated responses to the crisis? It was during this period that we find some of Douglass' most damning criticisms of Lincoln, and it is worthwhile to read these essays alongside his retrospective appreciation of Lincoln expressed in Selection 31. During the Civil War, Douglass had the opportunity to meet with Lincoln at the White House on three different occasions.[20] He came away quite impressed with Lincoln as a man, and, at some point during this period, he gained sufficient confidence in Lincoln's policies that he agreed to encourage African American enlistment in the Union Army. The classic expression of Douglass' recruitment pitch is to be found in "Why Should a Colored Man Enlist?" (Selection 25).

As the Civil War was drawing to a close, Douglass offered his thoughts on what postwar America ought to look like. He hoped that the "new birth of freedom," to borrow Lincoln's wonderful phrase, would be rooted in justice, fair play, and virtue. In "What the Black Man Wants" (Selection 26), Douglass demands "simply *justice*" for all Americans. By this, he meant that the rights of all people to life, liberty, political participation, and the equal opportunity to pursue happiness ought to be protected by a government that treats each individual as equal before the law. Douglass would develop the meaning of fair play in greater detail in later speeches, but in "What the Black Man Wants" we get a preview of what this idea entails. In order to meaningfully exercise one's rights, he concludes, one must have access not only to the "ballot box" and the "jury box" but also to equal opportunities to pursue education and achieve economic security. Finally, the idea of virtue was central to Douglass' postwar vision. In order to achieve personal success and social respectability, he contended in speech after speech, one must practice what we now call "bourgeois virtues" such as hard work, perseverance, reliability, and sobriety.[21]

Douglass lived for another three decades after the conclusion of the Civil War, and he continued his prolific career as a progressive writer, editor, and speaker. In addition, he was appointed to a variety of administrative positions

---

20. See generally, James Oakes, *The Radical and the Republican* (New York: W.W. Norton, 2007).

21. Deirdre McCloskey, *The Bourgeois Virtues* (Chicago: University of Chicago Press, 2010).

by Republican presidents from the early 1870s until the late 1880s. In Part V of this volume, "Reflections of an 'Old Watchman on the Walls of Liberty,'" I have tried to include essays and speeches that capture the four areas that mattered most to Douglass during this period: the quest for racial justice; the recognition of equal rights for women, immigrants, and laborers; the proper understanding of the meaning of the Civil War in American memory; and the promotion of moral excellence.

In "Sources of Danger to the Republic" (Selection 27), "Politics an Evil to the Negro?" (Selection 30), "West India Emancipation" (Selection 32), and "The Nation's Problem" (Selection 33), we find Douglass reflecting on the quest for racial justice in the United States after the Civil War. These essays and speeches span almost two decades, and in these selections we catch glimpses of Douglass' positive vision of what a genuine republic might look like. We also find some of his most powerful indictments of the failure to provide adequate redress and reconstruction for freed slaves after the war. Unfortunately, the forces opposed to Douglass' racial egalitarianism won most of the battles during the last three decades of the nineteenth century. One cannot read these selections without wondering: what if there had been sufficient political will to make policies closer to Douglass' vision of justice and fairness a reality for all Americans?

One of the most remarkable things about Douglass is the capaciousness of his reform agenda. While he is rightfully remembered as *the* great advocate for the rights of African Americans, he always aspired to be much more than that. From the earliest days of his public career until (quite literally) the day he died, Douglass was a fervent advocate for the rights of *all* people. In "Our Composite Nationality" (Selection 28), we find one of his great defenses of ethnic and religious pluralism. In this response to anti-immigrant sentiment against the Chinese, Douglass defended a vision of society in which individuals of various ethnic origins and religious creeds live side by side in an atmosphere of mutual respect.

In "Woman Suffrage Movement" (Selection 29) and his "Address to the Annual Meeting of the New England Woman Suffrage Association" (Selection 36), we find some representative examples of Douglass' deep commitment to the rights of women. He was present (and played an important role in) the famous convention for women's rights held at Seneca Falls in 1848, and from the earliest days of his career he was a staunch believer in the credo: "Right is of no sex." While questions of economic justice are central to many of Douglass' essays and speeches on racial justice, the rights of women, and the rights of immigrants, the essay "The Labor Question" (Selection 30) takes up the issue in a more direct and provocative way. We must never forget, Douglass argues in the essay, that the well-being of "Man," not the well-being of "Property," must be the guiding principle of our "civilization."

In his 1876 "Oration in Memory of Abraham Lincoln" (Selection 31), his 1881 speech on "John Brown" (Selection 33), and his 1882 defense of "Decoration Day" (Selection 34), Douglass concerned himself with the meaning of the long struggle to end slavery. These are three very different speeches, but they fit together because in each Douglass reflects on the lessons we ought to learn from the lives and deaths of Lincoln, Brown, and those who fought in the Civil War. Like his essays and speeches of the secession and Civil War era, Douglass' orations on Lincoln, Brown, and Decoration Day (what we now call "Memorial Day") are marked by one overriding moral conclusion: "there was a right side in the late war." This moral clarity, though, was not without nuance. In his remembrance of Lincoln, Douglass was careful to show the ways in which the sixteenth president failed when viewed from a "genuine abolition ground," while at the same time exhibiting some of the highest virtues of statesmanship. In his reflections on Brown, Douglass acknowledges the morally problematic nature of many of Brown's actions while at the same time defending him as a moral hero. Taken together, these speeches provide a remarkable portrait of Douglass' own reckoning with the meaning of the Civil War.

"It Moves" (Selection 35), "Self-Made Men" (Selection 38), and "Blessings of Liberty and Education" (Selection 39) are speeches that are about many things, but at their core we can find Douglass' explanation of the nature of moral excellence. In "It Moves," Douglass offers deeply philosophical ruminations on the moral responsibility all conscientious individuals have to contribute to efforts to make the world more just. For Douglass, there was no calling higher than the call of progressive reform.

"Self-Made Men" was the speech Douglass delivered more than any other during his long career of oratory.[22] In the speech, he offers a remarkable defense of the idea that each individual has it within his power to make himself (and remake himself). "Self-Made Men" is far more than a feel-good, motivational speech, and it is certainly not a simpleminded defense of a dog-eat-dog doctrine of individualism. Instead, it is a series of profound (and implicitly autobiographical) reflections of a man who had risen from slavery to international prominence and who was well aware that the doctrine of self-reliance was only defensible under conditions of justice and fairness. In the 1894 speech "Blessings of Liberty and Education" (Selection 39), Douglass builds on the understanding of moral excellence developed in "It Moves" and "Self-Made Men" by emphasizing the cultivation of the mind as essential to human flourishing. One cannot truly be free, he told his audience, without being educated.

---

22. See John W. Blassingame, ed. *The Frederick Douglass Papers: Series One*, vol. 5 (New Haven: Yale University Press, 1992), 544–45.

Douglass worried late in life that he would merely be remembered for his remarkable journey from slavery to a position of prominence within the abolitionist movement. While he is certainly most often recalled for his incredible life story, the writings and speeches assembled in this volume remind us that he ought to be remembered for far more than that. Douglass' name, in the words of the historian Philip S. Foner, should be "placed beside the names of Jefferson and Lincoln" as one of the greatest men of our history because, in the words of political theorist Herbert J. Storing, "few men deserve so fully the rank of American statesman."[23] Douglass' enduring relevance is to be found not in the fact that he rose from the depths of slavery to the heights of public life but in what he said and did once he got there.

---

23. Foner, *Life and Writings*, 11; Herbert J. Storing, "Frederick Douglass," in *Toward a More Perfect Union*, ed. Joseph M. Bessette (Washington, DC: AEI Press, 1995), 151.

Select Bibliography

Blassingame, John W., ed. *The Frederick Douglass Papers, Series One: Speeches, Debates, and Interviews.* 5 vols. New Haven, CT: Yale University Press, 1979–1992.

Blassingame, John W., et al. *The Frederick Douglass Papers, Series Two: Autobiographies.* 3 vols. New Haven, CT: Yale University Press, 1999–2012.

Blight, David. *Frederick Douglass' Civil War.* Baton Rouge: Louisiana State University Press, 1989.

Blight, David. *Frederick Douglass: A Life.* New York: Simon and Schuster, forthcoming.

Buccola, Nicholas. *The Political Thought of Frederick Douglass.* New York: New York University Press, 2012.

Foner, Philip S., ed. *The Life and Writings of Frederick Douglass.* 5 vols. New York: International Publishers, 1950–1975.

Gates, Henry Louis, ed. *Frederick Douglass: Autobiographies.* New York: Library of America, 1994.

Lawson, Bill, and Frank Kirkland, eds. *Frederick Douglass: A Critical Reader.* Malden, MA: Blackwell Publishing, 1999.

Martin, Waldo E. *The Mind of Frederick Douglass.* Chapel Hill: University of North Carolina Press, 1984.

McFeely, William S. *Frederick Douglass.* New York: W.W. Norton, 1991.

McKivigan, John., ed. *The Frederick Douglass Papers, Series 3: Correspondence.* Vol. 1. New Haven: Yale University Press, 2009.

Myers, Peter C. *Frederick Douglass: Race and the Rebirth of American Liberalism.* Lawrence: University Press of Kansas, 2008.

Oakes, James. *The Radical and the Republican: Frederick Douglass, Abraham Lincoln, and the Triumph of Antislavery Politics.* New York: W.W. Norton, 2008.

Preston, Dickson J. *Young Frederick Douglass: The Maryland Years.* Baltimore: Johns Hopkins University Press, 1985.

Quarles, Benjamin. *Frederick Douglass.* New York: Perseus Books, 1948.

Roberts, Neil, ed. *A Political Companion to Frederick Douglass.* Lexington: University Press of Kentucky, forthcoming.

Stauffer, John. *Giants: The Parallel Lives of Frederick Douglass and Abraham Lincoln.* New York: Twelve, 2008.

Turner, Jack. *Awakening to Race: Individualism and Social Consciousness in America.* Chicago: University of Chicago Press, 2012.

PART I
THE AUTIOBIOGRAPHY OF A SLAVE

1. "Gradual Initiation to the Mysteries of Slavery," Chapter V of *My Bondage and My Freedom* (New York: Miller, Orton, & Mulligan, 1855)[1]

Although my old master—Capt. Aaron Anthony—gave me at first [. . .] very little attention, and although that little was of a remarkably mild and gentle description, a few months only were sufficient to convince me that mildness and gentleness were not the prevailing or governing traits of his character.[2] These excellent qualities were displayed only occasionally. He could, when it suited him, appear to be literally insensible to the claims of humanity, when appealed to by the helpless against an aggressor, and he could himself commit outrages, deep, dark and nameless. Yet he was not by nature worse than other men. Had he been brought up in a free state, surrounded by the just restraints of free society—restraints which are necessary to the freedom of all its members, alike and equally—Capt. Anthony might have been as humane a man, and every way as respectable, as many who now oppose the slave system; certainly as humane and respectable as are members of society generally. The slaveholder, as well as the slave, is the victim of the slave system. A man's character greatly takes its hue and shape from the form and color of things about him. Under the whole heavens there is no relation more unfavorable to the development of honorable character, than that sustained by the slaveholder to the slave. Reason is imprisoned here, and passions run wild. Like the fires of the prairie, once lighted, they are at the mercy of every wind, and must burn, till they have consumed all that is combustible within their remorseless grasp. Capt. Anthony could be kind, and, at times, he even showed an affectionate disposition. Could the reader have seen him gently leading me by the hand— as he sometimes did—patting me on the head, speaking to me in soft, caressing tones and calling me his "little Indian boy," he would have deemed him a kind old man, and really, almost fatherly. But the pleasant moods of a slaveholder are remarkably brittle; they are easily snapped; they neither come often, nor

---

1. The early chapters of Douglass' autobiographies are full of valuable information about his life and his growing sense of the inhumanity of slavery. This excerpt was chosen because it provides one of Douglass' most powerful descriptions of the physical and psychological cruelty at the core of the institution of slavery.
2. Aaron Anthony was Douglass' first master. He managed Wye House, the plantation of Colonel Edward Lloyd.

remain long. His temper is subjected to perpetual trials; but, since these trials are never borne patiently, they add nothing to his natural stock of patience.

Old master very early impressed me with the idea that he was an unhappy man. Even to my child's eye, he wore a troubled, and at times, a haggard aspect. His strange movements excited my curiosity, and awakened my compassion. He seldom walked alone without muttering to himself; and he occasionally stormed about, as if defying an army of invisible foes. "He would do this, that, and the other; he'd be d—d if he did not," —was the usual form of his threats. Most of his leisure was spent in walking, cursing and gesticulating, like one possessed by a demon. Most evidently, he was a wretched man, at war with his own soul, and with all the world around him. To be overheard by the children, disturbed him very little. He made no more of our presence, than of that of the ducks and geese which he met on the green. He little thought that the little black urchins around him, could see, through those vocal crevices, the very secrets of his heart. Slaveholders ever underrate the intelligence with which they have to grapple. I really understood the old man's mutterings, attitudes and gestures, about as well as he did himself. But slaveholders never encourage that kind of communication, with the slaves, by which they might learn to measure the depths of his knowledge. Ignorance is a high virtue in a human chattel; and as the master studies to keep the slave ignorant, the slave is cunning enough to make the master think he succeeds. The slave fully appreciates the saying, "where ignorance is bliss, 'tis folly to be wise." When old master's gestures were violent, ending with a threatening shake of the head, and a sharp snap of his middle finger and thumb, I deemed it wise to keep at a respectable distance from him; for, at such times, trifling faults stood, in his eyes, as momentous offenses; and, having both the power and the disposition, the victim had only to be near him to catch the punishment, deserved or undeserved.

One of the first circumstances that opened my eyes to the cruelty and wickedness of slavery, and the heartlessness of my old master, was the refusal of the latter to interpose his authority, to protect and shield a young woman, who had been most cruelly abused and beaten by his overseer in Tuckahoe. This overseer—a Mr. Plummer—was a man like most of his class, little better than a human brute; and, in addition to his general profligacy and repulsive coarseness, the creature was a miserable drunkard. He was, probably, employed by my old master, less on account of the excellence of his services, than for the cheap rate at which they could be obtained. He was not fit to have the management of a drove of mules. In a fit of drunken madness, he committed the outrage which brought the young woman in question down to my old master's for protection. This young woman was the daughter of Milly, an own aunt of mine. The poor girl, on arriving at our house, presented a pitiable appearance. She had left in haste, and without preparation; and, probably, without the knowledge of Mr. Plummer. She had traveled twelve miles, bare-footed, bare-necked and bare-headed. Her neck and shoulders were covered with scars, newly made; and not content with marring her neck and shoulders, with the cowhide, the cowardly brute had dealt her a blow on the head with a hickory club, which cut a horrible gash, and left her face literally covered with blood. In this condition, the poor young woman came down, to implore protection at the hands of my old master. I expected to see him boil over with rage at the revolting deed, and to hear him fill the air with curses upon the brutal Plummer; but I was disappointed. He sternly told her, in an angry tone, he "believed she deserved every bit of it," and, if she did not go home instantly, he would himself take the remaining skin from her neck and back. Thus was the poor girl compelled to return, without redress, and perhaps to receive an additional flogging for daring to appeal to old master against the overseer.

Old master seemed furious at the thought of being troubled by such complaints. I did not, at that time, understand the philosophy of his treatment of my cousin. It was stern, unnatural, violent. Had the man no bowels of compassion? Was he dead to all sense of humanity? No. I think I now understand it. This treatment is a part of the system, rather than a part of the man. Were slaveholders to listen to complaints of this sort against the overseers, the luxury of owning large numbers of slaves, would be impossible. It would do away with the office of overseer, entirely; or, in other words, it would convert the master himself into an overseer. It would occasion great loss of time and labor, leaving the overseer in fetters, and without the necessary power to secure obedience to his orders. A privilege so dangerous as that of appeal, is, therefore, strictly prohibited; and any one exercising it, runs a fearful hazard. Nevertheless, when a slave has nerve enough to exercise it, and boldly approaches his master, with a well-founded complaint against an overseer, though he may be repulsed, and may even have that of which he complains repeated at the time, and, though he may be beaten by his master, as well as by the overseer, for his temerity, in the end the policy of complaining is, generally, vindicated by the relaxed rigor of the overseer's treatment. The latter becomes more careful, and less disposed to use the lash upon such slaves thereafter. It is with this final result in view, rather than with any expectation of immediate good, that the outraged slave is induced to meet his master with a complaint. The overseer very naturally dislikes to have the ear of the master disturbed by complaints; and, either upon this consideration, or upon advice and warning privately given him by his employers, he generally modifies the rigor of his rule, after an outbreak of the kind to which I have been referring.

Howsoever the slaveholder may allow himself to act toward his slave, and, whatever cruelty he may deem it wise, for example's sake, or for the gratification of his humor, to inflict, he cannot, in the absence of all provocation, look with pleasure upon the bleeding wounds of a defenseless slave-woman. When he drives her from his presence without redress, or the hope of redress, he acts, generally, from motives of policy, rather than from a hardened nature, or from innate brutality. Yet, let but his own temper be stirred, his own passions get loose, and the slave-owner will go *far beyond* the overseer in cruelty. He will convince the slave that his wrath is far more terrible and boundless, and vastly more to be dreaded, than that of the underling overseer. What may have been mechanically and heartlessly done by the overseer, is now done with a will. The man who now wields the lash is irresponsible. He may, if he pleases, cripple or kill, without fear of consequences; except in so far as it may concern profit or loss. To a man of violent temper—as my old master was—this was but a very slender and inefficient restraint. I have seen him in a tempest of passion, such as I have just described—a passion into which entered all the bitter ingredients of pride, hatred, envy, jealousy, and the thirst for revenge.

The circumstances which I am about to narrate, and which gave rise to this fearful tempest of passion, are not singular nor isolated in slave life, but are common in every slaveholding community in which I have lived. They are incidental to the relation of master and slave, and exist in all sections of slave-holding countries.

The reader will have noticed that, in enumerating the names of the slaves who lived with my old master, *Esther* is mentioned. This was a young woman who possessed that which is ever a curse to the slave-girl; namely—personal beauty. She was tall, well formed, and made a fine appearance. The daughters of Col. [Edward] Lloyd could scarcely surpass her in personal charms.[3] Esther was courted by Ned Roberts, and he was as fine looking a young man, as she was a woman. He was the son of a favorite slave of Col. Lloyd. Some slaveholders would have been glad to promote the marriage of two such persons; but, for some reason or other, my old master took it upon him to break up the growing intimacy between Esther and Edward. He strictly ordered her to quit the company of said Roberts, telling her that he would punish her severely if he ever found her again in Edward's company. This unnatural and heartless order was, of course, broken. A woman's love is not to be annihilated by the peremptory command of any one, whose breath is in his nostrils. It was impossible to keep Edward and Esther apart. Meet they would, and meet they did. Had old master been a man of honor and purity, his motives, in this matter, might have been viewed more favorably. As it was, his motives were as abhorrent, as his methods were foolish and contemptible. It was too evident that he was not concerned for the girl's welfare. It is one of the damning characteristics of the slave system, that it robs its victims of every earthly incentive to a holy life. The fear of God, and the hope of heaven, are found sufficient to sustain many slave-women, amidst the snares and dangers of their strange lot; but, this side of God and heaven, a

3. Colonel Edward Lloyd was the owner of Wye House, the plantation where Douglass spent part of his childhood.

slave-woman is at the mercy of the power, caprice and passion of her owner. Slavery provides no means for the honorable continuance of the race. Marriage as imposing obligations on the parties to it—has no existence here, except in such hearts as are purer and higher than the standard morality around them. It is one of the consolations of my life, that I know of many honorable instances of persons who maintained their honor, where all around was corrupt.

Esther was evidently much attached to Edward, and abhorred—as she had reason to do—the tyrannical and base behavior of old master. Edward was young, and fine looking, and he loved and courted her. He might have been her husband, in the high sense just alluded to; but WHO and *what* was this old master? His attentions were plainly brutal and selfish, and it was as natural that Esther should loathe him, as that she should love Edward. Abhorred and circumvented as he was, old master, having the power, very easily took revenge. I happened to see this exhibition of his rage and cruelty toward Esther. The time selected was singular. It was early in the morning, when all besides was still, and before any of the family, in the house or kitchen, had left their beds. I saw but few of the shocking preliminaries, for the cruel work had begun before I awoke. I was probably awakened by the shrieks and piteous cries of poor Esther. My sleeping place was on the floor of a little, rough closet, which opened into the kitchen; and through the cracks of its unplaned boards, I could distinctly see and hear what was going on, without being seen by old master. Esther's wrists were firmly tied, and the twisted rope was fastened to a strong staple in a heavy wooden joist above, near the fireplace. Here she stood, on a bench, her arms tightly drawn over her breast. Her back and shoulders were bare to the waist. Behind her stood old master, with cowskin in hand, preparing his barbarous work with all manner of harsh, coarse, and tantalizing epithets. The screams of his victim were most piercing. He was cruelly deliberate, and protracted the torture, as one who was delighted with the scene. Again and again he drew the hateful whip through his hand, adjusting it with a view of dealing the most pain-giving blow. Poor Esther had never yet been severely whipped, and her shoulders were plump and tender. Each blow, vigorously laid on, brought screams as well as blood. "*Have mercy; Oh! have mercy*" she cried; "*I won't do so no more*"; but her piercing cries seemed only to increase his fury. His answers to them are too coarse and blasphemous to be produced here. The whole scene, with all its attendants, was revolting and shocking, to the last degree; and when the motives of this brutal castigation are considered, —language has no power to convey a just sense of its awful criminality. After laying on some thirty or forty stripes, old master untied his suffering victim, and let her get down. She could scarcely stand, when untied. From my heart I pitied her, and—child though I was—the outrage kindled in me a feeling far from peaceful; but I was hushed, terrified, stunned, and could do nothing, and the fate of Esther might be mine next. The scene here described was often repeated in the case of poor Esther, and her life, as I knew it, was one of wretchedness.

2. "Life in Baltimore," Chapter X of *My Bondage and My Freedom* (New York: Miller, Orton, & Mulligan, 1855)[4]

Once in Baltimore, with hard brick pavements under my feet, which almost raised blisters, by their very heat, for it was in the height of summer; walled in on all sides by towering brick buildings; with troops of hostile boys ready to pounce upon me at every street corner; with new and strange objects glaring upon me at every step; and with startling sounds reaching my ears from all directions, I for a time thought that, after all, the home plantation was a more desirable place of residence than my home on Alliciana Street, in Baltimore. My country eyes and ears were confused and bewildered here; but the boys were my chief trouble. They chased me, and called me "*Eastern Shore man*" till really I almost wished myself back on the Eastern Shore. I had to undergo a sort of moral acclimation, and when that was over, I did much better. My new mistress[5] happily proved to be all she *seemed* to be, when, with her husband, she met me at the door, with a most beaming, benignant countenance. She was, naturally, of an excellent disposition, kind, gentle and cheerful. The supercilious contempt for the rights and feelings of the slave, and the petulance and bad humor which generally characterize slaveholding ladies, were all quite absent from kind "Miss" Sophia's manner and bearing toward me. She had, in truth, never been a slaveholder, but had—a thing quite unusual in the South—depended almost entirely upon her own industry for a living. To this fact the dear lady, no doubt, owed the excellent preservation of her natural goodness of heart, for slavery can change a saint into a sinner, and an angel into a demon. I hardly knew how to behave toward "Miss Sophia," as I used to call Mrs. Hugh Auld. I had been treated as a *pig* on the plantation; I was treated as a *child* now. I could not even approach her as I had formerly approached Mrs. Thomas Auld. How could I hang down my head, and speak with bated breath, when there was no pride to scorn me, no coldness to repel me, and no hatred to inspire me with fear? I therefore soon learned to regard her as something more akin to a mother, than a slaveholding mistress. The crouching servility of a slave, usually so acceptable a quality to the haughty slaveholder, was not understood nor desired by this gentle woman. So far from deeming it impudent in a

---

4. In 1826, Douglass was sent from "the country" (Wye House) to live with Hugh and Sophia Auld in "the city" Baltimore, Maryland. For an explanation of why this move occurred, see William S. McFeely, *Frederick Douglass* (New York: W.W. Norton, 1991), 22–25.
5. Miss Sophia Auld was the wife of Mr. Hugh Auld, Douglass' master in Baltimore.

slave to look her straight in the face, as some slaveholding ladies do, she seemed ever to say, "look up, child; don't be afraid; see, I am full of kindness and good will toward you." The hands belonging to Col. Lloyd's sloop, esteemed it a great privilege to be the bearers of parcels or messages to my new mistress; for whenever they came, they were sure of a most kind and pleasant reception. If little Thomas was her son, and her most dearly beloved child, she, for a time, at least, made me something like his half-brother in her affections. If dear Tommy was exalted to a place on his mother's knee, "Freddy" was honored by a place at his mother's side. Nor did he lack the caressing strokes of her gentle hand, to convince him that, though *motherless*, he was not *friendless*. Mrs. Auld was not only a kind-hearted woman, but she was remarkably pious; frequent in her attendance of public worship, much given to reading the Bible, and to chanting hymns of praise, when alone. Mr. Hugh Auld was altogether a different character. He cared very little about religion, knew more of the world, and was more of the world, than his wife. He set out, doubtless to be—as the world goes—a respectable man, and to get on by becoming a successful ship builder, in that city of ship building. This was his ambition, and it fully occupied him. I was, of course, of very little consequence to him, compared with what I was to good Mrs. Auld; and, when he smiled upon me, as he sometimes did, the smile was borrowed from his lovely wife, and, like all borrowed light, was transient, and vanished with the source whence it was derived. While I must characterize Master Hugh as being a very sour man, and of forbidding appearance, it is due to him to acknowledge, that he was never very cruel to me, according to the notion of cruelty in Maryland. The first year or two which I spent in his house, he left me almost exclusively to the management of his wife. She was my law-giver. In hands so tender as hers, and in the absence of the cruelties of the plantation, I became, both physically and mentally, much more sensitive to good and ill treatment; and, perhaps, suffered more from a frown from my mistress, than I formerly did from a cuff at the hands of Aunt Katy. Instead of the cold, damp floor of my old master's kitchen, I found myself on carpets; for the corn bag in winter, I now had a good straw bed, well furnished with covers; for the coarse corn-meal in the morning, I now had good bread, and mush occasionally; for my poor tow-linen shirt, reaching to my knees, I had good, clean clothes. I was really well off. My employment was to run errands, and to take care of Tommy; to prevent his getting in the way of carriages, and to keep him out of harm's way generally. Tommy, and I, and his mother, got on swimmingly together, for a time. I say *for a time*, because the fatal poison of irresponsible power, and the natural influence of slavery customs, were not long in making a suitable impression on the gentle and loving disposition of my excellent mistress. At first, Mrs. Auld evidently regarded me simply as a child, like any other child; she had not come to regard me as *property*. This latter thought was a thing of conventional growth. The first was natural and

spontaneous. A noble nature, like hers, could not, instantly, be wholly perverted; and it took several years to change the natural sweetness of her temper
into fretful bitterness. In her worst estate, however, there were, during the first
seven years I lived with her, occasional returns of her former kindly disposition.

The frequent hearing of my mistress reading the Bible for she often read
aloud when her husband was absent soon awakened my curiosity in respect to
this *mystery* of reading, and roused in me the desire to learn. Having no fear of
my kind mistress before my eyes (she had then given me no reason to fear), I
frankly asked her to teach me to read; and, without hesitation, the dear woman
began the task, and very soon, by her assistance, I was master of the alphabet,
and could spell words of three or four letters. My mistress seemed almost as
proud of my progress, as if I had been her own child; and, supposing that her
husband would be as well pleased, she made no secret of what she was doing for
me. Indeed, she exultingly told him of the aptness of her pupil, of her intention
to persevere in teaching me, and of the duty which she felt it to teach me, at
least to read *the bible*. Here arose the first cloud over my Baltimore prospects,
the precursor of drenching rains and chilling blasts.

Master Hugh was amazed at the simplicity of his spouse, and, probably
for the first time, he unfolded to her the true philosophy of slavery, and the
peculiar rules necessary to be observed by masters and mistresses, in the management of their human chattels. Mr. Auld promptly forbade continuance of
her instruction; telling her, in the first place, that the thing itself was unlaw-
ful[6]; that it was also unsafe, and could only lead to mischief. To use his own
words, further, he said, "if you give a nigger an inch, he will take an ell"; "he
should know nothing but the will of his master, and learn to obey it"; "if you
teach that nigger—speaking of myself—how to read the bible, there will be no
keeping him"; "it would forever unfit him for the duties of a slave"; and "as to
himself, learning would do him no good, but probably, a great deal of harm—
making him disconsolate and unhappy." "If you learn him now to read, he'll
want to know how to write; and, this accomplished, he'll be running away
with himself." Such was the tenor of Master Hugh's oracular exposition of the
true philosophy of training a human chattel; and it must be confessed that he
very clearly comprehended the nature and the requirements of the relation of
master and slave. His discourse was the first decidedly anti-slavery lecture to
which it had been my lot to listen. Mrs. Auld evidently felt the force of his
remarks; and, like an obedient wife, began to shape her course in the direction
indicated by her husband. The effect of his words, *on me*, was neither slight nor
transitory. His iron sentences—cold and harsh—sunk deep into my heart, and

6. For more information about legislation regulating the education of slaves, see generally,
Thomas D. Morris, *Southern Slavery and the Law* (Chapel Hill: University of North Carolina
Press, 1996), 347.

stirred up not only my feelings into a sort of rebellion, but awakened within me a slumbering train of vital thought. It was a new and special revelation, dispelling a painful mystery, against which my youthful understanding had struggled, and struggled in vain, to wit: the *white* man's power to perpetuate the enslavement of the *black* man. "Very well," thought I; "knowledge unfits a child to be a slave." I instinctively assented to the proposition; and from that moment I understood the direct pathway from slavery to freedom. This was just what I needed; and I got it at a time, and from a source, whence I least expected it. I was saddened at the thought of losing the assistance of my kind mistress; but the information, so instantly derived, to some extent compensated me for the loss I had sustained in this direction. Wise as Mr. Auld was, he evidently underrated my comprehension, and had little idea of the use to which I was capable of putting the impressive lesson he was giving to his wife. *He* wanted me to be *a slave*; I had already voted against that on the home plantation of Col. Lloyd. That which he most loved I most hated; and the very determination which he expressed to keep me in ignorance, only rendered me the more resolute in seeking intelligence. In learning to read, therefore, I am not sure that I do not owe quite as much to the opposition of my master, as to the kindly assistance of my amiable mistress. I acknowledge the benefit rendered me by the one, and by the other; believing, that but for my mistress, I might have grown up in ignorance. [. . .]

3. "The Last Flogging," Chapter XVII of *My Bondage and My Freedom* (New York: Miller, Orton, & Mulligan, 1855)[7]

Sleep itself does not always come to the relief of the weary in body, and the broken in spirit; especially when past troubles only foreshadow coming disasters. The last hope had been extinguished. My master, who I did not venture to hope would protect me as *a man*, had even now refused to protect me as *his property*; and had cast me back, covered with reproaches and bruises, into the hands of a stranger to that mercy which was the soul of the religion he professed. May the reader never spend such a night as that allotted to me, previous to the morning which was to herald my return to the den of horrors from which I had made a temporary escape.

I remained all night—sleep I did not—at St. Michael's; and in the morning (Saturday) I started off, according to the order of Master Thomas, feeling that I had no friend on earth, and doubting if I had one in heaven. I reached Covey's about nine o'clock; and just as I stepped into the field, before I had reached the house, Covey, true to his snakish [*sic*] habits, darted out at me from a fence corner, in which he had secreted himself, for the purpose of securing me. He was amply provided with a cowskin and a rope; and he evidently intended to *tie me up*, and to wreak his vengeance on me to the fullest extent. I should have been an easy prey, had he succeeded in getting his hands upon me, for I had taken no refreshment since noon on Friday; and this, together with the pelting, excitement, and the loss of blood, had reduced my strength. I, however, darted back into the woods, before the ferocious hound could get hold of me, and buried myself in a thicket, where he lost sight of me. The corn-field afforded me cover, in getting to the woods. But for the tall corn, Covey would have overtaken me, and made me his captive. He seemed very much chagrined that he did not catch me, and gave up the chase, very reluctantly; for I could see his angry movements, toward the house from which he had sallied, on his foray.

Well, now I am clear of Covey, and of his wrathful lash, for present. I am in the wood, buried in its somber gloom, and hushed in its solemn silence; hid

---

7. In 1833, Douglass was sent to live with Thomas Auld in St. Michaels, Maryland. In early 1834, Auld "hired" Douglass out to work on the farm of Edward Covey, who had a reputation for his harsh treatment of slaves. Douglass' encounter with Covey altered the course of his life in many ways, and this selection provides the reader with a sense of why the time on Covey's farm proved to be so important. For more on Douglass' time in St. Michaels and on Covey's farm, see McFeely, *Frederick Douglass*, 40–48.

from all human eyes; shut in with nature and nature's God, and absent from all human contrivances. Here was a good place to pray; to pray for help for deliverance—a prayer I had often made before. But how could I pray? Covey could pray—Capt. Auld could pray—I would fain pray; but doubts (arising partly from my own neglect of the means of grace, and partly from the sham religion which everywhere prevailed, cast in my mind a doubt upon all religion, and led me to the conviction that prayers were unavailing and delusive) prevented my embracing the opportunity, as a religious one. Life, in itself, had almost become burdensome to me. All my outward relations were against me; I must stay here and starve (I was already hungry) or go home to Covey's, and have my flesh torn to pieces, and my spirit humbled under the cruel lash of Covey. This was the painful alternative presented to me. The day was long and irksome. My physical condition was deplorable. I was weak, from the toils of the previous day, and from the want of food and rest; and had been so little concerned about my appearance, that I had not yet washed the blood from my garments. I was an object of horror, even to myself. Life, in Baltimore, when most oppressive, was a paradise to this. What had I done, what had my parents done, that such a life as this should be mine? That day, in the woods, I would have exchanged my manhood for the brutehood [*sic*] of an ox.

Night came. I was still in the woods, unresolved what to do. Hunger had not yet pinched me to the point of going home, and I laid myself down in the leaves to rest; for I had been watching for hunters all day, but not being molested during the day, I expected no disturbance during the night. I had come to the conclusion that Covey relied upon hunger to drive me home; and in this I was quite correct—the facts showed that he had made no effort to catch me, since morning.

During the night, I heard the step of a man in the woods. He was coming toward the place where I lay. A person lying still has the advantage over one walking in the woods, in the day time, and this advantage is much greater at night. I was not able to engage in a physical struggle, and I had recourse to the common resort of the weak. I hid myself in the leaves to prevent discovery. But, as the night rambler in the woods drew nearer, I found him to be a *friend*, not an enemy; it was a slave of Mr. William Groomes, of Easton, a kind hearted fellow, named "Sandy." Sandy lived with Mr. Kemp that year, about four miles from St. Michael's. He, like myself had been hired out by the year; but, unlike myself, had not been hired out to be broken. Sandy was the husband of a free woman, who lived in the lower part of "*Potpie Neck*," and he was now on his way through the woods, to see her, and to spend the Sabbath with her.

As soon as I had ascertained that the disturber of my solitude was not an enemy, but the good-hearted Sandy—a man as famous among the slaves of the neighborhood for his good nature, as for his good sense I came out from my hiding place, and made myself known to him. I explained the circumstances of the past two days, which had driven me to the woods, and he deeply compassionated my distress. It was a bold thing for him to shelter me, and I could not ask him to do so; for, had I been found in his hut, he would have suffered the penalty of thirty-nine lashes on his bare back, if not something worse. But Sandy was too generous to permit the fear of punishment to prevent his relieving a brother bondman from hunger and exposure; and, therefore, on his own motion, I accompanied him to his home, or rather to the home of his wife—for the house and lot were hers. His wife was called up—for it was now about midnight—a fire was made, some Indian meal was soon mixed with salt and water, and an ash cake was baked in a hurry to relieve my hunger. Sandy's wife was not behind him in kindness—both seemed to esteem it a privilege to succor me; for, although I was hated by Covey and by my master, I was loved by the colored people, because *they* thought I was hated for my knowledge, and persecuted because I was feared. I was the *only* slave *now* in that region who could read and write. There had been one other man, belonging to Mr. Hugh Hamilton, who could read (his name was "Jim"), but he, poor fellow, had, shortly after my coming into the neighborhood, been sold off to the far south. I saw Jim ironed, in the cart, to be carried to Easton for sale—pinioned like a yearling for the slaughter. My knowledge was now the pride of my brother slaves; and, no doubt, Sandy felt something of the general interest in me on that account. The supper was soon ready, and though I have feasted since, with honorable [*sic*], lord mayors and aldermen, over the sea, my supper on ash cake and cold water, with Sandy, was the meal, of all my life, most sweet to my taste, and now most vivid in my memory.

Supper over, Sandy and I went into a discussion of what was *possible* for me, under the perils and hardships which now overshadowed my path. The question was, must I go back to Covey, or must I now tempt to run away? Upon a careful survey, the latter was found to be impossible; for I was on a narrow neck of land, every avenue from which would bring me in sight of pursuers. There was the Chesapeake Bay to the right, and "Potpie" river to the left, and St. Michael's and its neighborhood occupying the only space through which there was any retreat.

I found Sandy an old advisor. He was not only a religious man, but he professed to believe in a system for which I have no name. He was a genuine African, and had inherited some of the so-called magical powers, said to be possessed by African and eastern nations. He told me that he could help me; that, in those very woods, there was an herb, which in the morning might be found, possessing all the powers required for my protection (I put his thoughts in my own language); and that, if I would take his advice, he would procure me the root of the herb of which he spoke. He told me further, that if I would take that root and wear it on my right side, it would be impossible for Covey to strike me a blow; that with this root about my person, no white man could whip me. He said he had carried it for years, and that he had fully tested its virtues. He had never received a blow from a slaveholder since he carried it; and he never expected to receive one, for he always meant to carry that root as a protection. He knew Covey well, for Mrs. Covey was the daughter of Mr. Kemp; and he (Sandy) had heard of the barbarous treatment to which I was subjected, and he wanted to do something for me.

Now all this talk about the root, was to me, very absurd and ridiculous, if not positively sinful. I at first rejected the idea that the simple carrying a root on my right side (a root, by the way, over which I walked every time I went into the woods) could possess any such magic power as he ascribed to it, and I was, therefore, not disposed to cumber my pocket with it. I had a positive aversion to all pretenders to "*divination*." It was beneath one of my intelligence to countenance such dealings with the devil, as this power implied. But, with all my learning—it was really precious little—Sandy was more than a match for me. "My book learning," he said, "had not kept Covey off me" (a powerful argument just then) and he entreated me, with flashing eyes, to try this. If it did me no good, it could do me no harm, and it would cost me nothing, any way Sandy was so earnest, and so confident of the good qualities of this weed, that, to please him, rather than from any conviction of its excellence, I was induced to take it. He had been to me the good Samaritan, and had, almost providentially, found me, and helped me when I could not help myself; how did I know but that the hand of the Lord was in it? With thoughts of this sort, I took the roots from Sandy, and put them in my right hand pocket.

This was, of course, Sunday morning. Sandy now urged me to go home, with all speed, and to walk up bravely to the house, as though nothing had happened. I saw in Sandy too deep an insight into human nature, with all his superstition, not to have some respect for his advice; and perhaps, too, a slight gleam or shadow of his superstition had fallen upon me. At any rate, I started off toward Covey's, as directed by Sandy. Having, the previous night, poured my griefs [*sic*] into Sandy's ears, and got him enlisted in my behalf, having made his wife a sharer in my sorrows, and having, also, become well refreshed by sleep and food, I moved off, quite courageously, toward the much dreaded Covey's. Singularly enough, just as I entered his yard gate, I met him and his wife, dressed in their Sunday best—looking as smiling as angels—on their way to church. The manner of Covey astonished me. There was something really benignant in his countenance. He spoke to me as never before; told me that the pigs had got into the lot, and he wished me to drive them out; inquired how I was, and seemed an altered man. This extraordinary conduct of Covey, really made me begin to think that Sandy's herb had more virtue in it than I, in my pride, had been willing to allow; and, had the day been other than Sunday, I should have attributed Covey's altered manner solely to the magic power of the root. I suspected, however, that the *Sabbath*, and not the *root*, was the real explanation of Covey's manner. His religion hindered him from breaking the Sabbath, but not from breaking my skin. He had more respect for the *day* than for the *man*, for whom the day was mercifully given; for while he would cut and slash my body during the week, he would not hesitate, on Sunday, to teach me the value of my soul, or the way of life and salvation by Jesus Christ.

All went well with me till Monday morning; and then, whether the root had lost its virtue, or whether my tormentor had gone deeper into the black art than myself (as was sometimes said of him), or whether he had obtained a special indulgence, for his faithful Sabbath day's worship, it is not necessary for me to know, or to inform the reader; but, this I *may* say—the pious and benignant smile which graced Covey's face on *Sunday*, wholly disappeared on *Monday*. Long before daylight, I was called up to go and feed, rub, and curry the horses. I obeyed the call, and would have so obeyed it, had it been made at an earlier hour, for I had brought my mind to a firm resolve, during that Sunday's reflection, viz: to obey every order, however unreasonable, if it were possible, and, if Mr. Covey should then undertake to beat me, to defend and protect myself to the best of my ability. My religious views on the subject of resisting my master, had suffered a serious shock, by the savage persecution to which I had been subjected, and my hands were no longer tied by my religion. Master Thomas's indifference had served the last link. I had now to this extent "backslidden" from this point in the slave's religious creed; and I soon had occasion to make my fallen state known to my Sunday-pious brother, Covey.

Whilst I was obeying his order to feed and get the horses ready for the field, and when in the act of going up the stable loft for the purpose of throwing down some blades, Covey sneaked into the stable, in his peculiar snake-like way, and seizing me suddenly by the leg, he brought me to the stable floor, giving my newly mended body a fearful jar. I now forgot my roots, and remembered my pledge to *stand up in my own defense*. The brute was endeavoring skillfully to get a slip-knot on my legs, before I could draw up my feet. As soon as I found what he was up to, I gave a sudden spring (my two day's rest had been of much service to me and by that means, no doubt, he was able to bring me to the floor so heavily. He was defeated in his plan of tying me. While down, he seemed to think he had me very securely in his power. He little thought he was—as the rowdies say—"in" for a "rough and tumble" fight; but such was the fact. Whence came the daring spirit necessary to grapple with a man who, eight-and-forty hours before, could, with his slightest word have made me tremble like a leaf in a storm, I do not know; at any rate, *I was resolved to fight*, and, what was better still, I was actually hard at it. The fighting madness had come upon me, and I found my strong fingers firmly attached to the throat of my cowardly tormentor; as heedless of consequences, at the moment, as though we stood as equals before the law. The very color of the man was forgotten. I felt as supple as a cat, and was ready for the snakish [*sic*] creature at every turn.

Every blow of his was parried, though I dealt no blows in turn. I was strictly on the *defensive*, preventing him from injuring me, rather than trying to injure him. I flung him on the ground several times, when he meant to have hurled me there. I held him so firmly by the throat, that his blood followed my nails. He held me, and I held him.

All was fair, thus far, and the contest was about equal. My resistance was entirely unexpected, and Covey was taken all aback by it, for he trembled in every limb. *"Are you going to resist,* you scoundrel?" said he. To which, I returned a polite *"Yes sir"*; steadily gazing my interrogator in the eye, to meet the first approach or dawning of the blow, which I expected my answer would call forth. But, the conflict did not long remain thus equal. Covey soon cried out lustily for help; not that I was obtaining any marked advantage over him, or was injuring him, but because he was gaining none over me, and was not able, single handed, to conquer me. He called for his cousin Hughs, to come to his assistance, and now the scene was changed. I was compelled to give blows, as well as to parry them; and, since I was, in any case, to suffer for resistance, I felt (as the musty proverb goes) that "I might as well be hanged for an old sheep as a lamb." I was still *defensive* toward Covey, but *aggressive* toward Hughs; and, at the first approach of the latter, I dealt a blow, in my desperation, which fairly sickened my youthful assailant. He went off, bending over with pain, and manifesting no disposition to come within my reach again. The poor fellow was in the act of trying to catch and tie my right hand, and while flattering himself with success, I gave him the kick which sent him staggering away in pain, at the same time that I held Covey with a firm hand.

Taken completely by surprise, Covey seemed to have lost his usual strength and coolness. He was frightened, and stood puffing and blowing, seemingly unable to command words or blows. When he saw that poor Hughes was standing half bent with pain—his courage quite gone, the cowardly tyrant asked if I "meant to persist in my resistance." I told him *"I did mean to resist, come what might"*; that I had been by him treated like a *brute*, during the last six months; and that I should stand it *no longer*. With that, he gave me a shake, and attempted to drag me toward a stick of wood, that was lying just outside the stable door. He meant to knock me down with it; but, just as he leaned over to get the stick, I seized him with both hands by the collar, and, with a vigorous and sudden snatch, I brought my assailant harmlessly, his full length, on the *not* overclean ground—for we were now in the cow yard. He had selected the place for the fight, and it was but right that he should have all the advantages of his own selection.

By this time, Bill, the hired-man, came home. He had been to Mr. Hemsley's, to spend the Sunday with his nominal wife, and was coming home on Monday morning, to go to work. Covey and I had been skirmishing from before daybreak, till now, that the sun was almost shooting his beams over the eastern woods, and we were still at it. I could not see where the matter was to termi- nate. He evidently was afraid to let me go, lest I should again make off to the woods; otherwise, he would probably have obtained arms from the house, to frighten me. Holding me, Covey called upon Bill for assistance. The scene here, had something comic about it. "Bill," who knew *precisely* what Covey wished him to do, affected ignorance, and pretended he did not know what to do. "What shall I do, Mr. Covey," said Bill. "Take hold of him—take hold of him!" said Covey. With a toss of his head, peculiar to Bill, he said, "Indeed, Mr. Covey I want to go to work." "*This is* your work," said Covey; "take hold of him." Bill replied, with spirit, "My master hired me here, to work, and *not* to help you whip Frederick." It was now my turn to speak. "Bill," said I, "don't put your hands on me." To which he replied, "My GOD! Frederick, I ain't goin' to tech ye," and Bill walked off, leaving Covey and myself to settle our matters as best we might.

But, my present advantage was threatened when I saw Caroline (the slave- woman of Covey) coming to the cow yard to milk, for she was a powerful woman, and could have mastered me very easily, exhausted as I now was. As soon as she came into the yard, Covey attempted to rally her to his aid. Strangely—and, I may add, fortunately—Caroline was in no humor to take a hand in any such sport. We were all in open rebellion, that morning. Caroline answered the command of her master to "*take hold of me,*" precisely as Bill had answered, but in *her*, it was at greater peril so to answer; she was the slave of Covey, and he could do what he pleased with her. It was *not* so with Bill, and Bill knew it. Samuel Harris, to whom Bill belonged, did not allow his slaves to be beaten, unless they were guilty of some crime which the law would punish. But, poor Caroline, like myself, was at the mercy of the merciless Covey; nor did she escape the dire effects of her refusal. He gave her several sharp blows.

Covey at length (two hours had elapsed) gave up the contest. Letting me go, he said—puffing and blowing at a great rate—"Now, you scoundrel, go to your work; I would not have whipped you half so much as I have had you not resisted." The fact was, *he had not whipped me at all*. He had not, in all the scuffle, drawn a single drop of blood from me. I had drawn blood from him; and, even without this satisfaction, I should have been victorious, because my aim had not been to injure him, but to prevent his injuring me.

During the whole six months that I lived with Covey, after this transaction, he never laid on me the weight of his finger in anger. He would, occasionally, say he did not want to have to get hold of me again—a declaration which I had no difficulty in believing; and I had a secret feeling, which answered, "You need not wish to get hold of me again, for you will be likely to come off worse in a second fight than you did in the first."

Well, my dear reader, this battle with Mr. Covey—undignified as it was, and as I fear my narration of it is—was the turning point in my "*life as a slave.*"

It rekindled in my breast the smoldering embers of liberty; it brought up my Baltimore dreams, and revived a sense of my own manhood. I was a changed being after that fight. I was *nothing* before; I WAS A MAN NOW. It recalled to life my crushed self-respect and my self-confidence, and inspired me with a renewed determination to be A FREEMAN. A man, without force, is without the essential dignity of humanity. Human nature is so constituted, that it cannot *honor* a helpless man, although it can *pity* him; and even this it cannot do long, if the signs of power do not arise.

He can only understand the effect of this combat on my spirit, who has himself incurred something, hazarded something, in repelling the unjust and cruel aggressions of a tyrant. Covey was a tyrant, and a cowardly one, withal. After resisting him, I felt as I had never felt before. It was a resurrection from the dark and pestiferous tomb of slavery, to the heaven of comparative freedom. I was no longer a servile coward, trembling under the frown of a brother worm of the dust, but, my long-cowed spirit was roused to an attitude of manly independence. I had reached the point, at which I was *not afraid to die*. This spirit made me a freeman in *fact*, while I remained a slave in *form*. When a slave cannot be flogged he is more than half free. He has a domain as broad as his own manly heart to defend, and he is really "*a power on earth*." While slaves prefer their lives, with flogging, to instant death, they will always find Christians enough, like unto Covey, to accommodate that preference. From this time, until that of my escape from slavery, I was never fairly whipped. Several attempts were made to whip me, but they were always unsuccessful. Bruises I did get, as I shall hereafter inform the reader; but the case I have been describing, was the end of the brutification to which slavery had subjected me.

The reader will be glad to know why, after I had so grievously offended Mr. Covey, he did not have me taken in hand by the authorities; indeed, why the law of Maryland, which assigns hanging to the slave who resists his master, was not put in force against me; at any rate, why I was not taken up, as is usual in such cases, and publicly whipped, for an example to other slaves, and as a means of deterring me from committing the same offense again. I confess, that the easy manner in which I got off, for a long time, [was] a surprise to me, and I cannot, even now, fully explain the cause.

The only explanation I can venture to suggest, is the fact, that Covey was, probably, ashamed to have it known and confessed that he had been mastered by a boy of sixteen. Mr. Covey enjoyed the unbounded and very valuable reputation, of being a first-rate overseer and *Negro breaker*. By means of this reputation, he was able to procure his hands for *very trifling* compensation, and with very great ease. His interest and his pride mutually suggested the wisdom of passing the matter by, in silence. The story that he had undertaken to whip a lad, and had been resisted, was, of itself, sufficient to damage him; for his bearing should, in the estimation of slaveholders, be of that imperial order that should make such an occurrence *impossible*. I judge from these circumstances, that Covey deemed it best to give me the go-by. It is, perhaps, not altogether creditable to my natural temper, that, after this conflict with Mr. Covey, I did, at times, purposely aim to provoke him to an attack, by refusing to keep with the other hands in the field, but I could never bully him to another battle. I had made up my mind to do him serious damage, if he ever again attempted to lay violent hands on me.

> *Hereditary bondmen, know ye not*
> *Who would be free, themselves must strike the blow?*[8]

---

8. Lord Byron, *Childe Harold's Pilgrimage*, Canto the Second, section LXXVI.

4. "Letter to Henry C. Wright," published in *The Liberator*, January 29, 1847[9]

DEAR FRIEND:

Your letter of the 12th December reached me at this place, yesterday. Please accept my heartfelt thanks for it. I am sorry that you deemed it necessary to assure me, that it would be the last letter of advice you would ever write me. It looked as if you were about to cast me off forever! I do not, however, think you meant to convey any such meaning; and if you did, I am sure you will see cause to change your mind, and to receive me again into the fold of those, whom it should ever be your pleasure to advise and instruct.

The subject of your letter is one of deep importance, and upon which, I have thought and felt much; and, being the party of all others most deeply concerned, it is natural to suppose I have an opinion, and ought to be able to give it on all fitting occasions. I deem this a fitting occasion and shall act accordingly.

You have given me your opinion: I am glad you have done so. You have given it to me direct, in your own emphatic way. You never speak insipidly, smoothly, or mincingly; you have strictly adhered to your custom, in the letter before me. I now take great pleasure in giving you my opinion, as plainly and unreservedly as you have given yours, and I trust with equal good feeling and purity of motive. I take it, that nearly all that can be said against my position is contained in your letter; for if any man in the wide world would be likely to find valid objections to such a transaction as the one under consideration, I regard you as that man. I must, however, tell you, that I have read your letter over, and over again, and have sought in vain to find anything like what I can regard a valid reason against the purpose of my body or against my receiving the manumission papers, if they are ever presented to me.

Let me, in the first place, state the facts and circumstances of the transaction which you so strongly condemn. It is your right to do so, and God forbid that I should ever cherish the slightest desire to restrain you in the exercise of that right. I say to you at once, and in all the fullness of sincerity, speak out; speak freely; keep nothing back; let me know your whole mind. "Hew to the line, though the chips fly in my face." Tell me, and tell me plainly, when you think

---

9. In this open letter to Henry C. Wright (1797–1870), a New England abolitionist with close ties to William Lloyd Garrison, Douglass defends the morality of the abolitionists who purchased his freedom from Thomas Auld.

I am deviating from the strict line of duty and principle; and when I become unwilling to hear, I shall have attained a character which I now despise, and from which I would hope to be preserved. But to the facts.

I am in England, my family are in the United States. My sphere of usefulness is in the United States; my public and domestic duties are there; and there it seems my duty to go. But I am legally the property of Thomas Auld, and if I go to the United States (no matter to what part, for there is no City of Refuge there, no spot sacred to freedom there) Thomas Auld, aided by the American government, can seize, bind and fetter, and drag me from my family, feed his cruel revenge upon me, and doom me to unending slavery. In view of this simple statement of facts, a few friends, desirous of seeing me released from the terrible liability, and to relieve my wife and children from the painful trepidation, consequent upon the liability, and to place me on an equal footing of safety with all other anti-slavery lecturers in the United States, and to enhance my usefulness by enlarging the field of my labors in the United States, have nobly and generously paid Hugh Auld, the agent of Thomas Auld, £150—in consideration of which, Hugh Auld (acting as his agent) and the government of the United States agree, that I shall be free from all further legal liability.

These, dear friend, are the facts of the whole transaction. The principle here acted on by my friends, and that upon which I shall act in receiving the manumission papers, I deem quite defensible.

First, as to those who acted as my friends, and their actions. The actuating motive was, to secure me from a liability full of horrible forebodings to myself and family. With this object, I will do you the justice to say, I believe you fully unite, although some parts of your letters would seem to justify a different belief.

Then, as to the measure adopted to secure this result. Does it violate a fundamental principle, or does it not? This is the question, and to my mind the only question of importance, involved in the discussion. I believe that, on our part, no just or holy principle has been violated.

Before entering upon the argument in support of this view, I will take the liberty (and I know you will pardon it) to say, I think you should have pointed out some principle violated in the transaction, before you proceeded to exhort me to repentance. You have given me any amount of indignation against "Auld" and the United States, in all which I cordially unite, and felt refreshed by reading; but it has no bearing whatever upon the conduct of myself, or friends, in the matter under consideration. It does not prove that I have done wrong, nor does it demonstrate what is right, or the proper course to be pursued. Now that the matter has reached its present point, before entering upon the argument, let me say one other word; it is this—I do not think you have acted quite consistently with your character for promptness, in delaying your advice till the transaction was completed. You knew of the movement at its conception, and have known it through its progress, and have never, to my knowledge, uttered one syllable against it, in conversation or letter, till now that the deed is done. I regret this, not because I think your earlier advice would have altered the result, but because it would have left me more free than I can now be, since the thing is done. Of course, you will not think hard of my alluding to this circumstance. Now, then, to the main question.

The principle which you appear to regard as violated by the transaction in question, may be stated as follows: —Every man has a natural and inalienable right to himself. The inference from this is, "that man cannot hold property in man"—and as man cannot hold property in man, neither can Hugh Auld nor the United States have any right of property in me—and having no right of property in me, they have no right to sell me—and, having no right to sell me, no one has a right to buy me. I think I have now stated the principle, and the inference from the principle, distinctly and fairly. Now, the question upon which the whole controversy turns is, simply, this: does the transaction, which you condemn, really violate this principle? I own that, to a superficial observer, it would seem to do so. But I think I am prepared to show, that, so far from being a violation of that principle, it is truly a noble vindication of it. Before going further, let me state here, briefly, what sort of a purchase would have been a violation of this principle, which, in common with yourself, I reverence, and am anxious to preserve inviolate.

1st. It would have been a violation of that principle, had those who purchased me done so, to make me a slave, instead of a freeman. And,

2ndly. It would have been a violation of that principle, had those who purchased me done so with a view to compensate the slaveholder, for what he and they regarded as his rightful property.

In neither of these ways was my purchase effected. My liberation was, in their estimation, of more value than £150; the happiness and repose of my family were, in their judgment, more than paltry gold. The £150 was paid to the remorseless plunderer, not because he had any just claim to it, but to induce him to give up his legal claim to something which they deemed of more value than money. It was not to compensate the slaveholder, but to release me from his power; not to establish my natural right to freedom, but to release me from all legal liabilities to slavery. And all this, you and I, and the slaveholders, and all who know anything of the transaction, very well understand. The very letter to Hugh Auld, proposing terms of purchase, informed him that those who gave, denied his right to it. The error of those, who condemn this transaction, consists in their confounding the crime of buying men into slavery, with the meritorious act of buying men out of slavery, and the purchase of legal freedom with abstract right and natural freedom. They say, "If you BUY, you recognize the right to sell. If you receive, you recognize the right of the giver to give." And this has a show of truth, as well as of logic. But a few plain cases will show its entire fallacy.

There is now, in this country, a heavy duty on corn. The government of this country has imposed it; and though I regard it a most unjust and wicked imposition, no man of common sense will charge me with endorsing or recognizing the right of this government to impose this duty, simply because, to prevent myself and family from starving, I buy and eat this corn.

Take another case: —I have had dealings with a man. I have owed him one hundred dollars, and have paid it; I have lost the receipt. He comes upon me the second time for the money. I know, and he knows, he had no right to it; but he is a villain, and has me in his power. The law is with him, and against me. I must pay or be dragged to jail. I choose to pay the bill a second time. To say I sanctioned his right to rob me, because I preferred to pay rather than go to jail, is to utter an absurdity, to which no sane man would give heed. And yet the principle of action, in each of these cases, is the same. The man might indeed say, the claim is unjust—and declare, I will rot in jail, before I will pay it. But this would not, certainly, be demanded by any principle of truth, justice, or humanity; and however much we might be disposed to respect his daring, but little deference could be paid to his wisdom. The fact is, we act upon this principle every day of our lives and we have an undoubted right to do so. When I came to this country from the United States, I came in the second cabin. And why? Not because my natural right to come in the first cabin was not as good as that of any other man, but because a wicked and cruel prejudice decided, that the second cabin was the place for me. By coming over in the second, did I sanction or justify this wicked prescription? Not at all. It was the best I could do. I acted from necessity.

One other case, and I have done with this view of the subject. I think you will agree with me, that the case I am now about to put is pertinent, though you may not readily pardon use for making yourself the agent of my illustration. The case respects the passport system on the continent of Europe. That system you utterly condemn. You look upon it as an unjust and wicked interference, a bold and infamous violation of the natural and sacred right of locomotion. You hold (and so do I) that the image of our common God ought to be a passport all over the habitable world. But bloody and tyrannical governments have ordained otherwise; they usurp authority over all, and decide for you, on what conditions you shall travel. They say, you shall have a passport, or you shall be put in prison. Now, the question is, have they a right to prescribe any such terms? and do you, by complying with these terms, sanction their interference? I think you will answer, no; submission to injustice, and sanction of injustice, are different things; and he is a poor reasoner [*sic*] who confounds the two, and makes them one and the same thing. Now, then, for the parallel, and the application of the passport system to my own case.

I wish to go to the United States. I have a natural right to go there, and be free. My natural right is as good as that of Hugh Auld, or James K. Polk[10]; but that plundering government says, I shall not return to the United States in safety—it says, I must allow Hugh Auld to rob me, or my friends, of £150, or be hurled into the infernal jaws of slavery. I must have a "bit of paper, signed and sealed," or my liberty must be taken from me, and I must be torn from my family and friends. The government of Austria said to you, "Dare to come upon my soil, without a passport, declaring you to be an American citizen (which you say you are not) you shall at once be arrested, and thrown into prison." What said you to that government? Did you say that the threat was a villainous one, and an infamous invasion of your right of locomotion? Did you say, "I will come upon your soil; I will go where I please! I dare and defy your government." Did you say, "I will spurn your passports; I would not stain my hand, and degrade myself, by touching your miserable parchment. You have no right to give it, and I have no right to take it. I trample your laws, and will put your constitutions under my feet! I will not recognize them!" Was this your course? No! dear friend, it was not. Your practice was wiser than your theory. You took the passport, submitted to be examined while traveling, and availed yourself of all the advantages of your "passport"—or, in other words, escaped all the evils which you ought to have done, without it, and would have done, but for the tyrannical usurpation in Europe.

I will not dwell longer upon this view of the subject; and I dismiss it, feeling quite satisfied of the entire correctness of the reasoning, and the principle attempted to be maintained. As to the expediency of the measures, different opinions may well prevail; but in regard to the principle, I feel it difficult to conceive of two opinions. I am free to say, that, had I possessed one hundred and fifty pounds, I would have seen Hugh Auld kicking, before I would have given it to him. I would have waited till the emergency came, and only given up the money when nothing else would do. But my friends thought it best to provide against the contingency; they acted on their own responsibility, and I am not disturbed about the result. But, having acted on a true principle, I do not feel free to disavow their proceedings.

In conclusion, let me say, I anticipate no such change in my position as you predict. I shall be Frederick Douglass still, and once a slave still. I shall neither be made to forget nor cease to feel the wrongs of my enslaved fellow-countrymen. My knowledge of slavery will be the same, and my hatred of it will be the same. By the way, I have never made my own person and suffering the theme of public discourse, but have always based my appeal upon the wrongs of the three millions now in chains; and these shall still be the burden

---

10. James K. Polk (1795–1849) was the eleventh president of the United States. He served from 1845 to 1849.

of my speeches. You intimate that I may reject the papers, and allow them to remain in the hands of those friends who have effected the purchase, and thus avail myself of the security afforded by them, without sharing any part of the responsibility of the transaction. My objection to this is one of honor. I do not think it would be very honorable on my part, to remain silent during the whole transaction, and giving it more than my silent approval; and then, when the thing is completed, and I am safe, attempt to play the hero, by throwing off all responsibility in the matter. It might be said, and said with great propriety, "Mr. Douglass, your indignation is very good, and has but one fault, and that is, it comes too late." It would be a show of bravery when the danger is over. From every view I have been able to take of the subject, I am persuaded to receive the papers, if presented, —not, however, as a proof of my right to be free, for that is self-evident but as a proof that my friends have been legally robbed of £150, in order to secure that which is the birthright of every man. And I will hold up those papers before the world, in proof of the plundering character of the American government. It shall be the brand of infamy, stamping the nation, in whose name the deed was done, as a great aggregation of hypocrites, thieves and liars, —and their condemnation is just. They declare that all men are created equal, and have a natural and inalienable right to liberty, while they rob me of £150, as a condition of my enjoying this natural and inalienable right. It will be their condemnation, in their own hand-writing and may be held up to the world as a means of humbling that haughty republic into repentance.

I agree with you, that the contest which I have to wage is against the government of the United States. But the representative of that government is the slaveholder, Thomas Auld. He is commander-in-chief of the army and navy. The whole civil and naval force of the nation are at his disposal. He may command all these to his assistance, and bring them all to bear upon me, until I am made entirely subject to his will, or submit to be robbed myself, or allow my friends to be robbed, of seven hundred and fifty dollars. And rather than be subject to his will, I have submitted to be robbed or allowed my friends to be robbed, of the seven hundred and fifty dollars.

Sincerely yours,
FREDERICK DOUGLASS.

5. "Letter to My Old Master [Thomas Auld]," published in *The Liberator*, September 22, 1848[11]

SIR:

The long and intimate, though by no means friendly relation which unhappily subsisted between you and myself, leads me to hope that you will easily account for the great liberty which I now take in addressing you in this open and public manner. The same fact may possibly remove any disagreeable surprise which you may experience on again finding your name coupled with mine, in any other way than in an advertisement, accurately describing my person, and offering a large sum for my arrest. In thus dragging you again before the public, I am aware that I shall subject myself to no inconsiderable amount of censure. I shall probably be charged with an unwarrantable, if not a wanton and reckless disregard of the rights and proprieties of private life. There are those North as well as South who entertain a much higher respect for rights which are merely conventional, than they do for rights which are personal and essential. Not a few there are in our country, who, while they have no scruples against robbing the laborer of the hard earned results of his patient industry, will be shocked by the extremely indelicate manner of bringing your name before the public. Believing this to be the case, and wishing to meet every reasonable or plausible objection to my conduct, I will frankly state the ground upon which I justify myself in this instance, as well as on former occasions when I have thought proper to mention your name in public. All will agree that a man guilty of theft, robbery, or murder, has forfeited the right to concealment and private life; that the community have a right to subject such persons to the most complete exposure. However much they may desire retirement, and aim to conceal themselves and their movements from the popular gaze, the public have a right to ferret them out, and bring their conduct before the proper tribunals of the country for investigation. Sir, you will undoubtedly make the proper application of these generally admitted principles, and will easily see the light in which you are regarded by me, I will not therefore manifest ill temper, by calling you hard names. I know you to be a man of some intelligence, and can readily determine the precise estimate which I entertain of your character. I may therefore indulge in language which may seem to others indirect and ambiguous, and yet be quite well understood by yourself.

---

11. In this "open letter" to his former master, Thomas Auld, Douglass offers a direct and powerful defense of his decision to escape.

I have selected this day on which to address you, because it is the anniversary of my emancipation; and knowing of no better way, I am led to this as the best mode of celebrating that truly important event. Just ten years ago this beautiful September morning, yon bright sun beheld me a slave—a poor, degraded chattel—trembling at the sound of your voice, lamenting that I was a man, and wishing myself a brute. The hopes which I had treasured up for weeks of a safe and successful escape from your grasp, were powerfully confronted at this last hour by dark clouds of doubt and fear, making my person shake and my bosom to heave with the heavy contest between hope and fear. I have no words to describe to you the deep agony of soul which I experienced on that never to be forgotten morning—(for I left by daylight). I was making a leap in the dark. The probabilities, so far as I could by reason determine them, were stoutly against the undertaking. The preliminaries and precautions I had adopted previously, all worked badly. I was like one going to war without weapons—ten chances of defeat to one of victory. One in whom I had confided, and one who had promised me assistance, appalled by fear at the trial hour, deserted me, thus leaving the responsibility of success or failure solely with myself. You, sir, can never know my feelings. As I look back to them, I can scarcely realize that I have passed through a scene so trying. Trying however as they were, and gloomy as was the prospect, thanks be to the Most High, who is ever the God of the oppressed, at the moment which was to determine my whole earthly career. His grace was sufficient, my mind was made up. I embraced the golden opportunity, took the morning tide at the flood, and a free man, young, active and strong, is the result.

I have often thought I should like to explain to you the grounds upon which I have justified myself in running away from you. I am almost ashamed to do so now, for by this time you may have discovered them yourself. I will, however, glance at them. When yet but a child about six years old, I imbibed the determination to run away. The very first mental effort that I now remember on my part, was an attempt to solve the mystery. Why am I a slave? and with this question my youthful mind was troubled for many days, pressing upon me more heavily at times than others. When I saw the slave-driver whip a slave woman, cut the blood out of her neck, and heard her piteous cries, I went away into the corner of the fence, wept and pondered over the mystery. I had, through some medium, I know not what, got some idea of God, the Creator of all mankind, the black and the white, and that he had made the blacks to serve the whites as slaves. How he could do this and be *good*, I could not tell. I was not satisfied with this theory, which made God responsible for slavery, for it pained me greatly, and I have wept over it long and often. At one time, your first wife, Mrs. Lucretia [Anthony Auld],[12] heard me singing and saw me

---

12. Lucretia Anthony Auld was the daughter of Douglass' first master, Aaron Anthony, and the wife of Douglass' second master, Thomas Auld.

shedding tears, and asked of me the matter, but I was afraid to tell her. I was puzzled with this question, till one night, while sitting in the kitchen, I heard some of the old slaves talking of their parents having been stolen from Africa by white men, and were sold here as slaves. The whole mystery was solved at once. Very soon after this my aunt Jinny and uncle Noah ran away, and the great noise made about it by your father-in-law, made me for the first time acquainted with the fact, that there were free States as well as slave States. From that time, I resolved that I would some day run away. The morality of the act, I dispose as follows: I am myself; you are yourself: we are two distinct persons, equal persons. What you are, I am. You are a man, and so am I. God created both, and made us separate beings. I am not by nature bound to you, or you to me. Nature does not make your existence depend upon me, or mine depend upon yours. I cannot walk upon your legs, or you upon mine. I cannot breathe for you, or you for me; I must breathe for myself, and you for yourself. We are distinct persons, and are each equally provided with faculties necessary to our individual existence. In leaving you, I took nothing but what belonged to me, and in no way lessened your means for obtaining an *honest* living. Your faculties remained yours, and mine became useful to their rightful owner. I therefore see no wrong in any part of the transaction. It is true, I went off secretly, but that was more your fault than mine. Had I let you into the secret, you would have defeated the enterprise entirely; but for this, I should have been really glad to have made you acquainted with my intentions to leave.

You may perhaps want to know how I like my present condition. I am free to say, I greatly prefer it to that which I occupied in Maryland. I am, however, by no means prejudiced against the state as such. Its geography, climate, fertility and products, are such as to make it a very desirable abode for any man; and but for the existence of slavery there, it is not impossible that I might again take up my abode in that state. It is not that I love Maryland less, but freedom more. You will be surprised to learn that people at the North labor under the strange delusion that if the slaves were emancipated at the South, they would flock to the North. So far from this being the case, in that event, you would see many old and familiar faces back again to the South. The fact is, there are few here who would not return to the South in the event of emancipation. We want to live in the land of our birth, and to lay our bones by the side of our fathers'; and nothing short of an intense love of personal freedom keeps us from the South. For the sake of this, most of us would live on a crust of bread and a cup of cold water.

Since I left you, I have had a rich experience. I have occupied stations which I never dreamed of when a slave. Three out of the ten years since I left you, I spent as a common laborer on the wharves of New Bedford, Massachusetts. It was there I earned my first free dollar. It was mine. I could spend it as I pleased. I could buy hams or herring with it, without asking any odds of anybody. That was a precious dollar to me. You remember when I used to make seven or eight, or even nine dollars a week in Baltimore, you would take every cent of it from me every Saturday night, saying that I belonged to you, and my earnings also. I never liked this conduct on your part—to say the best, I thought it a little mean. I would not have served you so. But let that pass. I was a little awkward about counting money in New England fashion when I first landed in New Bedford. I like to have betrayed myself several times. I caught myself saying phip [*sic*], for fourpence; and at one time a man actually charged me with being a runaway, whereupon I was silly enough to become one by running away from him, for I was greatly afraid he might adopt measures to get me again into slavery, a condition I then dreaded more than death.

I soon, however, learned to count money, as well as to make it, and got on swimmingly. I married soon after leaving you: in fact, I was engaged to be married before I left you; and instead of finding my companion a burden, she was truly a helpmeet. She went to live at service, and I to work on the wharf, and though we toiled hard the first winter, we never lived more happily. After remaining in New Bedford for three years, I met with Wm. Lloyd Garrison,[13] a person of whom you have *possibly* heard, as he is pretty generally known among slaveholders. He put it into my head that I might make myself service-able to the cause of the slave by devoting a portion of my time to telling my own sorrows, and those of other slaves which had come under my observation. This was the commencement of a higher state of existence than any to which I had ever aspired. I was thrown into society the most pure, enlightened and benevolent that the country affords. Among these I have never forgotten you, but have invariably made you the topic of conversation—thus giving you all the notoriety I could do. I need not tell you that the opinion formed of you in these circles, is far from being favorable. They have little respect for your honesty, and less for your religion.

But I was going on to relate to you something of my interesting experience. I had not long enjoyed the excellent society to which I have referred, before the light of its excellence exerted a beneficial influence on my mind and heart. Much of my early dislike of white persons was removed, and their manners, habits and customs, so entirely unlike what I had been used to in the kitchen-quarters on the plantations of the South, fairly charmed me, and gave me a strong disrelish for the coarse and degrading customs of my former condition. I therefore made an effort so to improve my mind and deportment, as to be somewhat fitted to the station to which I seemed almost providentially called. The transition from degradation to respectability was indeed great, and to get from one to the other without carrying some marks of one's former condition,

---

13. William Lloyd Garrison (1805–1879) was the editor of *The Liberator*, a leading antislavery newspaper in Boston, Massachusetts.

is truly a difficult matter. I would not have you think that I am now entirely clear of all plantation peculiarities, but my friends here, while they entertain the strongest dislike to them, regard me with that charity to which my past life somewhat entitles me, so that my condition in this respect is exceedingly pleasant. So far as my domestic affairs are concerned, I can boast of as comfortable a dwelling as your own. I have an industrious and neat companion, and four dear children—the oldest a girl of nine years, and three fine boys, the oldest eight, the next six, and the youngest four years old. The three oldest are now going regularly to school—two can read and write, and the other can spell with tolerable correctness words of two syllables: Dear fellows! they are all in comfortable beds, and are sound asleep, perfectly secure under my own roof. There are no slaveholders here to rend my heart by snatching them from my arms, or blast a mother's dearest hopes by tearing them from her bosom. These dear children are ours—not to work up into rice, sugar and tobacco, but to watch over, regard, and protect, and to rear them up in the nurture and admonition of the gospel to train them up in the paths of wisdom and virtue, and, as far as we can to make them useful to the world and to themselves. Oh! sir, a slaveholder never appears to me so completely an agent of hell, as when I think of and look upon my dear children. It is then that my feelings rise above my control. I meant to have said more with respect to my own prosperity and happiness, but thoughts and feelings which this recital has quickened unfits me to proceed further in that direction. The grim horrors of slavery rise in all their ghastly terror before me, the wails of millions pierce my heart, and chill my blood. I remember the chain, the gag, the bloody whip, the death-like gloom overshadowing the broken spirit of the fettered bondman, the appalling liability of his being torn away from wife and children, and sold like a beast in the market. Say not that this is a picture of fancy. You well know that I wear stripes on my back inflicted by your direction; and that you, while we were brothers in the same church, caused this right hand, with which I am now penning this letter, to be closely tied to my left, and my person dragged at the pistol's mouth, fifteen miles, from the Bay side to Easton, to be sold like a beast in the market, for the alleged crime of intending to escape from your possession. All this and more you remember, and know to be perfectly true, not only of yourself, but of nearly all of the slaveholders around you.

At this moment, you are probably the guilty holder of at least three of my own dear sisters, and my only brother in bondage. These you regard as your property. They are recorded on your ledger, or perhaps have been sold to human flesh mongers, with a view to filling your own ever-hungry purse. Sir, I desire to know how and where these dear sisters are. Have you sold them? or are they still in your possession? What has become of them? are they living or dead? And my dear old grandmother, whom you turned out like an old horse, to die in the woods—is she still alive? Write and let me know all about them.

If my grandmother be still alive, she is of no service to you, for by this time she must be nearly eighty years old—too old to be cared for by one to whom she has ceased to be of service, send her to me at Rochester, or bring her to Philadelphia, and it shall be the crowning happiness of my life to take care of her in her old age. Oh! she was to me a mother, and a father, so far as hard toil for my comfort could make her such. Send me my grandmother that I may watch over and take care of her in her old age. And my sisters, let me know all about them. I would write to them, and learn all I want to know of them, without disturbing you in any way, but that, through your unrighteous conduct, they have been entirely deprived of the power to read and write. You have kept them in utter ignorance, and have therefore robbed them of the sweet enjoyments of writing or receiving letters from absent friends and relatives. Your wickedness and cruelty committed in this respect on your fellow-creatures, are greater than all the stripes you have laid upon my back, or theirs. It is an outrage upon the soul—a war upon the immortal spirit, and one for which you must give account at the bar of our common Father and Creator.

The responsibility which you have assumed in this regard is truly awful—and how you could stagger under it these many years is marvelous. Your mind must have become darkened, your heart hardened, your conscience seared and petrified, or you would have long since thrown off the accursed load and sought relief at the hands of a sin-forgiving God. How, let me ask, would you look upon me, were I some dark night in company with a band of hardened villains, to enter the precincts of your elegant dwelling and seize the person of your own lovely daughter Amanda, and carry her off from your family, friends and all the loved ones of her youth—make her my slave—compel her to work, and I take her wages—place her name on my ledger as property—disregard her personal rights—fetter the powers of her immortal soul by denying her the right and privilege of learning to read and write—feed her coarsely—clothe her scantly, and whip her on the naked back occasionally; more and still more horrible, leave her unprotected—a degraded victim to the brutal lust of fiendish overseers, who would pollute, blight, and blast her fair soul—rob her of all dignity—destroy her virtue, and annihilate all in her person the graces that adorn the character of virtuous womanhood? I ask how would you regard me, if such were my conduct? Oh! the vocabulary of the damned would not afford a word sufficiently infernal, to express your idea of my God-provoking wickedness. Yet sir, your treatment of my beloved sisters is in all essential points, precisely like the case I have now supposed. Damning as would he such a deed on my part, it would be no more so than that which you have committed against me and my sisters.

I will now bring this letter to a close, you shall hear from me again unless you let me hear from you. I intend to make use of you as a weapon with which to assail the system of slavery—as a means of concentrating public attention on the system, and deepening their horror of trafficking in the souls and bodies of men. I shall make use of you as a means of exposing the character of the American church and clergy—and as a means of bringing this guilty nation with yourself to repentance. In doing this I entertain no malice toward you personally. There is no roof under which you would be more safe than mine, and there is nothing in my house which you might need for your comfort, which I would not readily grant. Indeed, I should esteem it a privilege, to set you an example as to how mankind ought to treat each other.

I am your fellow man, but not your slave,
FREDERICK DOUGLASS.

• not operating from a place of fear
↳ diminishing his previous master
↳ signifying his own freedom

Facts of living in South.
critique of Northern ppl. ⇒ slavery a preverted form
of aristocracy. features
returned.
[Place & Cond]
↳ even slave says = South is
home.
place of
birth.

PART II
DOUGLASS ON THE LAW, POLITICS, & MORALITY OF ABOLITION

6. "The Constitution and Slavery," an essay published in *The North Star*, March 16, 1849[1]

The assertion which we made five weeks ago, that "the Constitution, *if strictly construed according to its reading*," is not a pro-slavery instrument, has excited some interest amongst our anti-slavery brethren. Letters have reached us from different quarters on the subject. Some of these express agreement and pleasure with our views, and others, surprise and dissatisfaction. Each class of opinion and feeling is represented in the letters which we have placed in another part of this week's paper. The one from our friend Gerrit Smith,[2] represents the view which the Liberty Party takes of this subject, and that of Mr. Robert Forten[3] is consistent with the ground occupied by a majority of the American Anti-Slavery Society.

Whether we shall be able to set ourselves right in the minds of those on the one side of this question or the other, and at the same time vindicate the correctness of our former assertion, remains to be seen. Of one thing, however, we can assure our readers, and that is, that we bring to the consideration of this subject no partisan feelings, nor the slightest wish to make ourselves consistent with the creed of either anti-slavery party, and that our only aim is to know what is truth and what is duty in respect to the matter in dispute, holding ourselves perfectly free to change our opinion in any direction, and at any time which may be indicated by our immediate apprehension of truth, unbiased by the smiles or frowns of any class or party of abolitionists. The only truly consistent man is he who will, for the sake of being right today, contradict what he said wrong yesterday. "Sufficient unto the day is the evil thereof."[4] True stability consists not in being of the same opinion now as formerly, but in a fixed principle of honesty, even urging us to the adoption or rejection of that which may seem to us true or false at the ever-present now.

applies to everything

Before entering upon a discussion of the main question, it may be proper to remove a misapprehension into which Gerrit Smith and Robert Forten seem to have fallen, in respect to what we mean by the term, "strictly construed

---

1. This essay provides one example of Douglass defending the "Garrisonian" interpretation of the Constitution as a proslavery document.
2. Gerrit Smith (1797–1874) was an American abolitionist, philanthropist, and politician.
3. Robert Forten (1813–1864) was an American abolitionist.
4. Matthew 6:34 (all Bible references are from the King James version).

according to its reading," as used by us in regard to the Constitution. Upon a second reading of these words, we can readily see how easily they can be made to mean more than we intended. What we meant then, and what we would be understood to mean now, is simply this—that the Constitution of the United States, standing alone, and construed *only* in the light of its letter, without reference to the opinions of the men who framed and adopted it, or to the uniform, universal and undeviating practice of the nation under it, from the time of its adoption until now, is not a pro-slavery instrument. Of this admission we are perfectly willing to give our esteemed friend Gerrit Smith, and all who think with him on this subject, the fullest benefit; accompanied, however, with this explanation, that it was made with no view to give the public to understand that we held this construction to be the proper one of that instrument, and that it was drawn out merely because we were unwilling to go before the public on so narrow an issue, and one about which there could be so little said on either side. How a document would appear under one construction is one thing; but whether the construction be the right one is quite another and a very different thing. Confounding these two things has led Gerrit Smith to think too favorably of us, and Robert Forten too unfavorably. We may agree with the Roman Catholic, that the language of Christ, with respect to the sacrament, if construed according to reading, teaches the doctrine of transubstantiation. But the admission is not final, neither are we understood by doing so, to sanction that irrational though literal doctrine. Neither Roman Catholic nor Protestant could attach any importance to such an admission. It would neither afford pleasure to the Catholic, nor pain to the Protestant. Hoping that we have now made ourselves understood on this point, we proceed to the general question.

THE CONSTITUTIONALITY OF SLAVERY.

The Constitution of the United States. —What is it? Who made it? For whom and for what was it made? Is it from heaven or from men? How, and in what light are we to understand it? If it be divine, divine light must be our means of understanding it; if human, humanity, with all its vice and crimes, as well as its virtues, must help us to a proper understanding of it. All attempts to explain it in the light of heaven must fail. It is human, and must be explained in the light of those maxims and principles which human beings have laid down as guides to the understanding of all written instruments, covenants, contracts and agreements, emanating from human beings, and to which human beings are parties, both on the first and the second part. It is in such a light that we propose to examine the Constitution; and in this light we hold it to be a most cunningly-devised and wicked compact, demanding the most constant and earnest efforts of the friends of righteous freedom for its complete overthrow.

It was "conceived in sin, and shaped in iniquity."[5] But this will be called mere declamation, and assertion—mere "heat without light"—sound and fury signify nothing. —Have it so. Let us then argue the question with all the coolness and clearness of which an unlearned fugitive slave, smarting under the wrongs inflicted by this unholy Union, is capable. We cannot talk "lawyer like" about LAW—about its emanating from the bosom of God! —about government, and of its seat in the great heart of the Almighty! —nor can we, in connection with such an ugly matter-of-fact looking thing as the United States Constitution, bring ourselves to split hairs about the alleged legal rule of interpretation, which declares that an "act of the legislature may be set aside when it contravenes natural justice." We have to do with facts, rather than theory. The Constitution is not an abstraction. It is a living breathing fact, exerting a mighty power over the nation of which it is the bond of the Union.

Had the Constitution dropped down from the blue overhanging sky, upon a land uncursed by slavery, and without an interpreter, although some difficulty might have occurred in applying its manifold provisions, yet so cunningly is it framed, that no one would have imagined that it recognized or sanctioned slavery. But having a terrestrial, and not a celestial origin, we find no difficulty in ascertaining its meaning in all the parts which we allege to relate to slavery. Slavery existed before the Constitution, in the very states by whom it was made and adopted. —Slaveholders took a large share in making it. It was made in view of the existence of slavery, and in a manner well calculated to aid and strengthen that heaven-daring crime.

Take, for instance, article 1st, section 2d, to wit: "Representatives and direct taxes shall be apportioned among the several states which may be included within this Union, according to their respective numbers, which shall be determined by adding to the whole number of *free* persons, including those bound to service for a term of years, and including Indians not taxed, *three-fifths of all other persons.*"

A diversity of persons are here described—*persons* bound to service for a *term of years,* Indians not taxed, and three-fifths of *all other persons.* Now, we ask, in the name of common sense, can there be an honest doubt that, in states where there are slaves, that they are included in this basis of representation? To us, it is as plain as the sun in the heavens that this clause does, and was intended to mean, that the slave states should enjoy a representation of their human chattels under this Constitution. Besides, the term free, which is generally, though not always, used as the correlative of slave, "all other persons," settles the question forever that slaves are here included.

It is contended on this point by Lysander Spooner[6] and others, that the words, "all other persons," used in this article of the Constitution, relates *only*

---

5. Douglass paraphrases Psalms 51:5.
6. Lysander Spooner (1808–1887) was an American abolitionist and entrepreneur.

to aliens. We deny that the words bear any such construction. Are we to presume that the Constitution, which so carefully points out a class of persons for exclusion, such as "Indians not taxed," would be silent with respect to another class which it was meant equally to exclude? We have never studied logic, but it does seem to us that such a presumption would be very much like an absurdity. And the absurdity is all the more glaring, when it is remembered and the language used immediately after the words "excluding Indians not taxed," (having done with exclusions) it includes "*all other persons.*" It is as easy to suppose that the Constitution contemplates *including* Indians (against its express declaration to the contrary) as it is to suppose that it should be construed to mean the exclusion of slaves from the basis of representation, against the express language, "including all other persons." Where all are included, none remain to be excluded. The reasonings of those who are likely to take the opposite view of the clause, appear very much like quibbling, to use no harsher word. One thing is certain about this clause of the Constitution. It is this—that under it, the slave system has enjoyed a large and domineering representation in Congress, which has given laws to the whole Union in regard to slavery, ever since the formation of the government.

Satisfied that the view we have given of this clause of the Constitution is the only sound interpretation of it, we throw at once all those parts and particulars of the instrument which refer to slavery, and constitute what we conceive to be the slaveholding compromises of the Constitution, before the reader, and beg that he will look with candor upon the comments which we propose to make upon them.

"Art. 5th, Sect. 8th. —Congress shall have power to suppress insurrections."

"Art. 1st, Sect. 9th. —The migration or importation of any such persons as any of the states now existing shall think proper to admit, shall not be prohibited by Congress prior to the year one thousand eight hundred and eight; but a tax or duty may be imposed, not exceeding ten dollars each person."

"Art. 4th, Sec. 2nd. —No person held to service or labor in one state, escaping into another, shall in consequence of any law or regulation therein, be discharged from such service or labor, but shall be delivered up on claim of the party to whom such service or labor may be due."

"Art. 4th, Sec. 4th.—The United States shall guarantee to every state in this Union a Republican form of Government; and shall protect each of them against invasion; and on application of the Legislature, or of the Executive (when the Legislature cannot be convened) against Domestic violence."

The first article and ninth section is a full, complete and broad sanction of the slave trade for twenty years. In this compromise of the Constitution, the parties to it pledged the national arm to protect that infernal trade for twenty years. While all other subjects of commerce were left under the control of Congress, this species of commerce alone was constitutionally exempted. And why was this the case? Simply because South Carolina and Georgia declared, through their delegates that framed the Constitution, that they would not come into the Union if this traffic in human flesh should be prohibited. Mr. [John] Rutledge,[7] of South Carolina (a distinguished member of the convention that framed the Constitution) said, "if the convention thinks that North Carolina, South Carolina, and Georgia, will ever agree to the plan, *unless their right to import slaves be untouched*, the expectation is vain." Mr. [Charles] Pinckney[8] said, South Carolina could never receive the plan, "*if it prohibits the slave trade.*" In consequence of the determination of these states to stand out of the Union in case of the traffic in human flesh should be prohibited, and from one was adopted, as a *compromise*; and shameful as it is, it is by no means more shameful than others which preceded and succeeded it. The slaveholding South, by that unyielding tenacity and consistency which they usually contend for their measures, triumphed, and the doughface North was brought to the disgraceful terms in question, just as they have been ever since on all questions touching the subject of slavery.

As a compensation for their base treachery to human freedom and justice, the North were permitted to impose a tax of ten dollars for each person imported, with which to swell the coffers of the national treasury, thus baptizing the infant republic with the bloodstained gold.

Art. 4th, Sec. 2nd.—This article was adopted with a view to restoring fugitive slaves to their masters—ambiguous, to be sure, but sufficiently explicit to answer the end sought to be attained. Under it, and in accordance with it, the Congress enacted the atrocious "law of '93,"[9] making it penal in a high degree to harbor or shelter the flying fugitive. The whole nation that adopted it, consented to become kidnappers, and the whole land converted into slave-hunting ground.

Art. 4th, Sec. 4th.—Pledges the national arm to protect the slaveholder from *domestic violence*, and is the safeguard of the Southern tyrant against the vengeance of the outraged and plundered slave. Under it, the nation is bound to do the bidding of the slaveholder, to bring out the whole naval and military power of the country, to crush the refractory slaves into obedience to their cruel masters. Thus has the North, under the Constitution, not only consented to form bulwarks around the system of slavery, with all its bloody enormities, to prevent the slave from escape, but has planted its uncounted feet and tremendous weight on the heaving hearts of American bondmen, to prevent them

---

7. John Rutledge (1739–1800) was an American politician who was a signer of the US Constitution and the second chief justice of the US Supreme Court.
8. Charles Pinckney (1757–1824) was an American politician who was a signer of the US Constitution.
9. This is a reference to the Fugitive Slave Act of 1793.

from rising to gain their freedom. Could pandemonium devise a Union more inhuman, unjust, and affronting to God and man, than this? Yet such is the Union consummated under the Constitution of the United States. It is truly a compact demanding immediate disannulment, and one which, with our view of its wicked requirements, we can never enter.

We might just here drop the pen and the subject, and assume the Constitution to be what we have briefly attempted to prove it to be, radically and essentially pro-slavery, in fact as well as in its tendency; and regard our position to be correct beyond the possibility of an honest doubt, and treat those who differ from us as mere cavilers, bent upon making the worse appear the better reason; or we might anticipate the objections which are supposed to be valid against that position. We are, however, disposed to do neither. —We have too much respect for the men opposed to us to do the former, and have too strong a desire to have those objections put in their most favorable light, to do the latter. —We are prepared to hear all sides, and to give the arguments of our opponents a candid consideration. Where an honest expression of views is allowed, Truth has nothing to fear. [. . .]

7. "Change of Opinion Announced," an essay published in *The Liberator*, May 23, 1851[10]

The debate on the resolution relative to anti-slavery newspapers [at the annual meeting of the American Anti-Slavery Society][11] assumed such a character as to make it our duty to define the position of the *North Star* in respect to the Constitution of the United States. The ground having been directly taken, that no paper ought to receive the recommendation of the American Anti-Slavery Society that did not assume the Constitution to be a pro-slavery document, we felt in honor bound to announce at once to our old anti-slavery companions that we no longer possessed the requisite qualification for their official approval and commendation; and to assure them that we had arrived at the firm conviction that the Constitution, construed in the light of well established rules of legal interpretation, might be made consistent in its details with the noble purposes avowed in its preamble; and that hereafter we should insist upon the application of such rules to that instrument, and demand that it be wielded in behalf of emancipation. The change in our opinion on this subject has not been hastily arrived at. A careful study of the writings of Lysander Spooner, of Gerrit Smith, and of William Goodell,[12] has brought us to our present conclusion. We found, in our former position, that, when debating the question, we were compelled to go behind the letter of the Constitution, and to seek its meaning in the history and practice of the nation under it—a process always attended with disadvantages; and certainly we feel little inclination to shoulder disadvantages of any kind, in order to give slavery the slightest protection. In short, we hold it to be a system of lawless violence; that it *never was lawful, and never can be made so*; and that it is the first duty of every American citizen, whose conscience permits so to do, to use his *political* as well as his *moral* power for its overthrow. Of course, this avowal did not pass without animadversion, and it would have been strange if it had passed without some crimination; for it is hard for any combination or party to attribute good motives to anyone who differs from them in what they deem a vial point.

---

10. After much study, debate, and reflection, Douglass published this editorial announcing his rejection of the Garrisonian reading of the Constitution as proslavery in favor of the antislavery interpretation of the document defended by Gerrit Smith, William Goodell, Lysander Spooner, and others.

11. The American Anti-Slavery Society was founded by William Lloyd Garrison and several others in 1833.

12. William Goodell (1792–1878) was an American abolitionist.

Brother Garrison at once exclaimed, "There is roguery somewhere!" but we can easily forgive this hastily expressed imputation, falling, as it did, from the lips of one to whom we shall never cease to be grateful, and for whom we have cherished (and do now cherish) a veneration only inferior in degree to that which we own to our conscience and our God. [. . .]

• What if one was to place it in context?

8. "Is Civil Government Right?" an essay published in *Frederick Douglass' Paper*, October 23, 1851[13]

This question is raised and summarily disposed of in a letter, which appears in another column, addressed by Mr. [Henry C.] Wright to Gerrit Smith, Esq. The writer thinks a just civil government "*an impossibility.*" He does not, in this, object to the abuses of power, but to the power itself, and he classes the assumed right of government with robbery, piracy and slavery. "*To speak of a righteous human ruler is the same as to speak of a righteous thief, a righteous robber, a righteous murderer, a righteous pirate or a righteous slaveholder.*"

To those unacquainted with Mr. Wright's style, this letter will seem an outburst of unusual extravagance on his part; but we must pronounce it *tame* as compared with many of his productions, on this and on kindred subjects. There is in it an absence of startling assertion, and an attempt at reasoning such as Mr. Wright does not always condescend to in dealing with opponents. We, therefore, take pleasure in laying his letter before our readers, that they may have both sides of a subject which is to them, and to us, one of unspeakable interest.

Were we to presume to criticize Mr. Wright's letter, we should object to his limited statement of the assumed right upon which civil government is based. He says, "*the assumption is, that man is invested by God with power to dictate law to man and to punish him if he do not obey.*"

To this statement we object, that the vital principle of government is left out. It contains the skeleton, but the life is not there. —The bones and sinews are retained, but the vital spark which should animate them is gone. Were we to make an inquiry into the rightfulness of civil government, we should (perhaps owing to the diffuseness of our intellect) begin by assuming, first, that man is a social as well as an individual being; that he is endowed, by his Creator, with faculties and powers suited to his individuality and to society. Second, that individual isolation is unnatural, unprogressive and against the highest interests of man; and that society is required, by the natural wants and necessities inherent in human existence. —Third, that man is endowed with reason and understanding

13. Douglass wrote this essay in response to a critique of Gerrit Smith's involvement with the antislavery Liberty Party penned by Henry C. Wright, a prominent associate of William Lloyd Garrison. The dispute between Douglass and Smith on the one side and Wright and Garrison on the other reveals important philosophical differences between the Garrisonian doctrine of nonresistance and the core tenets of political abolitionism.

capable of discriminating between good and evil, right and wrong, justice and injustice. Fourth, that while man is constantly liable to do evil, he is still capable of apprehending and pursuing that which is good; and that, upon the whole, his evil tendencies are quite outweighed by the powers within him, impelling him to good. —In a word, that crime is the exception, and innocence is the rule of human nature. —Fifth, that rewards and punishments are natural agents for restraining evil and for promoting good, man being endowed with faculties keenly alive to both. Finally, that whatever serves to increase the happiness, to preserve the well-being, to give permanence, order and attractiveness to society, and leads to the very highest development of human perfection, is, unless positively prohibited by Divine command, to be esteemed innocent and right. The question then comes, Is human government right? Mark, the question is not, Is arbitrary, despotic, tyrannical, corrupt, unjust, capricious government right? but is society (that is a company of human beings) authorized by their Creator to institute a government for themselves, and to pass and enforce laws which are in accordance with justice, liberty and humanity? Mr. Wright says that they *have not*. His reasons are, that "*to admit the rightfulness of such government is to admit that human will or discretion is the only tenure by which we hold life, liberty or happiness. That the existence of each one is at the discretion of each and every other. That we must all live or die, be slaves or freemen, be happy or miserable, by act of Congress or Parliament,*" and much more in the same strain.

From a conclusion so revolting and terrible, he, naturally enough, recoils with a shudder. The fallacy and fatal error which form the basis of this reasoning, are the assumptions that human government is necessarily arbitrary and absolute; and that there is no difference between a righteous and a wicked government. Human government, from its very nature, is an organization, like every other human institution, limited in its powers, and subject to the very wants of human nature which call it into existence. A community of men who will organize a government, granting it the power to make them slaves or freemen, to kill them or to let them live, to make them happy or miserable at discretion, are in a pitiable condition, and far behind the Liberty Party[14] in right apprehensions of the nature and office of civil government.

"But," says Mr. Wright, "*if a man may rightfully tell his fellow-beings how to act, he may tell them how to speak, how to feel, and how to think.*" Well, what of it? Mr. Wright is constantly telling me how to act, how to think, how to feel, and how to speak; and it would be well for the world if it followed some of his telling at least. But we apprehend that the objection to government does not consist in its telling men how to think, speak, feel or act, but in the punishment

---

14. The Liberty Party was an antislavery political party founded in 1840. The party nominated Gerrit Smith as its presidential candidate in 1848 and William Goodell as its presidential candidate in 1852.

which government may see fit to inflict, and that involves the question of the rightfulness of physical force, of which we shall speak anon. Mr. Wright does not object to societies expressing by their votes their dissent or approval of the thoughts, sayings, feelings and actions of men. He, doubtless, deems this proper and praiseworthy; nor does he, as we understand him, object to the principle that majorities ought to rule; at any rate, he certainly cannot think that the minority of the members of the American Anti-Slavery Society ought to adopt measures which are condemned by the majority. Why is this respect to be shown to the majority? Simply because a majority of human hearts and intellects may be presumed, as a general rule, to take a wiser and more comprehensive view of the matters upon which they act than the minority. It is in accordance with the doctrine that good is the rule, and evil the exception in the character and constitution of man. If the fact were otherwise (that is, if men were more disposed to evil than to good) it would, indeed, be dangerous for men to enter into a compact, by which power should be wielded by the mass, for then evil being predominant in man, would predominate in the mass, and innumerable hardships would be inflicted upon the good. The old assertion of the wickedness of the masses, and their consequent unfitness to govern themselves, is the falsehood and corruption out of which have sprung the despotic and tyrannical conspiracies, calling themselves governments, in the old world. They are founded not in the aggregate morality and intelligence of the people, but in a fancied divine authority, resulting from the inherent incompetency of the people to direct their own temporal concerns. Kings and despots flourish in such a soil, poisoning the moral atmosphere with oppression and paralyzing the spirit of progress by choking the utterance of free speech from the platform and the press. It is confounding such government with a righteous democratic government, and charging the crimes of the former upon the latter, that has led such men as Mr. Wright to array themselves against the Liberty Party.

But how different is the ground assumed by Gerrit Smith and his associates, from that upon which despotic governments are based. The one assumes that the people may be trusted, and the other, that no confidence can be placed in them. The one that the people, the whole people, should have a voice in making the laws under which they live, and the other, that the people should have nothing to do with the laws but to obey them; or (to use a favorite sentiment of Mr. Wright) one regards institutions for men, and the other regards men for institutions. But it is alleged that the power claimed for government by the Liberty Party, is, in essence, the same as that which is claimed by despots, and is, therefore, to be rejected. This allegation is unfounded, since there is all the difference between the cases, that exists between limited and restricted power, and power unlimited and unrestricted. In the one case, the governing power is in the hands of the people, who are supposed to know their rights and to understand their interests; and in the other, the governing power is in the hands of an individual, who, from his very circumstances and environments, can be supposed to have very little sympathy with the people, or very little desire to promote their intelligence as to their best interests.

Mr. Wright will, however, insist that the exercise of governmental power is practically the same, whether it be wielded by King Individual or King Majority; that the will, caprice, or what not, of the majority is as imperious in its tone, and must be as implicitly obeyed as that of the king.

The answer is, that the Liberty Party concedes no governmental authority to pass laws, nor to compel obedience to any laws, against the natural rights and happiness of man. It affirms that the office of government is protection; and when it ceases to protect the rights of man, they repudiate it as a tyrannical usurpation. But our friend asks, "*Who is to decide?*" We answer, the Constitution and the common sense of the people, manifested in the choice of their law-makers. It may still be further asked, will they always decide rightly? They may not, for the individual does not always decide for himself what is for his best interest. What then? Shall we abolish the individual, and deny him the right to govern himself because he may sometimes govern wrongly? The reasoning which would deny the right of society to frame laws for its own protection, preservation and happiness, would, if rigidly adhered to, deny to man the right to govern himself; for is he not a frail mortal, and has he any more right to ruin himself than he has to ruin others? But again, the very fact that a government is instituted by all, and rests upon all for support and direction, is the strongest guarantee that can be given that it will be wielded justly and impartially. With all the drawbacks upon government which fancy can depict, or imagination conjure up, society possessing it is as paradise to pandemonium, compared with society without it.

Mr. Wright objects to civil government because "there is no crime which man may not and will not perpetrate against man." A strange reason against government truly. —We use the fact in favor of government, not against it. Because there are hardened villains, enemies to themselves and to the well-being of society, who will cheat, steal, rob, burn and murder their fellow-creatures, and because these are the exceptions to the mass of humanity, society has the right to protect itself against their depredations and aggressions upon the common weal. Society without law, is society with a curse, driving men into isolation and depriving them of one of the greatest blessings of which man is susceptible. It is no answer to this to say that if all men would obey the laws of God, lead virtuous lives, do by others as they would be done unto, human government would be unnecessary; for it is enough to know, as Mr. Wright declares, that "there are no crimes which man may not and will not perpetrate against his fellow-man," to justify society in resorting to force, as a means of protecting itself from crime and its consequences.

If it be alleged that to repel aggression by force is to promote aggression; and that to submit to be robbed, plundered and enslaved is the true way to establish justice and liberty among men, the answer is, that the theory is contradicted by the facts of human nature, and by the experience of men in all ages. —The present condition of the slave population of this country is a striking illustration of the fallacy that submission is the best remedy for the wrongs and injustice to which they are subjected. Here we have two hundred years of non-resisting submission, and equally two hundred years of cruel injustice; and so far from this submission serving as a remedy for the frightful injustice, it is urged by the oppressors as a reason for persisting in their course. Concessions do but lead to exactions, and submission, to the imposition of still greater hardships, and this is the lesson taught by the facts of human nature, and by the history of the world. Men need to be taught, not only the happy consequences arising from dealing justly, but the dreadful consequences which result from injustice; their fears, therefore, may be as legitimately appealed to as their hopes, and he who repudiates such appeals, throws away an important instrumentality for establishing justice among men, and promoting the peace and happiness of society. All tyrants, all oppressors should be taught, by precept and by example, that, in trampling wantonly and ruthlessly upon the lives and liberties of their unoffending brother-men, they forfeit their own right to liberty, and richly deserve the slavery and death that they inflict upon others. Mr. Wright may say that the slave should appeal to the humanity and to the sense of justice of his master, and thus overcome evil with good; but, once enslaved, the master may forbid such an appeal; for, to use the language of Mr. Wright, the power claimed is such as may enable the slave-holder to tell his slave, not only "how to act," but how to speak, think and feel; and he may deprive his victim of every means of reaching his sense of justice, except through his bodily fears. This, then, is our reasoning: that when every avenue to the understanding and heart of the oppressor is closed, when he is deaf to every moral appeal, and rushes upon his fellow-man to gratify his own selfish propensities at the expense of the rights and liberties of his brother-man, the exercise of physical force, sufficient to repel the aggression, is alike the right and the duty of society.

Truth may withstand falsehood, love may overcome hatred, opinion may be opposed to opinion, the theory of liberty may be opposed to slavery, and common sense alike teaches that physical resistance is the antidote for physical violence.

It is asked, in view of these conclusions, when will wars cease? We answer, when man shall learn to respect the rights of man: "*first pure, then peaceable.*"[15] There can be no peace while there is oppression. The true way to give peace to the world is, to establish justice in the world; and regarding righteous civil government as an important means to this great end, we unhesitatingly and heartily consecrate ourselves, within our humble sphere, to its advocacy.

---

15. James 3:17.

9. "What to the Slave Is the Fourth of July?" a speech delivered in Rochester, New York on July 5, 1852 and published as a pamphlet (Rochester: Lee, Mann, & Company, 1852)[16]

MR. PRESIDENT, FRIENDS AND FELLOW CITIZENS:

He who could address this audience without a quailing sensation, has stronger nerves than I have. I do not remember ever to have appeared as a speaker before any assembly more shrinkingly, nor with greater distrust of my ability, than I do this day. A feeling has crept over me, quite unfavorable to the exercise of my limited powers of speech. The task before me is one which requires much previous thought and study for its proper performance. I know that apologies of this sort are generally considered flat and unmeaning. I trust, however, that mine will not be so considered. Should I seem at ease, my appearance would much misrepresent me. The little experience I have had in addressing public meetings, in country school houses, avails me nothing on the present occasion.

The papers and placards say, that I am to deliver a Fourth of July oration. This certainly, sounds large, and out of the common way, for me. It is true that I have often had the privilege to speak in this beautiful hall, and to address many who now honor me with their presence. But neither their familiar faces, nor the perfect gage I think I have of Corinthian Hall, seems to free me from embarrassment.

The fact is, ladies and gentlemen, the distance between this platform and the slave plantation, from which I escaped, is considerable—and the difficulties to be overcome in getting from the latter to the former, are by no means slight. That I am here today, is, to me, a matter of astonishment as well as of gratitude. You will not, therefore, be surprised, if in what I *have* to say, I evince no elaborate preparation, nor grace my speech with any high sounding exordium. With little experience and with less learning, I have been able to throw my thoughts hastily and imperfectly together; and trusting to your patient and generous indulgence, I will proceed to lay them before you.

This, for the purpose of this celebration, is the Fourth of July. It is the birthday of your national independence, and of your political freedom. This,

16. As noted in the introduction, Douglass was invited by the Ladies Antislavery Society of Rochester to deliver an oration marking the "national anniversary" in 1852. It is widely considered to be not only one of Douglass' greatest speeches but one of the greatest speeches of the nineteenth century.

to you, is what the Passover was to the emancipated people of God. It carries your minds back to the day, and to the act of your great deliverance; and to the signs, and to the wonders, associated with that act that day. This celebration also marks the beginning of another year of your national life; and reminds you that the Republic of America is now seventy-six years old. I am glad, fellow citizens, that your nation is so young. Seventy-six years, though a good old age for a man, is but a mere speck in the life of a nation. "Three score years and ten"[17] is the allotted time for individual men; but nations number their years by thousands. According to this fact, you are, even now only in the beginning of your national career, still lingering in the period of childhood. I repeat, I am glad this is so. There is hope in the thought, and hope is much needed, under the dark clouds which lower above the horizon. The eye of the reformer is met with angry flashes, portending disastrous times; but his heart may well beat lighter at the thought that America is young, and that she is still in the impressible stage of her existence. May he not hope that high lessons of wisdom, of justice and of truth, will yet give direction to her destiny? Were the nation older, the patriot's heart might be sadder, and the reformer's brow heavier. Its future might be shrouded in gloom, and the hope of its prophets go out in sorrow. There is consolation in the thought, that America is young. —Great streams are not easily turned from channels, worn deep in the course of ages. They may sometimes rise in quiet and stately majesty, and inundate the land, refreshing and fertilizing the earth with their mysterious properties. They may also rise in wrath and fury, and bear away, on their angry waves, the accumulated wealth of years of toil and hardship. They, however, gradually flow back to the same old channel, and flow on as serenely as ever. But, while the river may not be turned aside, it may dry up, and leave nothing behind but the withered branch, and the unsightly rock, to howl in the abyss-sweeping wind, the sad tale of departed glory. As with rivers so with nations.

Fellow-citizens, I shall not presume to dwell at length on the associations that cluster about this day. The simple story of it is, that, 76 years ago, the people of this country were British subjects. The style and title of your "sovereign people" (in which you now glory) was not then born. You were under the British Crown. Your fathers esteemed the English government as the home government and England as the fatherland. This home government, you know, although a considerable distance from your home, did, in the exercise of its parental prerogatives, impose upon its colonial children, such restraints, burdens and limitations, as, in its mature judgment, it deemed wise, right and proper.

But, your fathers, who had not adopted the fashionable idea of this day, of the infallibility of government, and the absolute character of its acts, presumed

---

17. Psalms 90:10.

to differ from the home government in respect to the wisdom and the justice of some of those burdens and restraints. They went so far in their excitement as to pronounce the measures of government unjust, unreasonable, and oppressive, and altogether such as ought not to be quietly submitted to. I scarcely need say, fellow-citizens, that my opinion of those measures fully accords with that of your fathers. Such a declaration of agreement on my part, would not be worth much to anybody. It would, certainly, prove nothing, as to what part I might have taken, had I lived during the great controversy of 1776. To say *now* that America was right, and England wrong, is exceedingly easy. Everybody can say it; the dastard, not less than the noble brave, can flippantly discant on the tyranny of England toward the American colonies. It is fashionable to do so; but there was a time when, to pronounce against England, and in favor of the cause of the colonies, tried men's souls. They who did so were accounted in their day, plotters of mischief, agitators and rebels, dangerous men. To side with the right, against the wrong, with the weak against the strong, and with the oppressed against the oppressor! *here* lies the merit, and the one which, of all others, seems unfashionable in our day. The cause of liberty may be stabbed by the men who glory in the deeds of your fathers. But, to proceed.

Feeling themselves harshly and unjustly treated, by the home government, your fathers, like men of honesty, and men of spirit, earnestly sought redress. They petitioned and remonstrated; they did so in a decorous, respectful, and loyal manner. Their conduct was wholly unexceptionable. This, however, did not answer the purpose. They saw themselves treated with sovereign indifference, coldness and scorn. Yet they persevered. They were not the men to look back.

As the sheet anchor takes a firmer hold, when the ship is tossed by the storm, so did the cause of your fathers grow stronger, as it breasted the chilling blasts of kingly displeasure. The greatest and best of British statesmen admitted its justice, and the loftiest eloquence of the British senate came to its support. But, with that blindness which seems to be the unvarying characteristic of tyrants, since Pharaoh and his hosts were drowned in the Red Sea, the British government persisted in the exactions complained of.

The madness of this course, we believe, is admitted now, even by England; but, we fear the lesson is wholly lost on our present rulers.

Oppression makes a wise man mad.[18] Your fathers were wise men, and if they did not go mad, they became restive under this treatment. They felt themselves the victims of grievous wrongs, wholly incurable in their colonial capacity. With brave men there is always a remedy for oppression. Just here, the idea of a total separation of the colonies from the crown was born! It was a startling idea, much more so, than we, at this distance of time, regard it. The timid and the prudent (as has been intimated) of that day, were, of course, shocked and

---

18. Ecclesiastes 7:7.

alarmed by it. Such people lived then, had lived before, and will, probably, ever have a place on this planet; and their course, in respect to any great change (no matter how great the good to be attained, or the wrong to be redressed by it) may be calculated with as much precision as can be the course of the stars. They hate all changes, but silver, gold and copper change! Of this sort of change they are always strongly in favor.

These people were called Tories in the days of your fathers; and the appellation, probably, conveyed the same idea that is meant by a more modern, though a somewhat less euphonious term, which we often find in our papers, applied to some of our old politicians.

Their opposition to the then dangerous thought was earnest and powerful; but, amid all their terror and affrighted vociferations against it, the alarming and revolutionary idea moved on, and the country with it.

On the 2d of July, 1776, the old Continental Congress, to the dismay of the lovers of ease, and the worshippers of property, clothed that dreadful idea with all the authority of national sanction. They did so in the form of a resolution; and as we seldom hit upon resolutions, drawn up in our day, whose transparency is at all equal to this, it may refresh your minds and help my story if I read it.

"Resolved, That these united colonies *are*, and of right, ought to be free and Independent States; that they are absolved from all allegiance to the British Crown; and that all political connection between them and the State of Great Britain is, and ought to be, dissolved."

Citizens, your fathers made good that resolution. They succeeded; and today you reap the fruits of their success. The freedom gained is yours; and you, therefore, may properly celebrate this anniversary. The Fourth of July is the first great fact in your nation's history—the very ringbolt in the chain of your yet undeveloped destiny.

Pride and patriotism, not less than gratitude, prompt you to celebrate and to hold it in perpetual remembrance. I have said that the Declaration of Independence is the RINGBOLT to the chain of your nation's destiny; so, indeed, I regard it. The principles contained in that instrument are saving principles. Stand by those principles, be true to them on all occasions, in all places, against all foes, and at whatever cost.

From the round top of your ship of state, dark and threatening clouds may be seen. Heavy billows, like mountains in the distance, disclose to the leeward huge forms of flinty rocks! That *bolt* drawn, that *chain*, broken, and all is lost. *Cling to this day—cling to it*, and to its principles, with the grasp of a storm-tossed mariner to a spar at midnight.

The coming into being of a nation, in any circumstances, is an interesting event. But, besides general considerations, there were peculiar circumstances which make the advent of this republic an event of special attractiveness.

The whole scene, as I look back to it, was simple, dignified and sublime. The population of the country, at the time, stood at the insignificant number of three millions. The country was poor in the munitions of war. The population was weak and scattered, and the country a wilderness unsubdued. There were then no means of concert and combination, such as exist now. Neither steam nor lightning had then been reduced to order and discipline. From the Potomac to the Delaware was a journey of many days. Under these, and innumerable other disadvantages, your fathers declared for liberty and independence and triumphed.

Fellow citizens, I am not wanting in respect for the fathers of this republic. The signers of the Declaration of Independence were brave men. They were great men too—great enough to give fame to a great age. It does not often happen to a nation to raise, at one time, such a number of truly great men. The point from which I am compelled to view them is not, certainly the most favorable; and yet I cannot contemplate their great deeds with less than admiration. They were statesmen, patriots and heroes, and for the good they did, and the principles they contended for, I will unite with you to honor their memory.

They loved their country better than their own private interests; and, though this is not the highest form of human excellence, all will concede that it is a rare virtue, and that when it is exhibited, it ought to command respect. He who will, intelligently, lay down his life for his country, is a man whom it is not in human nature to despise. Your fathers staked their lives, their fortunes, and their sacred honor, on the cause of their country. In their admiration of liberty, they lost sight of all other interests.

They were peace men; but they preferred revolution to peaceful submission to bondage. They were quiet men; but they did not shrink from agitating against oppression. They showed forbearance; but that they knew its limits. They believed in order; but not in the order of tyranny. With them, nothing was "*settled*" that was not right. With them, justice, liberty and humanity were "*final*"; not slavery and oppression. You may well cherish the memory of such men. They were great in their day and generation. Their solid manhood stands out the more as we contrast it with these degenerate times.

How circumspect, exact and proportionate were all their movements! How unlike the politicians of an hour! Their statesmanship looked beyond the passing moment, and stretched away in strength into the distant future. They seized upon eternal principles, and set a glorious example in their defense. Mark them!

Fully appreciating the hardships to be encountered, firmly believing in the right of their cause, honorably inviting the scrutiny of an on-looking world, reverently appealing to heaven to attest their sincerity, soundly comprehending the solemn responsibility they were about to assume, wisely measuring the terrible odds against them, your fathers, the fathers of this republic, did, most deliberately, under the inspiration of a glorious patriotism, and with a sublime faith in the great principles of justice and freedom, lay deep, the cornerstone of the national super-structure, which has risen and still rises in grandeur around you.

Of this fundamental work, this day is the anniversary. Our eyes are met with demonstrations of joyous enthusiasm. Banners and pennants wave exultingly on the breeze. The din of business, too, is hushed. Even mammon seems to have quitted his grasp on this day. The ear-piercing fife and the stirring drum unite their accents with the ascending peal of a thousand church bells. Prayers are made, hymns are sung, and sermons are preached in honor of this day; while the quick martial tramp of a great and multitudinous nation, echoed back by all the hills, valleys and mountains of a vast continent, bespeak the occasion one of thrilling and universal interest—a nation's jubilee.

Friends and citizens, I need not enter further into the causes which led to this anniversary. Many of you understand them better than I do. You could instruct me in regard to them. That is a branch of knowledge in which you feel, perhaps, a much deeper interest than your speaker. The causes which led to the separation of the colonies from the British Crown have never lacked for a tongue. They have all been taught in your common schools, narrated at your firesides, unfolded from your pulpits, and thundered from your legislative halls, and are as familiar to you as household words. They form the staple of your national poetry and eloquence.

I remember, also, that, as a people, Americans are remarkably familiar with all facts which make in their own favor. This is esteemed by some as a national trait—perhaps a national weakness. It is a fact, that whatever makes for the wealth or for the reputation of Americans, and can be had *cheap!* will be found by Americans. I shall not be charged with slandering Americans, if I say I think the American side of any question may be safely left in American hands.

I leave, therefore, the great deeds of your fathers to other gentlemen whose claim to have been regularly descended will be less likely to be disputed than mine!

THE PRESENT.

My business, if I have any here today, is with the present. The accepted time with God and his cause is the ever-living now.

> *"Trust no future, however pleasant, Let the dead past bury its dead;*
> *Act, act in the living present, Heart within, and God overhead."*[19]

---

19. Henry Wadsworth Longfellow, "A Psalm of Life."

We have to do with the past only as we can make it useful to the present and to the future. To all inspiring motives, to noble deeds which can be gained from the past, we are welcome. But now is the time, the important time. Your fathers have lived, died, and have done their work, and have done much of it well. You live and must die, and you must do your work. You have no right to enjoy a child's share in the labor of your fathers, unless your children are to be blest by your labors. You have no right to wear out and waste the hard-earned fame of your fathers to cover your indolence. Sydney Smith tells us that men seldom eulogize the wisdom and virtues of their fathers, but to excuse some folly or wickedness of their own. This truth is not a doubtful one. There are illustrations of it near and remote, ancient and modern. It was fashionable, hundreds of years ago, for the children of Jacob to boast, we have "Abraham to our father,"[20] when they had long lost Abraham's faith and spirit. That people contented themselves under the shadow of Abraham's great name, while they repudiated the deeds which made his name great. Need I remind you that a similar thing is being done all over this country today? Need I tell you that the Jews are not the only people who built the tombs of the prophets, and garnished the sepulchers of the righteous? Washington could not die till he had broken the chains of his slaves. Yet his monument is built up by the price of human blood, and the traders in the bodies and souls of men, shout—"We have Washington to *our father.*"—Alas! that it should be so; yet so it is.

> "*The evil that men do, lives after them, The good is oft' interred with their bones.*"[21]

Fellow-citizens, pardon me, allow me to ask, why am I called upon to speak here today? What have I, or those I represent, to do with your national independence? Are the great principles of political freedom and of natural justice, embodied in that Declaration of Independence, extended to us? and am I, therefore, called upon to bring our humble offering to the national altar, and to confess the benefits and express devout gratitude for the blessings resulting from your independence to us?

Would to God, both for your sakes and ours, that an affirmative answer could be truthfully returned to these questions! Then would my task be light, and my burden easy and delightful. For *who* is there so cold, that a nation's sympathy could not warm him? Who so obdurate and dead to the claims of gratitude, that would not thankfully acknowledge such priceless benefits? Who so stolid and selfish, that would not give his voice to swell the hallelujahs of a nation's jubilee, when the chains of servitude had been torn from his limbs? I

---

20. Matthew 3:9.
21. William Shakespeare, *Julius Caesar*, act 3, sc. 2.

am not that man. In a case like that, the dumb might eloquently speak, and the "lame man leap as an hart."[22]

But, such is not the state of the case. I say it with a sad sense of the disparity between us. I am not included within the pale of this glorious anniversary! Your high independence only reveals the immeasurable distance between us. The blessings in which you, this day, rejoice, are not enjoyed in common. —The rich inheritance of justice, liberty, prosperity and independence, bequeathed by your fathers, is shared by you, not by me. The sunlight that brought life and healing to you, has brought stripes and death to me. This Fourth of July is *yours,* not *mine. You* may rejoice, *I must mourn.* To drag a man in fetters into the grand illuminated temple of liberty, and call upon him to join you in joyous anthems, were inhuman mockery and sacrilegious irony. Do you mean, citizens, to mock me, by asking me to speak today? If so, there is a parallel to your conduct. And let me warn you that it is dangerous to copy the example of a nation whose crimes, towering up to heaven, were thrown down by the breath of the Almighty, burying that nation in irrecoverable ruin! I can today take up the plaintive lament of a peeled and woe-smitten people!

"By the rivers of Babylon, there we sat down. Yea! we wept when we remembered Zion. We hanged our harps upon the willows in the midst thereof. For there, they that carried us away captive, required of us a song; and they who wasted us required of us mirth, saying, Sing us one of the songs of Zion. How can we sing the Lord's song in a strange land? If I forget thee, O Jerusalem, let my right hand forget her cunning. If I do not remember thee, let my tongue cleave to the roof of my mouth."[23]

Fellow citizens; above your national, tumultuous joy, I hear the mournful wail of millions! whose chains, heavy and grievous yesterday, are, today, rendered more intolerable by the jubilee shouts that reach them. If I do forget, if I do not faithfully remember those bleeding children of sorrow this day, "may my right hand forget her cunning, and may my tongue cleave to the roof of my mouth!" To forget them, to pass lightly over their wrongs, and to chime in with the popular theme, would be treason most scandalous and shocking, and would make me a reproach before God and the world. My subject, then, fellow-citizens, is AMERICAN SLAVERY. I shall see, this day, and its popular characteristics, from the slave's point of view. Standing, there, identified with the American bondman, making his wrongs mine, I do not hesitate to declare, with all my soul, that the character and conduct of this nation never looked blacker to me than on this Fourth of July! Whether we turn to the declarations of the past, or to the professions of the present, the conduct of the nation seems equally hideous and revolting. America is false to the past, false to the present,

---

22. Isaiah 35:6.
23. Psalms 137.

and solemnly binds herself to be false to the future. Standing with God and the crushed and bleeding slave on this occasion, I will, in the name of humanity which is outraged, in the name of liberty which is fettered, in the name of the Constitution and the Bible, which are disregarded and trampled upon, dare to call in question and to denounce, with all the emphasis I can command, everything that serves to perpetuate slavery—the great sin and shame of America! "I will not equivocate; I will not excuse";[24] I will use the severest language I can command; and yet not one word shall escape me that any man, whose judgment is not blinded by prejudice, or who is not at heart a slaveholder, shall not confess to be right and just.

But I fancy I hear some one of my audience say, it is just in this circumstance that you and your brother abolitionists fail to make a favorable impression on the public mind. Would you argue more, and denounce less, would you persuade more, and rebuke less, your cause would be much more likely to succeed. But, I submit, where all is plain there is nothing to be argued. What point in the anti-slavery creed would you have me argue? On what branch of the subject do the people of this country need light? Must I undertake to prove that the slave is a man? That point is conceded already. Nobody doubts it. The slaveholders themselves acknowledge it in the enactment of laws for their government. They acknowledge it when they punish disobedience on the part of the slave. There are seventy-two crimes in the State of Virginia, which, if committed by a black man (no matter how ignorant he be) subject him to the punishment of death; while only two of the same crimes will subject a white man to the like punishment. —What is this but the acknowledgement that the slave is a moral, intellectual and responsible being. The manhood of the slave is conceded. It is admitted in the fact that Southern statute books are covered with enactments forbidding, under severe fines and penalties, the teaching of the slave to read or to write. When you can point to any such laws, in reference to the beasts of the field, then I may consent to argue the manhood of the slave. When the dogs in your streets, when the fowls of the air, when the cattle on your hills, when the fish of the sea, and the reptiles that crawl, shall be unable to distinguish the slave from a brute, *then* will *I* argue with you that the slave is a man!

For the present, it is enough to affirm the equal manhood of the Negro race. Is it not astonishing that, while we are plowing, planting and reaping, using all kinds of mechanical tools, erecting houses, constructing bridges, building ships, working in metals of brass, iron, copper, silver and gold; that, while we are reading, writing and cyphering, acting as clerks, merchants and

---

24. Here Douglass quotes William Lloyd Garrison's 1831 editorial launching his antislavery newspaper, *The Liberator*. See "Commencement of *The Liberator*," in *Against Slavery*, ed. Mason Lowance (New York: Penguin, 2000), 104.

secretaries, having among us lawyers, doctors, ministers, poets, authors, editors, orators and teachers; that, while we are engaged in all manner of enterprises common to other men, digging gold in California, capturing the whale in the Pacific, feeding sheep and cattle on the hillside, living, moving, acting, thinking, planning, living in families as husbands, wives and children, and, above all, confessing and worshipping the Christian's God, and looking hopefully for life and immortality beyond the grave, we are called upon to prove that we are men!

Would you have me argue that man is entitled to liberty? that he is the rightful owner of his own body? You have already declared it. Must I argue the wrongfulness of slavery? Is that a question for Republicans? Is it to be settled by the rules of logic and argumentation, as a matter beset with great difficulty, involving a doubtful application of the principle of justice, hard to be understood? How should I look today, in the presence of Americans, dividing, and subdividing a discourse, to show that men have a natural right to freedom? speaking of it relatively, and positively, negatively, and affirmatively. To do so, would be to make myself ridiculous, and to offer an insult to your understanding. —There is not a man beneath the canopy of heaven, that does not know that slavery is wrong *for him.*

What, am I to argue that it is wrong to make men brutes, to rob them of their liberty, to work them without wages, to keep them ignorant of their relations to their fellow men, to beat them with sticks, to flay their flesh with the lash, to load their limbs with irons, to hunt them with dogs, to sell them at auction, to sunder their families, to knock out their teeth, to burn their flesh, to starve them into obedience and submission to their masters? Must I argue that a system thus marked with blood, and stained with pollution, is *wrong*? No I will not. I have better employment for my time and strength, than such arguments would imply.

What, then, remains to be argued? Is it that slavery is not divine; that God did not establish it; that our doctors of divinity are mistaken? There is blasphemy in the thought. That which is inhuman, cannot be divine! *Who* can reason on such a proposition? They that can, may; I cannot. The time for such argument is past.

At a time like this, scorching irony, not convincing argument, is needed. O! had I the ability, and could I reach the nation's ear, I would, to day, pour out a fiery stream of biting ridicule, blasting reproach, withering sarcasm, and stern rebuke. For it is not light that is needed, but fire; it is not the gentle shower, but thunder. We need the storm, the whirlwind, and the earthquake. The feeling of the nation must be quickened; the conscience of the nation must be roused; the propriety of the nation must be startled; the hypocrisy of the nation must be exposed; and its crimes against God and man must be proclaimed and denounced.

What, to the American slave, is your Fourth of July? I answer; a day that reveals to him, more than all other days in the year, the gross injustice and cruelty to which he is the constant victim. To him, your celebration is a sham; your boasted liberty, an unholy license; your national greatness, swelling vanity; your sounds of rejoicing are empty and heartless; your denunciations of tyrants, brass fronted impudence; your shouts of liberty and equality, hollow mockery; your prayers and hymns, your sermons and thanksgivings, with all your religious parade and solemnity, are, to him, mere bombast, fraud, deception, impiety, and hypocrisy—a thin veil to cover up crimes which would disgrace a nation of savages. There is not a nation on the earth guilty of practices, more shocking and bloody, than are the people of these United States, at this very hour.

Go where you may, search where you will, roam through all the monarchies and despotisms of the old world, travel through South America, search out every abuse, and when you have found the last, lay your facts by the side of the every day practices of this nation, and you will say with me, that, for revolting barbarity and shameless hypocrisy, America reigns without a rival.

THE INTERNAL SLAVE TRADE.

Take the American slave-trade, which we are told by the papers is especially prosperous just now. Ex-Senator [Thomas Hart] Benton[25] tells us that the price of men was never higher than now. He mentions the fact to show that slavery is in no danger. This trade is one of the peculiarities of American institutions. It is carried on in all the large towns and cities in one half of this confederacy; and millions are pocketed every year, by dealers in this horrid traffic. In several states, this trade is a chief source of wealth. It is called (in contradistinction to the foreign slave-trade) *"the internal slave-trade."* It is, probably, called so, too, in order to divert from it the horror with which the foreign slave-trade is contemplated. That trade has long since been denounced by this government, as piracy. It has been denounced with burning words, from the high places of the nation, as an execrable traffic. To arrest it, to put an end to it, this nation keeps a squadron, at immense cost, on the coast of Africa. Everywhere, in this country, it is safe to speak of this foreign slave-trade, as a most inhuman traffic, opposed alike to the laws of God and of man. The duty to extirpate and destroy it, is admitted even by our doctors of divinity. In order to put an end to it, some of these last have consented that their colored brethren (nominally free) should leave this country, and establish themselves on the western coast of Africa! It is, however, a notable fact, that, while so much execration is poured

---

25. Thomas Hart Benton (1782–1858) was a US senator from Missouri. He served from 1821 to 1851.

out by Americans, upon those engaged in the foreign slave-trade, the men engaged in the slave-trade between the states pass without condemnation, and their business is deemed honorable.

Behold the practical operation of this internal slave-trade, the American slave-trade, sustained by American politics and American religion. Here you will see men and women, reared like swine, for the market. You know what is a swine-drover? I will show you a man-drover. They inhabit all our Southern states. They perambulate the country, and crowd the highways of the nation, with droves of human stock. You will see one of these human flesh jobbers, armed with pistol, whip and bowie-knife, driving a company of a hundred men, women, and children, from the Potomac to the slave market at New Orleans. These wretched people are to be sold singly, or in lots, to suit purchasers. They are food for the cotton-field, and the deadly sugar-mill. Mark the sad procession, as it moves wearily along, and the inhuman wretch who drives them. Hear his savage yells and his blood-chilling oaths, as he hurries on his affrighted captives! There, see the old man, with locks thinned and gray. Cast one glance, if you please, upon that young mother, whose shoulders are bare to the scorching sun, her briny tears falling on the brow of the babe in her arms. See, too, that girl of thirteen, weeping, *yes*! weeping, as she thinks of the mother from whom she has been torn! The drove moves tardily. Heat and sorrow have nearly consumed their strength; suddenly you hear a quick snap, like the discharge of a rifle; the fetters clank, and the chain rattles simultaneously; your ears are saluted with a scream, that seems to have torn its way to the center of your soul! The crack you heard was the sound of the slave whip; the scream you heard was from the woman you saw with the babe. Her speed had faltered under the weight of her child and her chains! that gash on her shoulder tells her to move on. Follow this drove to New Orleans. Attend the auction; see men examined like horses; see the forms of women rudely and brutally exposed to the shocking gaze of American slave-buyers. See this drove sold and separated for ever; and never forget the deep, sad sobs that arose from that scattered multitude. Tell me citizens, WHERE, under the sun, you can witness a spectacle more fiendish and shocking. Yet this is but a glance at the American slave-trade, as it exists, at this moment, in the ruling part of the United States.

I was born amid such sights and scenes. To me the American slave-trade is a terrible reality. When a child, my soul was often pierced with a sense of its horrors. I lived on Philpot Street, Fell's Point, Baltimore, and have watched from the wharves, the slave ships in the Basin, anchored from the shore, with their cargoes of human flesh, waiting for favorable winds to waft them down the Chesapeake. There was, at that time, a grand slave mart kept at the head of Pratt Street, by Austin Woldfolk. His agents were sent into every town and county in Maryland, announcing their arrival, through the papers, and on flaming "*hand-bills*," headed CASH FOR NEGROES. These men were generally well-dressed men, and very captivating in their manners. Ever ready to drink, to treat, and to gamble. The fate of many a slave has depended upon the turn of a single card; and many a child has been snatched from the arms of its mother, by bargains arranged in a state of brutal drunkenness.

The flesh-mongers gather up their victims by dozens, and drive them, chained, to the general depot at Baltimore. When a sufficient number have been collected here, a ship is chartered, for the purpose of conveying the forlorn crew to Mobile, or to New Orleans. From the slave prison to the ship, they are usually driven in the darkness of night; for since the anti-slavery agitation, a certain caution is observed.

In the deep still darkness of midnight, I have been often aroused by the dead heavy footsteps, and the piteous cries of the chained gangs that passed our door. The anguish of my boyish heart was intense; and I was often consoled, when speaking to my mistress in the morning, to hear her say that the custom was very wicked; that she hated to hear the rattle of the chains, and the heart-rending cries. I was glad to find one who sympathized with me in my horror.

Fellow-citizens, this murderous traffic is, today, in active operation in this boasted republic. In the solitude of my spirit, I see clouds of dust raised on the highways of the South; I see the bleeding footsteps; I hear the doleful wail of fettered humanity, on the way to the slave-markets, where the victims are to be sold like *horses, sheep,* and *swine,* knocked off to the highest bidder. There I see the tenderest ties ruthlessly broken, to gratify the lust, caprice and rapacity of the buyers and sellers of men. My soul sickens at the sight.

> *"Is this the land your fathers loved, The freedom which they toiled to win? Is this the earth whereon they moved? Are these the graves they slumber in?"* [26]

But a still more inhuman, disgraceful, and scandalous state of things remains to be presented.

By an act of the American Congress,[27] not yet two years old, slavery has been nationalized in its most horrible and revolting form. By that act, Mason & Dixon's line has been obliterated; New York has become as Virginia; and the power to hold, hunt, and sell men, women and children, as slaves, remains no longer a mere state institution, but is now an institution of the whole United States. The power is co-extensive with the star-spangled banner, and American Christianity. Where these go, may also go the merciless slave-hunter. Where these are, man is not sacred. He is a bird for the sportsman's gun. By that most foul and fiendish of all human decrees, the liberty and person of every man are

---

26. John Greenleaf Whittier, "Stanzas for the Times."
27. Fugitive Slave Act of 1850.

put in peril. Your broad republican domain is hunting ground for *men. Not* for thieves and robbers, enemies of society, merely, but for men guilty of no crime. Your law-makers have commanded all good citizens to engage in this hellish sport. Your president, your secretary of state, your *lords, nobles,* and ecclesiastics, enforce, as a duty you owe to your free and glorious country, and to your God, that you do this accursed thing. Not fewer than forty Americans, have, within the past two years, been hunted down, and, without a moment's warning, hurried away in chains, and consigned to slavery, and excruciating torture. Some of these have had wives and children, dependent on them for bread; but of this, no account was made. The right of the hunter to his prey, stands superior to the right of marriage, and to *all* rights in this republic, the rights of God included! For black men there are neither law, justice, humanity, nor religion. The fugitives slave law makes MERCY TO THEM, A CRIME; and bribes the judge who tries them. An American JUDGE GETS TEN DOL-LARS FOR EVERY VICTIM HE CONSIGNS to slavery, and five, when he fails to do so. The oath of any two villains is sufficient, under this hell-black enactment, to send the most pious and exemplary black man into the remorse-less jaws of slavery! His own testimony is nothing. He can bring no witnesses for himself. The minister of American justice is bound by the law to hear but *one* side; and *that* side is the side of the oppressor. Let this damning fact be perpetually told. Let it be thundered around the world, that, in tyrant-killing, king-hating, people-loving, democratic, Christian America, the seats of justice are filled with judges, who hold their offices under an open and palpable *bribe,* and are bound, in deciding in the case of a man's liberty, *to hear only his accusers!*

In glaring violation of justice, in shameless disregard of the forms of admin-istering law, in cunning arrangement to entrap the defenseless, and in dia-bolical intent, this fugitive slave law stands alone in the annals of tyrannical legislation. I doubt if there be another nation on the globe, having the brass and the baseness to put such a law on the statute-book. If any man in this assembly thinks differently from me in this matter, and feels able to disprove my statements, I will gladly confront him at any suitable time and place he may select.

RELIGIOUS LIBERTY.

I take this law to be one of the grossest infringements of Christian liberty, and, if the churches and ministers of our country were not stupidly blind, or most wickedly indifferent, they, too, would so regard it.

At the very moment that they are thanking God for the enjoyment of civil and religious liberty, and for the right to worship God according to the dictates of their own consciences, they are utterly silent in respect to a law which robs religion of its chief significance, and makes it utterly worthless to a world lying in wickedness. Did this law concern the *"mint, anise* and *cumin,"*[28]—abridge the right to sing psalms, to partake of the sacrament, or to engage in any of the ceremonies of religion, it would be smitten by the thunder of a thousand pulpits. A general shout would go up from the church, demanding *repeal, repeal, instant repeal!*—And it would go hard with that politician who presumed to solicit the votes of the people without inscribing this motto on his banner. Further, if this demand were not complied with, another Scotland would be added to the history of religious liberty, and the stern old covenanters would be thrown into the shade. A John Knox[29] would be seen at every church door, and heard from every pulpit, and Fillmore would have no more quarter than was shown by Knox, to the beautiful, but treacherous Queen Mary of Scotland.[30] —The fact that the Church of our country (with fractional exceptions) does not esteem "the fugitive slave law" as a declaration of war against religious liberty, implies that that Church regards religion simply as a form of worship, an empty ceremony, and *not* a vital principle, requiring active benevolence, justice, love and good will toward man. It esteems sacrifice above mercy; psalm-singing above right doing; solemn meetings above practical righteousness. A worship that can be conducted by persons who refuse to give shelter to the houseless, to give bread to the hungry, clothing to the naked, and who enjoin obedience to a law forbidding these acts of mercy, is a curse, not a blessing to mankind. The Bible addresses all such persons as "scribes, Pharisees, hypocrites, who pay tithe of *mint, anise,* and *cumin,* and have omitted the weightier matters of the law, judgment, mercy and faith."[31]

THE CHURCH RESPONSIBLE.

But the Church of this country is not only indifferent to the wrongs of the slave, it actually takes sides with the oppressors. It has made itself the bulwark of American slavery, and the shield of American slave-hunters. Many of its most eloquent divines, who stand as the very lights of the church, have shamelessly given the sanction of religion, and the Bible, to the whole slave system. —They have taught that man may, properly, be a slave; that the relation of master and slave is ordained of God; that to send back an escaped bondman to his master is clearly the duty of all the followers of the Lord Jesus Christ; and this horrible blasphemy is palmed off upon the world for Christianity.

For my part, I would say, welcome infidelity! welcome atheism! welcome anything! in preference to the gospel, *as preached by those divines!* They convert

---

28. Matthew 23:23.
29. John Knox (1514?–1572) was a Scottish Protestant theologian and leader.
30. Queen Mary of Scotland (1542–1587) was Queen of Scotland from 1542 to 1567.
31. Matthew 23:23.

the very name of religion into an engine of tyranny, and barbarous cruelty, and serve to confirm more infidels, in this age, than all the infidel writings of Thomas Paine, Voltaire, and Bolingbroke,[32] put together, have done? These ministers make religion a cold and flinty-hearted thing, having neither principles of right action, nor bowels of compassion. They strip the love of God of its beauty, and leave the throne of religion a huge, horrible, repulsive form. It is a religion for oppressors, tyrants, man-stealers, and *thugs*. It is not that *"pure and undefiled religion"*[33] which is from above, and which is *"first pure, then peaceable, easy to be entreated,* full of mercy and good fruits, *without partiality, and without hypocrisy."*[34] But a religion which favors the rich against the poor; which exalts the proud above the humble; which divides mankind into two classes, tyrants and slaves; which says to the man in chains, *stay there*; and to the oppressor, *oppress on*; it is a religion which may be professed and enjoyed by all the robbers and enslavers of mankind; it makes God a respecter of persons,[35] denies his fatherhood of the race, and tramples in the dust the great truth of the brotherhood of man. All this we affirm to be true of the popular Church, and the popular worship of our land and nation—a religion, a Church and a worship which, on the authority of inspired wisdom, we pronounce to be an abomination in the sight of God. In the language of Isaiah, the American Church might be well addressed, "Bring no more vain oblations; incense is an abomination unto me: the new moons and Sabbaths, the calling of assemblies, I cannot away with; it is iniquity, even the solemn meeting. Your new moons, and your appointed feasts my soul hateth. They are a trouble to me; I am weary to bear them; and when ye spread forth your hands I will hide mine eyes from you. Yea! when ye make many prayers, I will not hear. YOUR HANDS ARE FULL OF BLOOD; cease to do evil, learn to do well; seek judgment; relieve the oppressed; judge for the fatherless; plead for the widow."[36]

The American Church is guilty, when viewed in connection with what it is doing to uphold slavery; but it is superlatively guilty when viewed in connection with its ability to abolish slavery.

The sin of which it is guilty is one of omission as well as of commission. Albert Barnes[37] but uttered what the common sense of every man at all observant of the actual state of the case will receive as truth, when he declared that

---

32. In this passage, Douglass refers to the English American writer and political activist Thomas Paine (1737–1809), the French writer Voltaire (1694–1778), and Henry St. John, First Viscount Bolingbroke (1678–1751), the English politician and philosopher.
33. Douglass paraphrases James 1:27.
34. James 3:17.
35. Acts 10:34.
36. Isaiah 1:13–17.
37. Albert Barnes (1798–1870) was an American theologian.

"There is no power out of the Church that could sustain slavery an hour, if it were not sustained in it."[38]

Let the religious press, the pulpit, the Sunday school, the conference meeting, the great ecclesiastical, missionary, Bible and tract associations of the land array their immense powers against slavery, and slave-holding; and the whole system of crime and blood would be scattered to the winds, and that they do not do this involves them in the most awful responsibility of which the mind can conceive.

In prosecuting the anti-slavery enterprise, we have been asked to spare the Church, to spare the ministry; but *how*, we ask, could such a thing be done? We are met on the threshold of our efforts for the redemption of the slave, by the Church and ministry of the country, in battle arrayed against us; and we are compelled to fight or flee. From *what* quarter, I beg to know, has proceeded a fire so deadly upon our ranks, during the last two years, as from the Northern pulpit? As the champions of oppressors, the chosen men of American theology have appeared—men, honored for their so-called piety, and their real learning. The LORDS of Buffalo, the SPRINGS of New York, the LATHROPS of Auburn, the COXES and SPENCERS of Brooklyn, the GANNETS and SHARPS of Boston, the DEWEYS of Washington,[39] and other great religious lights of the land, have, in utter denial of the authority of *Him*, by whom they professed to be called to the ministry, deliberately taught us, against the example of the Hebrews, and against the remonstrance of the apostles, they teach "*that we ought to obey man's law before the law of God.*"[40]

My spirit wearies of such blasphemy; and how such men can be supported, as the "standing types and representatives of Jesus Christ," is a mystery which I leave others to penetrate. In speaking of the American Church, however, let it be distinctly understood that I mean the *great mass* of the religious organizations of our land. There are exceptions, and I thank God that there are. Noble men may be found, scattered all over these Northern states, of whom Henry Ward Beecher, of Brooklyn, Samuel J. May, of Syracuse, and my esteemed friend [Rev. R. R. Raymond][41] on the platform, are shining examples; and let me say further, that, upon these men lies the duty to inspire our ranks with high religious faith and zeal, and to cheer us on in the great mission of the slave's redemption from his chains.

---

38. Albert Barnes, *Scriptural Views of Slavery* (Philadelphia: Perkins and Purves, 1846).

39. Here Douglass identifies several prominent religious leaders who defended the legitimacy of the Fugitive Slave Act.

40. Douglass inverts the message of Acts 5:29, which says, "we ought to obey God rather than man."

41. Henry Ward Beecher (1813–1887) was an abolitionist clergymen, Samuel J. May (1797–1871) was a Unitarian minister and abolitionist, and R. R. Raymond (?–1888) was a minister in Rochester, New York.

Main argument is religious (handwritten note)

RELIGION IN ENGLAND AND RELIGION IN AMERICA.

One is struck with the difference between the attitude of the American Church toward the anti-slavery movement, and that occupied by the churches in England toward a similar movement in that country. There, the Church, true to its mission of ameliorating, elevating, and improving the condition of mankind, came forward promptly, bound up the wounds of the West Indian slave, and restored him to his liberty. There, the question of emancipation was a high religious question. It was demanded, in the name of humanity, and according to the law of the living God. The Sharps, the Clarksons, the Wilberforces, the Buxtons, the Burchells and the Knibbs,[42] were alike famous for their piety, and for their philanthropy. The anti-slavery movement *there,* was not an anti-Church movement, for the reason that the Church took its full share in prosecuting that movement: and the anti-slavery movement in this country will cease to be an anti-church movement, when the church of this country shall assume a favorable, instead of a hostile position toward that movement.

Americans! your republican politics, not less than your republican religion, are flagrantly inconsistent. You boast of your love of liberty, your superior civilization, and your pure Christianity, while the whole political power of the nation (as embodied in the two great political parties) is solemnly pledged to support and perpetuate the enslavement of three millions of your countrymen. You hurl your anathemas at the crowned headed tyrants of Russia and Austria, and pride yourselves on your democratic institutions, while you yourselves consent to be the mere *tools* and *body-guards of* the tyrants of Virginia and Carolina. You invite to your shores fugitives of oppression from abroad, honor them with banquets, greet them with ovations, cheer them, toast them, salute them, protect them, and pour out your money to them like water; but the fugitives from your own land, you advertise, hunt, arrest, shoot and kill. You glory in your refinement, and your universal education; yet you maintain a system as barbarous and dreadful, as ever stained the character of a nation—a system begun in avarice, supported in pride, and perpetuated in cruelty. You shed tears over fallen Hungary, and make the sad story of her wrongs the theme of your poets, statesmen and orators, till your gallant sons are ready to fly to arms to vindicate her cause against her oppressors; but, in regard to the ten thousand wrongs of the American slave, you would enforce the strictest silence, and would hail him as an enemy of the nation who dares to make those wrongs the subject of public discourse! You are all on fire at the mention of liberty for France or for Ireland; but are as cold as an iceberg at the thought of liberty for the enslaved of America. —You discourse eloquently on the dignity of labor; yet, you sustain a system which, in its very essence, casts a stigma upon labor. You can bare your bosom to the storm of

---

42. Here Douglass identifies several important British abolitionists.

British artillery, to throw off a three-penny tax on tea; and yet wring the last hard-earned farthing from the grasp of the black laborers of your country. You profess to believe "that, of one blood, God made all nations of men to dwell on the face of all the earth,"[43] and hath commanded all men, everywhere to love one another; yet you notoriously hate (and glory in your hatred) all men whose skins are not colored like your own. You declare, before the world, and are understood by the world to declare, that you "*hold these truths to be self evident, that all men are created equal; and are endowed by their Creator with certain, inalienable rights; and that, among these are, life, liberty, and the pursuit of happiness*"; and yet, you hold securely, in a bondage, which according to your own Thomas Jefferson, "*is worse than ages of that which your fathers rose in rebellion to oppose,*"[44] a seventh part of the inhabitants of your country.

Fellow-citizens! I will not enlarge further on your national inconsistencies. The existence of slavery in this country brands your republicanism as a sham, your humanity as a base pretense, and your Christianity as a lie. It destroys your moral power abroad; it corrupts your politicians at home. It saps the foundation of religion; it makes your name a hissing, and a byword to a mocking earth. It is the antagonistic force in your government, the only thing that seriously disturbs and endangers your *Union*. It fetters your progress; it is the enemy of improvement, the deadly foe of education; it fosters pride; it breeds insolence; it promotes vice; it shelters crime; it is a curse to the earth that supports it; and yet, you cling to it, as if it were the sheet anchor of all your hopes. Oh! be warned! be warned! a horrible reptile is coiled up in your nation's bosom; the venomous creature is nursing at the tender breast of your youthful republic; *for the love of God, tear away*, and fling from you the hideous monster, and *let the weight of twenty millions crush and destroy it forever*!

THE CONSTITUTION.

But it is answered in reply to all this, that precisely what I have now denounced is, in fact, guaranteed and sanctioned by the Constitution of the United States; that, the right to hold, and to hunt slaves is a part of that Constitution framed by the illustrious fathers of this republic.

Then, *I* dare to affirm, notwithstanding all I have said before, your fathers stooped, basely stooped.

> "*To palter with us in a double sense: And keep the word of promise to the ear, But break it to the heart.*"[45]

---

43. Acts 17:26.
44. Douglass paraphrases Thomas Jefferson's language in a letter written to Jean Nicolas Demeunier, dated January 24, 1886.
45. William Shakespeare, *Macbeth*, act 5, sc. 8.

And instead of being the honest men I have before declared them to be, they were the veriest imposters that ever practiced on mankind. *This* is the inevitable conclusion, and from it there is no escape; but I differ from those who charge this baseness on the framers of the Constitution of the United States. *It is a slander upon their memory,* at least, so I believe. There is not time now to argue the constitutional question at length; nor have I the ability to discuss it as it ought to be discussed. The subject has been handled with masterly power by Lysander Spooner, Esq., by William Goodell, by Samuel E. Sewall, Esq.,[46] and last, though not least, by Gerrit Smith, Esq. These gentlemen have, as I think, fully and clearly vindicated the Constitution from any design to support slavery for an hour.

Fellow-citizens! there is no matter in respect to which, the people of the North have allowed themselves to be so ruinously imposed upon, as that of the pro-slavery character of the Constitution. In *that* instrument I hold there is neither warrant, license, nor sanction of the hateful thing; but interpreted, as it *ought* to be interpreted, the Constitution is a GLORIOUS LIBERTY DOCUMENT. Read its preamble, consider its purposes. Is slavery among them? Is it at the gateway? or is it in the temple? it is neither. While I do not intend to argue this question on the present occasion, let me ask, if it be not somewhat singular that, if the Constitution were intended to be, by its framers and adopters, a slave-holding instrument, why neither *slavery, slave-holding,* nor *slave* can anywhere be found in it. What would be thought of an instrument, drawn up, *legally* drawn up, for the purpose of entitling the city of Rochester to a track of land, in which no mention of land was made? Now, there are certain rules of interpretation, for the proper understanding of all legal instruments. These rules are well established. They are plain, common-sense rules, such as you and I, and all of us, can understand and apply, without having passed years in the study of law. I scout the idea that the question of the constitutionality, or unconstitutionality of slavery, is not a question for the people. I hold that every American citizen has a right to form an opinion of the Constitution, and to propagate that opinion, and to use all honorable means to make his opinion the prevailing one. Without this right, the liberty of an American citizen would be as insecure as that of a Frenchman. Ex-Vice-President [George] Dallas[47] tells us that the Constitution is an object to which no American mind can be too attentive, and no American heart too devoted. He further says, the Constitution, in its words, is plain and intelligible, and is meant for the homebred, unsophisticated understandings of our

---

46. Samuel Sewall (1652–1730) was a judge and writer in Massachusetts.
47. George Dallas (1792–1864) was an American politician. He served as the eleventh vice president of the United States.

fellow-citizens. Senator [John] Berrien[48] tells us that the Constitution is the fundamental law, that which controls all others. The charter of our liberties, which every citizen has a personal interest in understanding thoroughly. The testimony of Senator [Sidney] Breese,[49] Lewis Cass,[50] and many others that might be named, who are everywhere esteemed as sound lawyers, so regard the Constitution. I take it, therefore, that it is not presumption in a private citizen to form an opinion of that instrument.

Now, take the Constitution according to its plain reading, and I defy the presentation of a single proslavery clause in it. On the other hand it will be found to contain principles and purposes, entirely hostile to the existence of slavery.

I have detained my audience entirely too long already. At some future period I will gladly avail myself of an opportunity to give this subject a full and fair discussion.

Allow me to say, in conclusion, notwithstanding the dark picture I have this day presented, of the state of the nation, I do not despair of this country. There are forces in operation, which must inevitably, work the downfall of slavery. "*The arm of the Lord is not shortened*,"[51] and the doom of slavery is certain.

I, therefore, leave off where I began, with *hope*. While drawing encouragement from "the Declaration of Independence," the great principles it contains, and the genius of American institutions, my spirit is also cheered by the obvious tendencies of the age. Nations do not now stand in the same relation to each other that they did ages ago. No nation can now shut itself up, from the surrounding world, and trot round in the same old path of its fathers without interference. The time *was* when such could be done. Long established customs of hurtful character could formerly fence themselves in, and do their evil work with social impunity. Knowledge was then confined and enjoyed by the privileged few, and the multitude walked on in mental darkness. But a change has now come over the affairs of mankind. Walled cities and empires have become unfashionable. The arm of commerce has borne away the gates of the strong city. Intelligence is penetrating the darkest corners of the globe. It makes its pathway over and under the sea, as well as on the earth. Wind, steam, and lightning are its chartered agents. Oceans no longer divide, but link nations together. From Boston to London is now a holiday excursion. Space is comparatively annihilated. —Thoughts expressed on one side of the Atlantic, are distinctly heard on the other.

---

48. John Berrien (1781–1856) was an American politician. He served as a US senator from Georgia from 1825 to 1829 and then as attorney general of the United States before returning to the Senate to serve from 1841 to 1852.
49. Senator Sidney Breese (1800–1878) was a US senator from Illinois from 1843 to 1849.
50. Lewis Cass (1782–1866) was an American military official and politician. He served as a US senator from Michigan from 1857 to 1860.
51. Isaiah 59:1.

The far off and almost fabulous Pacific rolls in grandeur at our feet. The Celestial Empire, the mystery of ages, is being solved. The fiat of the Almighty, *"Let there be Light,"*[52] has not yet spent its force. No abuse, no outrage whether in taste, sport or avarice, can now hide itself from the all-pervading light. The iron shoe, and crippled foot of China must be seen, in contrast with nature. *Africa must rise and put on her yet unwoven garment. "Ethiopia shall stretch out her hand unto God."*[53] In the fervent aspirations of William Lloyd Garrison, I say, and let every heart join in saying it:

> *God speed the year of jubilee*
> *The wide world o'er!*
> *When from their galling chains set free, Th' oppress'd shall vilely bend the knee, And wear the yoke of tyranny*
> *Like brutes no more.*
> *That year will come, and freedom's reign, To man his plundered rights again Restore.*
> *God speed the day when human blood*
> *Shall cease to flow!*
> *In every clime be understood,*
> *The claims of human brotherhood,*
> *And each return for evil, good, Not blow for blow;*
> *That day will come all feuds to end,*
> *And change into a faithful friend*
> *Each foe.*
> *God speed the hour, the glorious hour, When none on earth*
> *Shall exercise a lordly power,*
> *Nor in a tyrant's presence cower; But all to manhood's*
> *stature tower, By equal birth!*
> *THAT HOUR WILL COME, to each, to all,*
> *And from his prison-house, the thrall Go forth.*
> *Until that year, day, hour, arrive,*
> *With head, and heart, and hand I'll strive, To break the rod,*
> *and rend the gyve, The spoiler of his prey deprive*
> *So witness Heaven!*
> *And never from my chosen post,*
> *Whate'er the peril or the cost,*
> *Be driven.*[54]

---

52. Genesis 1:3.
53. Psalms 68:31.
54. William Lloyd Garrison, "The Triumph of Freedom." *Selections from the Writings and Speeches of William Lloyd Garrison* (Boston: W.F. Wallcut, 1852), 316.

Conclusion?

10. "The Fugitive Slave Law," a speech delivered to the National Free Soil Convention in Pittsburgh, Pennsylvania on August 11, 1852 and published in *Frederick Douglass' Paper*, August 20, 1852[55]

Gentlemen, I take it that you are in earnest, and mean all you say by this call, and therefore I will address you. I am taken by surprise, but I never withhold a word on such an occasion as this. The object of this convention is to organize a party, not merely for the present, but a party identified with eternal principles and therefore permanent. I have come here, not so much of a free soiler as others have come. I am, of course, for circumscribing and damaging slavery in every way I can. But my motto is extermination—not only in New Mexico, but in New Orleans—not only in California but in South Carolina. Nowhere has God ordained that this beautiful land shall be cursed with bondage by enslaving men. Slavery has no rightful existence anywhere. The slaveholders not only forfeit their right to liberty, but to life itself. —The earth is God's, and it ought to be covered with righteousness, and not slavery. We expect this great national convention to lay down some such principle as this. What we want is not a temporary organization, for a temporary want, but a firm, fixed, immovable, Liberty Party. Had the old Liberty Party continued true to its principles, we never should have seen such a hell born enactment as the fugitive slave law.

In making your platform, nothing is to be gained by a timid policy. The more closely we adhere to principle, the more certainly will we command respect. Both national conventions acted in open contempt of the anti-slavery sentiment of the North, by incorporating, as the corner stone of their two platforms, the infamous law to which I have alluded—a law which, I think, will never be repealed—it is too bad to be repealed—a law fit only to be trampled under foot (suiting the action to the word). The only way to make the fugitive slave law a dead letter is to make half a dozen or more dead kidnappers. A half dozen more dead kidnappers carried down South would cool the ardor of Southern gentlemen, and keep their rapacity in check. That is perfectly right as long as the colored man has no protection. The colored men's rights are less than those of a jackass. No man can take away a jackass without submitting the

---

55. Douglass delivered this address at the convention of the new Free Soil Party in 1852. As noted in the introduction, the Free Soil Party emerged as an alternative for antislavery voters as the Liberty Party faded from the scene.

matter to twelve men in any part of this country. A black man may be carried away without any reference to a jury. It is only necessary to claim him, and that some villain should swear to his identity. There is more protection there for a horse, for a donkey, or anything, rather than a colored man—who is, therefore, justified in the eye of God, in maintaining his right with his arm.

A Voice. —Some of us do not believe that doctrine.

Douglass. —The man who takes the office of a bloodhound ought to be treated as a bloodhound; and I believe that the lines of eternal justice are sometimes so obliterated by a course of long continued oppression that it is necessary to revive them by deepening their traces with the blood of a tyrant. This fugitive slave law had the support of the Lords, and the Coxes, the Tyngs, the Sharps and the flats.[56] It is nevertheless a degradation and a scandalous outrage on religious liberty; and if the American people were not sunk into degradation too deep for one possessing so little eloquence as I do to describe, they would feel it, too. This vile, infernal law does not interfere with singing of psalms, or anything of that kind, but with the weightier matters of the law, judgment, mercy, and faith. It makes it criminal for you, sir, to carry out the principles of Christianity. It forbids you the right to do right—forbids you to show mercy—forbids you to follow the example of the good Samaritan.[57]

Had this law forbidden any of the rites of religion, it would have been a very different thing. Had it been a law to strike at baptism, for instance, it would have been denounced from a thousand pulpits, and woe to the politician who did not come to the rescue. —But, I am spending my strength for naught; what care we for religious liberty? what are we—an unprincipled set of knaves. You feel it to be so. Not a man of you that looks a fellow Democrat or Whig in the face, but knows it. But it has been said that this law is constitutional—if it were, it would be equally the legitimate sphere of government to repeal it. I am proud to be one of the disciples of Gerrit Smith, and this is his doctrine; and he only utters what all law writers have said who have risen to any eminence. Human government is for the protection of rights; and when human government destroys human rights, it ceases to be a government, and becomes a foul and blasting conspiracy; and is entitled to no respect whatever.

It has been said that our fathers entered into a covenant for this slave-catching. Who were your daddies? I take it they were men, and so are you. You are the sons of your fathers; and if you find your fathers exercising any rights that you don't find among your rights, you may be sure that they have transcended their limits. If they have made a covenant that you should do that which they

---

56. Douglass identifies a number of religious leaders who have defended the legitimacy of the Fugitive Slave Act.
57. Luke 10:25–37.

have no right to do themselves, they transcended their own authority, and surely it is not binding on you. If you look over the list of your rights, you do not find among them any right to make a slave of your brother.

Well, you have just as good a right to do so as your fathers had. It is a fundamental truth that every man is the rightful owner of his own body. If you have no right to the possession of another man's body your fathers had no such right. But suppose that they have written in a constitution that they have a right, you and I have no right to conform to it. Suppose you and I had made a deed to give away two or three acres of blue sky; would the sky fall—and would anybody be able to plow it? You will say that this is an absurdity, and so it is. The binding quality of law is its reasonableness. I am safe, therefore, in saying, that slavery cannot be legalized at all. I hope, therefore, that you will take the ground that this slavery is a system, not only of wrong, but is of a lawless character, and cannot be Christianized nor legalized.

Can you hear me in that end of the hall now? I trust that this convention will be the means of laying before the country the principles of the Liberty Party which I have the honor to represent, to some extent, on this floor. Slavery is such a piracy that it is known neither to law nor gospel—it is neither human nor divine—a monstrosity that cannot be legalized. If they took this ground it would be the handwriting on the wall to the Belshazzars of the South.[58] It would strip the crime of its legality, and all the forms of law would shrink back with horror from it. As I have always an object when speaking on such subjects as this, I wish you to supply yourselves with Gerrit Smith's pamphlet on civil government, which I now hold in my hand. I thought you doubted the impossibility of legalizing slavery.

Could a law be made to pass away any of your individual rights? No. And so neither can a law be made to pass away the right of the black man. This is more important than most of you seem to think. You are about to have a party, but I hope not such a party as will gather up the votes, here and there, to be swallowed up at a meal by the great parties. I think I know what some leading men are now thinking. We hear a great deal of the independent, free democracy—at one time independent and another time dependent—but I want always to be independent, and not hurried to and fro into the ranks of Whigs or Democrats. It has been said that we ought to take the position to gain the greatest number of voters, but that is wrong.

We have had enough of that folly. It was said in 1848 that Martin Van Buren[59] would carry a strong vote in New York; he did so but he almost ruined us. He merely looked at us as into the pigpen to see how the animal grew; but

---

58. Daniel 5.

59. Martin Van Buren (1782–1862) was a New York politician who served as vice president, secretary of state, and the eighth president of the United States.

the table was the final prospect in view; he regarded the Free Soil Party as a
fatling to be devoured. Numbers should not be looked to so much as right. The
man who is right is a majority. He who has God and conscience on his side,
has a majority against the universe. Though he does not represent the present
state, he represents the future state. If he does not represent what we are, he
represents what we ought to be. [. . .]

11. "Is It Right and Wise to Kill a Kidnapper?" an essay published in *Frederick Douglass' Paper*, June 2, 1854[60]

A Kidnapper has been shot dead, while attempting to execute the fugitive slave bill in Boston. The streets of Boston in sight of Bunker Hill Monument, have been stained with the warm blood of a man in the act of perpetrating the most atrocious robbery which one man can possibly commit upon another—even the wresting from him his very person and natural powers. The deed of blood, as of course must have been expected, is making a tremendous sensation in all parts of the country, and calling forth all sorts of comments. Many are branding the deed as "murder," and would visit upon the perpetrator the terrible penalty attached to that dreadful crime. The occurrence naturally brings up the question of the reasonableness, and the rightfulness of killing a man who is in the act of forcibly reducing a brother man who is guilty of no crime, to the horrible condition of a slave. The question bids fair to be one of important and solemn interest, since it is evident that the practice of slave-hunting and slave-catching, with all their attendant enormities, will either be pursued, indefinitely, or abandoned immediately according to the decision arrived at by the community.

Cherishing a very high respect for the opinions of such of our readers and friends as hold to the inviolability of the human life, and differing from them on this vital question, we avail ourselves of the present excitement in the public mind, calmly to state our views and opinions, in reference to the case in hand, asking for them an attentive and candid perusal.

Our moral philosophy on this point is our own—never having read what others may have said in favor of the views which we entertain.

The shedding of human blood at first sight, and without explanation is, and must ever be, regarded with horror; and he who takes pleasure in human slaughter is very properly looked upon as a moral monster. Even the killing of animals produces a shudder in sensitive minds, uncalloused by crime; and men are only reconciled to it by being shown, not only its reasonableness,

---

60. In 1854, a group of abolitionists attempted to liberate a fugitive slave named Anthony Burns in Boston. In a confrontation with deputies attempting to prevent this liberation, James Batchelder, "a twenty-four-year-old Irish-born Custom House truckman," was shot and killed by one of the abolitionists assisting Burns. The death of Batchelder brought the moral legitimacy of abolitionist violence to the fore as a central topic of debate. For more on the "Burns Affair," see Albert J. Von Frank, *The Trials of Anthony Burns* (Cambridge: Harvard University Press, 1998).

but its necessity. These tender feelings so susceptible to pain, are most wisely designed by the Creator, for the preservation of life. They are, especially, the affirmation of God, speaking through nature, and asserting man's right to live. Contemplated in the light or warmth of these feelings, it is in all cases, a crime to deprive a human being of life: but God has not left us solely to the guidance of our feelings, having endowed us with reason, as well as with feeling, and it is in the light of reason that this question ought to be decided.

All will agree that human life is valuable or worthless, as to the innocent or criminal use that is made of it. Most evidently, also, the possession of life was permitted and ordained for beneficent ends, and not to defeat those ends, or to render their attainment impossible. Comprehensively stated, the end of man's creation is his own good, and the honor of his Creator. Life, therefore, is but a means to an end, and must be held in reason to be not superior to the purposes for which it was designed by the All-Wise Creator. In this view there is no such thing as an absolute right to live; that is to say, the right to live, like any other human right, may be forfeited, and if forfeited, may be taken away. If the right to life stands on the same ground as the right to liberty, it is subject to all the exceptions that apply to the right to liberty. All admit that the right to enjoy liberty largely depends upon the use made of that liberty; hence society has erected jails and prisons, with a view to deprive men of their liberty when they are so wicked as to abuse it by invading the liberties of their fellows. We have a right to arrest the locomotion of a man who insists upon walking and trampling on his brother man, instead of upon the highway. This right of society is essential to its preservations; without it a single individual would have it in his power to destroy the peace and the happiness of ten thousand otherwise right minded people. Precisely on the same ground, we hold that a man may, properly, wisely and even mercifully be deprived of life. Of course life being the most precious is the most sacred of all rights, and cannot be taken away, but under the direst necessity; and not until all reasonable modes had been adopted to prevent this necessity, and to spare the aggressor.

It is no answer to this view, to say that society is selfish in sacrificing the life of an individual, or of many individuals, to save the mass of mankind, or society at large. It is in accordance with nature, and the examples of the Almighty, in the execution of his will and beneficent laws. When a man flings himself from the top of some lofty monument, against a granite pavement, in that act he forfeits his right to live. He dies according to law, and however shocking may be the spectacle he presents, it is no argument against the beneficence of the law of gravitation, the suspension of whose operation must work ruin to the well-being of mankind. The observance of this law was necessary to his preservation; and his wickedness or folly, in violating it, could not be excused without imperiling those who are living in obedience to it. The atheist sees no benevolence in the law referred to; but to such minds we address not this article. It is enough for us that the All-Wise has established the law, and determined its character, and the penalty of its violation; and however we may deplore the mangled forms of the foolish and the wicked who transgress it, the beneficence of the law itself is fully vindicated by the security it gives to all who obey it.

We hold, then, in view of this great principle, or rule, in the physical world, we may properly infer that other law or principle of justice is the moral and social world, and vindicate its practical application to the preservation of the rights and liberties of the race, as against such exceptions furnished in the monsters who deliberately violate it by taking pleasure in enslaving, imbruting and murdering their fellow-men. As human life is not superior to the laws for the preservation of the physical universe, so, too, it is not superior to the eternal law of justice, which is essential to the preservation of the rights, and the security, and happiness of the race.

The argument thus far is to the point, that society has the right to preserve itself even at the expense of the life of the aggressor; and it may be said that, while what we allege may be right enough, as regards society, it is false as vested in an individual, such as the poor, powerless, and almost friendless wretch, now in the clutches of this proud and powerful republican government. But we take it to be a sound principle, that when government fails to protect the just rights of any individual man, either he or his friends may be held in the sight of God and man, innocent, in exercising any right for his preservation which society may exercise for its preservation. Such an individual is flung, by his untoward circumstances, upon his original right of self defense. We hold, therefore, that when James Batchelder, the truckman of Boston, abandoned his useful employment, as a common laborer, and took upon himself the revolting business of a kidnapper, and undertook to play the bloodhound on the track of his crimeless brother Burns, he labeled himself the common enemy of mankind, and his slaughter was as innocent, in the sight of God, as would be the slaughter of a ravenous wolf in the act of throttling an infant. We hold that he had forfeited his right to live, and that his death was necessary, as a warning to others liable to pursue a like course.

It may be said, that though the right to kill in defense of one's liberty be admitted, it is still unwise for the fugitive slave or his friends to avail themselves of this right; and that submission, in the circumstances, is far wiser than resistance. To this it is a sufficient answer to show that submission is valuable only so long as it has some chance of being recognized as a virtue. While it has this chance, it is well enough to practice it, as it may then have some moral effect in restraining crime and shaming aggression, but no longer. That submission on the part of the slave, has ceased to be a virtue, is very evident. While fugitives quietly cross their hands to be tied, adjust their ankles to be chained, and march off unresistingly to the hell of slavery, there will ever be fiends enough to hunt them and carry them back. Nor is this all nor the worst. Such submission, instead of being set to the credit of the poor sable ones, only creates contempt for them in the public mind, and becomes an argument in the mouths of the community, that Negroes are, by nature, only fit for slavery; that slavery is their normal condition. Their patient and unresisting disposition, their unwillingness to peril their own lives, by shooting down their pursuers, is already quoted against them, as marking them as an inferior race. This reproach must be wiped out, and nothing short of resistance on the part of colored men, can wipe it out. Every slave-hunter who meets a bloody death in his infernal business is an argument in favor of the manhood of our race. Resistance is, therefore, wise as well as just. [. . .]

12. "Claims of the Negro Ethnologically Considered," a speech (commencement address) delivered on July 12, 1854 before the Literary Societies of Western Reserve College in Hudson, Ohio and published as a pamphlet (Rochester: Lee, Mann, and Company, 1854)[61]

Gentlemen, in selecting the claims of the Negro as the subject of my remarks today, I am animated by a desire to bring before you a matter of living importance—a matter upon which action, as well as thought is required. The relation subsisting between the white and black people of this country is the vital question of the age. In the solution of this question, the scholars of America will have to take an important and controlling part. This is the moral battlefield to which their country and their God now call them. In the eye of both, the neutral scholar is an ignoble man. Here, a man must be hot, or be accounted cold, or, perchance, something worse than hot or cold. The lukewarm and the cowardly, will be rejected by earnest men on either side of the controversy. The cunning man who avoids it, to gain the favor of both parties, will be rewarded with scorn; and the timid man who shrinks from it, for fear of offending either party, will be despised. To the lawyer, the preacher, the politician, and to the man of letters, there is no neutral ground. He that is not for us, is against us. Gentlemen, I assume at the start, that wherever else I may be required to speak with bated breath, here, at least, I may speak with freedom the thought nearest my heart. This liberty is implied, by the call I have received to be here; and yet I hope to present the subject so that no man can reasonably say, that an outrage has been committed, or that I have abused the privilege with which you have honored me. I shall aim to discuss the claims of the Negro, general and special, in a manner, though not scientific, still sufficiently clear and definite to enable my hearers to form an intelligent judgment respecting them.

The first general claim which may here be set up, respects the manhood of the Negro. This is an elementary claim, simple enough, but not without question. It is fiercely opposed. A respectable public journal, published in Richmond, Va., bases its whole defense of the slave system upon a denial of the Negro's manhood.

---

61. In this commencement address at Western Reserve College in Ohio, Douglass takes on the proponents of "scientific racism." Unlike most of the selections in this volume, this speech is edited a bit due to its extraordinary length, but the essence has been retained.

"The white peasant is free, and if he is a man of will and intellect, can rise in the scale of society; or at least his offspring may. He is not deprived by law of those 'inalienable rights [to] liberty and the pursuit of happiness,' by the use of it. But here is the essence of slavery—that we do declare the Negro destitute of these powers. We bind him by law to the condition of the laboring peasant forever, without his consent, and we bind his posterity after him. Now, the true question is, have we a right to do this? If we have not, all discussions about his comfortable situation, and the actual condition of free laborers elsewhere, are quite beside the point. If the Negro has the same right to his liberty and the pursuit of his own happiness that the white man has, then we commit the greatest wrong and robbery to hold him a slave—an act at which the sentiment of justice must revolt in every heart and Negro slavery is an institution which that sentiment must sooner or later blot from the face of the earth." —*Richmond Examiner.*

After stating the question thus, the *Examiner* boldly asserts that the Negro has no such right—BECAUSE HE IS NOT A MAN!

There are three ways to answer this denial. One is by ridicule; a second is by denunciation; and a third is by argument. I hardly know under which of these modes my answer today will fall. I feel myself somewhat on trial; and that this is just the point where there is hesitation, if not serious doubt. I cannot, however, argue; I must assert. To know whether a Negro is a man, it must first be known what constitutes a man. Here, as well as elsewhere, I take it, that the "coat must be cut according to the cloth." It is not necessary, in order to establish the manhood of anyone making the claim, to prove that such an one equals [Henry] Clay[62] in eloquence, or [Daniel] Webster[63] and [John C.] Calhoun[64] in logical force and directness; for, tried by such standards of mental power as these, it is apprehended that very few could claim the high designation of man. Yet something like this folly is seen in the arguments directed against the humanity of the Negro. His faculties and powers, uneducated and unimproved, have been contrasted with those of the highest cultivation; and the world has then been called upon to behold the immense and amazing difference between the man admitted, and the man disputed. The fact that these

---

62. Henry Clay (1777–1852) was a politician from Kentucky who served in the House of Representatives and the US Senate.
63. Daniel Webster (1782–1852) was a politician from Massachusetts who served in the US Senate and as secretary of state.
64. John C. Calhoun (1782–1850) was a politician from South Carolina who served in the House of Representatives, the US Senate, and as secretary of state, secretary of war, and vice president of the United States.

intellects, so powerful and so controlling, are almost, if not quite as exceptional to the general rule of humanity, in one direction, as the specimen Negroes are in the other, is quite overlooked.

Man is distinguished from all other animals, by the possession of certain definite faculties and powers, as well as by physical organization and proportions. He is the only two-handed animal on the earth—the only one that laughs, and nearly the only one that weeps. Men instinctively distinguish between men and brutes. Common sense itself is scarcely needed to detect the absence of manhood in a monkey, or to recognize its presence in a Negro. His speech, his reason, his power to acquire and to retain knowledge, his heaven-erected face, his habitudes, his hopes, his fears, his aspirations, his prophecies, plant between him and the brute creation, a distinction as eternal as it is palpable. Away, therefore, with all the scientific moonshine that would connect men with monkeys; that would have the world believe that humanity, instead of resting on its own characteristic pedestal—gloriously independent—is a sort of sliding scale, making one extreme brother to the orangutan, and the other to angels, and all the rest intermediates! Tried by all the usual, and all the unusual tests, whether mental, moral, physical, or psychological, the Negro is a MAN—considering him as possessing knowledge, or needing knowledge, his elevation or his degradation, his virtues, or his vices—whichever road you take, you reach the same conclusion, the Negro is a MAN. His good and his bad, his innocence and his guilt, his joys and his sorrows, proclaim his manhood in speech that all mankind practically and readily understand.

A very recondite author says, that "man is distinguished from all other animals, in that he resists as well as adapts himself to his circumstances." He does not take things as he finds them, but goes to work to improve them. Tried by this test, too, the Negro is a man. You may see him yoke the oxen, harness the horse, and hold the plow. He can swim the river; but he prefers to fling over it a bridge. The horse bears him on his back—admits his mastery and dominion. The barnyard fowl know his step, and flock around to receive their morning meal from his sable hand. The dog dances when he comes home, and whines piteously when he is absent. All these know that the Negro is a MAN. Now, presuming that what is evident to beast and to bird, cannot need elaborate argument to be made plain to men, I assume, with this brief statement, that the Negro is a man.

[. . . .]

Looking out upon the surface of the globe, with its varieties of climate, soil, and formations, its elevations and depressions, its rivers, lakes, oceans, islands, continents, and the vast and striking differences which mark and diversify its multitudinous inhabitants, the question has been raised, and pressed with increasing ardor and pertinacity (especially in modern times) can all these various tribes, nations, tongues, kindreds [*sic*], so widely separated, and so strangely dissimilar, have descended from a common ancestry? That is the question, and it has been answered variously by men of learning. Different modes of reasoning have been adopted, but the conclusions reached may be divided into two—the one YES, and the other NO. Which of these answers is most in accordance with facts, with reason, with the welfare of the world, and reflects most glory upon the wisdom, power, and goodness of the Author of all existence, is the question for consideration with us? On which side is the weight of the argument, rather than which side is absolutely proved?

It must be admitted at the beginning, that, viewed apart from the authority of the Bible, neither the unity, nor diversity of origin of the human family, can be demonstrated. To use the terse expression of the Rev. Dr. [Martin Brewer] Anderson,[65] who speaking on this point, says: "It is impossible to get far enough back for that." This much, however, can be done. The evidence on both sides, can be accurately weighed, and the truth arrived at with almost absolute certainty.

It would be interesting, did time permit, to give here, some of the most striking features of the various theories, which have, of late, gained attention and respect in many quarters of our country—touching the origin of mankind—but I must pass this by. The argument today, is to the unity, as against that theory, which affirms the diversity of human origin.

THE BEARINGS OF THE QUESTION.

A moment's reflection must impress all, that few questions have more important and solemn bearings, than the one now under consideration. It is connected with eternal as well as with terrestrial interests. It covers the earth and reaches heaven. The unity of the human race—the brotherhood of man—the reciprocal duties of all to each, and of each to all, are too plainly taught in the Bible to admit of cavil. —The credit of the Bible is at stake—and if it be too much to say, that it must stand or fall, by the decision of this question, it is proper to say, that the value of that sacred book—as a record of the early history of mankind—must be materially affected, by the decision of the question.

For myself I can say, my reason (not less than my feeling, and my faith) welcomes with joy, the declaration of the inspired apostle, "that God has made of one blood all nations of men for to dwell upon all the face of the earth."[66] But this grand affirmation of the unity of the human race, and many others like unto it, together with the whole account of the creation, given in the early Scriptures, must all get a new interpretation or be overthrown altogether, if a diversity of human origin can be maintained. —Most evidently, this aspect of

---

65. Martin Brewer Anderson (1815–1890) was the president of the University of Rochester.
66. Acts 17:26.

the question makes it important to those, who rely upon the Bible, as the sheet anchor of their hopes—and the framework of all religious truth. The young minister must look into this subject and settle it for himself, before he ascends the pulpit, to preach redemption to a fallen race.

The bearing of the question upon revelation, is not more marked and decided than its relation to the situation of things in our country, at this moment. One seventh part of the population of this country is of Negro descent. The land is peopled by what may be called the most dissimilar races on the globe. The black and the white—the Negro and the European—these constitute the American people—and, in all the likelihoods of the case, they will ever remain the principal inhabitants of the United States, in some form or other. The European population are greatly in the ascendant in numbers, wealth and power. They are the rulers of the country—the masters—the Africans, are the slaves—the proscribed portion of the people—and precisely in proportion as the truth of human brotherhood gets recognition, will be the freedom and elevation, in this country, of persons of African descent. In truth, this question is at the bottom of the whole controversy, now going on between the slaveholders on the one hand, and the abolitionists on the other. It is the same old question which has divided the selfish, from the philanthropic part of mankind in all ages. It is the question whether the rights, privileges, and immunities enjoyed by some ought not to be shared and enjoyed by all.

[. . . .]

It may be said, that views and opinions, favoring the unity of the human family, coming from one of lowly condition, are open to the suspicion, that "the wish is father to the thought," and so, indeed, it may be. —But let it be also remembered, that this deduction from the weight of the argument on the one side, is more than counterbalanced by the pride of race and position arrayed on the other. Indeed, ninety-nine out of every hundred of the advocates of a diverse origin of the human family[67] in this country, are among those who hold it to be the privilege of the Anglo-Saxon to enslave and oppress the African—and slaveholders, not a few, like the *Richmond Examiner* to which I have referred, have admitted, that the whole argument in defense of slavery, becomes utterly worthless the moment the African is proved to be equally a man with the Anglo-Saxon. The temptation therefore, to read the Negro out of the human family is exceedingly strong, and may account somewhat for the repeated attempts on the part of Southern pretenders to science, to cast a doubt over the scriptural account of the origin

---

67. Douglass had in mind several prominent authors such as Josiah Nott (1804–1873), who defended this thesis. The ideas of Nott and others like him are discussed at greater length in portions of this speech that were edited out due to space constraints.

of mankind. If the origin and motives of most works, opposing the doctrine of the unity of the human race, could be ascertained, it may be doubted whether one such work could boast an honest parentage. Pride and selfishness, combined with mental power, never want for a theory to justify them— and when men oppress their fellow-men, the oppressor ever finds, in the character of the oppressed, a full justification for his oppression. Ignorance and depravity, and the inability to rise from degradation to civilization and respectability, are the most usual allegations against the oppressed. The evils most fostered by slavery and oppression, are precisely those which slaveholders and oppressors would transfer from their system to the inherent character of their victims. Thus the very crimes of slavery become slavery's best defense. By making the enslaved a character fit only for slavery, they excuse themselves for refusing to make the slave a freeman. A wholesale method of accomplishing this result, is to overthrow the instinctive consciousness of the common brotherhood of man. For, let it be once granted that the human race are of multitudinous origin, naturally different in their moral, physical, and intellectual capacities, and at once you make plausible a demand for classes, grades and conditions, for different methods of culture, different moral, political, and religious institutions, and a chance is left for slavery, as a necessary institution. The debates in Congress on the Nebraska bill[68] during the past winter, will show how slaveholders have availed themselves of this doctrine in support of slaveholding.

[. . . .]

THE AFRICAN RACE BUT ONE PEOPLE.

But I must hasten. Having shown that the people of Africa are, probably, one people; that each tribe bears an intimate relation to other tribes and nations in that quarter of the globe, and that the Egyptians may have flung off the different tribes seen there at different times, as implied by the evident relations of their language, and by other similarities; it can hardly be deemed unreasonable to suppose, that the African branch of the human species—from the once highly civilized Egyptian to the barbarians on the banks of the Niger—may claim brotherhood with the great family of Noah, spreading over the more northern and eastern parts of the globe. I will now proceed to consider those physical peculiarities of form, features, hair and color, which are supposed by some men to mark the African, not only as an inferior race, but as a distinct species, naturally and originally different from the rest of mankind, and as really to place him nearer to the brute than to man.

---

68. This is a reference to the Kansas-Nebraska Act of 1854.

THE EFFECT OF CIRCUMSTANCES UPON
THE PHYSICAL MAN.

I may remark, just here, that it is impossible, even were it desirable, in a discourse like this, to attend to the anatomical and physiological argument connected with this part of the subject. I am not equal to that, and if I were, the occasion does not require it. The form of the Negro—[I use the term Negro, precisely in the sense that you use the term Anglo Saxon; and I believe, too, that the former will one day be as illustrious as the latter]—has often been the subject of remark. His flat feet, long arms, high cheek bones and retreating forehead, are especially dwelt upon, to his disparagement, and just as if there were no white people with precisely the same peculiarities. I think it will ever be found, that the well or ill condition of any part of mankind, will leave its mark on the physical as well as on the intellectual part of man. A hundred instances might be cited, of whole families who have degenerated, and others who have improved in personal appearance, by a change of circumstances. A man is worked upon by what he works on. He may carve out his circumstances, but his circumstances will carve him out as well. I told a boot maker, in New Castle upon Tyne, that I had been a plantation slave. He said I must pardon him; but he could not believe it; no plantation laborer ever had a high instep. He said he had noticed, that the coal heavers and work people in low condition, had, for the most part, flat feet, and that he could tell, by the shape of the feet, whether a man's parents were in high or low condition. The thing was worth a thought, and I have thought of it, and have looked around me for facts. There is some truth in it; though there are exceptions, in individual cases.

The day I landed in Ireland, nine years ago, I addressed . . . a large meeting of the common people of Ireland, on temperance. Never did human faces tell a sadder tale. More than five thousand were assembled; and I say, with no wish to wound the feelings of any Irishman, that these people lacked only a black skin and woolly hair, to complete their likeness to the plantation Negro. The open, uneducated mouth—the long, gaunt arm—the badly formed foot and ankle—the shuffling gait—the retreating forehead and vacant expression—and, their petty quarrels and fights—all reminded me of the plantation, and my own cruelly abused people. Yet, that is the land of Grattan, of Curran, of O'Connell, and of Sheridan.[69] Now, while what I have said is true of the common people, the fact is, there are no more really handsome people in the world, than the educated Irish people. The Irishman educated, is a model gentleman; the Irishman ignorant and degraded, compares in form and feature, with the Negro!

I am stating facts. If you go into Southern Indiana, you will see what climate and habit can do, even in one generation. The man may have come from

---

69. Douglass lists several important Irish reformers and political leaders.

New England, but his hard features, sallow complexion, have left little of New England on his brow. The right arm of the blacksmith is said to be larger and stronger than his left. The ship carpenter is at forty round shouldered. The shoemaker carries the marks of his trade. One locality becomes famous for one thing, another for another. Manchester and Lowell, in America, Manchester and Sheffield, in England, attest this. But what does it all prove? Why, nothing positively, as to the main point; still it raises the inquiry the fact is, there are no more really handsome people in the world, than the educated Irish people. The Irishman educated, is a model gentleman; May not the condition of men explain their various appearances? Need we go behind the vicissitudes of barbarism for an explanation of the gaunt, wiry, apelike appearance of some of the genuine Negroes? Need we look higher than a vertical sun, or lower than the damp, black soil of the Niger, the Gambia, the Senegal, with their heavy and enervating miasma, rising ever from the rank growing and decaying vegetation, for an explanation of the Negro's color? If a cause, full and adequate, can be found here, why seek further?

[. . . .]

A powerful argument in the favor of the oneness of the human family, is afforded in the fact that nations, however dissimilar, may be united in one social state, not only without detriment to each other, but, most clearly, to the advancement of human welfare, happiness and perfection. While it is clearly proved, on the other hand, that those nations freest from foreign elements, present the most evident marks of deterioration. Dr. James McCune Smith,[70] himself a colored man, a gentleman and scholar, alleges—and not without excellent reason—that this, our own great nation, so distinguished for industry and enterprise, is largely indebted to its composite character. We all know, at any rate, that now, what constitutes the very heart of the civilized world— (I allude to England)—has only risen from barbarism to its present lofty eminence, through successive invasions and alliances with her people. The Medes and Persians constituted one of the mightiest empires that ever rocked the globe. The most terrible nation which now threatens the peace of the world, to make its will the law of Europe, is a grand piece of mosaic work, in which almost every nation has its characteristic feature, from the wild Tartar to the refined Pole.

But, gentlemen, the time fails me, and I must bring these remarks to a close. My argument has swelled beyond its appointed measure. What I intended to make special, has become, in its progress, somewhat general. I meant to speak here today, for the lonely and the despised ones, with whom I was cradled, and with whom I have suffered; and now, gentlemen, in conclusion, what if all this reasoning be unsound? What if the Negro may not be able to prove his

---

70. James McCune Smith (1813–1865) was an American physician, abolitionist, and author.

relationship to Nubians, Abyssinians and Egyptians? What if ingenious men are able to find plausible objections to all arguments maintaining the oneness of the human race? What, after all, if they are able to show very good reasons for believing the Negro to have been created precisely as we find him on the Gold Coast along the Senegal and the Niger—I say, what of all this? —"A man's a man for a' that."[71] I sincerely believe, that the weight of the argument is in favor of the unity of origin of the human race, or species—that the arguments on the other side are partial, superficial, utterly subversive of the happiness of man, and insulting to the wisdom of God. Yet, what if we grant they are not so? What, if we grant that the case, on our part, is not made out? Does it follow, that the Negro should be held in contempt? Does it follow, that to enslave and imbrute him is either just or wise? I think not. Human rights stand upon a common basis; and by all the reason that they are supported, maintained and defended, for one variety of the human family, they are supported, maintained and defended for all the human family; because all mankind have the same wants, arising out of a common nature. A diverse origin does not disprove a common nature, nor does it disprove a united destiny. The essential characteristics of humanity are everywhere the same. In the language of the eloquent Curran, "No matter what complexion, whether an Indian or an African sun has burnt upon him," his title deed to freedom, his claim to life and to liberty, to knowledge and to civilization, to society and to Christianity, are just and perfect. It is registered in the courts of heaven, and is enforced by the eloquence of the God of all the earth.

I have said that the Negro and white man are likely ever to remain the principal inhabitants of this country. I repeat the statement now, to submit the reasons that support it. The blacks can disappear from the face of the country by three ways. They may be colonized, —they may be exterminated, —or, they may die out. Colonization is out of the question; for I know not what hardships the laws of the land can impose, which can induce the colored citizen to leave his native soil. He was here in its infancy; he is here in its age. Two hundred years have passed over him, his tears and blood have been mixed with the soil, and his attachment to the place of his birth is stronger than iron. It is not probable that he will be exterminated; two considerations must prevent a crime so stupendous as that—the influence of Christianity on the one hand, and the power of self interest on the other; and, in regard to their dying out, the statistics of the country afford no encouragement for such a conjecture. The history of the Negro race proves them to be wonderfully adapted to all countries, all climates, and all conditions. Their tenacity of life, their powers of endurance, their malleable toughness, would almost imply especial interposition on their behalf. The ten thousand horrors of slavery, striking hard upon

---

71. Douglass cites the title of a poem by Robert Burns, "A Man's a Man for A' That."

the sensitive soul, have bruised, and battered, and stung, but have not killed. The poor bondman lifts a smiling face above the surface of a sea of agonies, hoping on, hoping ever. His tawny brother, the Indian, dies, under the flashing glance of the Anglo Saxon. Not so the Negro; civilization cannot kill him. He accepts it—becomes a part of it. In the Church, he is an Uncle Tom, in the state, he is the most abused and least offensive. All the facts in his history mark out for him a destiny, united to America and Americans. Now, whether this population shall, by Freedom, Industry, Virtue and Intelligence, be made a blessing to the country and the world, or whether their multiplied wrongs shall kindle the vengeance of an offended God, will depend upon the conduct of no class of men so much as upon the scholars of the country. The future public opinion of the land, whether anti-slavery or pro-slavery, whether just or unjust, whether magnanimous or mean, must redound to the honor of the scholars of the country or cover them with shame. There is but one safe road for nations or for individuals. The fate of a wicked man and of a wicked nation is the same. The flaming sword of offended justice falls as certainly upon the nation as upon the man. God has no children whose rights may be safely trampled upon. The sparrow may not fall to the ground without the notice of His eye, and men are more than sparrows.

Now, gentlemen, I have done. The subject is before you. I shall not undertake to make the application. I speak as unto wise men. I stand in the presence of scholars. We have met here today from vastly different points in the world's condition. I have reached here—if you will pardon the egotism—by little short of a miracle; at any rate, by dint of some application and perseverance. Born, as I was, in obscurity, a stranger to the halls of learning, environed by ignorance, degradation, and their concomitants, from birth to manhood, I do not feel at liberty to mark out, with any degree of confidence, or dogmatism, what is the precise vocation of the scholar. Yet, this I can say, as a denizen of the world, and as a citizen of a country rolling in the sin and shame of slavery, the most flagrant and scandalous that ever saw the sun, "Whatsoever things are true, whatsoever things are honest, whatsoever things are just, whatsoever things are pure, whatsoever things are lovely, whatsoever things are of good report, if there be any virtue, and if there be any praise, think on these things."[72]

---

72. Philippians 4:8.

PART III

DOUGLASS REFLECTS ON THE IMPENDING CRISIS

13. "The Kansas-Nebraska Bill," a speech delivered in Chicago, Illinois on October 30, 1854 and published in *Frederick Douglass' Paper*, November 24, 1854[1]

FRIENDS AND FELLOW CITIZENS:

A great national question, a question of transcendent importance—one upon which the public mind is deeply moved, and not my humble name—has assembled this multitude of eager listeners in Metropolitan Hall this evening. You have come up here in obedience to a humane and patriotic impulse, to consider of the requirements of patriotism and humanity, at an important crisis in the affairs of this nation.

In this patriotic and holy purpose, I hail your presence here with grateful, sincere, and heart-felt pleasure. I am anxious to address you on the great subject which has called you together—and will do so—but circumstances will justify me in saying a few words first of a personal nature.

I have the misfortune of being deemed an intruder by some of your fellow citizens. —My visit among you is thought to be untimely, and to savor of impudence, and the like. Upon this matter I have a word to say in my own defense. A man that will not defend himself is not fit to defend a good cause.

And first, ladies and gentlemen, I am not sure that a visit on my part to Chicago would at any time afford those who are now complaining of me any special pleasure. But, gentlemen, I am not ashamed of being called an intruder. I have met it a thousand times in a thousand different places, and I am quite prepared to meet it now—and here, as I have met it, at other times and in other places.

Every inch of ground occupied by the colored man in this country is sternly disputed. At the ballot box and at the altar—in the church and in the state— he is deemed an intruder. He is, in fact, seldom a welcome visitor anywhere. Marvel not, therefore, if I seem somewhat used to the charge of intrusiveness, and am not more embarrassed in meeting it. Men have been known to get used to conditions and objects which, at the first, seemed utterly repulsive and insufferable. And so may I.

---

1. As noted in the introduction, the passage of the Kanas-Nebraska Act in 1854 proved to have a galvanizing effect on a wide range of antislavery figures, from the radical abolitionist John Brown to the moderate politician Abraham Lincoln. Douglass made his way to Illinois, the home of the bill's author Senator Stephen A. Douglas, to offer his critique of the legislation.

One reason why I am not ashamed to be here is this: I have a right to be here and a duty to perform here. That right is a constitutional right, as well as a natural right. It belongs to every citizen of the United States. It belongs not less to the humblest than to the most exalted citizens. The genius of American institutions knows no privileged class or classes. The plebian and the would be patrician stand here upon a common level of equality, and the last man in the world who should complain of this is the earnest advocate of popular sovereignty.

I have a right to come into this state to prosecute any lawful business in a lawful manner. This is a natural right, and is a part of the supreme law of the land. By that law the citizens of each state are the citizens of the United States, with rights alike and equal in all the states. The only question of right connected with my case here respects my citizenship. If I am a citizen, I am clothed all over with the star spangled banner and defended by the American Constitution, in every state of the American Union. That Constitution knows no man by the color of his skin. The men who made it were too noble for any such limitation of humanity and human rights. The word white is a modern term in the legislation of this country. It was never used in the better days of the republic, but has sprung up within the period of our national degeneracy.

I claim to be an American citizen. The Constitution knows but two classes: Firstly, citizens, and secondly, aliens. I am not an alien; and I am, therefore, a citizen. I am moreover a free citizen. Free, thank God, not only by the law of the state in which I was born and brought up but free by the laws of nature.

In the State of New York where I live, I am a citizen and a legal voter, and may therefore be presumed to be a citizen of the United States. I am here simply as an American citizen, having a stake in the weal or woe of the nation, in common with other citizens. I am not even here as an agent of any sect or party. Parties are too politic and sects are too sectarian, to select one of my odious class, and of my radical opinions, at this important time and place, to represent them. Nevertheless, I do not stand alone here. There are noble minded men in Illinois who are neither ashamed of their cause nor their company. Some of them are here tonight, and I expect to meet with them in every part of the state where I may travel. But, I pray, hold no man or party responsible for my words, for I am no man's agent; and I am no party's agent; and I beg that my respected friends—the reporters—will be good enough to make a note of that. I have a very good reason for making this request—a reason which I may some day give to the world, but which I need not give now.

One other remark; and it shall be in regard to a matter about which you wish to hear at once. It touches the matter involved on my mission here. I wish not only to stand within my rights as a man, but to stand approved at the bar of propriety as a gentleman, when, as in this case, I can do so without the sacrifice of principle. It has been given out, I believe, by some friends and also by some of the enemies of the principles I am here to sustain that I have come into this state to confront in public debate, my distinguished namesake, the Hon. Stephen A. Douglas.[2]

Fellow citizens, I wish to disclaim so much of this report as can possibly imply the slightest disrespect for the talents of your honorable senator. His fame as an orator, and as a man of energy and perseverance, has not risen higher anywhere than in my own judgment. He is a man of the people. He came up from among them, and that by the native energy of his character and his manly industry. I am ever pleased to see a man rise from among the people. Every such man is prophetic of the good time coming. I have watched him during the past winter, when apparently overwhelmed with learning and eloquence, rise again, and with more than the tact and skill of a veteran, drive all before him. There is perhaps something in a name, and that may possibly explain the peculiar interest with which I have watched and contemplated the fortune of Mr. S. A. Douglas.

This feeling, I think, you will admit, is quite natural. No man likes to read in a newspaper of the hanging of a man bearing his own name.

On the other hand, no man bearing the name of Douglas, would think less of his name, if this great nation should, in the abundance of goodness be pleased to place that name in the scroll of its presidents; and this, notwithstanding the trite saying, that a rose by any other name would smell as sweet.[3]

But the times, the times bid us to have done with names. Names have lost their significance, in more ways than one—deeds, not words, are the order of the day; names are valued so long as they are associated with honor, justice and liberty; and become execrable when associated with falsehood, treachery and tyranny.

It is alleged that I am come to this state to insult Senator Douglas. Among gentlemen, that is only an insult which is intended to be such, and I disavow all such intention. I am not even here with the desire to meet in public debate, that gentleman. I am here precisely as I was in this state one year ago—with no other change in my relations to you, or to the great question of human freedom, than time and circumstances have brought about. I shall deal with the subject in the same spirit now as then; approving such men and such measures as I look to the security of liberty in the land and with my whole heart condemning all men and measures as serve to subvert or endanger it.

If Hon. S. A. Douglas, your beloved and highly gifted senator, has designedly, or through mistaken notions of public policy ranged himself, on the side

---

2. Stephen A. Douglas (1813–1861) was an American politician who served in the House of Representatives and the US Senate and was the Democratic nominee for president of the United States in 1860.

3. Douglass quotes William Shakespeare, *Romeo and Juliet*, act 2, sc. 2.

of oppressors and the deadliest enemies of liberty, I know of no reason, either in this world or any other world, which should prevent me, or prevent anyone else, from thinking so, or from saying so.

The people in whose cause I come here tonight, are not among those whose right to regulate their own domestic concerns, is so feelingly and eloquently contended for in certain quarters. They have no Stephen Arnold Douglas—no Gen. Cass,[4] to contend at North Market Hall for their popular sovereignty. They have no national purse—no offices, no reputation, with which to corrupt Congress, or to tempt men, mighty in eloquence and influence into their service. Oh, no! They have nothing to commend them but their unadorned humanity. They are human—that's all—only human. Nature owns them as human—God owns them as human; but men own them as property!—Every right of human nature, as such, is denied them—they are dumb in their chains! To utter one groan, or scream, for freedom in the presence of the Southern advocate of popular sovereignty, is to bring down the frightful lash upon their quivering flesh. I knew this suffering people; I am acquainted with their sorrows; I am one with them in experience; I have felt the lash of the slave driver, and stand up here with all the bitter recollections of its horrors vividly upon me.

There are special reasons, therefore, why I should speak and speak freely. The right of speech is a very precious one, especially to the oppressed.

I understand that Mr. Douglas regards himself as the most abused man in the United States and that the greatest outrage ever committed upon him was in the case in which your indignation raised your voices so high that his could not be heard. No personal violence, as I understand, was offered him. It seems to have been a trial of vocal powers between the individual and the multitude; as might have been expected, the voice of one man was not equal in volume to the voice of five hundred.

I do not mention this circumstance to approve it; I do not approve it; I am for free speech as well as for freemen and free soil; but how ineffably insignificant is this wrong done in a single instance, and to a single individual, compared with the stupendous iniquity perpetrated against more than three millions of the American people, who are struck dumb by the very men in whose cause Mr. Senator Douglas was here to plead. While I would not approve the silencing of Mr. Douglas, may we not hope that this slight abridgment of his rights may lead him to respect in some degree the rights of other men, as good in the eyes of heaven, as himself.

Let us now consider the great question of the age; the only great national question which seriously agitates the public mind at this hour. It is called the vexed question and excites alarm in every quarter of the country.

---

4. Lewis Cass (1782–1866) was an American military official and politician. He served as a US senator from Michigan from 1857 to 1860.

Efforts have been made to set it at rest. —Statesmen, and political parties, and churches have exerted themselves to settle it forever. They sought to bind it with cords; to resist it with revolutions, and bury it under platforms; but all to no purpose. The waves of the ocean still roll, and the earthquakes still shake the earth, and men's hearts still fail them for fear of those judgments which threaten to come upon the land.

Fellow citizens: some things are settled, and settled forever—not by the laws of man, but by the laws of God; by the constitution of mankind; by the relations of things and by the facts of human experience.

It is, I think, pretty well settled, that liberty and slavery cannot dwell in the United States in peaceful relations; the history of the last five and twenty years settles that.

It is pretty well settled, too, that one or the other of these must go to the wall. The South must either give up slavery, or the North must give up liberty. The two interests are hostile, and are irreconcilable. —The just demands of liberty are inconsistent with the overgrown exactions of the slave power.

There is not a single tendency of slavery but is adverse to freedom. The one is adapted to progress, to industry, and to dignify industry. Slavery is anti-progressive—sets a premium on idleness, and degrades both labor and laborers. The fetters on the limbs of the slave, to be secure, must be accompanied with fetters on society as well. A free press and a free gospel, are as hostile as fire and gunpowder—separation or explosion, are the only alternatives.

No people in this country better understand this peculiarity than the slaveholders themselves. Hence the repeated violations of your post office laws in Southern towns and cities; hence the expurgations of Northern literature, and the barbarous outrages committed upon the persons of Northern travelers in the Southern states. Light and love, justice and mercy, must be guarded against in a community where the cruel lash is the law, and human lust is religion.

For a long time, it has been seen that the ideas and institutions of liberty, if allowed their natural course, would finally overthrow slavery. That slaveholders themselves would after a while come to loathe it.

Selfishness combined with this knowledge has at length ultimated [*sic*] into the formation of a party, ranged under the very taking appellation of national—the greatest business of which is to hold at bay, and restrain, and if possible to extinguish in the heart of this great nation every sentiment supposed to be at variance with the safety of slavery.

This party has arisen out of the teachings of that great man of perverted faculties, the late John C. Calhoun. No man of the nation has left a broader or a blacker mark on the politics of the nation, than he. In the eye of Mr. Calhoun every right guaranteed by the American Constitution, must be held in subordination to slavery. It was he who first boldly declared the self-evident truths of the Declaration of Independence, self-evident falsehoods. [. . .]

The very spirit of Mr. Calhoun animates the slavery party of today. His principles are its principles, and his philosophy its philosophy. He looked upon slavery as the great American interest. The slavery party of today so esteems it. To preserve it, shield it, and support it, is its constant duty, and the object and aim of all its exertions. With this party the right of free men, free labor, and a free North are nothing. Daniel Webster never said a truer word than at Marshfield, in '48—"Why the North? There is no North!" But there is a South and ever has been a South controlling both parties, at every period of their existence.

The grand inauguration of this slavery party took place in the summer of 1852. —That party was represented in both the great parties; and demanded as a condition of their very existence, that they should give their solemn endorsement, as a finality to the compromise measures of 1850. Abhorrent as were its demands, and arrogant and repulsive as was its manner of pressing them—that party was obeyed. Both conventions took upon them the mark of the beast; and called upon the whole North to do the same. —The Democratic Party consented to be branded thus:

"That Congress has no power, under the Constitution, to interfere with, or control the domestic institutions of the several states; and that such states are the sole and proper judges of everything appertaining to their own affairs, not prohibited by the Constitution—that all efforts of the abolitionists or others to induce Congress to interfere with the question of slavery, or to take incipient steps in relation thereto, are calculated to lead to the most alarming and dangerous consequences; and that all such efforts have an inevitable tendency to diminish the happiness of the people, and endanger the stability and permanency of the Union; and ought not to be countenanced by any friend of our political institution.

"*Resolved*, That the foregoing proposition covers and was intended to embrace the whole subject of the slavery agitation in Congress; and, therefore, the Democratic Party of this Union, standing on this national platform, will abide by, and adhere to a faithful execution of the acts known as the compromise measures, settled by the last Congress—the act for reclaiming fugitives from service or labor included, which act being decided to carry out an express provision of the Constitution, cannot, with fidelity, be repealed or be changed as to destroy or impair its efficacy.

"*Resolved*, That the Democratic party will resist all attempts at renewing, in Congress or out of it, the agitation of the slavery question, under whatever shape or color the attempt may be made."

Gentlemen: Such was the Democratic *mark*, and such was the Democratic *pledge*. It was taken in sight of all the nation, and in the sight of God, only two years ago. Has it kept that pledge? Does it stand acquitted today at the bar of public honor? or does it stand forth black with perfidy toward the

North, while it wallows in the mire of deeper servility to the South? Has the Democratic Party a single claim on your confidence, more than any notorious liar would have upon your credulity? Can you believe in a party that keeps its word, only as it has no temptation to break it? Is there a single man that can pretend to say that the Democrats—the Baltimore platform Democrats, have been true to their solemn declarations? Have they not renewed, and, in a manner to peril the cause of liberty—the agitation of slavery, which they solemnly promised to resist? Do you say they have not? Then there is no longer an intelligible proposition in the English language—nor is it possible to frame one.

But let me read to you the resolution imposed on the Whig National Convention, as the vital condition of its existence; and which was given to the world as the faith of that great organization, touching the matter of slavery. Here it is:

"That the series of acts, of the 31st Congress, known as the compromise, including the Fugitive Slave Act, are received and acquiesced in by the Whig party of the United States, as a final settlement, in principle and substance, of the dangerous and exciting subjects which they embrace; and so far as the fugitive slave law is concerned, we will maintain the same, and insist upon its strict enforcement, until time and experience shall demonstrate the necessity of further legislation to guard against the evasion of the laws on the one hand, and the abuse of their powers on the other—not impairing their present efficacy—and deprecate all further agitation of the questions thus settled, as dangerous to our peace; and we will discountenance a continuance or renewal of such agitation, whenever, wherever, or however, the attempt may be made; and we will maintain this system as essential to the nationality of the Whig party, and the integrity of the Union."

Now, fellow-citizens: In those platforms, and in the events which have since transpired, it is easy to read the designs of the slave power. Something is gained when the plans and purposes of an enemy are discovered.

I understand the first purpose of the slave power to be the suppression of all anti-slavery discussion. Next, the extension of slavery over all the territories. Next, the nationalizing of slavery, and to make slavery respected in every state in the Union.

First, the right of speech is assailed, and both parties pledge themselves to put it down. When parties make platforms, they are presumed to put nothing into them, which, if need be, they may not organize into law. These parties on this presumption, are pledged to put down free discussion by law—to make it an offense against the law to speak, write, and publish against slavery, here in the free states, just as it now is an offense against the law to do so in the slave states. One end of the slave's chain must be fastened to a padlock in the lips of Northern freemen, else the slave will himself become free.

Now, gentlemen, are you ready for this? —Are you ready to give up the right of speech, and suppress every human and Christ-inspired sentiment, lest the conscience of the guilty be disturbed?

Our parties have attempted to give peace to slaveholders. They have attempted to do what God has made impossible to be done; and that is to give peace to slaveholders. —"There is no peace to the wicked, sayeth my God."[5] In the breast of every slaveholder, God has placed, or stationed an anti-slavery lecturer, whose cry is *guilty*, guilty, guilty; "thou art verily guilty concerning thy brother."[6]

But now let me come to the points of this great question which touch us most nearly tonight.

I take the case to be this: The citizens of this state are now appealed to, to give their sanction to the repeal of the law, by which slavery has been, during a period of thirty-four years, restricted to the south of thirty-six deg. thirty min. of north latitude, in the territory acquired by the purchase of Louisiana.

This is but a simple and truthful statement of the real question.

The question is not, whether "popular sovereignty" is the true doctrine for the territories—it is not whether the chief agents in the repeal of that line, acted from good or bad motives; nor is it whether they are able or feeble men.

These are points of very little consequence in determining the path of duty in this case. When principles are at stake, persons are of small account; and the safety of a republic is found in a rigid adherence to principles. Once give up these, and you are a ship in a storm, without anchor or rudder.

Fellow-Citizens: The proposition to repeal the Missouri Compromise, was a stunning one. It fell upon the nation like a bolt from a cloudless sky. The thing was too startling for belief. You believed in the South, and you believed in the North; and you knew that the repeal of the Missouri Compromise was a breach of honor; and, therefore, you said the thing could not be done. Besides, both parties had pledged themselves directly, positively and solemnly against re-opening in Congress the agitation on the subject of slavery; and the president himself had declared his intention to maintain the national quiet. Upon those assurances you rested, and rested fatally.

But you should have learned long ago that "men do not gather grapes of thorns, nor figs of thistles."[7] It is folly to put faith in men who have broken faith with God. When a man has brought himself to enslave a child of God, to put fetters on his brother, he has qualified himself to disregard the most sacred of compacts—beneath the sky there is nothing more sacred than man, and nothing can be properly respected when manhood is despised and trampled

---

5. Douglass paraphrases Isaiah 48:22 (all biblical references are from the King James version).
6. Genesis 42:21.
7. Matthew 7:16.

upon. Now let us attend to the defense made before the people by the advocates of the Kansas-Nebraska bill.

They tell us that the bill does not open the territories to slavery, and complain that they are misrepresented and slandered by those charging them with flinging open the territories to slavery. I wish to slander no man. I wish to misrepresent no man. They point us to the bill itself as proof that no such opening of the territories to slavery is contemplated, or intended by it. I will read to you from the bill itself, to see what is relied upon at this point:

"It being the true intent and meaning of this act not to legislate slavery into any Territory or State; nor *to exclude it therefrom,* but to leave the people thereof perfectly free to form and regulate their domestic institutions in their own way; subject only to the Constitution of the United States."

One part of this declaration is true and carries the evidence of its truth on its face. It is true that it is no part of the true intent and meaning of the act to exclude slavery from any territory or state. If its true intent and meaning had been otherwise, it would not have repealed the law, the only law, which had excluded slavery from those territories, and from those states which may be formed out of them. I repeat, this part of the bill needs no explanation. It is plain enough already. There is not a slaveholder in the land, however ardent an advocate of slavery extension he may be, who has ever complained that the true intent and meaning of the Kansas-Nebraska bill was to exclude slavery from the territories in question, or from any states which might be formed out of them. Slaveholders do not so understand the bill. Had they so understood it, they would never have gone in a *body* to sustain the bill. It is very significant that on this part of this "stump speech" in the declaration, the country is agreed, everybody understanding it alike, while on the other hand, the words in the bill, directly preceding it, are the subject of controversy. Why is this so? You are told that it is owing to the perversity of man's understanding. But this is not the answer. I will tell you why it is. The people, like the old rat, do not deny that the white dust they see here is meal—real and genuine meal—but under the meal they detect the treacherous form of the cat. Under that smooth exterior there are the sharp teeth and destructive claws, and hence they avoid, shun and detest it.

But again: it is claimed that the Nebraska bill does not open the territories to slavery for another reason. It is said that slavery is the creature of positive law, and that it can only exist where it is sustained by positive law—that neither in Kansas nor in Nebraska is there any law establishing slavery, and that, therefore, the moment a slaveholder carries his slaves into those territories they are free, and restored to the rights of human nature. This is the ground taken by General Cass. He contended for it in the North Market Hall, with much eloquence and skill. I thought, while I was hearing him on this point, that slaveholders would not be likely to thank him for the argument. Theoretically the argument is good, practically the argument is bad. It is not true that slavery cannot exist without being established by positive law. On the contrary, the instance cannot be shown where a law was ever made establishing slavery, where the relation of master and slave did not previously exist. The law is always an after-coming consideration. Wicked men first overpower, and subdue their fellow-men to slavery, and then call in the law to sanction the deed.

Even in the slave states of America, slavery has never been established by positive law. It was not so established under the colonial charters of the original states, nor the constitution of the states. It is now, and always has been, a system of lawless violence.

On this proposition, I hold myself ready and willing to meet any defender of the Nebraska bill. I would not even hesitate to meet the author of that bill himself. I insist upon it that the very basis upon which this bill is defended, is utterly and entirely false as applied to the practice of slavery in this country. The South itself scouts the theory of Messrs. Douglas and Cass at this point, and esteem it simply as a gull trap in which to catch the simple. They look upon it simply as a piece of plausible stump oratory, and censure it as such. But that slavery is not the tame creature of law, as alleged, I will not rely solely on my own declaration.

Senator [James] Mason,[8] of Virginia, the author of the fugitive slave bill, and one of the most influential members of the American Senate, during the debate on the fugitive slave bill in 1850, scouted such a basis for slavery, and confessed that no such existed. He said, and I quote his own words:

"Then again, it is proposed (by one of the opponents of the bill) as a part of the proof to be adduced at the hearing after the fugitive has been recaptured, that evidence shall be brought by the claimant to show that slavery is established in the state from whence the fugitive has absconded. Now, this very thing, in a recent case in the city of New York, was required by one of the judges of that state, which case attracted the attention of the authorities of Maryland, and against which they protested, because of the indignities heaped upon their citizens, and the losses which they sustained in that city. In that case, the judge of the state court required proof that slavery was established in Maryland, and went so far as to say that the only mode of proving it was by reference to the statute book. Such proof is required in the senator's amendment; and if he means by this that proof shall be brought that slavery is established by existing laws, it is impossible to comply with the requisition, for no such proof can be produced, I apprehend, in any of the slave states. *I am not aware that there is a single state in which the institution is established by positive law.* On a former occasion, and on a different topic, it was my duty to endeavor to show

---

8. James Mason (1798–1871) was an American politician who served in the House of Representatives and the US Senate.

to the Senate that no such law was necessary for its establishment; certainly none could be found, and none was required in any of the states of the Union."

There you have it. It cannot be shown that slavery is established by law even in the slaveholding states. But slavery exists there—and so may it exist in Nebraska and in Kansas—and I had almost said that this is well known to the very men who are now trying to persuade the people of the North that it cannot.

But there is another defense set up for the repeal of the Missouri restriction. It is said to be a patriotic defense, supported by patriotic reasons. It is the defense which Senator Douglas uses with much effect wherever he goes.

He says he wants no broad black line across this continent. Such a line is odious and begets unkind feelings between the citizens of a common country.

Now, fellow-citizens, why is the line of thirty-six degrees thirty minutes, a broad black line? What is it that entitles it to be called a *black line*? It is the fashion to call whatever is odious in this country, black. —You call the devil black—and he may be, but what is there in the line of thirty-six degrees thirty minutes, which makes it blacker than the line which separates Illinois from Missouri, or Michigan from Indiana? I can see nothing in the line itself which should make it black or odious. It is a line, that's all.

If it is black, black and odious, it must be so not because it is a line, but because of the things it separates.

If it keeps asunder what God has joined together—or separates what God intended should be fused—then it may be called an odious line, a black line; but if on the other hand, it marks only a distinction—natural and eternal—a distinction, fixed in the nature of things by the Eternal God, then I say, withered be the arm and blasted be the hand that would blot it out.

But we are told that the people of the North were originally opposed to that line, that they burnt in effigy the men from the North who voted for it, and that it comes with a bad grace from the North now to oppose its repeal.

Fellow-citizens, this may do in the barroom. It may answer somewhere outside of where the moon rises, but it won't do among men of intelligence.

Why did the North condemn the Missouri line? This it was: they believed that it gave slavery an advantage to which slavery had no right. By establishing the Missouri Compromise line, slavery got all south of it. By repealing that line it may get all north of it. Now are any so blind as not to see that the same reasons for opposing the original line, are good against repeal.

Allow me to illustrate. Thirty-four years ago, a man succeeds in getting a decision unjustly, by which he comes in possession of one half of your farm. You protest against that decision, and say it is corrupt. But the man does not heed your protests. He builds his house upon it, and fences in his lands and warns you to keep off his premises. You cannot help yourself. You live by his side thirty-four years. You have lost the means of regaining your lost property. But just at this time there comes a new judge, a Daniel, a very Daniel, and he reverses so much of the judgment by which you lost the first half of your farm, and makes another decision by which you may lose the other half.

You meekly protest against this new swindle. When the judge in question, with great affectation of impartiality, denounces you as very difficult to please, and as flagrantly inconsistent.

Such, gentlemen, is the plain and simple truth in the matter.

By the Missouri Compromise, slavery—an alien to the republic, and enemy to every principle of free institutions, and having no right to exist anywhere—got one half of a territory rightfully belonging to freedom. —You complained of that. Now a law is repealed whereby you may lose the other half also, and you are forbidden to complain.

But hear again:

It is said with much adroitness by the advocates of the Nebraska bill, that we are unnecessarily solicitous for the rights of Negroes, that if the people of the territories can be trusted to make laws for white men, they may be safely left to make laws for black men. Now, gentlemen, this is a favorite point of the author of the Nebraska bill. Under its fair seeming front, is an appeal to all that is mean, cowardly, and vindictive in the breast of the white public. It implies that the opponents of the Nebraska bill feel a deeper concern for the Negroes as such, than for white men, that we are unnaturally sensitive to rights of the blacks, and unnaturally indifferent to the rights of the whites.

With such an unworthy implication on its face, I brand it as a mean, wicked and bitter appeal to popular prejudice, against a people wholly defenseless, and at the mercy of the public.

The argument of Senator Douglas at this point, assumes the absurd position that a slaveholding people will be as careful of the rights of their black slaves as they are of their own. They might as well say that wolves may be trusted to legislate for themselves, and why not for lambs, as to say that slaveholders may do so for themselves, and why not for their slaves?

Shame on the miserable sophistry, and shame on the spirit that prompted its utterance! There is nothing manly or honorable in either. Take another specimen of senatorial logic; a piece of the same roll to which I have just referred.

Senator Douglas tells you, that the people may be as safely left to make laws respecting slavery, as to regulate theft, robbery, or murder. Very well—so they may. There is no doubt about that; but as usual, the Hon. Senator fails to bring out the whole truth. —To bring out the whole truth here, is to cover him with shame.

To put the matter in its true light, let us suppose that in the Southern states of this union, the people are so benighted as to practice and support "theft," "robbery," and "murder," but that in the other states that practice is loathed and abhorred.

Suppose, also, that up to a certain line in a territory belonging alike and equally to all the states, these wicked practices were prohibited by law; and then, suppose a grave senator from a state where theft, robbery and murder are looked upon with horror, rising in his place in the national legislature and moving to repeal the line excluding "theft," "robbery" and "murder," and demanding that "theft," "robbery" and "murder," be placed upon the same footing with honesty, uprightness and innocence. —I say, suppose this, and you have a parallel to the conduct of Senator Douglas, in repealing the line of thirty-six deg. thirty min.

But the grand argument, and the one which seems to be relied upon as unanswerable and overwhelming, is this: The people of the territories are American citizens, and carry with them the right of self-government; that this Nebraska bill is based upon this great American principle of popular sovereignty, and that to oppose this principle, is to act as did King George toward the American colonies.

Let me answer this argument. It may not need an answer here in Chicago, for it has been answered here, and answered well. —Nevertheless, let me answer it again, and prove by the bill itself, that it is a stupendous shame with every motive to deceive without the power.

What is meant by popular sovereignty? —It is the right of the people to establish a government for themselves, as against all others. Such was its meaning in the days of the revolution. It is the independent right of a people to make their own laws, without dictation or interference from any quarter. A sovereign subject is a contradiction in terms, and is an absurdity. When sovereignty becomes subject, it ceases to be sovereignty. When what was future becomes the present, it ceases to be the future and so with sovereignty and subjection, they cannot exist at the same time in the same place, any more than an event can be future and present at the same time. This much is clear.

Now the question is, does the Kansas-Nebraska bill give to the people of these territories the sovereign right to govern themselves? Is there a man here who will say that it does?

The author of the bill, in his stump speeches in the country, says that it does; and some men think the statement correct. But what say you, who have read the bill?

Nothing could be further from the truth, than to say that popular sovereignty is accorded to the people who may settle the territories of Kansas and Nebraska.

The three great cardinal powers of government are the executive, legislative and judicial. Are these powers secured to the people of Kansas and Nebraska?

That bill places the people of that territory as completely under the powers of the federal government as Canada is under the British crown. By this Kansas-Nebraska bill the federal government has the substance of all governing power, while the people have the shadow. The judicial power of the territories is not from the people of the territories, who are so bathed in the sunlight of popular sovereignty by stump eloquence, but from the federal government. —The executive power of the territories derives its existence not from the overflowing fountain of popular sovereignty, but from the federal government. The secretaries of the territories are not appointed by the sovereign people of the territories, but are appointed independently of popular sovereignty.

But is there nothing in this bill which justifies the supposition that it contains the principle of popular sovereignty? No, not one word. Even the territorial councils, elected, not by the people who may settle in the territories, but by only certain descriptions of people are subject to a double veto power, vested first in a governor, which they did not elect, and second in the president of the United States. The only shadow of popular sovereignty is the power given to the people of the territories by this bill to have, hold, buy and sell human beings. The sovereign right to make slaves of their fellowmen if they choose is the only sovereignty that the bill secures.

In all else, popular sovereignty means only what the boy meant when he said he was going to live with his uncle Robert. He said he was going there, and that he meant while there, to do just as he pleased, if his uncle Robert would let him!

I repeat, that the only seeming concession to the idea of popular sovereignty in this bill is authority to enslave men, and to concede that right or authority is a hell black denial of popular sovereignty itself.

Whence does popular sovereignty take rise? What and where is its basis? I should really like to hear from the author of the Nebraska bill, a philosophical theory, of the nature and origin of popular sovereignty. I wonder where he would begin, how he would proceed and where he would end.

The only intelligible principle on which popular sovereignty is founded, is found in the declaration of American independence, there and in these words: We hold these truths to be self-evident, that all men are created equal and are endowed by their Creator with the right of life, liberty and the pursuit of happiness.

The right of each man to life, liberty and the pursuit of happiness, is the basis of all social and political right, and, therefore, how brass-fronted and shameless is that impudence, which while it aims to rob men of their liberty, and to deprive them of the right to the pursuit of happiness—screams itself hoarse to the words of popular sovereignty.

But again: This bill, this Nebraska bill, gives to the people of the territories the right to hold slaves. Where did this bill get this right, which it so generously gives away? Did it get it from Hon. Stephen A. Douglas? Then I demand where he got that right?—Who gave it to him? Was he born with it? Or has he acquired it by some noble action? I repeat, how came he by it, or with it, or to have it?

Did the people of this state, from whom he derived his political and legislative life, give him this right, the right to make slaves of men? Had he any such right?

The answer is, he had not. He is in the condition of a man who has given away that which is not his own.

But it may be said that Congress has the right to allow the people of the territories to hold slaves.

The answer is, that Congress is made up of men, and possesses only the rights of men, and unless it can be shown, that some men have a right to hold their fellow-men as property, Congress has no such right.

There is not a man within the sound of my voice, who has not as good a right to enslave a brother man, as Congress has. This will not be denied even by slaveholders.

Then I put the question to you, each of you, all of you, have you any such right?

To admit such a right is to charge God with folly, to substitute anarchy for order, and to turn earth into a hell. And you know it.

Now, friends and fellow-citizens, I am uttering no new sentiments at this point, and am making no new argument. In this respect there is nothing new under the sun.[9]

Error may be new or it may be old, since it is founded in a misapprehension of what truth is. It has its beginnings and has its endings. But not so with truth. Truth is eternal. Like the great God from whose throne it emanates, it is from everlasting unto everlasting, and can never pass away.

Such a truth is man's right to freedom. —He was born with it. It was his before he comprehended it. The title deed to it is written by the Almighty on his heart, and the record of it is in the bosom of the eternal—and never can Stephen A. Douglas efface it unless he can tear from the great heart of God this truth. And this mighty government of ours will never be at peace with God until it shall, practically and universally, embrace this great truth as the foundation of all its institutions, and the rule of its entire administration.

Now, gentlemen, I have done. I have no fear for the ultimate triumph of free principles in this country. The signs of the times are propitious. Victories have been won by slavery, but they have never been won against the onward march of anti-slavery principles. The progress of these principles has been constant, steady, strong and certain. Every victory won by slavery has had the effect to fling our principles more widely and favorably among the people. —The annexation of Texas—the Florida war—the war with Mexico[10]—the compromise measures and the repeal of the Missouri Compromise, have all signally vindicated the wisdom of that great God, who has promised to overrule the wickedness of men for His own glory—to confound the wisdom of the crafty[11] and bring to naught the counsels of the ungodly.[12]

---

9. Ecclesiastes 1:9.
10. Here Douglass references various territorial gains made by the United States that served to expand slavery in the country.
11. I Corinthians 1:27.
12. Psalms 1.

14. "What Is My Duty as an Anti-Slavery Voter?" an essay published in *Frederick Douglass' Paper*, April 25, 1856[13]

There are, and have been, for the last dozen years, a band of conscientious men in this country, who have insisted upon casting their votes at the ballot-box in a manner fully to indicate their earnest desire for the abolition of slavery. To these, the old Liberty Party of eight years ago furnished the required platform, and the natural channels of political cooperation. Under the banner of this party, with many, or with few, they felt at home, and ready to fall or flourish. It was a noble party, and was animated by a noble spirit. That party, as such, has almost vanished. Its members are scattered, and its old armor has been borne off to a party with another name, and of another spirit. Led by the Barnburners of New York,[14] it supported Martin Van Buren for the presidency in 1848. Since then, it has been in the wilderness, wandering in darkness. Active, to be sure, but making little progress toward the great end, which combined its original elements. A portion of those who have filled the ranks of this wandering army, are beginning to raise the enquiry which heads this article.

The aggressive front of slavery, openly declaring for the entire mastery of the country—the ready enrollment of the Democratic and Know Nothing[15] parties in the boldest enterprises of slavery—the shocking outrages perpetrated in Kansas—and the evident determination of the slave power to make slaveholding and slave buying and selling, the law of the whole land—have suggested the propriety of giving up the more radical and comprehensive measures of abolitionists at the ballot-box and the adoption of some one measure, upon which a large and important party can be united and organized to meet the slave power.

It is against this suggestion that we propose to offer a few remarks, remarks which, though coming from an humble source, may yet be deemed entitled to consideration by some sincere enquirer for the right way.

1. The ultimate success of the anti-slavery movement depends upon nothing, under God, more than upon the soundness of its principles, the earnestness,

---

13. With the rise of the Republican Party as a significant force in American politics, abolitionists like Douglass had to revisit the question of how to balance principle with the pragmatic demands of political life. This essay provides a glimpse at his thinking on these issues in early 1856.

14. A faction in the nineteenth-century New York Democratic Party.

15. The "Know Nothing Party" was a name commonly used for a political party originally called the "Native American Party" in 1845 and renamed the "American Party" in 1855. The Know Nothings are remembered primarily for their hostile anti-immigrant views.

stringency and faithfulness with which they are enforced, and the integrity, consistency and disinterestedness of those who stand forth as its advocates. The purity of the cause is the success of the cause. There can be very little necessity for sustaining this proposition by argument. We rely upon honesty, and not dishonesty, to uproot injustice and wrong. This element of power can be rallied and enlisted by its like—and only by its like. —"Men will not serve God if the devil bid them"[16]—and hence the necessity for purity and consistency in all who seek to leave the world better than they found it. The first duty of the reformer is to be right. If right, he may go forward; but if wrong, or partly wrong, he is as a house divided against itself, and will fall. He will move, if he moves at all, like a man in fetters, and to no valuable purpose. To succeed against slavery, the public must be brought to respect anti-slavery; and it cannot be respected unless consistent with itself, and its advocates are conscientiously consistent with it. The country must be made to feel the pulsation of an enlightened conscience, animating, supporting and directing that cause, before they will own it and bless it as a cause entitled to triumph.

2. That the national Republican Party, around whose standard abolitionists are now called upon to rally, does not occupy this high anti-slavery ground (and what is worse, does not mean to occupy it) is most painfully evident. From the hour that the old Liberty Party was swallowed up by the Van Buren Free Soil party in '48, the work of deterioration began, and has been continued until now. Instead of going upward, the political antislavery sentiment has been going downward. The Buffalo platform in '48 was lower than that of the Liberty Party; and the Pittsburgh platform of '56, is lower than that of '52. But not only is this deterioration shown in the platform of the Pittsburgh convention, recently adopted. It is painfully manifest in the spirit of the convention itself. There was a spirit of cold calculation, of deliberate contriving, so to pair off the edge of anti-slavery truth, and so to arrange and dispose of anti-slavery principles, as to draw into the Republican ranks men of all parties and sentiments, except the men of the Administration Party. No man could have been found in the Republican convention, held in Pittsburgh four years ago, bold enough to have proposed a slaveholder—an actual man-stealer—to preside over that convention of anti-slavery men. Such a proposition would have been scouted as an insult to the anti-slavery sentiment of the North. Then the tone of the speeches made on the occasion was lower and weaker than on any former occasion. The anti-slavery creed, after the filtration of this convention, came out simply a measure to restore the restriction against slavery to Kansas and Nebraska. Nothing said of the fugitive slave bill—nothing said of slavery in the District of Columbia—nothing said of the slave trade between states—nothing said of giving the dignity of the nation to liberty—nothing said of securing

---

16. William Shakespeare, *Othello*, act 1, sc. 1.

the rights of citizens, from the Northern states, in the constitutional right to enter and transact business in the slave states. There is not a single warm and living position, taken by the Republican Party, except freedom for Kansas. We need not ask radical anti-slavery men if this is the natural and desirable tendency of the political anti-slavery sentiment of the country. They instinctively recoil from it, as destructive of the great purpose of the anti-slavery movement of the country. They can only be induced to follow after the Republican movement under the teachings of a plausible and sinuous political philosophy, which is the grand corrupter of all reforms. The substance of this philosophy is, that the one thing needful, the thing to precede all else, is a large party; and in order to do this, we are at liberty to abandon almost everything but a name. Parties of this kind serve certain leading ones who get into office by them; but they seldom advance the case that gave them birth.

3. We hold that the true mode to prevent this falling away from anti-slavery truth and duty, and to save the anti-slavery movement from utter destruction, is to support candidates for the presidency and vice presidency, of tried anti-slavery character, and of decided anti-slavery principles. This is the true path of anti-slavery duty. The anti-slavery voters of the country must not allow themselves to be transferred from one political demagogue to another, until all vitality shall have departed from them. Nothing can be more certain, than that the habitual accommodation of anti-slavery men to the men opposed to them, has weakened the self-respect of the Anti-Slavery Party, and awakened the contempt of their opponents. The slaveholders themselves, seeing how ready we are to chase shadows, and to fight men of straw are perpetually leading us away from the main issue by these trifles. —We must show the slaveholders, and the country, that we are in earnest, and cannot be drawn away from our legitimate work. For this reason, we shall look to Syracuse, rather than to Philadelphia, for the candidates to be supported in the next presidential election. With the party at Syracuse, principles are more precious than numbers—and hence our cause is more safe there than elsewhere.

4. But it is said that by casting our votes for a man who duly represents our radical anti-slavery sentiments, in the coming presidential election, we shall probably give the government into the hands of the Democratic Party, and thereby establish slavery in Kansas, thus depriving the North of a free state, and adding its power to the slave states the better enabling the latter to perpetuate slavery.

This is very evidently a grave argument, and cannot be lightly disposed of. It is meet that it should be duly considered. Suppose, then, that by voting as above the result, which is possible, should occur—slavery should be established in Kansas, and Kansas added to the slave states. It then becomes us to estimate the loss which freedom would sustain, not as against the saving of Kansas to freedom, but as against the evils which would arise from the policy, which it is relied on, will save Kansas to freedom. This is the only consistent and certain method by which to arrive at the path of duty in the premise. Looking at the matter from this point then, we hold, that great as would be the misfortune to liberty should Kansas be given to slavery, tenfold greater would be the misfortune, should Kansas be saved by means which must certainly demoralize the anti-slavery sentiment of the North, and render it weak and inefficient for the greater work of saving the entire country to liberty. Keep in mind the fact that our aim is the entire abolition of slavery; that our work is not done till this is done; and that the real importance of establishing freedom in Kansas, is to be found in its effect to establish freedom in the country at large. We deliberately prefer the loss of Kansas to the loss of our anti-slavery integrity. With Kansas saved, and our anti-slavery integrity gone, our cause is ruined. With Kansas lost, and our anti-slavery integrity saved, we have, at least, means left us with which to continue the war upon slavery, and of final victory.

5. But this is arguing at great disadvantage, far greater than our position requires. We have granted more than there is any absolute necessity for granting. It is by no means certain that the Republican Party, even with the votes of abolitionists, can save Kansas. Freedom in Kansas depends, less upon politics, than upon the anti-slavery sentiment of the North, and the anti-slavery integrity of those who settle that territory from the North. —Dark indeed would be the prospect of freedom in Kansas, if it depended entirely upon the election of a Republican president for the next four years. If that is to decide the question, slavery has very little to fear and everything to hope. Republican enthusiasm may predict the election of a Republican president, but the calmer reason of that party must pronounce it strongly improbable. With the South united, and the North divided, it is easy to see which side will be victorious at the polls. Republicans will have an enemy to contend with at the North, which will require all its strength, flinging the South out of the question. Again we might claim that a strong vote for Radical Abolitionists would far more certainly help freedom in Kansas than a much stronger vote for the Republicans would do.

The whole slave population of this country whether in states, territories, dock yards, or on the high seas, must be emancipated. For this the true friends of the slave must toil and hope, and for nothing less than this. It is short-sighted, as a matter of policy, to aim lower than this, and it is cruel to those bleeding millions to do so. Our God, our country and the slave alike have called us to this great work, and we cannot come down from it to mingle in a less comprehensive or a less commanding struggle. Slavery is a sin now, a sin at all times, and a sin everywhere; and as we hold all human enactments designed to sustain it as of no binding authority, and utterly contrary to the Constitution of the United States the coast is clear for an open, and direct war upon slavery everywhere in the United States. —But should we not do one thing at a time? —Yes, one thing at a time; but let that thing be the abolition of slavery.

It is not doing one thing at a time, in any important sense, to limit the domain of slavery, and to leave its continuance unlimited. It is not doing one thing at a time to establish freedom for the white citizen in Kansas, and to hunt the black citizen from it, like a wolf; and if it is doing one thing at a time to do this, we hold that a strong vote for the radical abolition[17] candidate is the best way to accomplish that one thing at a time. —"Freedom for all, or chains for all."

---

17. The Radical Abolition Party was a short-lived political party in the United States. The party held a convention in New York in 1855 and Douglass, Gerrit Smith, William Goodell, and several other prominent political abolitionists were in attendance.

15. "Fremont and Dayton," an essay published in *Frederick Douglass' Paper*, August 15, 1856[18]

The readers of our journal will observe that the honored names which, for some time, stood at the head of our columns, as its candidates for the president and vice-president of the United States, have been withdrawn and although no other names have been or shall be placed at the head of our columns, we deem it proper frankly to announce our purpose to support, with whatever influence we possess, little or much, John C. Fremont[19] and William L. Dayton,[20] the candidates of the Republican Party for the presidency and vice presidency of the United States, in the present political canvass.

To a part of our readers, this announcement, considering our previous position, will be an unwelcome surprise. We have, hitherto, advocated to the best of our ability, a course of political action inconsistent with our present course. It is, therefore, eminently fit that we should accompany the foregoing announcement with something like a statement of reasons for our newly adopted policy.

1. A step so important as to lead to a separation in action, at least, between ourselves and of loved, honored, and tried friends, should not be hastily or inconsiderately taken. In full view of this truth, we have with much care examined and re-examined the subject of our political relations and duties regarding slavery and the colored people of the United States. Our position, as well as the suggestion of wisdom just referred to, very naturally cause hesitation. The name of Gerrit Smith has long been synonymous with us as genuine, unadulterated abolitionism. Of all men beneath the sky, we would rather see this just man made president. Our heart and judgment cling and twine around this man and his counsels as the ivy to the oak. To differ from him, and the beloved friends who may still intend to vote for him at the approaching election, is the result only of stern and irresistible conviction, the voice of which we cannot feel ourselves at liberty to disregard.

---

18. In this essay, Douglass rethinks the position he staked out in "What Is My Duty as an Anti-Slavery Voter?" (Selection 14). Reading the two essays side-by-side gives the reader a sense of the difficulties he confronted in trying to balance his commitment to principle with the practical demands of politics.

19. John C. Fremont (1813–1890) was an American politician and military officer who served in the US Senate and was the nominee of the Republican Party for president of the United States in 1856.

20. William L. Dayton (1807–1864) was an American politician and diplomat who was the nominee of the Republican Party for vice president in 1856.

2. The time has passed for an honest man to attempt any defense of a right to change his opinion as to political methods of opposing slavery. Anti-slavery consistency itself, in our view, requires of the anti-slavery voter that disposition of his vote and his influence, which, in all the circumstances and likelihoods of the case tend most to the triumph of free principles in the councils and government of the nation. It is not to be consistent to pursue a course politically this year, merely because that course seemed the best last year, or at any previous time. Right anti-slavery action is that which deals the severest deadliest blow upon slavery that can be given at that particular time. Such action is always consistent, however different may be the forms through which it expresses itself.

3. Again, in supporting Fremont and Dayton, we are in no wise required to abandon a single anti-slavery truth or principle which we have hitherto cherished, and publicly advocated. The difference between our paper this week and last week is a difference of policy, not of principle. Hereafter, as hitherto, we shall contend for every principle, and maintain [mutilated] the platform of the Radical Abolitionists. The unconstitutionality of slavery, the illegality of slavery, the right of the federal government to abolish slavery in every part of the republic, whether in states or territories, will be as firmly held, and as sternly insisted upon, as hitherto. Nor do we wish, by supporting the Republican candidate in the approaching election, to be understood as merging our individuality, body and soul, into that party, nor as separating ourselves from our radical abolition friends in their present endeavors to enforce the great principles of justice and liberty, upon which the radical abolition movement is based. Furthermore, we here concede, that upon radical abolition grounds, the final battle against slavery in this country must be fought out—slavery must be seen and felt to be a huge crime, a system of lawless violence, before it can be abolished. In our paper, upon the platform, at home and abroad, we shall endeavor to bring slavery before the people in this hateful light; and by so doing, shall really be upholding the radical abolition platform in the very ranks of the Republican Party.

4. Beyond all controversy, the commanding and vital issue with slavery at the approaching presidential election, is the extension or the limitation of slavery. The malign purpose of extending, strengthening, and perpetuating slavery, is the conclusion of the great mass of the slaveholders. The execution of this purpose upon Kansas, is plainly enough the business set down for the present by the friends of slavery, North and South. And it cannot be denied that the election either of [James] Buchanan[21] or [Millard]

---

21. James Buchanan (1791–1868) was an American politician and diplomat who served as a US senator and the secretary of state and was elected to be the fifteenth president of the United States in 1856.

Fillmore[22] would be the success of this malign purpose of slave power. Other elements enter into the issue, such, for instance, as Northern or Southern ascendency of the slave power in the councils of the nation, the continued humiliation of the Northern people, the reign of terror at Washington,[23] the crippling of the anti-slavery movement, and the security and preservation of slavery from inward decay or outside destroying influences. The fact that slaveholders had taken a united stand in favor of this measure, is, at least, an argument why anti-slavery men should take a stand to defeat them. The greatest triumphs of slavery have been secured by the division of its enemies, one party insisting on attacking one point, and another class equally in earnest bending their energies in another direction. Were it in our power, the order of battle between liberty and slavery would be arranged differently. Antislavery in our hands, at the ballot box, should be the aggressor; but it is not within our power, or within that of any other man, to control the order of events, or the circumstances which shape our course, and determine our conduct at particular times. All men will agree, that, generally speaking, the point attacked, is the point to be defended. The South has tendered to us the issue of slavery extension; and to meet the slave power here is to rouse its most devilish animosity. It is to strike hardest, where the slaveholders feel most keenly. The most powerful blow that could be given at that point would in our judgment, be the election to the presidency and vice presidency of the republic the candidates of the Republican Party.

5. Briefly, then, we shall support Fremont and Dayton in the present crisis of the anti-slavery movement, because they are, by position, and from the very nature of the organization which supports them, the admitted and recognized antagonists of the slave power, of gag law, and of all the hellish designs of the slave power to extend and fortify the accursed slave system. We shall support them because they are the most numerous anti-slavery party, and, therefore, the most powerful to inflict a blow upon, and the most likely to achieve a valuable victory over, the slave oligarchy. There is not a trafficker in the bodies and souls of men, from Baltimore to New Orleans, that would not crack his

---

22. Millard Fillmore (1800–1874) was an American politician who served in the House of Representatives, as the twelfth vice president of the United States, and as the thirteenth president of the United States. In 1856, he was the nominee of the American Party (also known as the "Know Nothing Party") for president of the United States.

23. It is unclear precisely what Douglass means by "reign of terror" here. The abolitionist Harriet Jacobs had referred to the passage of the Fugitive Slave Act in 1850 as "the beginning of a reign of terror to the colored population" in her book, *Incidents in the Life of a Slave Girl*. It is also possible that Douglass is referring to the 1856 attack on antislavery senator Charles Sumner on the floor of the US Senate. In May of 1856 Sumner was attacked by South Carolina congressman Preston Brooks and suffered severe injuries as a result of the attack. Thanks to an anonymous reviewer for suggesting this latter possibility.

bloody slave whip with fiendish delight over the defeat of Fremont and Dayton. Whereas, on the other hand, the moral effect of the radical abolition vote, separated as it must be from the great anti-slavery body of the North, must, from the nature of the case, be very limited for good, and only powerful for mischief, where its effect would be to weaken the Republican Party. We shall support Fremont and Dayton, because there is no chance whatever in the present contest of electing better men than they. And we are the more reconciled to accepting them, by the fact that they are surrounded by a party of progressive men. Take them, therefore, not merely for what they are, but for what we have good reason to believe they will become when they have lived for a time in the element of anti-slavery discussion. We shall support them by pen, by speech, by vote, because it is by no means certain that they can succeed in this state against the powerful combinations opposed to them without the support of the full and complete abolition vote. Bitter indeed, would be the reproach, and deep and pointed would be the regret, if, through the Radical Abolitionists, victory should perch on the bloody standard of slave rule, as would be the case if Fremont and Dayton were defeated, and Buchanan and [John C.] Breckenridge[24] elected. For one, we are not disposed to incur this reproach, nor to experience this regret, and shall, therefore, vote for Fremont and Dayton. In supporting them, we neither dishonor our principles nor lessen our means of securing their adoption and active application. We can reach the ears and heart of as great a number within the ranks of the Republican Party as we could possibly do by remaining outside of those ranks. We know of no law applicable to the progress and promulgation of radical abolition principles which would act less favorably toward our principles inside the party, than outside of it.

6. Another reason for supporting the Republican Party at the ballot-box and thus supporting the anti-slavery vote as a unit, is, that such action conforms exactly to the facts of our existing relations as citizens. There is now, evidently, but one great question of widespread and of all-commanding national interest; and that question is freedom or slavery. In reality, there can be but two parties to this question; and for ourselves, we wish it to be with the natural division for freedom, in form, as well as in fact.

7. It seems to us both the dictate of good morals and true wisdom, that if we cannot abolish slavery in all the states by our votes at the approaching election, we ought, if we can, keep slavery out of Kansas by our vote. To pursue any other policy is to abandon at present, practical advantage to freedom in an assertion of more comprehensive claims, right enough in themselves, but which reason and fact assure us can only be attained by votes in the future,

24. John C. Breckenridge (1821–1875) was an American politician who served in the House of Representatives and the US Senate and as the fourteenth vice president of the United States. In 1860, he ran unsuccessfully for president of the United States.

when the public mind shall have been educated up to those claims. We are quite well aware that to the foregoing, objections of apparent weight may be urged by those for whose conscientious convictions we cherish the profoundest respect. And although we do not propose to anticipate objections, but intend to meet them as they shall be presented in the progress of the canvass, we will mention and reply to one. Most plainly the greatest difficulty to be met with by a Radical Abolitionist in supporting Fremont and Dayton, is the fact that these candidates have not declared and do not declare any purpose to abolish slavery by legislation, in the states. They neither entertain nor declare any such purpose, and in this they are far from occupying the high anti-slavery position of the Radical Abolition Society. But let us not be unreasonable or impatient with the Republican Party. In considering this defect in the anti-slavery character and creed of the Republican candidates, it should be borne in mind that they stand now in respect to this doctrine precisely where the Liberty Party stood ten years ago. The right and duty of the federal government to abolish slavery everywhere in the United States, is entirely true and deeply important; and yet, it must be confessed that this doctrine has been made appreciable but to a few minds, the dwellers in the mountain peaks of the moral world, who catch the first beams of morning, long before the slumberers in the valleys awake from their dreams. This new doctrine, we think, may very properly be left to take its turn in the arena of discussion. Time and argument will do more for its progress, and its final adoption by the people, than can be done for it in the present crisis, by the few votes of the isolated Radical Abolitionists. In further extenuation or apology, it may be very properly urged, that while the Republican Party has not at this point adopted the abolition creed, it has laid down principles and promulgated doctrines, which in their application, directly tend to the abolition of slavery in the states. But the conclusive answer to all who object upon this ground is the indisputable truth, that neither in religion nor morals, can a man be justified in refusing to assist his fellow-men to accomplish a possible good thing, simply because his fellows refuse to accomplish some other good things which they deem impossible. Most assuredly, that theory cannot be a sound one which would prevent us from voting with men for the abolition of slavery in Maryland simply because our companions refuse to include Virginia. In such a case, the path of duty is plainly this; go with your fellow-citizens for the abolition of slavery in Maryland when they are ready to go for that measure, and do all you can, meanwhile, to bring them to whatever work of righteousness may remain and which has become manifest to your clearer vision. Such, then, is the conclusion forced upon us by the philosophy of the facts of our condition as a nation. A great crime against freedom and civilization is about to be perpetrated. The slave power is resolved to plant the deadly Upas, slavery, in the virgin soil of Kansas. This great evil may be averted, and all the likelihoods of the case, the election of John C. Fremont and William

L. Dayton, will be instrumental in averting it. Their election will prevent the establishment of slavery in Kansas, overthrow slave rule in the republic, protect liberty of speech and of the press, give ascendency to Northern civilization over the bludgeon and blood-hound civilization of the South, and the mark of national condemnation on slavery, scourge doughfaces[25] from place and from power, and inaugurate a higher and purer standard of politics and government. Therefore, we go for Fremont and Dayton.

---

25. The term "doughface" is used here as a reference to Northerners who support the political positions of what Douglass and other abolitionists called "the slave power" in the South.

16. "The Dred Scott Decision," a speech delivered at the anniversary of the American Anti-Slavery Society in New York, New York on May 14, 1857 and published as a pamphlet (Rochester: C. P. Dewey, 1857)[26]

MR. CHAIRMAN, FRIENDS, AND FELLOW CITIZENS:

While four millions of our fellow countrymen are in chains—while men, women, and children are bought and sold on the auction-block with horses, sheep, and swine—while the remorseless slave-whip draws the warm blood of our common humanity—it is meet that we assemble as we have done today, and lift up our hearts and voices in earnest denunciation of the vile and shocking abomination. It is not for us to be governed by our hopes or our fears in this great work; yet it is natural on occasions like this, to survey the position of the great struggle which is going on between slavery and freedom, and to dwell upon such signs of encouragement as may have been lately developed, and the state of feeling these signs or events have occasioned in us and among the people generally. It is a fitting time to take an observation to ascertain where we are, and what our prospects are.

To many, the prospects of the struggle against slavery seem far from cheering. Eminent men, North and South, in church and state, tell us that the omens are all against us. Emancipation, they tell us, is a wild, delusive idea; the price of human flesh was never higher than now; slavery was never more closely entwined about the hearts and affections of the Southern people than now; that whatever of conscientious scruple, religious conviction, or public policy, which opposed the system of slavery forty or fifty years ago, has subsided; and that slavery never reposed upon a firmer basis than now. Completing this picture of the happy and prosperous condition of this system of wickedness, they tell us that this state of things is to be set to our account. Abolition agitation has done it all. How deep is the misfortune of my poor, bleeding people, if this be so! How lost their condition, if even the efforts of their friends but sink them deeper in ruin!

---

26. In this speech, Douglass reacts to the infamous Supreme Court decision on *Dred Scott v. Sandford* (1857). The details of this decision are described in the introduction to this collection. The speech provides not only Douglass' critique of the decision but also a further elaboration of his antislavery reading of the Constitution and his views on the shortcomings of Garrisonian political morality.

Without assenting to this strong representation of the increasing strength and stability of slavery, without denouncing what of untruth pervades it, I own myself not insensible to the many difficulties and discouragements, that beset us on every hand. They fling their broad and gloomy shadows across the pathway of every thoughtful colored man in this country. For one, I see them clearly, and feel them sadly. With an earnest, aching heart, I have long looked for the realization of the hope of my people. Standing, as it were, barefoot, and treading upon the sharp and flinty rocks of the present, and looking out upon the boundless sea of the future, I have sought, in my humble way, to penetrate the intervening mists and clouds, and, perchance, to descry, in the dim and shadowy distance, the white flag of freedom, the precise speck of time at which the cruel bondage of my people should end, and the long entombed millions rise from the foul grave of slavery and death. But of that time I can know nothing, and you can know nothing. All is uncertain at that point. One thing, however, is certain; slaveholders are in earnest, and mean to cling to their slaves as long as they can, and to the bitter end. They show no sign of a wish to quit their iron grasp upon the sable throats of their victims. Their motto is, "a firmer hold and a tighter grip" for every new effort that is made to break their cruel power. The case is one of life or death with them, and they will give up only when they must do that or do worse.

In one view the slaveholders have a decided advantage over all opposition. It is well to notice this advantage—the advantage of complete organization. They are organized; and yet were not at the pains of creating their organizations. The state governments, where the system of slavery exists, are complete slavery organizations. The church organizations in those states are equally at the service of slavery; while the federal government, with its army and navy, from the chief magistracy in Washington, to the Supreme Court, and thence to the chief marshal-ship at New York, is pledged to support, defend, and propagate the crying curse of human bondage. The pen, the purse, and the sword, are united against the simple truth, preached by humble men in obscure places.

This is one view. It is, thank God, only one view; there is another, and a brighter view. David, you know, looked small and insignificant when going to meet Goliath,[27] but looked larger when he had slain his foe. The Malakoff was, to the eye of the world, impregnable, till the hour it fell before the shot and shell of the allied army. Thus hath it ever been. Oppression, organized as ours is, will appear invincible up to the very hour of its fall. Sir, let us look at the other side, and see if there are not some things to cheer our heart and nerve us up anew in the good work of emancipation.

Take this fact—for it is a fact—the antislavery movement has, from first to last, suffered no abatement. It has gone forth in all directions, and is now felt

---

27. I Samuel 17.

in the remotest extremities of the republic. It started small, and was without capital either in men or money. The odds were all against it. It literally had nothing to lose, and everything to gain. There was ignorance to be enlightened, error to be combatted, conscience to be awakened, prejudice to be overcome, apathy to be aroused, the right of speech to be secured, mob violence to be subdued, and a deep, radical change to be inwrought in the mind and heart of the whole nation. This great work, under God, has gone on, and gone on gloriously. Amid all changes, fluctuations, assaults, and adverses [*sic*] of every kind, it has remained firm in its purpose, steady in its aim, onward and upward, defying all opposition, and never losing a single battle. Our strength is in the growth of anti-slavery conviction, and this has never halted.

There is a significant vitality about this abolition movement. It has taken a deeper, broader, and more lasting hold upon the national heart than ordinary reform movements. Other subjects of much interest come and go, expand and contract, blaze and vanish, but the huge question of American slavery, comprehending, as it does, not merely the weal or the woe of four millions, and their countless posterity, but the weal or the woe of this entire nation, must increase in magnitude and in majesty with every hour of its history. From a cloud not bigger than a man's hand, it has overspread the heavens. It has risen from a grain not bigger than a mustard seed.[28] Yet see the fowls of the air, how they crowd its branches.

Politicians who cursed it, now defend it; ministers, once dumb, now speak in its praise; and presses, which once flamed with hot denunciations against it, now surround the sacred cause as by a wall of living fire.[29] Politicians go with it as a pillar of cloud by day, and the press as a pillar of fire by night.[30] With these ancient tokens of success, I, for one, will not despair of our cause.

Those who have undertaken to suppress and crush out this agitation for liberty and humanity, have been most woefully disappointed. Many who have engaged to put it down, have found themselves put down. The agitation has pursued them in all their meanderings, broken in upon their seclusion, and, at the very moment of fancied security, it has settled down upon them like a mantle of unquenchable fire. Clay, Calhoun, and Webster each tried his hand at suppressing the agitation; and they went to their graves disappointed and defeated.

Loud and exultingly have we been told that the slavery question is settled, and settled forever. You remember it was settled thirty-seven years ago, when Missouri was admitted into the Union with a slaveholding constitution, and slavery prohibited in all territory north of thirty-six degrees of north latitude.

---

28. I Kings 18:44; Luke 13:19.
29. Douglass paraphrases Zechariah 2:5.
30. Exodus 13:21.

Just fifteen years afterward, it was settled again by voting down the right of petition, and gagging down free discussion in Congress. Ten years after this it was settled again by the annexation of Texas, and with it the war with Mexico. In 1850 it was again settled. This was called a final settlement. By it slavery was virtually declared to be the equal of liberty, and should come into the Union on the same terms. By it the right and the power to hunt down men, women, and children, in every part of this country, was conceded to our Southern brethren, in order to keep them in the Union. Four years after this settlement, the whole question was once more settled, and settled by a settlement which unsettled all the former settlements.

The fact is, the more the question has been settled, the more it has needed settling. The space between the different settlements has been strikingly on the decrease. The first stood longer than any of its successors. There is a lesson in these decreasing spaces. The first stood fifteen years—the second, ten years—the third, five years—the fourth stood four years—and the fifth has stood the brief space of two years.

This last settlement must be called the Taney settlement.[31] We are now told, in tones of lofty exultation, that the day is lost—all lost—and that we might as well give up the struggle. The highest authority has spoken. The voice of the Supreme Court has gone out over the troubled waves of the national conscience, saying peace, be still.[32]

This infamous decision of the slaveholding wing of the Supreme Court maintains that slaves are within the contemplation of the Constitution of the United States, property; that slaves are property in the same sense that horses, sheep, and swine are property; that the old doctrine that slavery is a creature of local law is false; that the right of the slaveholder to his slave does not depend upon the local law, but is secured wherever the Constitution of the United States extends; that Congress has no right to prohibit slavery anywhere; that slavery may go in safety anywhere under the star-spangled banner; that colored persons of African descent have no rights that white men are bound to respect; that colored men of African descent are not and cannot be citizens of the United States.

You will readily ask me how I am affected by this devilish decision—this judicial incarnation of wolfishness? My answer is, and no thanks to the slaveholding wing of the Supreme Court, my hopes were never brighter than now.

I have no fear that the national conscience will be put to sleep by such an open, glaring, and scandalous tissue of lies as that decision is, and has been, over and over, shown to be.

---

31. This is a reference to the *Dred Scott v. Sandford* (1857) decision of the US Supreme Court. This decision is described in the introduction to this volume.
32. Mark 4:39.

The Supreme Court of the United States is not the only power in this world. It is very great, but the Supreme Court of the Almighty is greater. Judge Taney can do many things, but he cannot perform impossibilities. He cannot bale out the ocean, annihilate the firm old earth, or pluck the silvery star of liberty from our Northern sky. He may decide, and decide again; but he cannot reverse the decision of the Most High. He cannot change the essential nature of things— making evil good, and good evil. Happily for the whole human family, their rights have been defined, declared, and decided in a court higher than the Supreme Court. "There is a law," says Brougham,[33] "above all the enactments of human codes, and by that law, unchangeable and eternal, man cannot hold property in man."

Your fathers have said that man's right to liberty is self-evident. There is no need of argument to make it clear. The voices of nature, of conscience, of reason, and of revelation, proclaim it as the right of all rights, the foundation of all trust, and of all responsibility. Man was born with it. It was his before he comprehended it. The *deed* conveying it to him is written in the center of his soul, and is recorded in heaven. The sun in the sky is not more palpable to the sight than man's right to liberty is to the moral vision. To decide against this right in the person of Dred Scott, or the humblest and most whip-scarred bondman in the land, is to decide against God. It is an open rebellion against God's government. It is an attempt to undo what God has done, to blot out the broad distinction instituted by the *All-Wise* between men and things, and to change the image and superscription of the ever-living God into a speechless piece of merchandise.

Such a decision cannot stand. God will be true though every man be a liar.[34] We can appeal from this hell black judgment of the Supreme Court, to the court of common sense and common humanity. We can appeal from man to God. If there is no justice on earth, there is yet justice in heaven. You may close your Supreme Court against the black man's cry for justice, but you cannot, thank God, close against him the ear of a sympathizing world, nor shut up the Court of Heaven. All that is merciful and just, on earth and in heaven, will execrate and despise this edict of Taney.

If it were at all likely that the people of these free states would tamely submit to this demonical judgment, I might feel gloomy and sad over it, and possibly it might be necessary for my people to look for a home in some other country. But as the case stands, we have nothing to fear.

In one point of view, we, the abolitionists and colored people, should meet this decision, unlooked for and monstrous as it appears, in a cheerful spirit. This very attempt to blot out forever the hopes of an enslaved people may be

---

33. Henry Peter Brougham (1778–1868) was a British politician and writer.
34. Romans 3:4.

one necessary link in the chain of events preparatory to the downfall and complete overthrow of the whole slave system.

The whole history of the anti-slavery movement is studded with proof that all measures devised and executed with a view to allay and diminish the anti-slavery agitation, have only served to increase, intensify, and embolden that agitation. This wisdom of the crafty has been confounded, and the counsels of the ungodly brought to naught. It was so with the fugitive slave bill. It was so with the Kansas-Nebraska bill; and it will be so with this last and most shocking of all pro-slavery devices, this Taney decision.

When great transactions are involved, where the fate of millions is concerned, where a long enslaved and suffering people are to be delivered, I am superstitious enough to believe that the finger of the Almighty may be seen bringing good out of evil, and making the wrath of man[35] redound to his honor, hastening the triumph of righteousness.

The American people have been called upon, in a most striking manner, to abolish and put away forever the system of slavery. The subject has been pressed upon their attention in all earnestness and sincerity. The cries of the slave have gone forth to the world, and up to the throne of God. This decision, in my view, is a means of keeping the nation awake on the subject. It is another proof that God does not mean that we shall go to sleep, and forget that we are a slaveholding nation.

Step by step we have seen the slave power advancing; poisoning, corrupting, and perverting the institutions of the country; growing more and more haughty, imperious, and exacting. The white man's liberty has been marked out for the same grave with the black man's.

The ballot box is desecrated, God's law set at naught, armed legislators stalk the halls of Congress, freedom of speech is beaten down in the Senate.[36] The rivers and highways are infested by border ruffians, and white men are made to feel the iron heel of slavery. This ought to arouse us to kill off the hateful thing. They are solemn warnings to which the white people, as well as the black people, should take heed.

If these shall fail, judgment, more fierce or terrible, may come. The lightning, whirlwind, and earthquake may come. Jefferson said that he trembled for his country when he reflected that God is just, and his justice cannot sleep forever.[37] The time may come when even the crushed worm may turn under the tyrant's feet. Goaded by cruelty, stung by a burning sense of wrong, in an

---

35. Psalms 76:10.
36. This is a reference to the 1856 attack on antislavery senator Charles Sumner on the floor of the US Senate. In May of 1856 Sumner was attacked by South Carolina congressman Preston Brooks and suffered severe injuries as a result of the attack.
37. Douglass refers to Thomas Jefferson's *Notes on the State of Virginia*, Query XVIII.

awful moment of depression and desperation, the bondman and bondwoman at the South may rush to one wild and deadly struggle for freedom. Already slaveholders go to bed with bowie knives, and apprehend death at their dinners. Those who enslave, rob, and torment their cooks, may well expect to find death in their dinner-pots.

The world is full of violence and fraud, and it would be strange if the slave, the constant victim of both fraud and violence, should escape the contagion. He, too, may learn to fight the devil with fire, and for one, I am in no frame of mind to pray that this may be long deferred.

[. . . .]

By all the laws of nature, civilization, and of progress, slavery is a doomed system. Not all the skill of politicians, North and South, not all the sophistries of judges, not all the fulminations of a corrupt press, not all the hypocritical prayers, or the hypocritical refusals to pray of a hollow-hearted priesthood, not all the devices of sin and Satan, can save the vile thing from extermination.

Already a gleam of hope breaks upon us from the southwest. One Southern city has grieved and astonished the whole South by a preference for freedom. The wedge has entered. Dred Scott, of Missouri, goes into slavery, but St. Louis declares for freedom. The judgment of Taney is not the judgment of St. Louis.

It may be said that this demonstration in St. Louis is not to be taken as an evidence of sympathy with the slave; that it is purely a white man's victory. I admit it. Yet I am glad that white men, bad as they generally are, should gain a victory over slavery. I am willing to accept a judgment against slavery, whether supported by white or black reasons—though I would much rather have it supported by both. He that is not against us, is on our part.

Come what will, I hold it to be morally certain that, sooner or later, by fair means or foul means, in quiet or in tumult, in peace or in blood, in judgment or in mercy, slavery is doomed to cease out of this otherwise goodly land, and liberty is destined to become the settled law of this republic.

I base my sense of the certain overthrow of slavery, in part, upon the nature of the American government, the Constitution, the tendencies of the age, and the character of the American people; and this, notwithstanding the important decision of Judge Taney. I know of no soil better adapted to the growth of reform than American soil. I know of no country where the conditions for affecting great changes in the settled order of things, for the development of right ideas of liberty and humanity, are more favorable than here in these United States.

The very groundwork of this government is a good repository of Christian civilization. The Constitution, as well as the Declaration of Independence, and the sentiments of the founders of the republic, give us a platform broad enough, and strong enough, to support the most comprehensive plans for the freedom and elevation of all the people of this country, without regard to color, class, or clime.

There is nothing in the present aspect of the anti-slavery question which should drive us into the extravagance and nonsense of advocating a dissolution of the American union as a means of overthrowing slavery, or freeing the North from the malign influence of slavery upon the morals of the Northern people. While the press is at liberty, and speech is free, and the ballot-box is open to the people of the sixteen free states; while the slaveholders are but four hundred thousand in number, and we are fourteen millions; while the mental and moral power of the nation is with us; while we are really the strong and they are the weak, it would look worse than cowardly to retreat from the Union.

If the people of the North have not the power to cope with these four hundred thousand slaveholders inside the Union, I see not how they could get out of the Union. The strength necessary to move the Union must ever be less than is required to break it up. If we have got to conquer the slave power to get out of the Union, I for one would much rather conquer, and stay in the Union. The latter, it strikes me, is the far more rational mode of action.

I make these remarks in no servile spirit, nor in any superstitious reverence for a mere human arrangement. If I felt the Union to be a curse, I should not be far behind the very chiefest [*sic*] of the disunion abolitionists in denouncing it. But the evil to be met and abolished is not in the Union. The power arrayed against us is not a parchment.

It is not in changing the dead form of the Union, that slavery is to be abolished in this country. We have to do not with the dead, but the living[38]; not with the past, but the living present.

Those who seek slavery in the Union, and who are everlastingly dealing blows upon the Union, in the belief that they are killing slavery, are most woefully mistaken. They are fighting a dead form instead of a living and powerful reality. It is clearly not because of the peculiar character of our Constitution that we have slavery, but the wicked pride, love of power, and selfish perverseness of the American people. Slavery lives in this country not because of any paper Constitution, but in the moral blindness of the American people, who persuade themselves that they are safe, though the rights of others may be struck down.

Besides, I think it would be difficult to hit upon any plan less likely to abolish slavery than the dissolution of the Union. The most devoted advocates of slavery, those who make the interests of slavery their constant study, seek a dissolution of the Union as their final plan for preserving slavery from abolition, and their ground is well taken. Slavery lives and flourishes best in the absence

---

38. Matthew 22:32.

of civilization; a dissolution of the Union would shut up the system in its own congenial barbarism.

The dissolution of the Union would not give the North one single additional advantage over slavery to the people of the North, but would manifestly take from them many which they now certainly possess.

Within the Union we have a firm basis of anti-slavery operation. National welfare, national prosperity, national reputation and honor, and national scrutiny; common rights, common duties, and common country, are so many bridges over which we can march to the destruction of slavery. To fling away these advantages because James Buchanan is president, or Judge Taney gives a lying decision in favor of slavery, does not enter into my notion of common sense.

Mr. Garrison and his friends have been telling us that, while in the Union, we are responsible for slavery; and in so telling us, he and they have told us the truth. But in telling us that we shall cease to be responsible for slavery by dissolving the Union, he and they have not told us the truth.

There now, clearly, is no freedom from responsibility for slavery, but in the abolition of slavery. We have gone too far in this business now to sum up our whole duty in the cant phrase of "no Union with slaveholders."

To desert the family hearth may place the recreant husband out of the sight of his hungry children, but it cannot free him from responsibility. Though he should roll the waters of three oceans between him and them, he could not roll from his soul the burden of his responsibility to them; and, as with the private family, so in this instance with the national family. To leave the slave in his chains, in the hands of cruel masters who are too strong for him, is not to free ourselves from responsibility. Again: If I were on board of a pirate ship, with a company of men and women whose lives and liberties I had put in jeopardy, I would not clear my soul of their blood by jumping in the long boat, and singing out no union with pirates. My business would be to remain on board, and while I never would perform a single act of piracy again, I should exhaust every means given me by my position, to save the lives and liberties of those against whom I had committed piracy. In like manner, I hold it is our duty to remain inside this Union, and use all the power to restore to enslaved millions their precious and God-given rights. The more we have done by our voice and our votes, in times past, to rivet their galling fetters, the more clearly and solemnly comes the sense of duty to remain, to undo what we have done. Where, I ask, could the slave look for release from slavery if the Union were dissolved? I have an abiding conviction founded upon long and careful study of the certain effects of slavery upon the moral sense of slaveholding communities, that if the slaves are ever delivered from bondage, the power will emanate from the free states. All hope that the slaveholders will be self-moved to this great act of justice, is groundless and delusive. Now, as of old, the Redeemer must come from above, not from beneath. To dissolve the Union would be to withdraw the emancipating power from the field.

But I am told this is the argument of expediency. I admit it, and am prepared to show that what is expedient in this instance is right. "Do justice, though the heavens fall." Yes, that is a good motto, but I deny that it would be doing justice to the slave to dissolve the Union and leave the slave in his chains to get out by the clemency of his master, or the strength of his arms. Justice to the slave is to break his chains, and going out of the Union is to leave him in his chains, and without any probable chance of getting out of them.

But I come now to the great question as to the constitutionality of slavery. The recent slaveholding decision, as well as the teachings of anti-slavery men, make this a fit time to discuss the constitutional pretensions of slavery.

The people of the North are a law-abiding people. They love order and respect the means to that end. This sentiment has sometimes led them to the folly and wickedness of trampling upon the very life of law, to uphold its dead form. This was so in the execution of that thrice accursed fugitive slave bill. Burns and Simms[39] were sent back to the hell of slavery after they had looked upon Bunker Hill, and heard liberty thunder in Faneuil Hall. The people permitted this outrage in obedience to the popular sentiment of reverence for law. While men thus respect law, it becomes a serious matter so to interpret the law as to make it operate against liberty. I have a quarrel with those who fling the supreme law of this land between the slave and freedom. It is a serious matter to fling the weight of the Constitution against the cause of human liberty, and those who do it, take upon them a heavy responsibility. Nothing but absolute necessity, shall, or ought to drive me to such a concession to slavery.

When I admit that slavery is constitutional, I must see slavery recognized in the Constitution. I must see that it is there plainly stated that one man of a certain description has a right of property in the body and soul of another man of a certain description. There must be no room for a doubt. In a matter so important as the loss of liberty, everything must be proved beyond all reasonable doubt.

The well known rules of legal interpretation bear me out in this stubborn refusal to see slavery where slavery is not, and only to see slavery where it is.

The Supreme Court has, in its day, done something better than make slaveholding decisions. It has laid down rules of interpretation which are in harmony with the true idea and object of law and liberty.

It has told us that the intention of legal instruments must prevail; and that this must be collected from its words. It has told us that language must be construed strictly in favor of liberty and justice.

It has told us where rights are infringed, where fundamental principles are overthrown, where the general system of the law is departed from, the legislative

---

39. Douglass refers to two prominent fugitive slave cases.

intention must be expressed with irresistible clearness, to induce a court of justice to suppose a design to effect such objects.

These rules are as old as law. They rise out of the very elements of law. It is to protect human rights, and promote human welfare. Law is in its nature opposed to wrong, and must everywhere be presumed to be in favor of the right. The pound of flesh, but not one drop of blood,[40] is a sound rule of legal interpretation. Besides there is another rule of law as well of common sense, which requires us to look to the ends for which a law is made, and to construe its details in harmony with the ends sought.

Now let us approach the Constitution from the standpoint thus indicated, and instead of finding in it a warrant for the stupendous system of robbery, comprehended in the term slavery, we shall find it strongly against that system.

"We, the people of the United States, in order to form a more perfect Union, establish justice, insure domestic tranquility, provide for the common defense, promote the general welfare, and secure the blessings of liberty to ourselves and our posterity, do ordain and establish this Constitution for the United States of America."

Such are the objects announced by the instrument itself, and they are in harmony with the Declaration of Independence, and the principles of human well-being. Six objects are here declared, "Union," "defense," "welfare," "tranquility," and "justice," and "liberty."

Neither in the preamble nor in the body of the Constitution is there a single mention of the term *slave* or *slave holder, slave* master or *slave state,* neither is there any reference to the color, or the physical peculiarities of any part of the people of the United States. Neither is there anything in the Constitution standing alone, which would imply the existence of slavery in this country.

"We, the people"—not we, the white people—not we, the citizens, or the legal voters—not we, the privileged class, and excluding all other classes but we, the people; not we, the horses and cattle, but we the people—the men and women, the human inhabitants of the United States, do ordain and establish this Constitution, &c.

I ask, then, any man to read the Constitution, and tell me where, if he can, in what particular that instrument affords the slightest sanction of slavery? Where will he find a guarantee for slavery? Will he find it in the declaration that no person shall be deprived of life, liberty, or property, without due process of law? Will he find it in the declaration that the Constitution was established to secure the blessing of liberty? Will he find it in the right of the people to be secure in their persons and papers, and houses, and effects? Will he find it in the clause prohibiting the enactment by any state of a bill of attainder?

---

40. William Shakespeare, *Merchant of Venice,* act 4, sc. 1.

These all strike at the root of slavery, and any one of them, but faithfully carried out, would put an end to slavery in every state in the American Union. [. . . .]

While this and much more can be said, and has been said, and much better said, by Lysander Spooner, William Goodell, Beriah Green,[41] and Gerrit Smith, in favor of the entire unconstitutionality of slavery, what have we on the other side? How is the constitutionality of slavery made out, or attempted to be made out? First, by discrediting and casting away as worthless the most beneficent rules of legal interpretation; by disregarding the plain and common sense reading of the instrument itself; by showing that the Constitution does not mean what it says, and says what it does not mean, by assuming that the written Constitution is to be interpreted in the light of a secret and unwritten understanding of its framers, which understanding is declared to be in favor of slavery. It is in this mean, contemptible, underhand method that the Constitution is pressed into the service of slavery.

They do not point us to the Constitution itself, for the reason that there is nothing sufficiently explicit for their purpose; but they delight in supposed intentions—intentions nowhere expressed in the Constitution, and everywhere contradicted in the Constitution.

Judge Taney lays down this system of interpreting in this wise:

"The general words above quoted would seem to embrace the whole human family, and, if they were used in a similar instrument at this day, would be so understood. But it is too clear for dispute that the enslaved African race were not intended to be included, and formed no part of the people who framed and adopted this declaration; for if the language, as understood in that day, would embrace them, the conduct of the distinguished men who framed the Declaration of Independence would have been utterly and flagrantly inconsistent with the principles they asserted; and instead of the sympathy of mankind, to which they appealed, they would have deserved and received universal rebuke and reprobation."

"It is difficult, at this day, to realize the state of public opinion respecting that unfortunate class with the civilized and enlightened portion of the world at the time of the Declaration of Independence and the adoption of the Constitution; but history shows they had, for more than a century, been regarded as beings of an inferior order, and unfit associates for the white race, either socially or politically, and had no rights which white men are bound to respect; and the black man might be reduced to slavery, bought and sold, and treated as an ordinary article of merchandise. This opinion, at that time, was fixed and universal with the civilized portion of the white race. It was regarded as an axiom of morals, which no one thought of disputing, and everyone habitually

---

41. Beriah Green (1795–1874) was an American abolitionist.

acted upon it, without doubting, for a moment, the correctness of the opinion. And in no nation was this opinion more fixed, and generally acted upon, than in England; the subjects of which government not only seized them on the coast of Africa, but took them, as ordinary merchandise, to where they could make a profit on them. The opinion, thus entertained, was universally maintained on the colonies this side of the Atlantic; accordingly, Negroes of the African race were regarded by them as property, and held and bought and sold as such in every one of the thirteen colonies, which united in the Declaration of Independence, and afterwards formed the Constitution."

The argument here is, that the Constitution comes down to us from a slaveholding period and a slaveholding people; and that, therefore, we are bound to suppose that the Constitution recognizes colored persons of African descent, the victims of slavery at that time, as debarred forever from all participation in the benefit of the Constitution and the Declaration of Independence, although the plain reading of both includes them in their beneficent range.

As a man, an American, a citizen, a colored man of both Anglo-Saxon and African descent, I denounce this representation as a most scandalous and devilish perversion of the Constitution, and a brazen misstatement of the facts of history.

[. . . .]

The American people have made void our Constitution by just such traditions as Judge Taney and Mr. Garrison have been giving to the world of late, as the true light in which to view the Constitution of the United States. I shall follow neither. It is not what Moses allowed for the hardness of heart,[42] but what God requires, ought to be the rule.

It may be said that it is quite true that the Constitution was designed to secure the blessings of liberty and justice to the people who made it, and to the posterity of the people who made it, but was never designed to do any such thing for the colored people of African descent.

This is Judge Taney's argument, and it is Mr. Garrison's argument, but it is not the argument of the Constitution. The Constitution imposes no such mean and satanic limitations upon its own beneficent operation. And, if the Constitution makes none, I beg to know what right has anybody, outside of the Constitution, for the special accommodation of slaveholding villainy, to impose such a construction upon the Constitution?

The Constitution knows all the human inhabitants of this country as "the people." It makes, as I have said before, no discrimination in favor of, or against, any class of the people, but is fitted to protect and preserve the rights of all, without reference to color, size, or any physical peculiarities. Besides, it has been shown by William Goodell and others, that in eleven out of the old

---

42. Matthew 19:8.

thirteen states, colored men were legal voters at the time of the adoption of the Constitution.

In conclusion, let me say, all I ask of the American people is, that they live up to the Constitution, adopt its principles, imbibe its spirit, and enforce its provisions. When this is done, the wounds of my bleeding people will be healed, the chain will no longer rust on their ankles, their backs will no longer be torn by the bloody lash, and liberty, the glorious birthright of our common humanity, will become the inheritance of all the inhabitants of this highly favored country.

17. "Letter to James Redpath," published in *The Liberator*, July 27, 1860[43]

MY DEAR SIR:

Your kind note, inviting me to meet with yourself and other friends on the Fourth of July, at North Elba, came into my hands only yesterday. Had it reached me only a day or two earlier, I certainly should have complied with it. Very gladly would I assemble with you and the others on that revolutionary day, to do honor to the memory of one whom I regard as THE man of the nineteenth century. Little, indeed, can you and I do to add luster to his deathless fame. —The principles of John Brown,[44] attested by a life of spotless integrity and sealed by his blood, are self-vindicated. His name is covered with a glory so bright and enduring, as to require nothing at our hands to increase or perpetuate it. Only for our own sake, and that of enslaved and imbruted humanity must we assemble. To have been acquainted with John Brown, shared his counsels, enjoyed his confidence, and sympathized with the great objects of his life and death, I esteem as among the highest privileges of my life. We do but honor to ourselves in doing honor to him, for it implies the possession of qualities akin to his.

I have little hope of the freedom of the slave by peaceful means. A long course of peaceful slaveholding has placed the slaveholders beyond the reach of moral and humane considerations. They have neither ears nor hearts for the appeals of justice and humanity. While the slave will tamely submit his neck to the yoke, his back to the lash, and his ankle to the fetter and chain, the Bible will be quoted, and learning invoked to justify slavery. The only penetrable point of a tyrant is the fear of death. The outcry that they make, as to the danger of having their throats cut is because they deserve to have them cut. The efforts of John Brown and his brave associates, though apparently unavailing, have done more to upset the logic and shake the security of slavery, than all other efforts in that direction for twenty years.

---

43. Douglass had been invited by the radical journalist James Redpath (1833–1891) to a celebration of the life of John Brown. Douglass' open letter in response to the invitation provides a sense of how Douglass viewed Brown's radical antislavery activities. The ideas expressed here receive fuller development in Douglass' later speeches on Brown, including one included in this volume.
44. John Brown (1800–1859) was an American abolitionist who participated in guerilla warfare over the slavery issue in Kansas and led the raid of the federal arsenal on Harpers Ferry, which is described in the introduction.

The sleeping dust, over which yourself and friends proposed to meet on the 4th, cannot be revived; but the noble principles and disinterested devotion which led John Brown to step serenely to the gallows and lay down his life will never die. They are all the more potent for his death.

Not unwisely are the eyes and hearts of the American slaves and their friends turned to the lofty peaks of the Alleghenies. The innumerable glens, caves, ravines and rocks of those mountains, will yet be the hiding-places of hunted liberty. The eight-and-forty hours of John Brown's school in the mountains of Virginia taught the slaves more than they could have otherwise learned in a half-century. Even the mistake of remaining in the arsenal after the first blow was struck, may prove the key to future success. The tender regard which the dear old man evinced for the life of the tyrants—and which should have secured him his life—will not be imitated by future insurgents. Slaveholders are as insensible to magnanimity as to justice, and the measure they meter must be meted to them again. My heart is with you.

Very truly,
Fred'k Douglass

18. "The Prospect in the Future," an essay published in *Douglass' Monthly*, August 1860

The future of the anti-slavery cause is shrouded in doubt and gloom. The labors of a quarter of a century, instead of culminating in success, seem to have reached a point of weary hopelessness, so far as Radical Abolitionists are concerned. The great work of enlightening the people as to the wicked enormities of slavery, is well nigh accomplished, but the practical results of this work have disappointed our hopes. The grim and bloody tragedies of outrage and cruelty are rehearsed day by day to the ears of the people, but they look on as coolly indifferent as spectators in a theatre. The dangers to our common country produce as little emotion as the revelation of the wrongs of our common humanity. They assent to all the horrid truths which reveal the inhuman secrets of the gloomy prison house, but are not moved to action. They commend the iron-linked logic, and soul-born eloquence of abolitionists, but never practice the principles laid bare by the one, or act upon the emotions called up by the other. An able advocate of human rights gratifies their intellectual tastes, pleases their imaginations, titillates their sensibilities into a momentary sensation, but does not move them from the downy seat of inaction. They are familiar with every note in the scale of abstract rights, from the Declaration of Independence to the orations of Charles Sumner,[45] but seem to regard the whole as a grand operatic performance, of which they are mere spectators. You cannot relate a new fact, or frame an unfamiliar argument on this subject. —Reason and morality have emptied their casket of richest jewels in to the lap of this cause, in vain. Religion has exhausted her volleyed thunders of denunciation upon the head of this gigantic crime, but it stands unmoved and defiant. She has poured out floods of the tears of love and sympathy before this people, but their hearts have never been so melted as to produce an appropriate response to her divine ardor. Art, literature and poetry have all expended their treasures to arouse the callous hearts of the American people to the duty of letting the oppressed go free, and yet four millions struggle out their lives in blood-rusted chains. Europe is rocking and heaving with the struggle for liberty, while America is comparatively indifferent under a system of bondage more terrible than Europe has known for centuries. GARIBALDI[46] lands on

---

45. Charles Sumner (1811–1874) was an American politician who served as a US senator from Massachusetts.
46. Giuseppe Garibaldi (1807–1882) was an Italian general and politician.

the coast of Sicily with a few hundred men, as the forlorn hope of Italian freedom, and a brave and generous and appreciating people flock to his standard, and drive the tyrant of Naples from his bloody throne. JOHN BROWN takes up arms against a system of tyranny more cruel and barbarous than that of the murderer of Palermo, and is hung on a Virginia gallows, while thirty millions of people, whose civil catechism is the Declaration of Independence, look on unmoved to interference.

What is the explanation of this terrible paradox of passing history? Are the people of this country of an inferior race? Are they lacking in physical courage? Do they fail to appreciate the value of liberty? Our history, if we shall confine its revelations to the descendants of the Anglo Saxon, the Teutonic, or the Celtic races, answers all these questions in the negative. This conglomerate people, made-up from the crossing of all these races, have shown great courage and patriotism in defending *their own freedom*, but have utterly failed in the magnanimity and philanthropy necessary to prompt respect for the rights of another and a weaker race than those mentioned above. It is not because we fail to appreciate or lack the courage to defend our own rights that we permit the existence of slavery among us, but it is because our patriotism is intensely selfish, our courage lacks generosity, and our love of liberty is circumscribed by our narrow and wicked selfhood, that we quietly permit a few tyrants to crush a weak people in our midst. Whoever levies a tax upon our Bohea or Young Hyson, will find the whole land blazing with patriotism and bristling with bayonets the next morning. Let the mightiest maritime nation on the globe but impress a few Yankee sailors, and our merchant ships will be punctured with port holes, and manned with sailors who fight like heroes. Let any power on earth claim sovereignty over a single rood of the scraggy pine woods of Maine, or a foot of the drifted sand of some island on our western border, and Congress will burst forth with such a flood of pyrotechnic oratory as to stir our warlike blood to the tune of battle. But millions of a foreign race may be stolen from their homes, and reduced to hopeless and inhuman bondage among us and we either approve the deed, or protest as gently as "sucking doves." Our courage, our love of liberty, our statesmanship, our literature, our ethics, and our religion, are all most intensely and wickedly selfish. Our national character fails to present a single fulcrum for the lever of justice or humanity. We only ask to be permitted to enjoy our own heritage and on this condition are content to see others crushed in our midst. Ours is the philosophy, of CAIN. When God and humanity cry out against the oppression of the African, we coolly ask what of it? "Am I my brother's keeper?"[47] If his blood cry to us for redress, we say, "let it cry; it is not our blood." If his children are stolen and enslaved, we look on and say "they are not our children; don't you see their

---

47. Genesis 4:9.

noses are flat and their hair curls." If his daughters are debauched, our blood remains cool, for they are neither our daughters nor sisters. If his wife is stolen, we have nothing to do so long as our wives are protected by law. If the way to heaven is open to the white man, and we have a chance to "land our souls in glory," we are sublimely indifferent to the fact that the Bible and the Gospel are withheld from the Negro, and go on shouting our amens, and singing our anthems so loud that nobody but GOD can hear his wail of agony above the din of our voiceful, but heartless piety. Heaven help the poor slave, whose only hope of freedom is in the selfish hearts of such a people! —Nor can heaven help him, except by moving him to help himself. The motive power which shall liberate the slave must be looked for in slavery itself—must be generated in the bosom of the bondman. Outside philanthropy never disenthralled any people. It required a SPARTACUS,[48] himself a Roman slave and gladiator, to arouse the servile population of Italy, and defeat some of the most powerful armies of Rome, at the head of an army of slaves; and the slaves of America await the advent of an African SPARTACUS.

There is one element of American character which has as yet never been fairly appealed to in behalf of the slave. Our philanthropy melts itself away into maudlin tears at the story of his wrongs. Our sense of justice kicks the beam when his master's cotton bales are in the adverse scale. Our religion whines and snivels over his sufferings, but cannot leave its formal devotions long enough to bind up his wounds. Our politics bellow in his behalf on the stump, but only employ his cause as a stalking horse for party effect, and to carry self-seekers into power. But there is a latent element in our national character which, if fairly called into action, will sweep everything down in its course. The American people admire courage displayed in defense of liberty, and will catch the flame of sympathy from the sparks of its heroic fire. —The strength of this trait of character has been long manifest in the reception of the patriots who have been cast upon our shores from the wrecks of European revolutions; and when some African EUNUS[49] or SALVIUS[50] shall call the servile population of the South to arms, and inspire them to fight a few desperate battles for freedom, the mere animal instincts and sympathies of this people will do more for them than has been accomplished by a quarter of a century of oratorical philanthropy. We can never cease to regret that an appeal to the higher and better elements of human nature is, in this case, so barren of fitting response. But so it is, and until this people have passed through several generations of humanitarian culture, so it will be. —In the meantime the slave must continue to suffer or

---

48. Spartacus (111–71 BC) was a Thracian gladiator.
49. Eunus was a slave who led a revolt in ancient Sicily.
50. Salvius was a slave who led a revolt in ancient Sicily.

rebel, and did they know their strength they would not wait the tardy growth of our American sense of justice.

To the Negro-hating conservative this language sounds harsh and vengeful, no doubt. But that same law-and-order conservative reads of the glorious deeds of GARABALDI and the Sicilian insurrectionists, with a shout of responsive enthusiasm springing to his lips, and rejoices at the downfall of the tyrants of Naples. The cruelties inflicted by the brutal police of Francis II,[51] are reproduced every week on hundreds of plantations in America, and a people far outnumbering the Sicilians are crushed under the heel of a democracy which is far heavier than that of any crowned and booted Bourbon. Why should we shout when a tyrant is driven from his throne by GARABALDI'S bayonets, and shudder and cry peace at the thought that the American slave may one day learn the use of bayonets also?

---

51. Francis II (1836–1894) was a political leader in Sicily who Garibaldi was attempting to overthrow.

PART IV
DOUGLASS ON SECESSION AND CIVIL WAR

19. "The Dissolution of the American Union," an essay published in *Douglass' Monthly*, January 1861[1]

The event so long and so loudly threatened by the State of South Carolina, and dreaded by the other states, has at last happened, and is a matter of history. She has seceded, separated, repealed, quitted, dissolved the Union, declared her independence, set up for herself, assumed a place among the sisterhood of nations, pulled down the star spangled banner of the great American Confederacy, and up on innumerable pine poles have unfurled the Palmetto flag, preferring to be a large piece of nothing, to being any longer a small piece of something. Her ordinance of secession passed unanimously. Her people (except those of them held in slavery, which are more than half her population) have hailed the event as another and far more glorious Fourth of July, and are celebrating it with plenty of gunpowder, bad brandy, but as yet no balls, except those where perfumed ladies and gentlemen move their feet to the inspiring notes of the fiddle. Other balls may yet come; and unless South Carolina shall retreat, or the federal government shall abdicate its functions, they must come. But for the present all is remarkably pleasant and agreeable. Secession seems a newly invented game, and the people are much delighted with it. They play it over and over again—never tire of it. They play till midnight, and sing "We'll not go home till morning." For once the Palmetto state seems happy. Once in a while there is a word of apprehension, a murmur, that all is not well, from a thoughtful source; but this is soon hashed in the general hilarity of her people, on account of their transition from federal bondage to national independence and freedom. South Carolina is very happy indeed. She sends word to the world on the wings of lightning, that she has met with a change, and is attesting her great joy by bonfires, pyrotechnics, cannons, illuminations, music and dancing. And yet, as we have said, there is an under current of doubt, uncertainty, distrust, and foreboding. The fact is, the new republic has cleared, taken her papers, but has not yet weighed anchor, drawn a hawser, or set a single thread of canvas. —There is much noise, much pulling and hauling, and a lively stir generally; but the ship is still anchored in the safe harbor of the Union, and those having her in charge seem, after all, rather reluctant about venturing out upon the untried billows of the dissolution sea. We think,

---

1. The election of Abraham Lincoln as president of the United States in 1860 was perceived by many in the South as a threat to the continued existence of the institution of slavery. In this essay, Douglass responds to the secession of the State of South Carolina from the Union.

however, she will not hesitate much longer, but will soon fire a parting salute, and bid the Union defiance, instead of an affectionate farewell.

To speak plainly, South Carolina is out of the Union, just as the non-voting abolitionists are out of the Union—the former to preserve slavery, and the latter to abolish slavery. She is out of the Union, on paper, in speeches, letters, resolutions and telegrams. The head and front of her independence hath this extent, no more. The postal arrangements of the United States are still extended over her; the revenue laws of the United States are still enforced in her ports, and no hand, thus far, has been lifted against the one or the other. The United States flag yet waves over Fort Moultrie, and a United States revenue cutter is lying in Charleston Harbor. The South Carolinians have accomplished what they call peaceful secession—a thing quite as easily done as the leaving of a society of Odd Fellows, or bidding good night to a spiritual circle.

But, unfortunately, human governments are neither held together, nor broken up by such mild and gentle persuasives as are implied in the soft phrase—peaceful secession. Theirs is a voice of command, not of persuasion. They rest not upon paper, but upon power. They do not solicit obedience as a favor, but compel it as a duty. The work is not done yet. Though boasting of her sovereignty, her independence, and her freedom, instead of being out of the Union, South Carolina has really accomplished little more than to make known to the world the wish of certain politicians to take her out, and their design, either to take her out or to *scare* the Northern people and the Republican Party into such guarantees for slavery, as even an Algerine pirate, on the score of humanity, might hesitate to grant. Nothing short of irrepealable and eternal bondage will satisfy South Carolina. She can only be satisfied when cotton is declared king, and South Carolina admitted to be the kingdom of cotton. Evidently, however, if she really means to go out of the Union, she has yet an immensely difficult and dangerous work before her. The moorings that bind these states together can only be broken by opinion, backed up by force.

She must exclude the mail service, put an end to United States post offices, drive United States custom house officers from her ports, capture public property, take the forts and arsenals, and drive out every officer from her borders who holds and exercises any authority whatsoever under the government of the U.S. This may be an easy task, and may also be, under Mr. BUCHANAN (who is clearly in the plot) speedily done; but even when this is done, South Carolina is still in the Union. —The incoming president is elected to preside over the *United* States and if any of them have been permitted, by the treachery and weakness of his predecessor, to break away from the government, his business will be to bring them back, and see that the laws of the United States are duly extended over them, and faithfully executed. The coolest and wisest statesmen of the republic deny the right of peaceful secession. They admit the right of revolution; but revolution in this country is rebellion, and rebellion is treason, and treason is levying war against the United States, with something more substantial than paper resolutions and windy declamations. —There must be swords, guns, powder, balls, and men behind them to use them.

Now, when matters reach that point, South Carolina must conquer the United States, or the United States must conquer South Carolina. The right of South Carolina to secede, therefore, depends upon her ability to do so, and to stay so. If she can whip the federal government and scourge and keep it beyond her borders, and compel the United States to regard her as other than a revolted province, she can get out of the Union. But until she does all this, ABRAHAM LINCOLN is bound by his oath of office to regard her as one of the United States, and subject to the "Union, the Constitution and the laws."

Such everybody knows to be the true legal view of secession; but the question comes—is there virtue enough in the federal government to enforce the law. When a poor slave escapes to Boston, and hides in the cellars and garrets of humane men, the U.S. Government is strong. It can line the streets with soldiers, surround the granite court house with chains, and convert the temple of justice into a prison to catch, hold and hurl the fugitive back into the house of bondage; but has that government virtue enough to enforce the laws against the slaveholding, women-whipping rebels of Charleston? We do not ask, has Mr. BUCHANAN the virtue to do this? The fact is, that old man is in a fair way to win for himself the infamy of another BENEDICT ARNOLD.[2] Only under his fostering care could the state of disorder and alarm have reached its present magnitude. His message was a virtual invitation to the slave states to secede from the Union, assuring them that no force would be employed against them. Of all old sinners, there is less hope of him who paints his crimes with prayers, who prays for light when he means to walk in darkness, who repents only of righteousness and clings to wrong, turns his back on justice, and flings around slavery the mantle of religion. Of such a man there is no hope. Even should he resist, it would be a sham resistance, more to show the enemies of the government in a favorable light, than to punish and to subdue them to law and order. Of him nothing can be expected but weakness, cunning, treachery and gross hypocrisy; and we believe naught else is expected of him. Like LOUIS XI,[3] he can pray and poison, count beads and cutthroats. In the crafty wording of his proclamation of fast, you might suppose that Mr. BUCHANAN had slavery in his eye as one of the sins of the nation; but we have only to read his message to know what he regards as our great sin. It is *opposition* to slavery, to making merchandise of men, to trading in human flesh, to selling women at

---

2. Benedict Arnold (1741–1801) was a general in the Continental Army during the American Revolution before he defected to the side of Great Britain. His name has become synonymous with traitorousness.
3. Louis XI (1423–1483) was the king of France from 1461 to 1483.

auction, to driving them to toil, and giving them naught for their work. It is anti-slavery, according to this old saint, not slavery, that has brought the frown of heaven upon our land! Oh! what a stench arises from the rottenness of such piety; and yet such is the current religion of the Bell-Everett[4] and squatter sovereignty[5] religion of the national fusion parties of the country. Nothing will so rapidly and effectually bring religion into utter contempt, as this making it the mantle to hide the monstrous and shocking enormities, the blood-chilling and unutterable cruelty and wickedness of slavery. Mr. BUCHANAN threw around his character the very poetry of villainy, when he called upon the nation to join him in prayer and fasting.

But to the dissolution of the Union, and its chances of success. Conquering a federal army, and driving out all federal officers, is not the only difficulty to be overcome. The slave population of South Carolina may at last prove the most serious check upon disunion. They are more than equal to the whites in number, and cannot have failed to learn something from passing events. All the precautions of their tyrant masters have not hid from them the fact that *they*, in some sort, have a direct interest in the controversy between the state and the federal government. It is more than probable that they have given Mr. LINCOLN credit for having intentions toward them far more benevolent and just than any he is known to cherish. —His pledges to protect and uphold slavery in the states have not reached them; while certain dim, undefined, but large and exaggerated notions of his emancipating purposes have taken firm hold of them, and have grown larger and firmer with every look, nod and undertone of their oppressors. They were taught to look for freedom by the election of JOHN C. FREMONT. He failed; but he so nearly succeeded, that hope was entertained that another trial would bring certain victory. That victory they have been taught to believe has now been achieved; that a friend of theirs is now about to take the reins of government; that he is a "*Black Republican*"[6]; that his mission is to free the slaves. Let them learn that there is enmity between the state and the federal government, and that South Carolina has broken away from the Union to defeat their liberation from bondage; that ABRAHAM LINCOLN, the president, is on their side, and against their

---

4. John Bell (1796–1869) was an American politician who served as secretary of war as well as in the House of Representatives and the US Senate. He ran for president of the United States on the Constitutional Union ticket in 1860. Edward Everett (1794–1865) was an American politician and diplomat who served as secretary of state as well as in the House of Representatives and the Senate of the United States. He was nominated as the candidate for vice president by the Constitutional Union Party in 1860.

5. This is a reference to the doctrine of "popular sovereignty" being defended by Senator Stephen A. Douglas and others. This doctrine is described in the introduction to this volume.

6. A term used by critics of the Republican Party that implied a commitment to radical racial views.

masters; that he has only been defeated in giving them their liberty by taking the state out of the Union, and it is easy to see that such impressions and ideas might burst forth and spread havoc and death among slaveholders to an extent never surpassed even in the annals of St. Domingo. South Carolina, in such an event, would be more likely to fight her way back into the Union, than to fight her way out of it. Her salvation as a slave state might be made to depend upon federal arms.

But will not the cotton states join South Carolina? They probably will; but the elements of weakness would be the same. South Carolina would only be presented on a larger scale: with her, those cotton states have to extinguish the life of the federal government within their limits, and keep that extinguished. This can only be done *by force, by treachery, or by negotiation*; and to neither will ABRAHAM LINCOLN succumb. To do so would be to put the razor to the throat of his party, write himself down a coward, make political platforms, worse than a mockery, and to become the pliant tool of the very barbarism which he was elected to restrain, and "place it where the public mind would rest in the belief in its ultimate extinction."[7] —He is pledged to the maintenance of the Union; and if he has the *will*, he will not lack the power to maintain it against all foes. But if the Union can only be maintained by new concessions to the slaveholders; if it can only be stuck together and held together by a new drain on the Negro's blood; if the North is to forswear the exercise of all rights incompatible with the safety and perpetuity of slavery; that slavery shall be the only right, the only system superior to investigation, and superior to progress—we say, if this (and it is all demanded) be the price of the Union, then will every right minded man and woman in the land say, let the Union perish, and perish forever. As against compromises and national demoralization, welcome, ten thousand times over, the hardships consequent upon a dissolution of the Union.

---

7. Douglass quotes a phrase Lincoln used on several occasions to describe his hopes for the future extinction of slavery in the United States.

20. "The New President," an essay published in *Douglass' Monthly*, March 1861[8]

Of one satisfaction, one ray of hope amid the darkness of the passing hour, and the reign of doubt and distraction, we may now safely begin to assure ourselves. Before we can again speak to our respected readers through this channel, the long desired 4th of March will have come, LINCOLN will be inaugurated at Washington, and his policy declared. Whatever that policy may be toward the seceded and confederated states; whatever it may be toward slavery, the ruling cause of our nation's troubles, it will at least be a great relief to know it, to rejoice in and defend it, if right, and to make war upon it if wrong. To know what it is, is now the main thing. If he is going to abandon the principles upon which he was elected, compliment the South for being wrong, and censure himself and friends for being right, court treason and curse loyalty, desert his friends and cleave to his enemies, turn his back on the cause of freedom and give new guarantees to the system of slavery—whatever policy, whether of peace or war, or neither, it will be a vast gain at least to know what it is. Much of the present trouble is owing to the doubt and suspense caused by the shuffling, do-nothing policy of Mr. BUCHANAN. —No man has been able to tell an hour beforehand what to expect from that source. However well disposed he may have been, the slaveholding thieves and traitors about him have had him under their thumb from the beginning until now. Every man who wishes well to the country will rejoice at his out going, and feel that though he leaves the body politic weakened, and the nation's Constitution shattered, his out going, like the subsidence of some pestilence walking in darkness, is a cause for devout thanksgiving. A month longer in power, and perhaps, the epitaph of the American republic might, if it may not now, be written, and its death consigned to the moldy tombs of once great, but now extinct nations.

While not at all too confident of the incorruptible purity of the new president (for we remember the atmosphere of Washington, and the subtle devices of the enemies of liberty, among whom he has now gone) still we hope something from him. His stately silence during these last tumultuous and stormy three months, his stern refusal thus far to commit himself to any of the much advocated schemes of compromise, his refusal to have concessions extorted from him under the terror instituted by thievish conspirators and traitors, the

---

8. In this essay, Douglass offers some thoughts on the new president of the United States, Abraham Lincoln.

cool and circumspect character of his replies to the various speeches, some delicate, appropriate, and sensible, and some rudely curious and prying, made to him during his circuitous route to Washington, the modesty with which he has pushed aside the various compliments bestowed upon him, all prove that he has not won deceitfully the title of Honest Old Abe. True, indeed, he has made no immoderate promises to the cause of freedom. His party has made none. But what were small in Chicago, will be found large at Washington, and what were moderate in the canvass, have become much augmented by the frowning difficulties since flung in the way of their accomplishment by the movement for disunion. It was a small thing six months ago to say, as the Republican Party did say, that the Union shall be preserved, but events have now transpired, which make this a very solemn matter to reduce to practice. Most things are easier said than done, and this thing belongs to the general rule. That declaration in the Chicago platform implied that those who uttered it, believed that this government possesses ample power for its own preservation, and that those powers should be in their hands, faithfully wielded for that purpose. This, then, is the first question: Will Mr. LINCOLN boldly grapple with the monster of disunion, and bring down his proud looks?

Will he call upon the haughty slave masters, who have risen in arms, to break up the government, to lay down those arms, and return to loyalty, or meet the doom of traitors and rebels? He must do this, or do worse. —He must do this, or consent to be the despised representative of a defied and humbled government. He must do this, or own that party platforms are the merest devices of scheming politicians to cheat the people, and to enable them to crawl up to place and power. He must do this, or compromise the fundamental principle upon which he was elected, to wit, the right and duty of Congress to prohibit the farther extension of slavery. Will he compromise? Time and events will soon answer this question. For the present, there is much reason to believe that he will not consent to any compromise which will violate the principle upon which he was elected; and since none which does not utterly trample upon that principle can be accepted by the South, we have a double assurance that there will be no compromise, and that the contest must now be decided, and decided forever, which of the two, freedom or slavery, shall give law to this republic. Let the conflict come, and God speed the right, must be the wish of every true-hearted American, as well as of that of an onlooking world.

21. "The Inaugural Address," an essay published in *Douglass' Monthly*, April 1861[9]

Elsewhere in the columns of our present monthly, our readers will find the inaugural address of Mr. ABRAHAM LINCOLN, delivered on the occasion of his induction to the office of president of the United States. The circumstances under which the address was delivered, were the most extraordinary and portentous that ever attended any similar occasion in the history of the country. Threats of riot, rebellion, violence and assassination had been freely, though darkly circulated, as among the probable events to occur on that memorable day. The life of Mr. LINCOLN was believed, even by his least timid friends, to be in most imminent danger. No mean courage was required to face the probabilities of the hour. He stood up before the pistol or dagger of the sworn assassin, to meet death from an unknown hand, while upon the very threshold of the office to which the suffrages of the nation had elected him. The outgoing administration, either by its treachery or weakness, or both, had allowed the government to float to the very verge of destruction. A fear, amounting to agony in some minds, existed that the great American republic would expire in the arms of its newly elected guardian upon the very moment of his inauguration. For weeks and months previously to the 4th of March, under the wise direction and management of General [Winfield] SCOTT,[10] elaborate military preparations were made with a view to prevent the much apprehended outbreak of violence and bloodshed, and secure the peaceful inauguration of the president elect. How much the notion is indebted to General SCOTT for its present existence, it is impossible to tell. No doubt exists that to him, rather than to any forbearance of the rebels, Washington owes its salvation from bloody streets on the 4th of March. The manner in which Mr. LINCOLN entered the capital was in keeping with the menacing and troubled state of the times. He reached the capital as the poor, hunted fugitive slave reaches the North, in disguise, seeking concealment, evading pursuers, by the Underground Railroad, between two days, not during the sunlight, but crawling and dodging under the sable wing of night. He changed his program, took another route, started at another hour, traveled in other company, and arrived

---

9. In this essay, Douglass offers a moral critique of the conciliatory rhetoric used by President Lincoln in his first inaugural address.
10. Winfield Scott (1786–1866) was an American general and politician. He was the nominee of the Whig Party for the presidency of the United States in 1852.

at another time in Washington. We have no censure for the president at this point. He only did what braver men have done. It was, doubtless, galling to his very soul to be compelled to avail himself of the methods of a fugitive slave, with a nation howling on his track. It is hard to think of anything more humiliating. The great party that elected him fairly wilted under it. The act, in some sense, was an indication of the policy of the new government—more cunning than bold, evading rather than facing danger, outwitting rather than bravely conquering and putting down the enemy. The whole thing looked bad, but it was not adopted without reason. Circumstances gave to an act which, upon its face, was cowardly and mean, the merit of wisdom, forethought and discretion.

Once in Washington, Mr. LINCOLN found himself in the thick atmosphere of treason on the one hand, and a cowardly, sentimental and deceitful profession of peace on the other. With such surroundings, he went to work upon his inaugural address, and the influence of those surroundings may be traced in the whole character of his performance. Making all allowance for circumstances, we must declare the address to be but little better than our worst fears, and vastly below what we had fondly hoped it might be. It is a double-tongued document, capable of two constructions, and conceals rather than declares a definite policy. No man reading it could say whether Mr. LINCOLN was for peace or war, whether he abandons or maintains the principles of the Chicago convention upon which he was elected. The occasion required the utmost frankness and decision. Overlooking the whole field of disturbing elements, he should have boldly rebuked them. He saw seven states in open rebellion, the Constitution set at naught, the national flag insulted, and his own life murderously sought by slave-holding assassins. Does he expose and rebuke the enemies of his country, the men who are bent upon ruling or ruining the country? Not a bit of it. But at the very start he seeks to court their favor, to explain himself where nobody misunderstands him, and to deny intentions of which nobody had accused him. He turns away from his armed enemy and deals his blows on the head of an innocent bystander. He knew, full well, that the grand objection to him and his party respected the one great question of slavery extension. The South want to extend slavery, and the North want to confine it where it is, "where the public mind shall rest in the belief of its ultimate extinction." This was the question which carried the North and defeated the South in the election which made Mr. ABRAHAM LINCOLN president. Mr. LINCOLN knew this, and the South has known it all along; and yet this subject only gets the faintest allusion, while others, never seriously in dispute, are dwelt upon at length.

Mr. LINCOLN opens his address by announcing his complete loyalty to slavery in the slave states, and quotes from the Chicago platform a resolution affirming the rights of property in slaves, in the slave states. He is not content with declaring that he has no lawful power to interfere with slavery in the states, but he also denies having the least "*inclination*" to interfere with slavery in the states. This denial of all feeling against slavery, at such a time and in such circumstances, is wholly discreditable to the head and heart of Mr. LINCOLN. Aside from the inhuman coldness of the sentiment, it was a weak and inappropriate utterance to such an audience, since it could neither appease nor check the wild fury of the rebel slave power. Any but a blind man can see that the disunion sentiment of the South does not arise from any misapprehension of the disposition of the party represented by Mr. LINCOLN. The very opposite is the fact. The difficulty is, the slaveholders understand the position of the Republican Party too well. Whatever maybe the honied [*sic*] phrases employed by Mr. LINCOLN when confronted by actual disunion; however silvery and beautiful may be the subtle rhetoric of his long-headed secretary of state, when wishing to hold the government together until its management should fall into other hands; all know that the masses at the North (the power behind the throne) had determined to take and keep this government out of the hands of the slave-holding oligarchy, and administer it hereafter to the advantage of free labor as against slave labor. The slaveholders knew full well that they were hereafter to change the condition of rulers to that of being ruled; they knew that the mighty North is outstripping the South in numbers, and in all the elements of power, and that from being the superior, they were to be doomed to hopeless inferiority. This is what galled them. They are not afraid that LINCOLN will send out a proclamation over the slave states declaring all the slaves free, nor that Congress will pass a law to that effect. They are no such fools as to believe any such thing; but they do think, and not without reason, that the power of slavery is broken, and that its prestige is gone whenever the people have made up their minds that liberty is safer in the hands of freemen than in those of slaveholder? To those sagacious and crafty men, schooled into mastery over bondmen on the plantation, and thus the better able to assume the airs of superiority over Northern doughfaces, Mr. LINCOLN'S disclaimer of any power, right or inclination to interfere with slavery in the states, does not amount to more than a broken shoestring! They knew it all before, and while they do not accept it as a satisfaction, they do look upon such declarations as the evidence of cowardly baseness, upon which they may safely presume.

The slaveholders, the parties especially addressed, may well inquire if you, Mr. LINCOLN, and the great party that elected you, honestly entertain this very high respect for the rights of slave property in the states, how happens it that you treat the same rights of property with scorn and contempt when they are setup in the territories of the United States? —If slaves are property, and our rights of property in them are to be so sacredly guarded in the states, by what rule of law, justice or reason does that property part with the attributes of property, upon entering into a territory owned in part by that same state? The fact is, the slaveholders have the argument all their own way, the moment that the right of property in their slaves is conceded under the Constitution. It was, therefore weak, uncalled for and useless for Mr. LINCOLN to begin his inaugural address by thus at the outset prostrating himself before the foul and withering curse of slavery. The time and the occasion called for a very different attitude. Weakness, timidity and conciliation toward the tyrants and traitors had emboldened them to a pitch of insolence which demanded an instant check. Mr. LINCOLN was in a position that enabled him to wither at a single blast their high blown pride. The occasion was one for honest rebuke, not for palliations and apologies. The slaveholders should have been told that their barbarous system of robbery is contrary to the spirit of the age, and to the principles of liberty in which the federal government was founded, and that they should be ashamed to be everlastingly pressing that scandalous crime into notice. Some thought we had in Mr. LINCOLN the nerve and decision of an OLIVER CROMWELL[11]; but the result shows that we merely have a continuation of the PIERCES[12] and BUCHANANS, and that the Republican president bends the knee to slavery as readily as any of his infamous predecessors. Not content with the broadest recognition of the right of property in the souls and bodies of men in the slave states, Mr. LINCOLN next proceeds, with nerves of steel, to tell the slaveholders what an excellent slave hound he is, and how he regards the right to recapture fugitive slaves a constitutional duty; and lest the poor bondman should escape being returned to the hell of slavery by the application of certain well known rules of legal interpretation, which any and every white man may claim in his own case, Mr. LINCOLN proceeds to cut off the poor, trembling Negro who had escaped from bondage from all advantages from such rules. He will have the pound of flesh, blood or no blood, be it more or less, a just pound or not. The SHYLOCKS of the South, had they been after such game, might have exclaimed, in joy, an ABRAHAM come to judgment! But they were not to be caught with such fodder. The hunting down a few slaves, the sending back of a few LUCY BAGLEYS,[13] young and beautiful though they be, to the lust and brutality of the slaveholders and slave-breeders of the border states, is to the rapacity of the rebels only as a drop of water upon a house in flames. The value of the thing was wholly in its quality. "Mr. LINCOLN, you will catch and return our slaves if they run away from us, and will help us hold them where they are; what cause, then, since you have descended to this depth of wickedness, withholds you from coming down to us entirely? Indeed, in what respect are

---

11. Oliver Cromwell (1599–1658) was an English military leader and politician who held power from 1653 to 1658.
12. Douglass refers to Franklin Pierce (1804–1869), an American politician who served in the House of Representatives and the US senate before serving as the fourteenth president of the United States.
13. Douglass refers here to a fugitive slave.

you better than ourselves, or our overseers and drivers who hunt and flog our Negroes into obedience?" —Again, the slaveholders have a decided advantage over Mr. LINCOLN, and over his party. He stands upon the same moral level with them, and is in no respect better than they. If we held the Constitution, as held by Mr. LINCOLN, no earthly power could induce us to swear to support it. The fact is (following the lead of the Dred Scott decision, and all the Southern slaveholding politicians, with all the doughfaces of the North who have been engaged in making a Constitution, for years, outside of the Constitution of 1789) Mr. LINCOLN has taken everything at this point in favor of slavery for granted. He is like the great mass of his countrymen, indebted to the South for both law and gospel.

But the inaugural does not admit of entire and indiscriminate condemnation. It has at least one or two features which evince the presence of something like a heart as well as a head. Horrible as is Mr. LINCOLN'S admission of the constitutional duty of surrendering persons claimed as slaves, and heartily as he seems determined that that revolting work shall be performed, he has sent along with his revolting declaration a timid suggestion which, tame and spiritless as it is, must prove as unpalatable as gall to the taste of slaveholders. He says: "In any law on this subject, ought not all the safeguards of liberty known in humane and civilized jurisprudence be introduced, so that a free man be not in any case, surrendered as a slave." For so much, little as it is, let the friends of freedom thank Mr. LINCOLN. This saves his address from the gulf of infamy into which the Dred Scott decision sunk the Supreme Court of the United States. Two ideas are embraced in this suggestion: First, a black man's rights should be guarded by all the safeguards known to liberty and to humane jurisprudence; secondly, that slavery is an inhuman condition from which a free man ought by all lawful means to be saved. When we remember the prevailing contempt for the rights of all persons of African descent, who are mostly exposed to the operation of these slave-catching laws, and the strenuous efforts of the American Church and clergy to make slavery a divine relation, and especially blissful to our much hated variety of the human family, we are disposed to magnify and rejoice over even this slight recognition of rights, and this implied acknowledgment of the hatefulness of slavery. One of the safeguards of liberty is trial in open court. Another is the right of bringing evidence in one's own favor, and of confronting and questioning opposing witnesses. Another is the trial by a jury of our peers. Another is that juries are judges both of the law and the evidence in the case. There are other safeguards of liberty which we might specify, any one of which, faithfully applied, would not only make it difficult to surrender a free man as a slave, but would make it almost impossible to surrender any man as such. Thanking Mr. LINCOLN for even so much, we yet hold him to be the most dangerous advocate of slave-hunting and slave-catching in the land.

He has laid down a general rule of legal interpretation which, like most, if not all general rules, may be stretched to cover almost every conceivable villainy. "*The intention of the lawgiver is the law,*" says Mr. LINCOLN. But we say that this depends upon whether the *intention* itself is lawful. If law were merely an arbitrary rule, destitute of all idea of, right and wrong, the intention of the lawgiver might indeed be taken as the law, provided that intention were certainly known. But the very idea of law carries with it ideas of right, justice and humanity. Law, according to [William] BLACKSTONE,[14] commands that which is right and forbids that which is wrong. A law authorizing murder is no law, because it is an outrage upon all the elements out of which laws originate. Any man called to administer and execute such a law is bound to treat such an edict as a nullity, having no binding authority over his action or over his conscience. He would have a right to say, upon the authority of the Supreme Court, that "laws against fundamental morality are void"; that a law for murder is an absurdity, and not only from the purpose of all law and government, but wholly at war with every principle of law. —It would be no avail in such a case to say that the "intention of lawmakers is the law." To prove such an intention is only to destroy the validity of the law.

But the case is not murder, but simply the surrendering of a person to slavery who has made his or her escape from slavery into a free state. But what better is an act of this kind than murder? Would not Mr. LINCOLN himself prefer to see a dagger plunged to the hilt into the heart of his own daughter, than to see that daughter given up to the lust and brutality of the slaveholders of Virginia, as was poor, trembling LUCY BAGLEY given up a few weeks ago by the Republicans of Cleveland? What is slavery but a slow process of soul murder? What but murder is its chief reliance? How do slaveholders hold their slaves except by asserting their right and power to murder their slaves if they do not submit to slavery? Does not the whole slave system rest upon a basis of murder? Your money or your life, says the pirate; your liberty or your life, says the slaveholder. —And where is the difference between the pirate and the slaveholder?

But the "intention of the law is the law." Well, suppose we grant it in the present case, that the intention of the law-maker is the law, and two very important questions arise—first, as to who were the makers, and, secondly, by what means are we required to learn their intentions. Who made the Constitution? The preamble to the Constitution answers that question. "We, the people, do ordain and establish this Constitution." The people, then, made the law. How stood their intention as to the surrender of fugitive slaves? Were they all agreed in this intention to send slaves to bondage who might escape from it? Or were only a part? and if a part, how many? Surely, if a minority only were

---

14. William Blackstone (1723–1780) was an English politician and writer.

of that intention, that intention could not be the law, especially as the law itself expresses no such intention. The fact is, there is no evidence whatever that any considerable part of the people who made and adopted the American Constitution intended to make that instrument a slave-hunting or a slaveholding instrument, while there is much evidence to prove the very reverse. DANIEL WEBSTER, even in his infamous 7th of March speech, was sufficiently true to the letter of the Constitution, and to the history of the times in which the Constitution was framed and adopted, to deny that the Constitution required slaves to be given up, and quoted Mr. JAMES MADISON[15] in corroboration of his statement. This is Mr. WEBSTER'S language: —'It may not be improper here to allude to that—I had almost said celebrated—opinion of Mr. MADISON. You observe, sir, that the term slavery is not used in the Constitution. The Constitution does not require that fugitive slaves shall be delivered up; it requires that persons bound to service in one state escaping into another, shall be delivered up. Mr. MADISON opposed the introduction of the term slave, or slavery, into the Constitution; for he said he did not wish to see it recognized by the Constitution of the United States of America, that there could be property in men.'

How sadly have the times changed, not only since the days of MADISON—the days of the Constitution—but since the days even of DANIEL WEBSTER. Cold and dead as that great bad man was to the claims of humanity, he was not sufficiently removed from the better days of the republic to claim, as Mr. LINCOLN does, that the surrender of fugitive slaves is a plain requirement of the Constitution.

But here comes along a slight gleam of relief. Mr. LINCOLN tremblingly ventures to *inquire* (for he is too inoffensive to the slave-holders to assert and declare, except when the rights of black men are asserted and declared away) if it "might not be well to provide by law for the enforcement of that clause in the Constitution which guarantees that the citizens of each state shall be entitled to all the privileges and immunities of citizens in the several states."

Again we thank Mr. LINCOLN. He has, however, ventured upon a hazardous suggestion. The man has not quite learned his lesson. He had not been long enough in Washington to learn that Northern citizens, like persons of African descent, have no rights, privileges or immunities that slaveholders are bound to respect. To break open a man's trunk, to read the letters from his wife, and daughters, to tar and feather him, to ride him on a rail and give him the alternative of being hanged or of leaving town the same hour, simply because he resides in a free state, is a privilege and immunity which our Southern

---

15. James Madison (1751–1836) was an American politician and diplomat. He was a delegate to the Constitutional Convention, a member of the House of Representatives, secretary of state, and the fourth president of the United States.

brethren will not give up, though the requirement were made in every line of the Constitution. Yet, we say, we are thankful. It is something even to have a sickly intimation that other American citizens, not belonging to the privileged slaveholding class, have rights which it *"might be well"* to secure by law, and that the mere fact of living in a free state ought not to subject the unfortunate traveler either to being whipped, hanged or shot. Yes, this is something to be thankful for and is more than any other American president has ever ventured to say, either in his inaugural speech or annual message. It is perhaps, this latter fact that gives Mr. LINCOLN'S casual remark its chief importance. — Hitherto our presidents had pictured the South as the innocent lamb, and the greedy North as the hungry wolf, ever ready to tear and devour.

From slave-catching, Mr. LINCOLN proceeds to give a very lucid exposition of the nature of the federal Union, and shows very conclusively that this government, from its own nature and the nature of all governments, was intended to be perpetual, and that it is revolutionary, insurrectionary and treasonable to break it up. His argument is excellent; but the difficulty is that the argument comes too late. When men deliberately arm themselves with the avowed intention of breaking up the government; when they openly insult its flag, capture its forts, seize its munitions of war, and organize a hostile government, and boastfully declare that they will fight before they will submit, it would seem of little use to argue with them. If the argument was merely for the loyal citizen, it was unnecessary. If it was for those already in rebellion, it was casting pearls before swine. No class of men in the country understand better than the rebels themselves the nature of the business on which they are engaged. —They tell us this in the thousands of pounds of powder they have been buying, and the millions of money and arms they have been stealing. They know that unless the government is a miserable and contemptible failure, destitute of every attribute of a government except the name, that that government must meet them on the field and put them down, or be itself put down. To parley with traitors is but to increase their insolence and audacity.

It remains to be seen whether the federal government is really able to do more than hand over some JOHN BROWN to be hanged, suppress a slave insurrection, or catch a runaway slave—whether it is powerless for liberty, and only powerful for slavery. Mr. LINCOLN says, "I shall take care that the laws of the Union shall be faithfully executed in all the states"—that is, he will do so as *"as far as practicable,"* and *unless* the American people, his masters, shall, in some authoritative manner direct the contrary. To us, both these provisos had better have been omitted. They imply a want of confidence in the ability of the government to execute its own laws, and opens its doors to all that border tribe who have nothing but smiles for the rebels and peace lecturers for the government. The American people have placed the government in the hands of ABRAHAM LINCOLN for the next four years, and his instructions are in the

Constitution, he had no right to suppose that they will reverse those instructions in a manner to give immunity to traitors; and it was a mistake to admit such a possibility, especially in the presence of the very traitors themselves. But we are dwelling longer upon Mr. LINCOLN'S speech than we had intended, and longer than we are warranted either by the patience of our readers, or the extent of our space. The perusal of it has left no very hopeful impression upon our mind for the cause of our down-trodden and heart-broken countrymen. Mr. LINCOLN has avowed himself ready to catch them if they run away, to shoot them down if they rise against their oppressors, and to prohibit the federal government *irrevocably* from interfering for their deliverance. With such declarations before them, coming from our first modern anti-slavery president, the abolitionists must know what to expect during the next four years (should Mr. LINCOLN not be, as he is likely to be, driven out of Washington by his rival, Mr. JEFF. DAVIS,[16] who has already given out that should Mr. LINCOLN attempt to do, what he has sworn to do—namely, execute the laws, fifty thousand soldiers will march directly upon Washington!). This might be taken as an empty threat on the part of the president of the confederated states, if we did not see with what steadiness, promptness and certainty the rebels have from the first executed all their designs, and fulfilled all their promises. A thousand things are less probable than that Mr. LINCOLN and his cabinet will be driven out of Washington, and made to go out, as they came in, by the Underground Railroad. The game is completely in the hands of Mr. JEFFERSON DAVIS, and no doubt he will avail himself of every advantage.

---

16. Jefferson Davis (1808–1889) was an American politician who served as secretary of war, in the House of Representatives, and in the US Senate. He was president of the Confederate States of America during the Civil War (1861–1865).

22. "Substance of a Lecture [on Secession and the Civil War]," a speech delivered at Zion Church in Rochester, New York on June 16, 1861 and published in *Douglass' Monthly*, July 1861[17]

I am not surprised, my respected hearers, though I am most deeply gratified by the continued interest which you have manifested in these now somewhat protracted anti-slavery lectures. The subject of slavery is a most fruitful one, and it seems impossible to exhaust it. I seldom retire from this place without thinking of something left unsaid, which might have been said to profit.

More than thirty years of earnest discussion has augmented rather than diminished the interest which surrounds the subject. Tongues the most eloquent, and pens the most persuasive, the highest talent and genius of the country have been arduously employed in the attempt to unfold the matchless and measureless abominations comprehended in that one little word—slavery. Yet those who have succeeded best, own that they have fallen far short of the terrible reality. You, yourselves, have read much, thought much, and have felt much respecting the slave system, and yet you come up here and crowd this church every Sunday to hear the subject further discussed.

Vain as I may be, I have not the vanity to suppose that you come here because of any eloquence of mine, or any curiosity to hear a colored man speak—for I have been speaking among you more or less frequently nearly a score of years; and I recognize among my hearers today some of those kind friends who greeted me the first time I attempted to plead the cause of the slave in this city. No—the explanation of this continued, and I may say increasing interest, is not to be found in your humble speaker; nor can it be ascribed altogether to the temper of the times, and the mighty events now transpiring in the country. We shall find it in the deep significance, the solemn importance and unfathomable fullness of the subject itself. It sweeps the whole horizon of human rights, powers, duties, and responsibilities. The grand primal principles which form the basis of human society are here.

Those who love peace more than justice; those who prefer grim and hoary oppression to agitation and liberty, condemn the discussion of slavery because

---

17. This speech is called "The Decision of the Hour" in Foner's *The Life and Writings of Frederick Douglass*, and it is called "American Apocalypse" in Blassingame's *Frederick Douglass Papers*. With the Civil War now under way, Douglass articulated his views on the meaning of the war and what its objectives ought to be.

it is an exciting subject. They cry, away with it; we have had enough of it; it excites the people, excites the Church, excites Congress, excites the North, excites the South, and excites everybody. It is, in a word, an exciting subject. I admit it all. The subject is, indeed, an exciting one. Herein is one proof of its importance. Small pots boil quick; empty barrels make the most noise when rolled; but that which has the power to stir a nation's heart, and shake the foundations of church and state, is something more than empty clamor. Individual men of excitable temperament may be moved by trifles; they may give to an inch the importance of a mile—elevate a mote to the grandeur of a mountain—but the masses of men are not of this description. Only mighty forces, resting deep down among the foundations of nature and life, can lash the deep and tranquil sea of humanity into a storm, like that which the world is now witnessing.

The human mind is so constructed as that, when left free from the binding and hardening power of selfishness, it bows reverently to the mandates of truth and justice. It becomes loyal and devoted to an idea. Good men, once fully possessed of this loyalty, this devotion, have bravely sacrificed fortune, reputation, and life itself. All the progress toward perfection ever made by mankind, and all the blessings which are now enjoyed, are ascribable to some brave and good man, who, catching the illuminations of a heaven-born truth, has counted it a joy, precious and unspeakable, to toil, suffer, and often die for the glorious realization of that heaven-born truth. Hence the excitement. Cold water added to cold water, makes no disturbance. Error added to error causes no jar. Selfishness and selfishness walk together in peace, because they are agreed; but when fire is brought in direct contact with water, when flaming truth grapples with some loathsome error, when the clear and sweet current of benevolence sets against the foul and bitter stream of selfishness, when mercy and humanity confront iron-hearted cruelty, and ignorant brutality, there cannot fail to be agitation and excitement.

Men have their choice in this world. They can be angels, or they can be demons. In the apocalyptic vision, John describes a war in heaven.[18] You have only to strip that vision of its gorgeous Oriental drapery, divest it of its shining and celestial ornaments, clothe it in the simple and familiar language of common sense, and you will have before you the eternal conflict between right and wrong, good and evil, liberty and slavery, truth and falsehood, the glorious light of love, and the appalling darkness of human selfishness and sin. The human heart is a seat of constant war. Michael and his angels are still contending against the infernal host of bad passions, and excitement will last while the fight continues, and the fight will continue till one or the other is subdued. Just what takes place in individual human hearts, often takes place between

---

18. Revelation 12:7 (all biblical references are from the King James version).

nations, and between individuals of the same nation. Such is the struggle now going on in the United States. The slaveholders had rather reign in hell than serve in heaven.

What a whirlwind, what a tempest of malignant passion greets us from that quarter! Behold how they storm with rage, and yet grow pale with terror! Their demonstrations of offended pride are only equaled by their consummate impudence and desperate lying. Let me read you a paragraph from a recent speech of Mr. Henry A. Wise,[19] as a specimen of the lies with which the leaders of this slaveholding rebellion inflame the base passions of their ignorant followers. He lyingly [*sic*] says of the Northern people:

"Your political powers and rights, which were enthroned in the Capitol when you were united with them under the old constitutional bond of the Confederacy, have been annihilated. They have undertaken to annul laws within their own limits that would render your property unsafe within those limits. They have abolitionized [*sic*] your border, as the disgraced Northwest will show. They have invaded your moral strongholds, and the rights of your religion, and have undertaken to teach you what should be the moral duties of men. They have invaded the sanctity of your home and firesides, and endeavored to play master, father, and husband for you in your households."

Such lies answer themselves at the North, but do their work at the South. The strong and enduring power which anti-slavery truth naturally exercises upon the minds of men, when earnestly presented, is explained, as I have already intimated, not by the cunning arts of rhetoric, for often the simplest and most broken utterances of the uneducated fugitive slave, will be far more touching and powerful than the finest flights of oratory. The explanation of the power of anti-slavery is to be found in the inner and spontaneous consciousness, which every man feels of the comprehensive and stupendous criminality of slavery. There are many wrongs and abuses in the world that shock and wound the sensibilities of men. They are felt to be narrow in their scope, and temporary in their duration, and to require little effort for their removal. But not so can men regard slavery. It compels us to recognize it, as an ever active, ever increasing, all comprehensive crime against human nature. It is not an earthquake swallowing up a town or city, and then leaving the solid earth undisturbed for centuries. It is not a Vesuvius which, belching forth its fire and lava at intervals, causes ruin in a limited territory; but slavery is felt to be a moral volcano, a burning lake, a hell on earth, the smoke and stench of whose torments ascend upward forever. Every breeze that sweeps over it comes to us tainted with its foul miasma, and weighed down with the sighs and groans of its victim. It is a compendium of all the wrongs which one man can inflict upon a helpless brother. It does not

---

19. Henry A. Wise (1806–1876) was an American politician and diplomat who served in the House of Representatives and as governor of Virginia.

cut off a right hand, nor pluck out a right eye, but strikes down at a single blow the god-like form of man. It does not merely restrict the rights, or lay heavy burdens upon its victims, grievous to be borne; but makes deliberate and constant war upon human nature itself, robs the slave of personality, cuts him off from the human family, and sinks him below even the brute. It leaves nothing standing to tell the world that here was a man and a brother.

In the eye of the law of slavery, the slave is only property. He cannot be a father, a husband, a brother, or a citizen, in any just sense of these words. To be a father, a husband, a brother, and a citizen, implies the personal possession of rights, powers, duties, and responsibilities, all of which are denied the slave. Slavery being the utter and entire destruction of all human relations, in opposing it, we are naturally enough bound to consideration of a wide range of topics, involving questions of the greatest importance to all men. But for the universal character of the anti-slavery question, it would have been impossible to have held the public mind suspended upon this discussion during the space of thirty years. The best informed men have candidly confessed that anti-slavery meetings have been the very best schools of the nation during the last quarter of a century. The nation has been taught here, as nowhere else, laws, morals and Christianity. Untrammelled by prescription, unrestrained by popular usage, unfettered by moudly [sic] creeds, despising all the scorn of vulgar prejudice, our anti-slavery speakers and writers have dared to call in question every doctrine and device of man, which could strengthen the hands of tyrants, and bind down the bodies and souls of men. The manhood of the slave has been the test of all our laws, customs, morals, civilization, governments, and our religions. With a single eye here, the whole anti-slavery body has been full of light. With the golden rule, they have measured American Christianity, and found it hollow—its votaries doing precisely unto others which they would shoot, stab, burn and devour others for doing unto themselves. To all who press the Bible into the service of slavery, we have said, if you would not be the slave, you cannot be the master.

The fact is, slavery is at the bottom of all mischief among us, and will be until we shall put an end to it. We have seen three attempts within less than thirty years to break up the American government in this the first century of its existence, and slavery has been the moving cause in each instance. The attempt was made in 1832, again in 1850, and again in 1860. Some of us were surprised and astonished that the slaveholders should rebel against the American government, simply because they could not rule the government to the full extent of their wishes. Little cause had we for such surprise and astonishment. We ought to have known slaveholders better.

What is a slaveholder but a rebel and a traitor? That is, and must be in the nature of his vocation, his true character. Treason and rebellion are the warp and woof of the relation of master and slave. A man cannot be a slaveholder without being a traitor to humanity and a rebel against the law and government of the ever-living God. He is a usurper, a spoiler. His patriotism means plunder, and his principles are those of a highway robber. Out of such miserable stuff you can make nothing but conspirators and rebels.

So far as the American government is entitled to the loyal support and obedience of American citizens, so far that government is, in the main, in harmony with the highest good and the just convictions of the people. Justice, goodness, conscience are divine. Conformity to these, on the part of human governments, make them binding and authoritative. These attributes, wherever exhibited, whether in the government of states, in the government of families, or wherever else exhibited, command the reverence and loyal regard of honest men and women. But slaveholders, by the very act of slaveholding, have thrown off all the trammels of conscience and right. They are open, brazen, self-declared rebels and traitors to all that makes loyalty a virtue, and fidelity a duty. The greater includes the lesser crime. In the one high handed act of rebellion against truth, justice and humanity, comprehended in making one man the slave of another, we have the ascertained sum of treason and rebellion which now rages and desolates the whole slaveholding territory in the United States.

This is no new idea in these lectures. I have presented it before, and shall probably repeat it again. I wish at any rate to underscore it now, for I deem it important that we should thoroughly understand the foe with which we have to deal. Let it, then, be written down in every man's mind, as no longer a matter of dispute, that a thief and a robber cannot be safely trusted; that a slaveholder cannot be a good citizen of a free republic; and that the relation of master and slave is, in the nature of it, treason and rebellion. It has long been obvious to common sense—it is now known to common experience—that a slaveholder who is a slaveholder at heart is a natural born traitor and rebel. He is a rebel against manhood, womanhood and brotherhood. The essence of his crime is nothing less than the complete destruction of all that dignifies and ennobles human character.

I don't know how it seems to you, in reading the authoritative utterances of our government, and the officers of our army, respecting slavery; but it really seems to me that they are woefully mistaken if they think this country can ever have peace while slavery is allowed to live. Every little while you learn that slaves have been sent back to their loyal masters. We hear that while other property is freely confiscated, this peculiar property is only held to the end of the war, and the inference seems to be that these slaves, by and by, are to enter into the basis of negotiations between the government and the slaveholding rebels. I am anxious to look charitably upon everything looking to the suppression of rebellion and treason. I want to see the monster destroyed; but I think that while our government uses its soldiers to catch and hold slaves, and offers to put down slave insurrections, and subject them to the control and authority of their rebel masters will make precious little headway in putting down the rebels, or in establishing the peace of the country hereafter.

There is still an effort to conciliate the border states. Our government does not know slavery. Our rulers do not yet know slaveholders. We are likely to find them out after a while. We are just now in a pretty good school. The revolution through which we are passing is an excellent instructor. We are likely to find out what is meant by Southern chivalry and Southern honor. When you have watched a while longer the course of Southern men, whether in the cotton states or in the slave-breeding states you will have become convinced that they are all of the same species, and that the border states are as bad as any. JOHN BELL, the Union man, is as much a traitor as FRANK PICKENS of South Carolina. We shall learn by and by that such men as [JOHN] LECHTER of Virginia, [CLAIBORNE] JACKSON of Missouri, [BERIAH] MAGOFFIN of Kentucky, were traitors and rebels in the egg, only waiting to be hatched by the heat of surrounding treason.[20] The ties that bind slaveholders together are stronger than all other ties, and in every state where they hold the reins of government, they will take sides openly or secretly with the slaveholding rebels. Conciliation is out of the question. They know no law, and will respect no law but the law of force. The safety of the government can be attained only in one way, and that is, by rendering the slaveholders powerless.

Slavery, like all other gross and powerful forms of wrong which appeal directly to human pride and selfishness, when once admitted into the framework of society, has the ability and tendency to beget a character in the whole network of society surrounding it, favorable to its continuance. The very law of its existence is growth and dominion. Natural and harmonious relations easily repose in their own rectitude, while all such as are false and unnatural are conscious of their own weakness, and must seek strength from without. Hence the explanation of the uneasy, restless, eager anxiety of slaveholders. Our history shows that from the formation of this government, until the attempt now making to break it up, this class of men has been constantly pushing schemes for the safety and supremacy of the slave system. They have had marvelous success. They have completely destroyed freedom in the slave states, and were doing their best to accomplish the same in the free states. He is a very imperfect reasoner who attributes the steady rise and ascendancy of slavery to anything else than the nature of slavery itself. Truth may be careless and forgetful, but a lie cannot afford to be either. Truth may repose upon its inherent strength,

---

20. Douglass identifies a number of politicians who proclaimed loyalty to the Union while at the same time arguing for the perpetuation of slavery (John Bell, John Lechter, Claiborne Jackson, and Beriah Magoffin) and argues that they are not to be trusted any more than the secessionist Frank Pickens (1805–1869), who was then governor of South Carolina.

but a falsehood rests for support upon external props. Slavery is the most stupendous of all lies, and depends for existence upon a favorable adjustment of all its surroundings. Freedom of speech, of the press, of education, of labor, of locomotion, and indeed all kinds of freedom, are felt to be a standing menace to slavery. Hence, the friends of slavery are bound by the necessity of their system to do just what the history of the country shows they have done—that is, to seek to subvert all liberty, and to pervert all the safeguards of human rights. They could not do otherwise. It was the controlling law of their situation.

Now, if these views be sound, and are borne out by the whole history of American slavery, then for the statesman of this hour to permit any settlement of the present war between slavery and freedom, which will leave untouched and undestroyed the relation of master and slave, would not only be a great crime, but a great mistake, the bitter fruits of which would poison the life blood of unborn generations. No grander opportunity was ever given to any nation to signalize, either its justice and humanity, or its intelligence and statesmanship, than is now given to the loyal American people. We are brought to a point in our national career where two roads meet and diverge. It is the critical moment for us. The destiny of the mightiest republic in the modern world hangs upon the decision of that hour. If our government shall have the wisdom to see, and the nerve to act, we are safe. If it fails, we perish, and go to our own place with those nations of antiquity long blotted from the maps of the world. I have only one voice, and this neither loud nor strong. I speak to but few, and have little influence; but whatever I am or may be, I may, at such a time as this, in the name of justice, liberty and humanity, and in that of the permanent security and welfare of the whole nation, urge all men, and especially the government, to the abolition of slavery. Not a slave should be left a slave in the returning footprints of the American army gone to put down this slaveholding rebellion. Sound policy, not less than humanity, demands the instant liberation of every slave in the rebel states.

23. "The Slaveholders' Rebellion," a speech delivered at Himrods Corners, New York, July 4, 1862, published in *Douglass' Monthly*, August 1862[21]

FELLOW CITIZENS:

Eighty-six years ago the Fourth of July was consecrated and distinguished among all the days of the year as the birthday, of American liberty and independence. The fathers of the republic recommended that this day be celebrated with joy and gladness by the whole American people, to their latest posterity. Probably not one of those fathers ever dreamed that this hallowed day could possibly be made to witness the strange and portentous events now transpiring before our eyes, and which even now cast a cloud of more than midnight blackness over the face of the whole country. We are the observers of strange and fearful transactions.

Never was this national anniversary celebrated in circumstances more trying, more momentous, more solemn and perilous, than those by which this nation is now so strongly environed. We present to the world at this moment, the painful spectacle of a great nation, undergoing all the bitter pangs of a gigantic and bloody revolution. We are torn and rent asunder, we are desolated by large and powerful armies of our own kith and kin, converted into desperate and infuriated rebels and traitors, more savage, more fierce and brutal in their modes of warfare, than any recognized barbarians making no pretensions to civilization.

In the presence of this troubled and terrible state of the country, in the appalling jar and rumbling of this social earthquake, when sorrow and sighing are heard throughout our widely extended borders, when the wise and brave men of the land are everywhere deeply and sadly contemplating this solemn crisis as one which may permanently decide the fate of the nation I should greatly transgress the law of fitness, and violate my own feelings and yours, if I should on this occasion attempt to entertain you by delivering anything of the usual type of our Fourth of July orations.

The hour is one for sobriety, thoughtfulness and stern truthfulness. When the house is on fire, when destruction is spreading its baleful wings everywhere,

---

21. As the Civil War progressed, Douglass continued to use his voice and his pen to promote a particular conception of the meaning of the war and the path to meaningful victory. This Fourth of July oration is especially important because Douglass offers a detailed explanation of "the nature of the rebellion" and reveals the distance between the principles of the Confederate revolutionaries and the American revolutionaries of 1776.

when helpless women and children are to be rescued from devouring flames a true man can neither have ear nor heart for anything but the thrilling and heart rending cry for help. Our country is now on fire. No man can now tell what the future will bring forth. The question now is whether this great republic before it has reached a century from its birth, is to fall in the wake of unhappy Mexico, and become the constant theatre of civil war or whether it shall become like old Spain, the mother of Mexico, and by folly and cruelty part with its renown among the nations of the earth, and spend the next seventy years in vainly attempting to regain what it has lost in the space of this one slaveholding rebellion.

Looking thus at the state of the country, I know of no better use to which I can put this sacred day, I know of no higher duty resting upon me, than to enforce my views and convictions, and especially to hold out to reprobation, the short sighted and ill judged, and inefficient modes adopted to suppress the rebels. The past may be dismissed with a single word. The claims of our fathers upon our memory, admiration and gratitude, are founded in the fact that they wisely, and bravely, and successfully met the crisis of their day. And if the men of this generation would deserve well of posterity they must like their fathers, discharge the duties and responsibilities of their age.

Men have strange notions nowadays as to the manner of showing their respect for the heroes of the past. They everywhere prefer the form to the substance, the seeming to the real. One of our generals, and some of our editors seem to think that the fathers are honored by guarding a well, from which those fathers may have taken water, or the house in which they may have passed a single night, while our sick soldiers need pure water, and are dying in the open fields for water and shelter. This is not honoring, but dishonoring your noble dead. Nevertheless, I would not even in words do violence to the grand events, and thrilling associations, that gloriously cluster around the birth of our national independence. There is no need of any such violence. The thought of today and the work of today, are alike linked, and interlinked with the thought and work of the past. The conflict between liberty and slavery, between civilization and barbarism, between enlightened progress and stolid indifference and inactivity is the same in all countries, in all ages, and among all peoples. Your fathers drew the sword for free and independent government, Republican in its form, Democratic in its spirit, to be administered by officers duly elected by the free and un-bought suffrages of the people; and the war of today on the part of the loyal North, the east and the west, is waged for the same grand and all commanding objects. We are only continuing the tremendous struggle, which your fathers, and my fathers began eighty-six years ago. Thus identifying the present with the past, I propose to consider the great present question, uppermost and all absorbing in all minds and hearts throughout the land.

I shall speak to you of the origin, the nature, the objects of this war, the manner of conducting, and its possible and probable results.

ORIGIN OF THE WAR.

It is hardly necessary at this very late day of this war, and in view of all the discussion through the press and on the platform which has transpired concerning it, to enter now upon any elaborate enquiry or explanation as to whence came this foul and guilty attempt to break up and destroy the national government. All but the willfully blind or the malignantly traitorous, know and confess that this whole movement, which now so largely distracts the country, and threatens ruin to the nation, has its root and its sap, its trunk and its branches, and the bloody fruit it bears only from the one source of all abounding abomination, and that is slavery. It has sprung out of a malign selfishness and a haughty and imperious pride which only the practice of the most hateful oppression and cruelty could generate and develop. No ordinary love of gain, no ordinary love of power, could have stirred up this terrible revolt. The legitimate objects of property, such as houses, lands, fruits of the earth, the products of art, science and invention, powerful as they are, could never have stirred and kindled this malignant flame, and set on fire this rebellious fury. The monster was brought to its birth, by pride, lust and cruelty which could not brook the sober restraints of law, order and justice. The monster publishes its own parentage. Grim and hideous as this rebellion is, its shocking practices, digging up the bones of our dead soldiers slain in battle, making drinking vessels out of their skulls, drumsticks out of their arm bones, slaying our wounded soldiers on the field of carnage, when their gaping wounds appealed piteously for mercy, poisoning wells, firing upon unarmed men, stamp it with all the horrid characteristics of the bloody and barbarous system and society from which it derived its life.

[. . . .]

There is however one false theory of the origin of the war to which a moment's reply may be properly given here. It is this. The abolitionists by their insane and unconstitutional attempt to abolish slavery, have brought on the war. All that class of men who opposed what they were pleased to call coercion at the first, and a vigorous prosecution of the war at the present, charge the war directly to the abolitionists. In answer to this charge, I lay down this rule as a basis to which all candid men will assent. Whatever is said or done by any class of citizens, strictly in accordance with rights guaranteed by the Constitution, cannot be fairly charged as against the Union, or as inciting to a dissolution of the Union.

Now the slaveholders came into the Union with their eyes wide open, subject to a constitution wherein the right to be abolitionists was sacredly guaranteed to all the people. They knew that slavery was to take its chance with all other evils against the power of free speech, and national enlightenment. They came on board the national ship subject to these conditions, they signed the articles after having duly read them, and the fact that those rights, plainly written, have been exercised is no apology whatever for the slaveholders' mutiny and their attempt to lay piratical hands on the ship, and its officers. When therefore I hear a man denouncing abolitionists on account of the war, I know that I am listening to a man who either does not know what he is talking about, or to one who is a traitor in disguise.

THE NATURE OF THE REBELLION.

There is something quite distinct and quite individual in the nature and character of this rebellion. In its motives and objects it stands entirely alone, in the annals of great social disturbances. Rebellion is no new thing under the sun. The best governments in the world are liable to these terrible social disorders. All countries have experienced them. Generally however, rebellions are quite respectable in the eyes of the world, and very properly so. They naturally command the sympathy of mankind, for generally they are on the side of progress. They would overthrow and remove some old and festering abuse not to be otherwise disposed of, and introduce a higher civilization, and a larger measure of liberty among men. But this rebellion is in no wise analogous to such. The pronounced and damning peculiarity of the present rebellion, is found in the fact, that it was conceived, undertaken, planned, and persevered in, for the guilty purpose of handing down to the latest generations the accursed system of human bondage. Its leaders have plainly told us by words as well as by deeds, that they are fighting for slavery. They have been stirred to this perfidious revolt, by a certain deep and deadly hate, which they warmly cherish toward every possible contradiction of slavery whether found in theory or in practice. For this cause they hate free society, free schools, free states, free speech, the freedom asserted in the Declaration of Independence, and guaranteed in the Constitution. Herein is the whole secret of the Rebellion. The plan is and was to withdraw the slave system from the hated light of liberty, and from the natural operations of free principles. While the slaveholders could hold the reins of government they could and did pervert the free principles of the Constitution to slavery, and could afford to continue in the Union, but when they saw that they could no longer control the Union as they had done for sixty years before, they appealed to the sword and struck for a government which should forever shut out all light from the Southern conscience, and all hope of emancipation from the Southern slave. This rebellion therefore, has no point of comparison with that which has brought liberty to America, or with those of Europe, which have been undertaken from time to time, to throw off the galling yoke of despotism. It stands alone in its infamy.

Our slaveholding rebels with an impudence only belonging to themselves, have sometimes compared themselves to Washington, Jefferson, and the long list of worthies who led in the revolution of 1776, when in fact they would hang either of those men if they were no living, as traitors to slavery, because, they each and all, considered the system an evil.

THE CONFLICT UNAVOIDABLE.

I hold that this conflict is the logical and inevitable result of a long and persistent course of national transgression. Once in a while you will meet with men who will tell you that this war ought to have been avoided. In telling you this, they only make the truth serve the place and perform the office of a lie. I too say that this war ought never to have taken place. The combustible material which has produced this terrible explosion ought long ago to have been destroyed. For thirty years the abolitionists have earnestly sought to remove this guilty cause of our troubles. There was a time when this might have been done, and the nation set in permanent safety. Opportunities have not been wanting. They have passed by unimproved. They have sometimes been of a character to suggest the very work which might have saved us from all the dreadful calamities, the horrors and bloodshed, of this war. Events, powerful orators, have eloquently pleaded with the American people to put away the hateful slave system. For doing this great work we have had opportunities innumerable. One of these was presented upon the close of the war for independence; the moral sentiment of the country was purified by that great struggle for national life. At that time slavery was young and small, the nation might have easily abolished it, and thus relieved itself forever of this alien element, the only disturbing and destructive force in our republican system of government. Again there was another opportunity, for putting away this evil in 1789, when we assembled to form the Constitution of the United States. At that time the anti-slavery sentiment was strong both in church and state, and many believed that by giving slavery no positive recognition in the Constitution and providing for the abolition of the slave trade, they had given slavery its death-blow already. They made the great mistake of supposing that the existence of the slave trade was necessary to the existence of slavery, and having provided that the slave trade should cease, they flattered themselves, that slavery itself must also speedily cease. They did not comprehend the radical character of the evil. Then again in 1819 the Missouri question gave us another opportunity to seal the doom of the slave system, by simply adhering to the early policy of the fathers and sternly refusing the admission of another state into the Union with a Constitution tolerating slavery. Had this been done in the case of Missouri, we should not now be cursed with this terrible rebellion. Slavery would have fallen into gradual decay. The moral sentiment of the country, instead of being vitiated as it is, would have been healthy and strong against the slave system. Political parties and politicians would not as they have done since, courted the slave power for votes and thus increased the importance of slavery.

THE FIRST PALPABLE DEPARTURE FROM RIGHT POLICY.

The date of the Missouri Compromise forms the beginning of that political current which has swept us on to this rebellion, and made the conflict unavoidable. From this dark date in our nation's history, there started forth a new political and social power. Until now slavery had been on its knees, only asking time to die in peace. But the Missouri Compromise gave it a new lease of life. It became at once a tremendous power. The line of thirty-six degrees, thirty minutes, at once stamped itself upon our national politics, our morals, manners, character and religion. From this time there was a South side to everything American, and the country was at once subjected to the slave power, a power as restless and vigilant as the eye of an escaping murderer. We became under its sway an illogical nation. Pure and simple truth lost its attraction for us. We became a nation of compromisers.

It is curious to remark the similarity of national, to individual demoralization. A man sets out in life with honest principles and with high purposes inspired at the family hearthstone, and for a time steadily and scrupulously keeps them in view. But at last under the influence of some powerful temptation he is induced to violate his principles and push aside his sense of right. The water from the first moment is smooth about him, but soon he finds himself in the rapids. He has lost his footing. The broad flood, resistless as the power of fate, sweeps him onward, from bad to worse, he becomes more hardened, blind and shameless in his crimes till he is overtaken by dire calamity, and at last sinks to ruin. Precisely this has been the case with the American people. No people ever entered upon the pathway of nations, with higher and grander ideas of justice, liberty and humanity than ourselves. There are principles in the Declaration of Independence which would release every slave in the world and prepare the earth for a millennium of righteousness and peace. But alas! We have seen that declaration intended to be viewed like some colossal statue at the loftiest altitude, by the broad eye of the whole world, meanly subjected to a microscopic examination and its glorious universal truths craftily perverted into seeming falsehoods. Instead of treating it, as it was intended to be treated, as a full and comprehensive declaration of the equal and sacred rights of mankind, our contemptible Negro-hating and slaveholding critics, have endeavored to turn it into absurdity by treating it as a declaration of the equality of man in his physical proportions and mental endowments. This gross and scandalous perversion of the true intents of meaning of the declaration did not long stand alone. It was soon followed by the heartless dogma, that the rights declared in that instrument did not apply to any but white men. The slave power at last succeeded, in getting this doctrine proclaimed from the bench of the Supreme Court of the United States. It was there decided that "all men" only means some men, and those white men. And all this in face of the fact, that white people only form one fifth of the whole human family—and that some who pass for white are nearly as black as your humble speaker. While all this was going on, lawyers, priests and politicians were at work upon national prejudice against the colored man. They raised the cry and put it into the mouth of the ignorant, and vulgar and narrow minded, that "this is the white man's country," and other cries which readily catch the ear of the crowd. This popular method of dealing with an oppressed people has while crushing the blacks, corrupted and demoralized the whites. It has cheered on the slave power, increased its pride and pretension, till ripe for the foulest treason against the life of the nation. Slavery, that was before the Missouri Compromise couchant, on its knees, asking meekly to be let alone within its own limits to die, became in a few years after rampant, throttling free speech, fighting friendly Indians, annexing Texas, warring with Mexico, kindling with malicious hand the fires of war and bloodshed on the virgin soil of Kansas, and finally threatening to pull down the pillars of the republic, if you Northern men should dare vote in accordance with your constitutional and political convictions. You know the history, I will not dwell upon it. What I have said, will suffice to indicate the point at which began the downward career of the republic. It will be seen that it began by bartering away an eternal principle of right for present peace. We undertook to make slavery the full equal of liberty, and to place it on the same footing of political right with liberty. It was by permitting the dishonor of the Declaration of Independence, denying the rights of human nature to the man of color, and by yielding to the extravagant pretensions, set up by the slaveholder under the plausible color of state rights. In a word it was by reversing the wise and early policy of the nation, which was to confine slavery to its original limits, and thus leave the system to die out under the gradual operation of the principles of the Constitution and the spirit of the age. Ten years had not elapsed, after this compromise, when the demon disunion lifted its ugly front, in the shape of nullification. The plotters of this treason, undertook the work of disunion at that time as an experiment. They took the tariff, as the basis of action. The tariff was selected, not that it was the real object, but on the wisdom of the barber, who trains his green hands on wooden heads before allowing them to handle the razor on the faces of living men.

You know the rest. The experiment did not succeed. Those who attempted it were thirty years before their time. There was no BUCHANAN in the presidential chair, and no COBBS,[22] and FLOYDS[23] in the cabinet. CAL-HOUN and his treasonable associates were promptly assured, on the highest authority that their exit out of the Union was possible only by one way and that by way of the gallows. They were defeated, but not permanently. They dropped the tariff and openly adopted slavery as the ostensible, as well as the real ground of disunion. After thirty years of persistent preparatory effort, they have been able under the fostering care of a traitorous Democratic president, to inaugurate at last this enormous rebellion. I will not stop here to pour out loyal indignation on that arch traitor, who while he could find power in the Constitution to hunt down innocent men all over the North for violating the thrice accursed fugitive slave bill, could find no power in the Constitution to punish slaveholding traitors and rebels, bent upon the destruction of the government. That bad old man is already receiving a taste of the punishment due to his crimes. To live amid all the horrors, resulting from his treachery is of itself a terrible punishment. He lives without his country's respect. He lives a despised old man. He is no doubt still a traitor, but a traitor without power, a serpent without fangs, and in the agony of his torture and helplessness will probably welcome the moment which shall remove him from the fiery vision of the betrayed and half ruined country.

THE CONDUCT OF THE WAR.

Today we have to deal not with dead traitors, such as James Buchanan, Howell Cobb, Floyd, Thompson[24] and others, but with a class of men incomparably more dangerous to the country. They are our weak, paltering and incompetent rulers in the cabinet at Washington and our rebel worshipping generals in the field, the men who sacrifice the brave loyal soldiers of the North by thousands, while refusing to employ the black man's arm in suppressing the rebels, for fear of exasperating these rebels: men who never interfere with the orders of generals, unless those orders strike at slavery, the heart of the Rebellion. These are the men to whom we have a duty to discharge today, when the country is bleeding at every pore, and when disasters thick and terrible convert this national festal day, into a day of alarm and mourning. I do not underrate the power of the rebels, nor the vastness of the work required for suppressing them. Jefferson Davis is a powerful man, but Jefferson Davis has no such power to blast the hope and break down the strong heart of this nation, as that possessed and exercised by ABRAHAM LINCOLN. With twenty millions of men

---

22. Howell Cobb (1815–1868) was the secretary of the treasury under President James Buchanan.
23. John Floyd (1806–1863) was the secretary of war under President James Buchanan.
24. Possibly a reference to William Tappan Thompson (1812–1882), a proslavery journalist in Georgia.

behind him, with wealth and resources at his command such as might pride the heart of the mightiest monarch of Europe, and with a cause which kindles in every true heart the fires of valor and patriotism, we have a right to hold Abraham Lincoln, sternly responsible for any disaster or failure attending the suppression of this rebellion. I hold that the rebels can do us no serious harm, unless it is done through the culpable weakness, imbecility or unfaithfulness of those who are charged with the high duty, of seeing that the supreme law of the land is everywhere enforced and obeyed. Common sense will confess that five millions ought not to be a match for twenty millions. I know of nothing in the mettle of the slaveholder which should make him superior in any of the elements of a warrior to an honest Northern man. One slaveholder ought not longer to be allowed to maintain the boast that he is equal to three Northern men; and yet that boast will not be entirely empty, if we allow those five millions much longer to thwart all our efforts to put them down. It will be most mortifyingly shown that after all our appliances, our inventive genius, our superior mechanical skill, our great industry, our muscular energy, our fertility in strategy, our vast powers of endurance, our overwhelming numbers, and admitted bravery, that the eight or ten rebel slave states, sparsely populated, and shut out from the world by our possession of the sea, are invincible to the arms, of the densely populated, and every way powerful twenty free states. I repeat, these rebels can do nothing against us, cannot harm a single hair of the national head, if the men at Washington, the president and cabinet, and the commanding generals in the field will but earnestly do their most obvious duty. I repeat Jeff. Davis and his malignant slaveholding republic, can do this Union no harm except by the permission of the reigning powers at Washington.

I am quite aware that some who hear me will question the wisdom of any criticisms upon the conduct of this war at this time and will censure me for making them. I do not dread those censures. I have on many occasions, since the war began, held my breath when even the stones of the street would seem to cry out. I can do so no longer. I believe in the absence of martial law, a citizen may properly express an opinion as to the manner in which our government has conducted, and is still conducting this war. I hold that it becomes this country, the men who have to shed their blood and pour out their wealth to sustain the government at this crisis, to look very sharply into the movements of the men who have our destiny in their hands.

Theoretically this is a responsible government. Practically it can be made the very reverse. Experience demonstrates that our safety as a nation depends upon our holding every officer of the nation strictly responsible to the people for the faithful performance of duty. This war has developed among other bad tendencies, a tendency to shut our eyes to the mistakes and blunders of those in power. When the president has avowed a policy, sanctioned a measure, or commended a general, we have been told that his action must be treated as final.

I scout this assumption. A doctrine more slavish and abject than this does not obtain under the walls of St. Peter's. Even in the rebel states, the Confederate government is sharply criticized, and Jefferson Davis is held to a rigid responsibility. There is no reason of right or of sound policy for a different course toward the federal government. Our rulers are the agents of the people. They are fallible men. They need instruction from the people, and it is no evidence of a factitious disposition that any man presumes to condemn a public measure if in his judgment that measure is opposed to the public good.

This is already an old war. The statesmanship at Washington with all its admitted wisdom and sagacity, utterly failed for a long time to comprehend the nature and extent of this rebellion. Mr. Lincoln and his cabinet will have by and by to confess with many bitter regrets, that they have been equally blind and mistaken as to the true method of dealing with the rebels. They have fought the rebels with the olive branch. The people must teach them to fight them with the sword. They have sought to conciliate obedience. The people must teach them to compel obedience.

There are many men connected with the stupendous work of suppressing this slaveholding rebellion, and it is the right of the American people to keep a friendly and vigilant eye upon them all, but there are three men in the nation, from whose conduct the attention of the people should never be withdrawn: the first is President Lincoln, the commander in chief of the army and navy. The single word of this man can set a million of armed men in motion: He can make and unmake generals, can lift up or cast down at will. The other two men are MCCLELLAN and HALLECK. Between these two men nearly a half a million of your brave and loyal sons are divided. The one on the Potomac and the other on the Mississippi. They are the two extended arms of the nation, stretched out to save the Union.

Are those two men loyal? are they in earnest? are they competent? We have a right, and it is our duty to make these inquiries, and report and act in reference to them according to the truth.

Whatever may be said of the loyalty or competency of McClellan, I am fully persuaded by his whole course that he is not in earnest against the rebels, that he is today, as heretofore, in war, as in peace a real pro-slavery Democrat. His whole course proves that his sympathies are with the rebels, and that his ideas of the crisis make him unfit for the place he holds. He kept the Army of the Potomac standing still on that river, marching and countermarching, giving show parades during six months. He checked and prevented every movement which was during that time proposed against the rebels East and West.

Bear in mind the fact that this is a slaveholding rebellion, bear in mind that slavery is the very soul and life of all the vigor which the rebels have thus far been able to throw into their daring attempt to overthrow and ruin this country. Bear in mind that in time of war, it is the right and duty of each belligerent to adopt that course which will strengthen himself and weaken his enemy.

Bear in mind also that nothing could more directly and powerfully tend to break down the rebels, and put an end to the struggle than the insurrection or the running away of a large body of their slaves, and then, read General McClellan's proclamation, declaring that any attempt at a rising of the slaves against their rebel masters would be put down, and put down with an iron hand. Let it be observed too, that it has required the intervention of Congress, by repeated resolutions to prevent this general from converting the Army of the Potomac from acting as the slave dogs of the rebels, and that even now while our army are compelled to drink water from muddy swamps, and from the Pamunky River, forbidden by George B. McClellan to take pure water from the rebel General [Robert E.] LEE's[25] well. Let it be understood that Northern loyal soldiers, have been compelled by the orders of this same general, to keep guard over the property of a leading rebel, because of a previous understanding between the loyal, and the traitor general. Bear in mind the fact that this general has, in deference to the slave-holding rebels, forbidden the singing of anti-slavery songs in his camp, and you will learn that this general's ideas of the demands of the hour are most miserably below the mark, and unfit for the place he fills. Take another fact into account, General McClellan is at this moment the favorite general of the Richardsons, the Ben Woods, the Vallandighams,[26] and the whole school of proslavery Buchanan politicians of the North, and that he is reported in the Richmond *Dispatch*, to have said that he hated to war upon Virginia, and that he would far rather war against Massachusetts. This statement of the Richmond *Dispatch* in itself is not worth much, but if we find as I think we do find, in General McClellan's every movement an apparent reluctance to strike at Virginia rebels, we may well fear that his words have been no better than his deeds. Again, take the battles fought by him and under his order, and in every instance the rebels have been able to claim a victory, and to show as many prisoners and spoils taken as we. At Ball's Bluff, McClellan's first battle on the Potomac, it is now settled, that our troops were marched up only to be slaughtered. Nine hundred and thirty of our brave Northern soldiers were deliberately murdered, as much so as if they had each been stabbed, bayoneted, shot, or otherwise killed when asleep by some midnight assassin, for they were so ordered and handled, that they were perfectly harmless to their deadly foes, and helpless in their own defense. Then the Battle of

---

25. Robert E. Lee (1807–1870) was a Confederate military commander.
26. Douglass identifies several political leaders who were either against the Civil War or thought to be sympathetic to the Confederacy.

Seven Pines, where General [Silas] Casey's[27] division was pushed out like an extended finger four miles beyond the lines of our army, toward the rebels, as if for no other purpose than to be cut to pieces or captured by the rebels, and then the haste with which this same division was censured by Gen. McClellan, are facts looking all the same way. This is only one class of facts. They are not the only facts, nor the chief ones that shake my faith in the general of the Army of the Potomac.

Unquestionably, Time is the mightiest ally that the rebels can rely on. Every month they can hold out against the government gives them power at home, and prestige abroad, and increases the probabilities of final success. Time favors foreign intervention, time favors heavy taxation upon the loyal people, time favors reaction, and a clamor for peace. Time favors fevers, and pestilence, wasting and destroying our army. Therefore *time, time* is the great ally of the rebels.

Now I undertake to say that General McClellan has from the beginning so handled the Army of the Potomac as to give the rebels the grand advantage of time. From the time he took command of the Potomac army in August 1861 until now, he has been the constant cause of delay, and probably would not have moved when he did, but that he was compelled to move or be removed. Then behold his movement. He moved upon Manassas when the enemy had been gone from there seven long days. When he gets there he is within sixty miles of Richmond. Does he go on? Oh! no, but he just says hush, to the press and the people, I am going to do something transcendentally brilliant in strategy. Three weeks pass away, and knowing ones wink and smile as much as to say you will see something wonderful soon. And so indeed we do; at the end of three weeks we find that General McClellan has actually marched back from Manassas to the Potomac, gotten together an endless number of vessels at a cost of untold millions, to transport his troops to Yorktown, where he is just as near to Richmond and not a bit nearer than he was just three weeks before, and where he is opposed by an army every way as strongly posted as any he could have met with by marching straight to Richmond from Manassas. Here we have two hundred and thirty thousand men moved to attack empty fortifications, and moved back again.

Now what is the state of facts concerning the nearly four months of campaign between the James and the York rivers? The first is that Richmond is not taken, and in all the battles yet fought, the rebels have claimed them as victories. We have lost between thirty and forty thousand men, and the general impression is that there is an equal chance that our army will be again repulsed before Richmond, and driven away.

---

27. Silas Casey (1807–1882) was a major general in the Union Army during the Civil War.

You may not go the length that I do, in regard to Gen. McClellan, at this time, but I feel quite sure that this country will yet come to the conclusion that Geo. B. McClellan, is either a cold-blooded traitor, or that he is an unmitigated military impostor. He has shown no heart in his conduct, except when doing something directly in favor of the rebels, such as guarding their persons and property and offering his service to suppress with an iron hand any attempt on the part of the slaves against their rebel masters.

THE POLICY OF THE ADMINISTRATION.

I come now to the policy of President Lincoln in reference to slavery. An administration without a policy, is confessedly an administration without brains, since while a thing is to be done, it implies a known way to do it and he who professes his ability to do it, but cannot show how it is to be done, confesses his own imbecility. I do not undertake to say that the present administration has no policy, but if it has, the people have a right to know what it is, and to approve or disapprove of it as they shall deem it wise or unwise.

Now the policy of an administration can be learned in two ways. The first by what it says, and the second by what it does, and the last is far more certain and reliable, than the first. It is by what President Lincoln has done in reference to slavery, since he assumed the reins of government that we are to know what he is likely to do, and deems best to do in the premises. We all know how he came into power. He was elected and inaugurated as the representative of the anti-slavery policy of the Republican Party. He had laid down and maintained the doctrine that liberty and slavery were the great antagonistic political elements in this country. That the Union of these states could not long continue half free and half slave, that they must in the end be all free or all slave.

In the conflict between these two elements he arrayed himself on the side of freedom, and was elected with a view to the ascendancy of free principles. Now what has been the tendency of his acts since he became commander in chief of the army and navy? I do not hesitate to say, that whatever may have been his intentions, the action of President Lincoln has been calculated in a marked and decided way to shield and protect slavery from the very blows which its horrible crimes have loudly and persistently invited. He has scornfully rejected the policy of arming the slaves, a policy naturally suggested and enforced by the nature and necessities of the war. He has steadily refused to proclaim, as he had the constitutional and moral right to proclaim, complete emancipation to all the slaves of rebels who should make their way into the lines of our army. He has repeatedly interfered with, and arrested the anti-slavery policy of some of his most earnest and reliable generals. He has assigned to the most important positions, generals who are notoriously pro-slavery, and hostile to the party and principles which raised him to power. He has permitted rebels to recapture their runaway slaves in sight of the capital. He has allowed General Halleck, to openly violate the spirit of a solemn resolution by Congress forbidding the army of the United States to return the fugitive slaves to their cruel masters, and has evidently from the first submitted himself to the guidance of the half loyal slave states, rather than to the wise and loyal suggestions of those states upon which must fall, and have fallen, the chief expense and danger involved in the prosecution of the war. It is from such action as this, that we must infer the policy of the administration. To my mind that policy is simply and solely to reconstruct the Union on the old and corrupting basis of compromise; by which slavery shall retain all the power that it ever had, with the full assurance of gaining more, according to its future necessities.

The question now arises, "Is such a reconstruction possible or desirable?" To this I answer from the depths of my soul, no. Mr. Lincoln is powerful, Mr. Lincoln can do many things, but Mr. Lincoln will never see the day when he can bring back or charm back, the scattered fragments of the Union into the shape and form they stood when they were shattered by this slaveholding rebellion.

What does this policy of bringing back the Union imply? It implies first of all, that the slave states will promptly and cordially, and without the presence of compulsory and extraneous force, cooperate with the free states under the very Constitution, which they have openly repudiated, and attempted to destroy. It implies that they will allow and protect the collection of the revenue in all their ports. It implies the regular election of the members of the Senate and the House of Representatives and the prompt and complete execution of all the federal laws within their limits. It implies that the rebel states will repudiate the rebel leaders, and that they shall be punished with perpetual political degradation. So much it implies on the part of the rebel states. And the bare statement, with what we know of the men engaged in the war, is sufficient to prove the impossibility of their fulfillment while slavery remains.

What is implied by a reconstruction of the Union on the old basis so far as concerns the Northern and loyal states? It implies that after all we have lost and suffered by this war to protect and preserve slavery, the crime and scandal of the nation, that we will as formerly act the disgusting part of the watch dogs of the slave plantation, that we will hunt down the slaves at the North, and submit to all the arrogance, bluster, and pretension of the very men who have imperiled our liberties and baptized our soil with the blood of our best and bravest citizens. Now I hold that both parties will reject these terms with scorn and indignation.

Having thus condemned as impossible and undesirable the policy which seems to be that of the administration you will naturally want to know what I consider to be the true policy to be pursued by the government and people in relation to slavery and the war. I will tell you: Recognize the fact, for it is the great fact, and never more palpable than at the present moment, that the only choice left to this nation, is abolition or destruction. You must abolish slavery or abandon the Union. It is plain that there can never be any union between the North and the South, while the South values slavery more than nationality. A union of interest is essential to a union of ideas, and without this union of ideas, the outward form of the union will be but as a rope of sand.

Now it is quite clear that while slavery lasts at the South, it will remain hereafter as heretofore, the great dominating interest, overtopping all others, and shaping the sentiments, and opinions of the people in accordance with itself. We are not to flatter ourselves that because slavery has brought great troubles upon the South by this war, that therefore the people of the South will be stirred up against it. If we can bear with slavery after the calamities it has brought upon us, we may expect that the South will be no less patient. Indeed we may rationally expect that the South will be more devoted to slavery than ever. The blood and treasure poured out in its defense will tend to increase its sacredness in the eyes of Southern people, and if slavery comes out of this struggle, and is retaken under the forms of old compromises, the country will witness a greater amount of insolence and bluster in favor of the slave system, than was ever shown before in or out of Congress.

But it is asked, how will you abolish slavery? You have no power over the system before the Rebellion is suppressed, and you will have no right or power when it is suppressed. I will answer this argument when I have stated how the thing may be done. The fact is there would be no trouble about the way, if the government only possessed the will. But several ways have been suggested. One is a stringent confiscation bill by Congress. Another is by a proclamation by the president at the head of the nation. Another is by the commanders of each division of the army. Slavery can be abolished in any or all these ways.

There is plausibility in the argument that we cannot reach slavery until we have suppressed the Rebellion. Yet it is far more true to say that we cannot reach the Rebellion until we have suppressed slavery. For slavery is the life of the Rebellion. Let the loyal army but inscribe upon its banner, emancipation and protection to all who will rally under it, and no power could prevent a stampede from slavery, such as the world has not witnessed since the Hebrews crossed the Red Sea. I am convinced that this rebellion and slavery are twin monsters, and that they must fall or flourish together, and that all attempts at upholding one while putting down the other, will be followed by continued trains of darkening calamities, such as make this anniversary of our national independence, a day of mourning instead of a day of transcendent joy and gladness.

But a proclamation of emancipation, says one, would only be a paper order. I answer so is any order emanating from our government. The president's proclamation calling his countrymen to arms, was a paper order. The proposition to retake the property of the federal government in the Southern states, was a paper order. Laws fixing the punishment of traitors are paper orders. All laws, all written rules for the government of the army and navy and people, are "paper orders," and would remain only such were they not backed up by force, still we do not object to them as useless, but admit their wisdom and necessity. Then these paper orders, carry with them a certain moral force which makes them in a large measure self-executing. I know of none which would possess this self-executing power in larger measure than a proclamation of emancipation. It would act on the rebel masters, and even more powerfully upon the slaves. It would lead the slaves to run away, and the masters to emancipate, and thus put an end to slavery. The conclusion of the whole matter is this: The end of slavery and only the end of slavery, is the end of the war, the end of secession, the end of disunion, and the return of peace, prosperity and unity to the nation. Whether emancipation comes from the North or from the South, from Jeff. Davis or from Abraham Lincoln, it will come alike for healing of the nation, for slavery is the only mountain interposed to make enemies of the North and South.

FELLOW CITIZENS: let me say in conclusion. This slavery begotten and slavery sustained, and slavery animated war, has now cost this nation more than a hundred thousand lives, and more than five hundred millions of treasure. It has weighed down the national heart with sorrow and heaviness, such as no speech can portray. It has cast a doubt upon the possibility of liberty and self-government which it will require a century to remove. The question is, shall this stupendous and most outrageous war be finally and forever ended? or shall it be merely suspended for a time, and again revived with increased and aggravated fury in the future? Can you afford a repetition of this costly luxury? Do you wish to transmit to your children the calamities and sorrows of today? The way to either class of these results is open to you. By urging upon the nation the necessity and duty of putting an end to slavery, you put an end to the war, and put an end to the cause of the war, and make any repetition of it impossible. But, just take back the pet monster again into the bosom of the nation, proclaim an amnesty to the slaveholders, let them have their slaves, and command your services in helping to catch and hold them, and so sure as like causes will ever produce like effects, you will hand down to your children here, and hereafter, born and to be born all the horrors through which you are now passing. I have told you of great national opportunities in the past, greater than any in the past is the opportunity of the present. If now we omit the duty it imposes, steel our hearts against its teachings, or shrink in cowardice from the work of today, your fathers will have fought and bled in vain to establish free institutions, and American republicanism will become a hissing and a by-word to a mocking earth.[28]

---

28. Douglass paraphrases Deuteronomy 28:37.

24. "The President and His Speeches," an essay published in *Douglass' Monthly*, September 1862[29]

The president of the United States seems to possess an ever increasing passion for making himself appear silly and ridiculous, if nothing worse. Since the publication of our last number he has been unusually garrulous, characteristically foggy, remarkably illogical and untimely in his utterances, often saying that which nobody wanted to hear, and studiously leaving unsaid about the only things which the country and the times imperatively demand of him. Our garrulous and joking president has favored the country and the world with two speeches, which if delivered by any other than the president of the United States, would attract no more attention than the funny little speeches made in front of the arcade by our friend John Smith, inviting customers to buy his razor strops. —One of the speeches of the president was made at a war meeting in Washington in vindication of Mr. [Edwin M.] Stanton,[30] and in justification of himself against the charge that he had failed to send reinforcements to Gen. McClellan. Very little need be said of this first speech. In comparison with some speeches made on that occasion, the president's is short, but in comparison to the amount of matter it contains, it is tediously long, full of repetitions, and so remarkably careless in style that it reminds one strongly of the gossiping manner in which a loquacious old woman discusses her neighbors and her own domestic affairs, and explaining herself so lucidly that her audience, after listening with all due patience, are in the end as well informed about the subject in question as before the exposition. In short, the speech does not prove anything except that the secretary of war is not responsible, but that the president is responsible for the failure to send reinforcements to General McClellan. We may at once have done with this speech, especially since the information it contains was explicitly given to the country full three weeks before its utterance at the war meeting in Washington.

The other and more important communication of the president it appears was delivered in the White House before a committee of colored men assembled by his invitation. In this address Mr. Lincoln assumes the language and arguments of an itinerant colonization lecturer, showing all his inconsistencies,

29. Douglass took to the pages of his newspaper to offer this stinging critique of President Abraham Lincoln's rhetoric and policy during the first half of the Civil War.
30. Edwin M. Stanton (1814–1869) was an American politician who served as secretary of war under President Abraham Lincoln.

his pride of race and blood, his contempt for Negroes and his canting hypocrisy. How an honest man could creep into such a character as that implied by this address we are not required to show. The argument of Mr. Lincoln is that the difference between the white and black races renders it impossible for them to live together in the same country without detriment to both. Colonization, therefore, he holds to be the duty and the interest of the colored people. Mr. Lincoln takes care in urging his colonization scheme to furnish a weapon to all the ignorant and base, who need only the countenance of men in authority to commit all kinds of violence and outrage upon the colored people of the country. Taking advantage of his position and of the prevailing prejudice against them he affirms that their presence in the country is the real first cause of the war, and logically enough, if the premises were sound, assumes the necessity of their removal.

It does not require any great amount of skill to point out the fallacy and expose the unfairness of the assumption, for by this time every man who has an ounce of brain in his head, no matter to which party he may belong, and even Mr. Lincoln himself, must know quite well that the mere presence of the colored race never could have provoked this horrid and desolating rebellion. Mr. Lincoln knows that in Mexico, Central America and South America, many distinct races live peaceably together in the enjoyment of equal rights, and that the civil wars which occasionally disturb the peace of those regions never originated in the difference of the races inhabiting them. A horse thief pleading that the existence of the horse is the apology for his theft or a highway man contending that the money in the traveler's pocket is the sole first cause of his robbery are about as much entitled to respect as is the president's reasoning at this point. No, Mr. President, it is not the innocent horse that makes the horse thief, not the traveler's purse that makes the highway robber, and it is not the presence of the Negro that causes this foul and unnatural war, but the cruel and brutal cupidity of those who wish to possess horses, money and Negroes by means of theft, robbery, and rebellion. Mr. Lincoln further knows or ought to know at least that Negro hatred and prejudice of color are neither original nor invincible vices, but merely the offshoots of that root of all crimes and evils—slavery. If the colored people instead of having been stolen and forcibly brought to the United States had come as free immigrants, like the German and the Irish, never thought of as suitable objects of property, they never would have become the objects of aversion and bitter persecution, nor would there ever have been divulged and propagated the arrogant and malignant nonsense about natural repellancy and the incompatibility of races.

Illogical and unfair as Mr. Lincoln's statements are, they are nevertheless quite in keeping with his whole course from the beginning of his administration up to this day, and confirm the painful conviction that though elected as an anti-slavery man by Republican and Abolition voters, Mr. Lincoln is quite a genuine representative of American prejudice and Negro hatred and far more concerned for the preservation of slavery, and the favor of the border slave states, than for any sentiment of magnanimity or principle of justice and humanity. This address of his leaves us less ground to hope for anti-slavery action at his hands than any of his previous utterances. Notwithstanding his repeated declarations that he considers slavery an evil, every step of his presidential career relating to slavery proves him active, decided, and brave for its support, and passive, cowardly, and treacherous to the very cause of liberty to which he owes his election. This speech of the president delivered to a committee of free colored men in the capital explains the animus of his interference with the memorable proclamation of General Fremont. A man who can charge this war to the presence of colored men in this country might be expected to take advantage of any legal technicalities for arresting the cause of emancipation, and the vigorous prosecution of the war against slaveholding rebels. To these colored people, without power and without influence, the president is direct, undisguised, and unhesitating. He says to the colored people: I don't like you, you must clear out of the country. So too in dealing with anti-slavery generals the president is direct and firm. He is always brave and resolute in his interferences in favor of slavery, remarkably unconcerned about the wishes and opinions of the people of the North; apparently wholly indifferent to the moral sentiment of civilized Europe; but bold and self-reliant as he is in the ignominious service of slavery, he is as timid as a sheep when required to live up to a single one of his anti-slavery testimonies. He is scrupulous to the very letter of the law in favor of slavery, and a perfect latitudinarian as to the discharge of his duties under a law favoring freedom. When Congress passed the confiscation bill,[31] made the emancipation of the slaves of rebels the law of the land, authorized the president to arm the slaves which should come within the lines of the federal army, and thus removed all technical objections, everybody who attached any importance to the president's declarations of scrupulous regard for law, looked at once for a proclamation emancipating the slaves and calling the blacks to arms. But Mr. Lincoln, formerly so strict and zealous in the observance of the most atrocious laws which ever disgraced a country, has not been able yet to muster courage and honesty enough to obey and execute that grand decision of the people. He evaded his obvious duty, and instead of calling the blacks to arms and to liberty he merely authorized the military commanders to use them as laborers, without even promising them their freedom at the end of their term of service to the government, and thus destroyed virtually the very object of the measure. Further when General Halleck issued his odious order

---

31. Congress passed the first Confiscation Act in 1861 and the second in 1862. The acts were intended to establish a legal framework through which the property of those in rebellion against the Union might be confiscated.

No. 3, excluding fugitive slaves from our lines, an order than which none could be more serviceable to the slaveholding rebels, since it was a guarantee against the escape of their slaves, Mr. Lincoln was deaf to the outcry and indignation which resounded through the North and West, and saw no occasion for interference, though that order violated a twice adopted resolution of Congress. When General McClellan employed our men guarding rebel property and even when Gen. [Benjamin] Butler[32] committed the outrage paralleled only by the atrocities of the rebels—delivering back into bondage thousands of slaves—Mr. Lincoln again was mute and did not feel induced to interfere in behalf of outraged humanity.

The tone of frankness and benevolence which he assumes in his speech to the colored committee is too thin a mask not to be seen through. The genuine spark of humanity is missing in it, no sincere wish to improve the condition of the oppressed has dictated it. It expresses merely the desire to get rid of them, and reminds one of the politeness with which a man might try to bow out of his house some troublesome creditor or the witness of some old guilt. We might also criticize the style adopted, so exceedingly plain and coarse threaded as to make the impression that Mr. L. had such a low estimate of the intelligence of his audience, as to think any but the simplest phrases and constructions would be above their power of comprehension. As Mr. Lincoln however in all his writings has manifested a decided awkwardness in the management of the English language, we do not think there is any intention in this respect, but only the incapacity to do better.

---

32. Benjamin F. Butler (1818–1893) was an American politician and military leader who served as a major general for the Union army during the Civil War.

25. "Remarks of Frederick Douglass [on the Emancipation Proclamation]," a speech delivered at Zion Church in Rochester, New York on December 28, 1862 and published in *Douglass' Monthly*, January 1863[33]

MY FRIENDS: —

This is scarcely a day for prose. It is a day for poetry and song, a new song. These cloudless skies, this balmy air, this brilliant sunshine (making December as pleasant as May) are in harmony with the glorious morning of liberty about to dawn upon us. Out of a full heart and with sacred emotion, I congratulate you my friends, and fellow citizens, on the high and hopeful condition, of the cause of human freedom and the cause of our common country, for these two causes are now one and inseparable and must stand or fall together. We stand today in the presence of a glorious prospect. —This sacred Sunday in all the likelihoods of the case, is the last which will witness the existence, of legal slavery in all the rebel slaveholding states of America. Henceforth and forever, slavery in those states is to be recognized, by all the departments the American government, under its appropriate character, as an unmitigated robber and pirate, branded as the sum of all villainy, an outlaw having no rights which any man white or colored is bound to respect. It is difficult for us who have toiled so long and hard, to believe that this event, so stupendous, so far reaching and glorious is even now at the door. It surpasses our most enthusiastic hopes that we live at such a time and are likely to witness the downfall, at least the legal downfall of slavery in America. It is a moment for joy thanksgiving and praise.

Among the first questions that tried the strength of my childhood mind— was first why are colored people slaves, and the next was will their slavery last forever. From that day onward, the cry that has reached the most silent chambers of my soul, by day and by night has been How long! How long oh! Eternal Power of the Universe, how long shall these things be?

This inquiry is to be answered on the first of January 1863.

---

33. In the summer of 1862, President Lincoln circulated early drafts of what would become the Emancipation Proclamation. By late 1863, news of the forthcoming proclamation was circulating in the country and many, including Douglass, were waiting in joyful anticipation. Douglass recognized the practical limitations of the Proclamation (which declared only those slaves in rebel States to be free), but he believed it had crucial symbolic importance and marked a turning point in the Civil War.

That this war is to abolish slavery I have no manner of doubt. The process may be long and tedious but that that result must at last be reached is among the undoubted certainties of the future! Slavery once abolished in the rebel states, will give the death wound to slavery in the border states. When Arkansas is a free state Missouri cannot be a slave state.

Nevertheless, this is no time for the friends of freedom, to fold their hands and consider their work at an end. The price of liberty is eternal vigilance. Even after slavery has been legally abolished, and the Rebellion substantially suppressed, even when their shall come representatives to Congress from the states now in rebellion, and they shall have repudiated the miserable and disastrous error of disunion, or secession, and the country, shall have reached a condition of comparative peace, there will still remain an urgent necessity for the benevolent activity of the men and the women who have from the first opposed slavery from high moral conviction.

Slavery has existed in this country too long and has stamped its character too deeply and indelibly, to be blotted out in a day or a year, or even in a generation. The slave will yet remain in some sense a slave, long after the chains are taken from his limbs, and the master, will retain much of the pride, the arrogance, imperiousness and conscious superiority, and love of power, acquired by his former relation of master. Time, necessity, education, will be required to bring all classes into harmonious and natural, relations.

But the South will not be the only part of the country demanding vigilance and exertion on the part of the true friends of the colored people. Our chief difficulty will hereafter as it has been here to fore with pro-slavery doughfaces, at the North. A dog will continue to scratch his neck even after the collar is removed. The sailor a night or two after reaching land feels his bed swimming from side to side, as if tossed by the sea. Daniel Webster received a large vote in Massachusetts after he was dead. It will not be strange if many Northern men whose politics, habits of thought, and accustomed submission to the slave power, leads them to continue to go through the forms, of their ancient servility long after their old master slavery is in his grave.

Law and the sword can and will, in the end abolish slavery. But law and the sword cannot abolish the malignant slaveholding sentiment which has kept the slave system, alive in this country during two centuries. Pride of race, prejudice against color, will raise their hateful clamor for oppression of the Negro as heretofore. The slave having ceased to be the abject slave of a single master, his enemies will endeavor to make him the slave of society at large.

For a time at least, we may expect that this malign purpose and principle of wrong will get itself, more or less expressed in party presses and platforms, pro-slavery political writers and speakers, will not fail to inflame the ancient prejudice against the Negro, by exaggerating his faults and concealing or disparaging his virtues. A crime committed by one of the hated race, while any excellence found in one black man will grudgingly beset to his individual credit. Hence we say that the friends of freedom, the men and women of the land who regard slavery as a crime and the slave as a man will still be needed even after slavery is abolished.

26. "Why Should a Colored Man Enlist?" an essay published in *Douglass' Monthly*, April 1863[34]

This question has been repeatedly put to us while raising men for the 54th Massachusetts regiment daring the past five weeks, and perhaps we cannot at present do a better service to the cause of our people or to the cause of the country than by giving a few of the many reasons why a colored man should enlist.

1st. You are a man, although a colored man. If you were only a horse or an ox, incapable of deciding whether the rebels are right or wrong, you would have no responsibility, and might like the horse or the ox go on eating your corn or grass, in total indifference, as to which side is victorious or vanquished in this conflict. You are however no horse, and no ox, but a man, and whatever concerns man should interest you. He who looks upon a conflict between right and wrong, and does not help the right against the wrong, despises and insults his own nature, and invites the contempt of mankind. As between the North and South, the North is clearly in the right and the South is flagrantly in the wrong. You should therefore, simply as a matter of right and wrong, give your utmost aid to the North. In presence of such a contest there is no neutrality for any man. You are either for the government or against the government. Manhood requires you to take sides, and you are mean or noble according to how you choose between action and inaction. —If you are sound in body and mind, there is nothing in your *color* to excuse you from enlisting in the service of the republic against its enemies. If *color* should not be a criterion of rights, neither should it be a standard of duty. The whole duty of a man, belongs alike to white and black.

> *"A man's a man for a' that."*

2d. You are however, not only a man, but an American citizen, so declared by the highest legal adviser of the government, and you have hitherto expressed in various ways, not only your willingness but your earnest desire to fulfill any and every obligation which the relation of citizenship imposes. Indeed, you have hitherto felt wronged and slighted, because while white men of all

---

34. In the wake of the Emancipation Proclamation, Douglass became a strong supporter of the enlistment of free blacks in the Union cause. This essay provides a good example of Douglass' recruiting pitch.

other nations have been freely enrolled to serve the country, you a native born citizen have been coldly denied the honor of aiding in defense of the land of your birth. The injustice thus done you is now repented of by the government and you are welcomed to a place in the army of the nation. Should you refuse to enlist now, you will justify the past contempt of the government toward you and lead it to regret having honored you with a call to take up arms in its defense. You cannot but see that here is a good reason why you should promptly enlist.

3d. A third reason why a colored man should enlist is found in the fact that every Negro hater and slavery-lover in the land regards the arming of Negroes as a calamity and is doing his best to prevent it. Even now all the weapons of malice, in the shape of slander and ridicule are used to defeat the filling up of the 54th Massachusetts (colored) regiment. In nine cases out of ten, you will find it safe to do just what your enemy would gladly have you leave undone. What helps you hurts him. Find out what he does not want and give him plenty of it.

4th. You should enlist to learn the use of arms, to become familiar with the means of securing, protecting and defending your own liberty. A day may come when men shall learn war no more, when justice shall be so clearly apprehended, so universally practiced, and humanity shall be so profoundly loved and respected, that war and bloodshed, shall be confined only to beasts of prey. Manifestly however, that time has not yet come, and while all men should labor to hasten its coming, by the cultivation of all the elements conducive to peace, it is plain that for the present no race of men can depend wholly upon moral means for the maintenance of their rights. Men must either be governed by love or by fear. They must love to do right or fear to do wrong. The only way open to any race to make their rights respected is to learn how to defend them. When it is seen that black men no more than white men can be enslaved with impunity, men will be less inclined to enslave and oppress them. Enlist therefore, that you may learn the art and assert the ability to defend yourself and your race.

5th. You are a member of a long enslaved and despised race. Men have set down your submission to slavery and insult, to a lack of manly courage. They point to this fact as demonstrating your fitness only to be a servile class. You should enlist and disprove the slander, and wipe out the reproach. When you shall be seen nobly defending the liberties of your own country against rebels and traitors—brass itself will blush to use such arguments imputing cowardice against you.

6th. Whether you are or are not, entitled to all the rights of citizenship in this country has long been a matter of dispute to your prejudice. By enlisting in the service of your country at this trial hour, and upholding the national flag, you will stop the months of traducers and win applause even from the iron lips of ingratitude. Enlist and you make this your country in common with all other men born in the country or out of it.

7th. Enlist for your own sake. Decried and derided as you have been and still are you need an act of this kind by which to recover your own self-respect. You have to some extent rated your value by the estimate of your enemies and hence have counted yourself less than you are. You owe it to yourself and your race to rise from your social debasement and take your place among the soldiers of your country, a man among men. Depend upon it, the subjective effect of this one act of enlisting will be immense and highly beneficial. You will stand more erect, walk more assured, feel more at ease, and be less liable to insult than you ever were before. He who fights the battles of America may claim America as his country—and have that claim respected. Thus in defending your country now against rebels and traitors you are defending your own liberty, honor, manhood and self-respect.

8th. You should enlist because your doing so will be one of the most certain means of preventing the country from drifting back into the whirlpool of pro-slavery compromise at the end of the war, which is now our greatest danger. He who shall witness another compromise with slavery in this country will see the free colored man of the North more than ever a victim of the pride, lust, scorn and violence of all classes of white men. The whole North will be but another Detroit, where every white fiend may with impunity revel in unrestrained beastliness toward people of color; they may burn their houses, insult their wives and daughters, and kill indiscriminately. If you mean to live in this country now is the time for you to do your full share in making it a country where you and your children after you can live in comparative safety. Prevent a compromise with the traitors, compel them to come back to the Union whipped and humbled into obedience and all will be well. But let them come back as masters and all their hate and hellish ingenuity will be exerted to stir up the ignorant masses of the North to hate, hinder and persecute the free colored people of the North. That most inhuman of all modern enactments, with its bribed judges, and summary process, the fugitive slave law, with all its infernal train of canting divines, preaching the gospel of kidnapping, as twelve years ago, will be revived against the free colored people of the North. One or two black brigades will do much to prevent all this.

9th. You should enlist because the war for the Union, whether men so call it or not, is a war for emancipation, The salvation of the country, by the inexorable relation of cause and effect, can be secured only by the complete abolition of slavery. The president has already proclaimed emancipation to the slaves in the rebel states which is tantamount to declaring emancipation in all the states, for slavery must exist everywhere in the South in order to exist anywhere in the South. Can you ask for a more inviting, ennobling and soul enlarging work, than that of making one of the glorious band who shall carry liberty to your long enslaved people. Remember that identified with the slave in color, you will have a power that white soldiers have not, to attract them to your lines and induce them to take up arms in a common cause. One black brigade will, for this work, be worth more than two white ones. Enlist, therefore, enlist without delay, enlist now, and forever put an end to the human barter and butchery which have stained the whole South with the warm blood of your people, and loaded its air with their groans. Enlist, and deserve not only well of your country, and win for yourselves, a name and a place among men, but secure to yourself what is infinitely more precious the fast dropping tears of gratitude of your kith and kin marked out for distraction, and who are but now ready to perish.

When time's ample curtain shall fall upon our national tragedy, and our hillsides and valleys shall neither redden with the blood nor whiten with the bones of kinsmen and country men who have fallen in the sanguinary and wicked strife; when grim visaged war has smoothed his wrinkled front and our country shall have regained its normal condition as a leader of nations in the occupation and blessings of peace—and history shall record the names of heroes and martyrs—who bravely answered the call of patriotism and liberty—against traitors thieves and assassins—let it not be said that in the long list of glory, composed of men of all nations—there appears the name of no colored man.

27. "What the Black Man Wants," a speech delivered at the Annual Meeting of the Massachusetts Anti-Slavery Society in Boston, Massachusetts, January 26, 1865 and published in *The Liberator*, February 10, 1865[35]

MR. PRESIDENT:
[. . . .]

I have had but one idea for the last three years to present to the American people, and the phraseology in which I clothe it is the old abolition phraseology. I am for the "immediate, unconditional, and universal" enfranchisement of the black man, in every state in the Union. Without this, his liberty is a mockery; without this, you might as well almost retain the old name of slavery for his condition; for in fact, if he is not the slave of the individual master, he is the slave of society, and holds his liberty as a privilege, not as a right. He is at the mercy of the mob, and has no means of protecting himself.

It may be objected, however, that this pressing of the Negro's right to suffrage is premature. Let us have slavery abolished, it may be said, let us have labor organized, and then, in the natural course of events, the right of suffrage will be extended to the Negro. I do not agree with this. The Constitution of the human mind is such, that if it once disregards the conviction forced upon it by a revelation of truth, it requires the exercise of a higher power to produce the same conviction afterward. The American people are now in tears. The Shenandoah has run blood—the best blood of the North. All around Richmond, the blood of New England and of the North has been shed—of your sons, your brothers and your fathers. We all feel, in the existence of this Rebellion, that judgments terrible, wide-spread, far-reaching, overwhelming, are abroad in the land; and we feel, in view of these judgments, just now, a disposition to learn righteousness. This is the hour. Our streets are in mourning, tears are falling at every fireside, and under the chastisement of this Rebellion we have almost come up to the point of conceding this great, this all-important right of suffrage. I fear that if we fail to do it now, if abolitionists fail to press it now, we may not see, for centuries to come, the same disposition that exists at this moment. Hence, I say, now is the time to press this right.

---

35. With Union victory near in the Civil War, Douglass and other reformers began to turn their attention to the aftermath of the war. This speech captures some of Douglass' early thoughts on the prospects for the "Reconstruction" of the South and the achievement of justice for liberated slaves.

It may be asked, "Why do you want it? Some men have got along very well without it. Women have not this right." Shall we justify one wrong by another? This is a sufficient answer. Shall we at this moment justify the deprivation of the Negro of the right to vote, because someone else is deprived of that privilege? I hold that women, as well as men, have the right to vote, and my heart and my voice go with the movement to extend suffrage to woman; but that question rests upon another basis than that on which our right rests. We may be asked, I say, why we want it. I will tell you why we want it. We want it because it is our right, first of all. No class of men can, without insulting their own nature, be content with any deprivation of their rights. We want it again, as a means for educating our race. Men are so constituted that they derive their conviction of their own possibilities largely from the estimate formed of them by others. If nothing is expected of a people, that people will find it difficult to contradict that expectation. By depriving us of suffrage, you affirm our incapacity to form an intelligent judgment respecting public men and public measures; you declare before the world that we are unfit to exercise the elective franchise, and by this means lead us to undervalue ourselves, to put a low estimate upon ourselves, and to feel that we have no possibilities like other men. Again, I want the elective franchise, for one, as a colored man, because ours is a peculiar government, based upon a peculiar idea, and that idea is universal suffrage. If I were in a monarchial government, or an autocratic or aristocratic government, where the few bore rule and the many were subject, there would be no special stigma resting upon me, because I did not exercise the elective franchise. It would do me no great violence. Mingling with the mass I should partake of the strength of the mass; I should be supported by the mass, and I should have the same incentives to endeavor with the mass of my fellow-men; it would be no particular burden, no particular deprivation; but here where universal suffrage is the rule, where that is the fundamental idea of the government, to rule us out is to make us an exception, to brand us with the stigma of inferiority, and to invite to our heads the missiles of those about us; therefore, I want the franchise for the black man.

There are, however, other reasons, not derived from any consideration merely of our rights, but arising out of the conditions of the South, and of the country—considerations which have already been referred to by Mr. Wendell Phillips—considerations which must arrest the attention of statesmen. I believe that when the tall heads of this Rebellion shall have been swept down, as they will be swept down, when the Davises and Toombses and Stephenses,[36] and others who are leading this Rebellion shall have been blotted out, there will be this rank undergrowth of treason, to which reference has been made, growing up there, and interfering with, and thwarting the quiet operation of the federal government in those states. You will see those traitors, handing down, from sire to son, the same malignant spirit which they have manifested,

---

36. Douglass identifies several important Confederate leaders.

and which they are now exhibiting, with malicious hearts, broad blades, and bloody hands in the field, against our sons and brothers. That spirit will still remain; and whoever sees the federal government extended over those Southern states will see that government in a strange land, and not only in a strange land, but in an enemy's land. A post-master of the United States in the South will find himself surrounded by a hostile spirit; a collector in a Southern port will find himself surrounded by a hostile spirit; a United States marshal or United States judge will be surrounded there by a hostile element. That enmity will not die out in a year, will not die out in an age. The federal government will be looked upon in those states precisely as the governments of Austria and France are looked upon in Italy at the present moment. They will endeavor to circumvent, they will endeavor to destroy, the peaceful operation of this government. Now, where will you find the strength to counterbalance this spirit, if you do not find it in the Negroes of the South? They are your friends, and have always been your friends. They were your friends even when the government did not regard them as such. They comprehended the genius of this war before you did. It is a significant fact, it is a marvelous fact, it seems almost to imply a direct interposition of Providence, that this war, which began in the interest of slavery on both sides, bids fair to end in the interest of liberty on both sides. It was begun, I say, in the interest of slavery on both sides. The South was fighting to take slavery out of the Union, and the North fighting to keep it in the Union; the South fighting to get it beyond the limits of the United States Constitution, and the North fighting to retain it within those limits; the South fighting for new guarantees, and the North fighting for the old guarantees; — both despising the Negro, both insulting the Negro. Yet, the Negro, apparently endowed with wisdom from on high, saw more clearly the end from the beginning than we did. When [William Henry] Seward[37] said the status of no man in the country would be changed by the war, the Negro did not believe him. When our generals sent their underlings in shoulder-straps to hunt the flying Negro back from our lines into the jaws of slavery, from which he had escaped, the Negroes thought that a mistake had been made, and that the intentions of the government had not been rightly understood by our officers in shoulder-straps, and they continued to come into our lines, threading their way through bogs and fens, over briers and thorns, fording streams, swimming rivers, bringing us tidings as to the safe path to march, and pointing out the dangers that threatened us. They are our only friends in the South, and we should be true to them in this their trial hour, and see to it that they have the elective franchise.

I know that we are inferior to you in some things—virtually inferior. We walk about among you like dwarfs among giants. Our heads are scarcely seen above the great sea of humanity. The Germans are superior to us; the Irish are

---

37. William Henry Seward (1801–1872) was an American politician who served as Secretary of State under President Abraham Lincoln.

superior to us; the Yankees are superior to us; they can do what we cannot, that is, what we have not hitherto been allowed to do. But while I make this admission, I utterly deny, that we are originally, or naturally, or practically, or in any way, or in any important sense, inferior to anybody on this globe. This charge of inferiority is an old dodge. It has been made available for oppression on many occasions. It is only about six centuries since the blue-eyed and fair-haired Anglo Saxons were considered inferior by the haughty Normans, who once trampled upon them. If you read the history of the Norman Conquest, you will find that this proud Anglo-Saxon was once looked upon as of coarser clay than his Norman master, and might be found in the highways and byways of Old England laboring with a brass collar on his neck, and the name of his master marked upon it. You were down then! You are up now. I am glad you are up, and I want you to be glad to help us up also.

The story of our inferiority is an old dodge, as I have said; for wherever men oppress their fellows, wherever they enslave them, they will endeavor to find the needed apology for such enslavement and oppression in the character of the people oppressed and enslaved. When we wanted, a few years ago, a slice of Mexico, it was hinted that the Mexicans were an inferior race, that the old Castilian blood had become so weak that it would scarcely run downhill, and that Mexico needed the long, strong and beneficent arm of the Anglo-Saxon care extended over it. We said that it was necessary to its salvation, and a part of the "manifest destiny" of this republic, to extend our arm over that dilapidated government. So, too, when Russia wanted to take possession of a part of the Ottoman Empire, the Turks were "an inferior race." So, too, when England wants to set the heel of her power more firmly in the quivering heart of old Ireland, the Celts are an "inferior race." So, too, the Negro, when he is to be robbed of any right which is justly his, is an "inferior man." It is said that we are ignorant; I admit it. But if we know enough to be hanged, we know enough to vote. If the Negro knows enough to pay taxes to support the government, he knows enough to vote; taxation and representation should go together. If he knows enough to shoulder a musket and fight for the flag, fight for the government, he knows enough to vote. If he knows as much when he is sober as an Irishman knows when drunk, he knows enough to vote, on good American principles.

But I was saying that you needed a counterpoise in the persons of the slaves to the enmity that would exist at the South after the Rebellion is put down. I hold that the American people are bound, not only in self-defense, to extend this right to the freedmen of the South, but they are bound by their love of country, and by all their regard for the future safety of those Southern states, to do this—to do it as a measure essential to the preservation of peace there. But I will not dwell upon this. I put it to the American sense of honor. The honor of a nation is an important thing. It is said in the Scriptures, "What doth it profit a man if he gain the whole world, and lose his own soul?"[38] It may be said, also, What doth it profit a nation if it gain the whole world, but lose its honor? I hold that the American government has taken upon itself a solemn obligation of honor, to see that this war—let it be long or let it be short, let it cost much or let it cost little—that this war shall not cease until every freedman at the South has the right to vote. It has bound itself to it. What have you asked the black men of the South, the black men of the whole country, to do? Why, you have asked them to incur the deadly enmity of their masters, in order to befriend you and to befriend this government. You have asked us to call down, not only upon ourselves, but upon our children's children, the deadly hate of the entire Southern people. You have called upon us to turn our backs upon our masters, to abandon their cause and espouse yours; to turn against the South and in favor of the North; to shoot down the Confederacy and uphold the flag—the American flag. You have called upon us to expose ourselves to all the subtle machinations of their malignity for all time. And now, what do you propose to do when you come to make peace? To reward your enemies, and trample in the dust your friends? Do you intend to sacrifice the very men who have come to the rescue of your banner in the South, and incurred the lasting displeasure of their masters thereby? Do you intend to sacrifice them and reward your enemies? Do you mean to give your enemies the right to vote, and take it away from your friends? Is that wise policy? Is that honorable? Could American honor withstand such a blow? I do not believe you will do it. I think you will see to it that we have the right to vote. There is something too mean in looking upon the Negro, when you are in trouble, as a citizen, and when you are free from trouble, as an alien. When this nation was in trouble, in its early struggles, it looked upon the Negro as a citizen. In 1776 he was a citizen. At the time of the formation of the Constitution the Negro had the right to vote in eleven states out of the old thirteen. In your trouble you have made us citizens. In 1812 Gen. Jackson addressed us as citizens—"fellow-citizens." He wanted us to fight. We were citizens then! And now, when you come to frame a conscription bill, the Negro is a citizen again. He has been a citizen just three times in the history of this government, and it has always been in time of trouble. In time of trouble we are citizens. Shall we be citizens in war, and aliens in peace? Would that be just?

I ask my friends who are apologizing for not insisting upon this right, where can the black man look, in this country, for the assertion of this right, if he may not look to the Massachusetts Anti-Slavery Society? Where under the whole heavens can he look for sympathy, in asserting this right, if he may not look to this platform? Have you lifted us up to a certain height to see that we are men, and then are any disposed to leave us there, without seeing that we

---

38. Matthew 16:26.

are put in possession of all our rights? We look naturally to this platform for the assertion of all our rights, and for this one especially. I understand the anti-slavery societies of this country to be based on two principles, —first, the freedom of the blacks of this country; and, second, the elevation of them. Let me not be misunderstood here. I am not asking for sympathy at the hands of abolitionists, sympathy at the hands of any. I think the American people are disposed often to be generous rather than just. I look over this country at the present time, and I see educational societies, sanitary commissions, freedmen's associations, and the like, —all very good: but in regard to the colored people there is always more that is benevolent, I perceive, than just, manifested toward us. What I ask for the Negro is not benevolence, not pity, not sympathy, but simply *justice*. The American people have always been anxious to know what they shall do with us. [. . .] Everybody has asked the question, and they learned to ask it early of the abolitionists, "What shall we do with the Negro?" I have had but one answer from the beginning. Do nothing with us! Your doing with us has already played the mischief with us. Do nothing with us! If the apples will not remain on the tree of their own strength, if they are worm-eaten at the core, if they are early ripe and disposed to fall, let them fall! I am not for tying or fastening them on the tree in any way, except by nature's plan, and if they will not stay there, let them fall. And if the Negro cannot stand on his own legs, let him fall also. All I ask is, give him a chance to stand on his own legs! Let him alone! If you see him on his way to school, let him alone, don't disturb him! If you see him going to the dinner-table at a hotel, let him go! If you see him going to the ballot-box, let him alone, don't disturb him! If you see him going into a work-shop, just let him alone, —your interference is doing him a positive injury. . . . Let him fall if he cannot stand alone! If the Negro cannot live by the line of eternal justice . . . the fault will not be yours, it will be his who made the Negro, and established that line for his government. Let him live or die by that. If you will only untie his hands, and give him a chance, I think he will live. He will work as readily for himself as the white man. [. . .]

PART V

REFLECTIONS OF AN "OLD WATCHMAN ON THE WALLS OF LIBERTY": DOUGLASS AFTER THE CIVIL WAR

28. "Sources of Danger to the Republic," a speech delivered in St. Louis, Missouri, February 7, 1867 and published in the *St. Louis Missouri Democrat*, February 8, 1867[1]

Ladies and Gentlemen:

I know of no greater misfortunes to individuals than an over confidence in their own perfections, and I know of fewer misfortunes that can happen to a nation greater than an over confidence in their own perfections, and I know of fewer misfortunes that can happen to a nation greater than an over confidence in the perfection of its government. It is common on great occasions to hear men speak of our republican form of government as a model of surpassing excellence—the best government on earth—a masterpiece of statesmanship—and destined at some period not very remote to supersede all other forms of government among men; and when our patriotic orators would appear in some degree recondite as well as patriotic, they treat us to masterly disquisitions upon what they are pleased to term "the admirable mechanism of our Constitution." They discourse wisely of its checks and balances, and the judicious distribution of the various powers.

I am certainly not here this evening rudely to call in question these very pleasing assumptions of governmental superiority on our part; they are perfectly natural; they are consistent with our natural self-love and our national pride; and when they are not employed, as they too often are, in the bad service of a blind, unreasoning, stubborn conservatism, to shelter old time abuses and discourage manly criticism, and to defeat needed measures of amendment, they are comparatively harmless, though we may not always be able to assent to the good taste with which they are urged. It is well enough, however, once in a while to remind Americans that they are not alone in this species of self-laudation; that in fact there are men, reputed wise and good men, living in other parts of the planet, under other forms of government, aristocratic, autocratic, oligarchic, and monarchical, who are just as confident of the good qualities of their government as we are of our own. It is true, also, that many good men, at home and abroad, and especially abroad, looking upon our republican experiment from afar, in the cool, calm light of their philosophy, have already discovered, or think that they have discovered, a decline or decay, and the

---

1. With the Civil War over and debates over Reconstruction at the center of national life, Douglass offers some thoughts on what must be done to secure the rights of all Americans and what might be done to reform flaws in the American political system.

certain downfall of our republican institutions, and the speedy substitution of some other form of government for our democratic institutions. Those who entertain these opinions of our government are not entirely without reason, plausible reason, in support of it. The fact that the ballot box, upon which we have relied so long as the chief source of strength, is the safety valve of our institutions through which the explosive passions of the populace could pass off harmlessly, has failed us—broken down under us, and that a formidable rebellion has arisen, the minority of the people in one section of the country united, animated and controlled by a powerful sectional interest, have rebelled, and for four long years disputed the authority of the constitutional majority of the people, is regarded as a telling argument against the prevailing assumption of our national stability and the impregnability of our institutions. Besides, they point us, and very decidedly, to the fact that there seemed to be no adequate comprehension of the character of this rebellion at the beginning of it, and seemed also to be nothing like a proper spirit of enthusiasm manifested by the people in support of the government. They point us to the tardiness and hesitation and doubt, and the disposition to yield up the government to the arrogant demands of conspirators; and they profess themselves now able to see the same want of spirit, manliness and courage in the matter of reconstruction since the rebellion has been suppressed. They point us also to the fact that so far as the government is concerned, there must be either an indisposition or an inability either to punish traitors or to reward and protect loyal men; and they say, very wisely, as I think, that a nation that cannot hate treason cannot love loyalty.

They point us also to the fact that there are growing antagonisms, forces bitter and unrelenting between the different branches of our government— the executive against the legislative, and the judicial in some instances against both. They point us also to the obvious want of gratitude on the part of the nation, its disposition to sacrifice its best friends and to make peace with its bitterest enemies; the fact that it has placed its only true allies under the political heels of the very men who with broad blades and bloody hands sought the destruction of the republic. They point us to the fact that loyal men by the score, by the hundred, have been deliberately and outrageously, and in open daylight, slaughtered by the known enemies of the country, and thus far that the murderers are at large: unquestioned by the law, unpunished by justice, unrebuked even by the public opinion of the localities where the crimes were committed. Under the whole heavens you cannot find any government besides our own thus indifferent to the lives of its loyal subjects. They tell us, moreover, that the lives of republics have been short, stormy, and saddening to the hopes of the friends of freedom, and they tell us, too, that ours will prove no exception to this general rule.

Now, why have I referred to these unfavorable judgments of American institutions? Not, certainly, to endorse them; neither to combat them; but as offering a reason why the Americans should take a little less extravagant view of the excellencies of our institutions. We should scrutinize them a little more closely and weigh their value a little more impartially than we are accustomed to do. We ought to examine our government, and I am here tonight, and I rejoice that in St. Louis that there is liberty enough, civilization enough, to tolerate free inquiry at this point as well as any other. I am here tonight in a little different capacity from what I ordinarily am, or what I have been before the American people. In other days—darker days than these—I appeared before the American people simply as a member of a despised, outraged and down-trodden race; simply to plead that the chains of the bondmen be broken; simply to plead that the auction block shall no more be in use for the sale of human flesh. I appear here no longer as a whipped, scarred slave—no longer as the advocate merely of an enslaved race, but in the high and commanding character of an American citizen having the interest that every true citizen should have in the welfare, stability, the permanence and the prosperity of our free institutions, and in this spirit I shall criticize our government tonight.

In one respect we here have decided advantage over the subjects of the "divine right" governments of Europe. We can at least examine our government. We can at least look into it—into every feature of it, and estimate it at its true value. No divine pretension stands athwart the pathway of free discussion here. The material out of which men would weave if they could a superstitious reverence for the Constitution of the United States, is an exceedingly slender and scarce commodity, and there is nothing upon which such a superstition can well be based. There were neither thunderings, nor lightnings, nor earthquakes, nor tempests, nor any other disturbance of nature when this great law was given to the world. It is at least an honest Constitution and asks to be accepted upon its own merits. . . . It is purely a human contrivance, designed with more or less wisdom, for human purposes; to combine liberty with order; to make society possible; or, to use its own admirable language, "to form a more perfect Union"; to establish justice; to provide for the common defense; and to secure the blessings of liberty to ourselves and all posterity, we the people, the *people*, the PEOPLE—*we, the people*, do ordain and establish this Constitution. There we stand on the main foundation.

Now, while I discard all Fourth of July extravagances about the Constitution, and about its framers, even I can speak respectfully of that instrument and respectfully of the men who framed it. To be sure my early condition in life was not very favorable to the growth of what men call patriotism and reverence for institutions—certainly not for the "peculiar institution" from which I graduated—yet even I can speak respectfully of the Constitution. For one thing I feel grateful—at least I think the fathers deserve homage of mankind for this—that against the assumptions, against the inducements to do otherwise, they have given us a Constitution commensurate in its beneficent arrangements with the wants of common humanity; that it embraces man as man. There is nothing in it of a narrow description. They could establish a Constitution free from bigotry, free from superstition, free from sectarian prejudices, caste or political distinction.

In the eye of that great instrument we are neither Jews, Greeks, Barbarians or Cythians, but fellow-citizens of a common country, embracing all men of all colors. The fathers of this republic did not learn to insert the word white, or to determine men's rights by their color. They did not base their legislation upon the differences among men in the length of their noses or the twist of their hair, but upon the broad fact of a common human nature.

I doubt if at any time during the last fifty years we could have received a constitution so liberal from the sons as we have received from the fathers of the republic. They were above going down, as certain men Caucasian and Teutonic ethnologists—have recently done, on their knees and measuring the human heel to ascertain the amount of intelligence he should have. They were above that. That is a modern improvement or invention.

Some have undertaken to prove the identity of the Negro, or the relationship of the Negro with the monkey from the length of his heel, forgetting what is the fact, that the monkey has no heel at all, and that in fact the longer a man's heel is the further he is from the monkey. Our fathers did not fall into this mistake. They made a constitution for men, not for color, not for features. In the eye of that great instrument the moment the chains are struck from the limbs of the humblest and most whip scarred slave he may rise to any position for which his talents and character fit him. For this I say the fathers are entitled to the profound gratitude of mankind—that against all temptations to do otherwise, they have given us a liberal constitution.

But wise and good as that instrument is; at this point and at many others, it is simply a human contrivance. It is the work of man and men struggling with many of the prejudices and infirmities common to man, and it is not strange that we should find in their constitution some evidences of their infirmity and prejudices. Time and experience and the ever increasing light of reason are constantly making manifest those defects and those imperfections, and it is for us, living eighty years after them, and therefore eighty years wiser than they, to remove those defects—to improve the character of our Constitution at this point where we find those defects.

I was rather glad at one feature in the effect produced by the rebellion. It for a time depressed the national exultation over the perfection of the Constitution of the United States. The uprising of that rebellion was a severe blow to our national extravagance at this point, but the manner in which we have met the rebellion, and as soon as we have succeeded in suppressing it, conquering the rebels and scattering their military forces, our old time notions of our perfect system of government have revived, and there is an indisposition on the part of some men to entertain propositions for amending the Constitution. But I think that a right view of our trouble, instead of increasing our confidence in the perfection of the fundamental structure of the government, ought to do quite the reverse; it ought to impress us with the sense of our national insecurity by disclosing, as it does disclose, the slenderness of the thread on which the national life was suspended, and showing us how small a circumstance might have whelmed our government in the measureless abyss of ruin, prepared for it by the rebels.

We succeeded in putting down the rebellion. And wherein is the secret of that success? Not in, I think, the superior structure of our government, by any means. We succeeded in that great contest because, during at least the latter part of the war, the loyal armies fought on the side of human nature; fought on the side of justice, civil order and liberty. This rebellion was struck with death the instant Abraham Lincoln inscribed on our banner the word "Emancipation." Our armies went up to battle thereafter for the best aspirations of the human soul in every quarter of the globe, and we conquered. The rebel armies fought well, fought bravely, fought desperately, but they fought in fetters. Invisible chains were about them. Deep down in their own consciences there was an accusing voice reminding them that they were fighting for chains and slavery, and not for freedom. They were in chains—entangled with the chains of their own slaves. They not only struggled with our gigantic armies and with the skill of our veteran generals, but they fought against the moral sense of the nineteenth century—they fought against their own better selves—they fought against the good in their own souls; they were weakened thereby; their weakness was our strength, hence our success. And our success over the rebels is due to another cause quite apart from the perfection of our structure of government. It is largely owing to the fact that the nation happened—for it only happened—we happened to have in the presidential chair, an honest man. It might not have been otherwise. It was our exceeding good fortune that Abraham Lincoln, not Wm. H. Seward—received the nomination at Chicago in 1860. Had Wm. H. Seward—judging him by his present position—had Franklin Pierce, had Millard Fillmore, had James Buchanan, or had that other embodiment of political treachery, meanness, baseness, ingratitude, the vilest of the vile, the basest of the base, the most execrable of the execrable of modern times—he who shall be nameless, occupied the presidential chair your magnificent republic might have been numbered with the things that were.

We talk about the power of the people over this government, of its admirable checks and balances, its wisely arranged machinery; but remember those three months, the last three months of Buchanan's administration. It is impossible to think wisely and deeply without learning a lesson of the inherent weakness of our republican structure. For three long months the nation saw their army and their navy scattered and the munitions of war of the government placed in the hands of its enemies. The people could do nothing but bite their lips in silent agony. They were on a mighty stream afloat, with all their liberties at stake and a faithless pilot on their boat. They could not help this. They were in a current which they could neither resist nor control. In the rapids of a political Niagara, sweeping the nation on and on, in silent agony toward the awful cataract in the distance to receive it. Our power was unable to stay the treachery.

We appealed, to be sure—we pointed out through our principles the right way—but we were powerless, and we saw no help till the man, Lincoln, appeared on the theater of action and extended his honest hand to save the republic. No; we owe nothing to our form of government for our preservation as a nation—nothing whatever—nothing to its checks, nor to its balances, nor to its wise division of powers and duties. It was an honest president backed up by intelligent and loyal people—men, high minded men that constitute the state, who regarded society as superior to its forms, the spirit as above the letter—men as more than country, and as superior to the Constitution. They resolved to save the country with the Constitution if they could, but at any rate to save the country. To this we owe our present safety as a nation.

Because a defective ship with a skillful captain, a hard-handed and honest crew, may manage to weather a considerable storm, is no proof that our old bark is sound in all her planks, bolts and timbers—because by constant pumping and extraordinary exertions we have managed to keep afloat and at last reach the shore.

I propose to speak to you of the sources of danger to our republic. These may be described under two heads, those which are esoteric in their character and those which are exoteric. I shall discourse of these in the order now stated. Let it not, however, be supposed by my intelligent audience that I concede anything to those who hold to the inherent weakness of a republican form of government. Far from this. The point of weakness in our government [does not] touch its republican character. On the contrary I hold that a republican form of government is the strongest government on earth when it is thoroughly republican. Our republican government is weak only as it touches or partakes of the character of monarchy or an aristocracy or an oligarchy. In its republican features it is strong. In its despotic features it is weak. Our government, in its ideas, is a government of the people. But unhappily it was framed under conditions, unfavorable to purely republican results, it was projected and completed under the influence of institutions quite unfavorable to a pure republican form of government—slavery on the one hand, monarchy on the other.

Late in a man's life his surroundings exert but a limited influence upon him—they are usually shaken off; but only a hero may shake off the influences of birth and early surroundings; the champion falls—the cause remains. Such is the constitution of the human mind, that there can be no such thing as immediate emancipation, either from slavery or from monarchy. An instant is sufficient to snap the chains; a century is not too much to obliterate all traces of former bondage.

It was easy for the fathers of the republic, comparatively so at least, to drive the redcoats from our continent, but it was not easy to drive the ideas and associations that surrounded the British throne and emanated from the monarch of this country. Born, as the fathers of this republic were, under monarchical institutions, they very naturally, when they came to form a government—although they assented to what Rufus Choate[2] called "the glittering generalities of the Declaration of Independence," they were disposed to blend something of the old error with the new truth, or of the newly discovered truth of liberty asserted in the Declaration of Independence. The eclectic principle may work pretty well in some governments, but it does not work well in our government. Here there must be unity; unity of idea; unity of object and accord of motive as well as of principles; in order to [achieve] a harmonious, happy and prosperous result.

The idea of putting new wine into old bottles or mending old garments with new cloth was not peculiar to the Jew; it came down to the fathers, and it is showing itself now among us. We are disposed to assent to the abolition of slavery, but we wish to retain something of slavery in the new dispensation. We are willing that the chains of the slave shall be broken if a few links can be left on his arm or on his leg. Your fathers were in some respects after the same pattern. They gave us a Constitution made in the shadow of slavery and of monarchy, and in its character it partakes in some of its features of both those unfavorable influences. Now, as I have said, I concede nothing to those who hold to the inherent weakness of our government or a republican form of government. The point of weakness or the features that weaken our government are exotic. They have been incorporated and interposited from other forms of government, and it is the business of this day and this generation to purge them from the Constitution.

In fact, I am here tonight as a democrat, a genuine democrat dyed in the wool. I am here to advocate a genuine democratic republic; to make this a republican form of government, purely a republic, a genuine republic; free it from everything that looks toward monarchy; eliminate all foreign elements, all alien elements from it; blot out from it everything antagonistic of republicanism declared by the fathers—that idea was that all governments derived their first powers from the consent of the governed; make it a government of the people, by the people and for the people, and for all the people, each for all and all for each; blot out all discriminations against any person, theoretically or practically, and make it conform to the great truths laid down by the fathers;

---

2. Rufus Choate (1799–1859) was an American politician who served in the House of Representatives and the US senate.

keep no man from the ballot box or jury box or the cartridge box, because of his color—exclude no woman from the ballot box because of her sex. Let the government of the country rest securely down upon the shoulders of the whole nation; let there be no shoulder that does not bear up its proportion of the burdens of the government. Let there [be] no conscience, no intellect in the land not directly responsible for the moral character of the government—for the honor of the government. Let it be a genuine republic, in which every man subject to it is represented in it, and I see no reason why a republic may not stand while the world stands.

Now, the first source of weakness to a republican government is the one-man power. I rejoice that we are at last startled into a consciousness of the existence of this one-man power. If it was necessary for Jeff Davis and his peculiar friends to resort to arms in order to show the danger of tolerating the slave power in our government, we are under great obligations to Andrew Johnson[3] for disclosing to us the unwisdom of tolerating the one-man power in their government. And if now we shall be moved, as I hope we shall, to revise our Constitution so as to entirely free it from the one-man power, to curtail or abridge that power, and reduce [it] to a manageable point, his accidental occupancy of the presidential chair will not be the unmitigated calamity we have been accustomed to regard it. It will be a blessing in disguise—though pretty heavily disguised. For disguise it we will, this one-man power is in our Constitution. It has its sheet anchor firmly in the soil of our Constitution. Mr. Johnson has sometimes overstepped this power, in certain conditions of his mind, which are quite frequent, and mistaken himself for the United States instead of the president of the United States. The fault is not entirely due to his marvelous vanity, but to the Constitution under which he lives. It is there in that Constitution. The "fantastic tricks" recently played "before high heaven"[4] by that dignitary when sandwiched between a hero of the land and sea, and swinging around the circle from the Atlantic to the Mississippi—we must break down the mainspring of those tricks in the Constitution before we shall get rid of them elsewhere.

It is true that our president is not our king for life; he is there only temporarily. I say king. Mr. Seward, you know, took it upon himself to introduce Andrew Johnson to the simple-hearted people of Michigan as king. "Will you have him as your president or as your king," said the astute secretary of state, evidently regarding the one title as appropriate to Andy Johnson as the other. There is a good deal of truth in it, for in fact he is invested with kingly power,

---

3. Andrew Johnson (1808–1875) was an American politician who served in the House of Representatives and the US senate, as governor of Tennessee, as vice president of the United States, and as president of the United States after the assassination of Abraham Lincoln.
4. William Shakespeare, *Measure for Measure*, act 2, sc. 2.

with an arbitrariness equal to any crown head in Europe. Spite of our boasts of the power of the people, your president can rule you as with a rod of iron. It is true he is only elected for four years—he is only a four-year-old—and the brief time of the term would seem to be a security against misbehavior; a security and a guarantee of good conduct, for the most turbulent of men can manage to behave themselves for short periods—always excepting the "humble individual." But the brief time—this brief time is no security—to my mind it furnishes impunity rather than security. We bear, in one of these presidents' behavior, arrogance and arbitrariness that we would not bear with but for the limited term of his service. We would not bear it an hour—the disgrace and scandal that we now stagger under—did we not know that two short, silent years will put an end to our misery in this respect.

It is true that we choose our president, and that would seem to show that the people after all rule. Well, we do choose him; we elect him, and we are free while we are electing him. When I was a slave; when I was first the privilege given hereafter of choosing my own master at the end of the year I was very much delighted. It struck me as a large concession to my manhood, the idea that I had the right to choose a master at the end of the year, and if I was kicked, and cuffed, bruised and beaten, during the year it was some satisfaction to know that after all, old fellow, I will shake you off at the end of the year. I thought it a great thing to be able to choose my own master. I was quite intoxicated with this little bit of liberty—and I would dance from Christmas to New Year on the strength of it. But, as I grew older and a trifle wiser, I began to be dissatisfied with this liberty, the liberty of choosing another master. I found that what I wanted, that what I needed was essential to my manhood was not another master, not a new master, not an old master, but the right to the power under the law to be my own master. From this little bit of experience—slave experience—I have elaborated quite a lengthy chapter of political philosophy, applicable to the American people. You are free to choose, but after you have chosen your freedom is gone, just as mine was gone, and our power is gone to a large extent under the framework of our government when you have chosen. You are free to choose, free while you are voting, free while you are dropping a piece of paper into the box with some names on it—I won't tell how those names got on it; that would evince, perhaps, a culpable familiarity with politics to do that. But you are free while you are dropping in your vote—going, going, gone. When your president is elected, once familiarly seated in the national saddle, his feet in the stirrups, his hand on the reins, he can drive the national animal almost where he will. He can administer this government with a contempt for public opinion, for the opinions and wishes of the people, such as no crowned head in Europe imitates toward his subjects.

Take, for instance, the government of England. It is sufficiently despotic and autocratic, but after all that government is administered with a deference for popular opinion far superior—far greater than our own. When the prime minister of England finds himself out-voted on the floor of the House of Commons by the people's representatives, what does he do? He lays the seals of his office at the foot of the throne; calls upon the national sovereignty to organize another government, more in harmony with the wishes and opinions of the people than he is able to be. He construes a vote against any great measure of his as a vote of want of confidence, and he is not willing to hold power when he is convinced that the people of the country are against him. He resigns.

But whoever heard of anybody in America resigning? Why, Congress might vote down Johnson every month and Seward every morning and they would stick to their offices just the same. They would hold on. Their theory is that when the people agree with them. They are right, but when the people differ from them they are simply mistaken. They go on in their accustomed ways. Whoever heard of anybody's resigning because he didn't represent the wishes of those who elected him? I have heard of a great many being invited, but I never heard of one accepting the invitation.

[. . . .] What I needed for my manhood was, that I should be my own master. What the American people need for their manhood and their national security is, that the people shall, in time of war, and in time of peace be the masters of their own government.

Now what are the elements that enter into this one-man power and swell it to the formidable measure at which we find it at this time? The first thing is the immense patronage of the president of the United States—the patronage of money, of honor, of place and power. He is able to divide among his friends and among his satellites—attaching men to his person and to his political fortunes—a hundred million of dollars per annum in time of peace, and uncounted thousands of millions of dollars in time of war are virtually at his disposal. This is an influence which can neither be weighed, measured nor otherwise estimated. The very thought of it is overwhelming. This amount of money lodged outside of the government in unfriendly hands could be made a formidable lever for the destruction of the government. It is a direct assault upon the national virtue. While the president of the United States can exalt whom he will, cast down whom he will; he can place A into office for agreeing with him in opinion, and cause B to be put out of office because of an honest difference of opinion with him. Who does not see that the tendency to agreement will be a million times stronger than the tendency to differ, even though truth should be in favor of difference. From this power—this patronage—has arisen the popular political maxim that "to the victors belong the spoils," and that other vulgar expression of the same idea by Postmaster General [Edwin M.] Randall, that no man shall eat the president's "bread and butter" who does not indorse the president's "policy." The first thing that an American is taught at the cradle side is never to fight against his bread and butter.

Now I hold that this patronage should be abolished, that is to say that the president's control over it should be abolished. The Constitution evidently contemplated that the large arm of our government should control the matter of appointments. It declares that the president may appoint by and with the consent and with the advice of the Senate; he must get the Senate's advice and consent, but custom and a certain laxity of administration has almost obliterated this feature of the Constitution, and now the president appoints, he not only appoints by and with the consent, but he has the power of removal, and with this power he virtually makes the agency of the Senate of the United States of no effect in the matter of appointments. I am very glad to see that a movement is on foot in Congress to make the appointments by the president or removal by the president alone illegal. The security which you and I will have against the president is that the same power that is required to appoint shall be required to remove; that if the president can only appoint with the advice and consent of the Senate, he shall remove with the advice and consent of the Senate. If the president's power at this point were abridged to this extent the case would be helped materially.

Another source of evil in the one-man power is the veto power. I am in favor of abolishing the veto power completely. It has no business in our Constitution. It is alien to every idea of republican government—borrowed from the Old World, from king craft and priest craft, and all other adverse craft to republican government. It is anti-republican, anti-democratic, anti-common-sense. It is based upon the idea, the absurdity that one man is more than many men—that one man separate from the people by his exalted station—one man sitting apart from the people in his room, surrounded by his friends, his cliques, his satellites, will be likely to bring to the consideration of public measures, a higher wisdom, a larger knowledge, a purer patriotism, than will the representatives of the republic in the face and in the presence of the multitude with the flaming sword of the press waving over them, directly responsible to their constituents, immediately in communication with the great heart of the people—that one man will be likely to govern more wisely than will a majority of the people. It is borrowed from the Old World; it is alien to our institutions; it is opposed to the very genius of free institutions, and I want to see it struck out of our Constitution. I believe that two heads are better than one, and I shall not stultify myself by saying that one head, even though it be the head of Andrew Johnson, is more than almost two-thirds of the representatives of the American people. Is that republicanism? Is that democracy? Is that consistent with the idea that the people shall rule? I think not.

But it is said that we must have a check somewhere. We are great on checks. We must have some checks against these fanatical majorities, and we have recently been told that majorities can be as destructive and more arbitrary than individual despots, especially when the individuals are humble "Uriah

Heeps."[5] If this be so; if this is the truth, I think that we ought to part with republican government at once. If it is to be true that one man is likely to be wiser, or is likely to be wiser than the majority—that one man is likely to wield the government more entirely [in] the interest of the people than will a majority, if one man is a safer guide for the people than nearly two-thirds of the best representatives—if that be true, let us have a one-man government at once, let us have done with republicanism—let us try the experiment of the one man government. And I would advise you to begin with a legitimate scion of some of the great families of Europe. Let us take a genuine sprig of the article. We can easily get one—they are becoming very abundant in Europe I am told. There is one now, I think, one that is out of place, and you need not send across the Atlantic for him. He is driving about down here in Mexico. You might send for Maximilian, and have a one-man government alone. And we should have the veto legitimate.

I believe majorities can be despotic and have been arbitrary, but arbitrary to whom? Arbitrary when arbitrary at all, always to unrepresented classes. What is the remedy? A consistent republic in which there shall be no unrepresented classes. For when all classes are represented the rights of all classes will be respected. It is a remarkable fact, and we Americans may well ponder it, that although the veto is entirely consistent with monarchical government and entirely inconsistent with republican government, the government of England, which is a monarchy, has not exercised the veto power once in 150 years. There where it is consistent it is never used. Here where it is inconsistent, and at war with the genius of our institutions we can have a little veto every morning. Where the people rule they are the vetoed. When any measure passes the House of Commons or House of Lords, it is sure of the royal assent. Popular as Queen Victoria is, honored as she is queen, loved as she is a mother, as a good citizen of the realm, it would cost her crown to veto a measure passed by the people's representatives in the House of Commons and by the House of Lords. But here the people have got used to it, like the eels that got used to being skinned—so used to it that they feel no indignation at the arrogance and presumption that one man exhibits in opposing his judgment to the judgment of the people's representatives. You have got used to it. I see no indignation at all at this impertinence. We have become so listless and indifferent about the dignity of the people, that we can see it insulted with a veto every month.

Now, I have looked down on the House of Commons and the House of Lords, and I have listened to the eloquence of their noblest orators, Sir Robert Peel, Lord John Russell, Richard Cobden and John Bright[6]—a man whose name should never be mentioned in an American audience without moving

---

5. Uriah Heep is a fictional character in Charles Dickens' *David Copperfield*.
6. Douglass identifies a number of prominent British statesmen.

it. I have listened to Lord Brougham and to Lord Palmerston,[7] and I have also looked down on the Senate of the United States, and heard the debates there, and I am free to say, without wishing to disparage the English House of Parliament, in all the elements going to exalt and dignify a high deliberative assembly, our Senate compares favorably with the House of Lords. I think it the superior of the House of Lords and our House of Representatives fully the equal of the House of Commons in England. And if in a monarchy the representatives of the people can be trusted to govern themselves without the veto, Republican Americans can't you? Have done with that veto. It is a fruitful source of mischief, and bad bold men. A man of vigorous intellect, imperious will, fiery temper and boundless ambition finds in that veto a convenient instrument for the gratification of all his desires and his base ambition. Do away with it; blot it out from your government, and you will have done with the antagonism between the legislative arm and the executive arm of the government. Make your president what you ought to be, not more than he ought to be, and you should see to it that such changes should be made in the Constitution of the United States that your president is simply your executive, that he is there not to make laws, but to enforce them; not to defy your will, but to enforce your high behests.

Another thing I would do. I would abolish, if I had it in my power, the two-term principle. Away with that. While that principle remains in the Constitution while the president can be his own successor, and is eligible to succeed himself, he will not be warm in his seat in the presidential chair (such is poor human nature), before he will begin to scheme for a second election. It is a standing temptation to him to use the powers of his office in such a manner as to promote his own political fortune. The presidency is too valuable to allow man who occupies the position the means of perpetuating himself in that office. Another objection to this provision of the Constitution is, that we have a divided man in the presidential chair. The duties of the presidency are such as to require a whole man, the whole will, and the whole work; but the temptation of a president is to make himself a president of a presidential party as well as of the country, and the result is that we are only half served. What we want is the entire service of a man reduced to one term, and then he can bring to the service of his country an undivided man, an undivided sense of duty and devote his energies to the discharge of his office without selfish ends or aims. Blot out this two-term system.

Another thing I would abolish—the pardoning power. I should take that right out of the hands of this one man. The argument against it is in some respects similar to that used against the veto power. Those against the veto power are equally persistent against the pardoning power, and there is a good

---

7. Douglass identifies two more prominent British statesmen.

reason why we should do away with the pardoning power in the hands of the president, that is that our government may at some time be in the hands of a bad man. When in the hands of a good man it is all well enough, and we ought to have our government so shaped that even when in the hands of a bad man we shall be safe. And we know that the people are usually well intentioned. A certain percentage are thieves, a certain percentage are robbers, murderers, assassins, blind, insane and idiots. But the great mass of men are well intentioned, and we should watch the individual. Trust the masses always. That is good democracy, is it not? Not modern, but old-fashioned. But my argument is this: A bad president, for instance, has the power to do what? What can he not do? If he wanted to revolutionize this government, he could easily do it with this ponderous power; it would be an auxiliary power. He could cry "havoc, and let slip the dogs of war,"[8] and say to the conspirators: "I am with you. If you succeed, all is well. If you fail, I will interpose the shield of my pardon, and you are safe. If your property is taken away from you by Congress, I will pardon and restore your property. Go on and revolutionize the government; I will stand by you." The bad man will say or might say this. I am not sure but we have got a man now who comes very near saying it. Let us have done with this pardoning power. We have had enough of this. Pardoning! How inexpressibly base have been the uses made by this power—this beneficent power. It has been that with which a treacherous president has trafficked. He has made it the means of securing adherents to himself instead of securing allegiance to the government. Let us have done with closet pardons—pardons obtained by bad men—pardons obtained by questionable women—pardons obtained in the most disgraceful and scandalous manner. Drive this pardoning power out of the government and put it in the legislative arm of the government in some way. Let a committee of the House of Representatives and Senate of the United States determine who shall be the recipients of the clemency at the hands of the nation. Let it not come from an individual, but let it come from the people. An outraged people know to whom to extend this clemency.

Another thing I am in favor of. I am in favor of abolishing the office of the vice-president. Let us have no more vice-presidents. We have had bad luck with them. We don't need them. There is no more need of electing a vice-president at the same time we elect a president than there is need of electing a second wife when we have got one already. "Sufficient unto the day is the evil thereof."[9] The argument against the vice presidency is to me very conclusive. It may be briefly stated thus: The presidency of the United States, like the crown of a monarchy, is a tempting bauble. It is a very desirable thing. Men are men. Ambition is ambition the world over. History is constantly repeating

---

8. William Shakespeare, *Julius Caesar*, act 3, sc. 1.

9. Matthew 6:34 (all biblical references are from the King James version).

itself. There is not a single crown in Europe that has not at some time been stained with innocent blood—not one. For the crown, men have murdered their friends who have dined at the table with them; for the crown, men have sent the assassin to the cells of their own brothers and their own sisters, and plunged the dagger into their own warm, red blood. For the crown all manner of crimes have been committed. The presidency is equally a tempting bauble in this country. I am not for placing that temptation so near any man as it is placed when we elect a vice-president. I am not for electing a man to the presidential chair, and then putting a man behind him with his ambition all leading that way—with his desires, his thoughts, all directed upon that chair, with a knowledge, at the same time, that only the president's life stands between him and the object of his ambition. I am not for placing a man behind the president, within striking distance of him, whose interest, whose ambition, whose every inclination is to be sub-served by his getting that chair. The wall of assassination is too thin to be placed between a man and the presidency of the United States. Let your vice-president be, unknown to himself and unknown to the people. Let him be in the mass till there is need for him. Don't plump him right upon the president. Your president is unsafe while the shadow of the vice-president falls upon the presidential chair. How easy it would be to procure the death of any man where there are such temptations as that offered. A clique, a clan, a ring, usually forms about the vice-president.

How would you administer the government if you were president? Who would you send to the court of St. James? Who would you send to the court of France? Who would you appoint postmaster general? Who would you appoint collector of the port of New Orleans, or New York or of St. Louis? What would you do if you were president? "I would do so and so." "It suits us to a dot." The president dies, and in steps the vice-president. He is reminded at once of his old pledges, and he begins to try to redeem them by turning against the party who elected him. It is a remarkable fact that in no instance has any vice-president followed out the policy of the president that he was elected with. Elected on the same ticket, on the same platform, at the same time, at the instant the president is taken off the vice-president has reversed the machinery of the policy on which he was elected in every instance.

General [William Henry] Harrison[10] was the first man suspected of entertaining opinions unfavorable to slavery. He died in a month. He was succeeded by whom? By John Tyler[11]—one of the most violent propagandists of slavery

---

10. William Henry Harrison (1773–1841) was an American military officer and politician. Harrison was the ninth president of the United States, but he died soon after taking office.
11. John Tyler (1790–1862) was an American politician who became the tenth president of the United States upon the death of President William Henry Harrison in 1841.

that ever trod this continent. Where was the Whig Party that elected him? Nowhere. Where was the policy on which he was elected? Nowhere.

General [Zachary] Taylor,[12] though a slaveholding man and an honest man toward his constituents and the people of the country, the moment it was ascertained he was in favor of admitting California as a free state if she saw fit to come with a constitution of that character and was opposed to paying ten millions of dollars to Texas on account of the claim on New Mexico there were means at hand to kill him. He died and was followed by whom? By a vile sycophant who spit on the policy of his predecessor, and put himself in the service of the very men whom that president had offended. Well, they tried to murder even James Buchanan in order that he should be followed by a younger, stronger traitor than himself. They put Mr. Breckinridge behind him, and when he went down to Washington they carried him to the national hotel and helped him to a large dose of poison. But in that instance the poison met its match. Who doubts that James Buchanan was poisoned? It was notorious at the time, and no doubt poisoned for a purpose.

Today, today we mourn, the nation has to mourn, that the nation has a president, made president by the bullet of an assassin. I do not say that he knew that his noble predecessor was to be murdered. I do not say that he had any hand in it; but this I do say, without fear of contradiction, that the men who murdered Abraham Lincoln knew Andrew Johnson as we know him now. Let us have done with these vice-presidents. The nation can easily call a man to fill the presidential chair in case of death; besides, he is not half so likely to die. It is a little remarkable, too, that while presidents die, vice-presidents never die. There is nobody behind them.

Well I had marked a number of points I intended to dwell upon. I am taking up perhaps too much of your time, to go further with internal sources of danger to the republic. I had purposed to have spoken specially of secret diplomacy, but I pass it over as one of the sources of weakness to our republican form of government. I may be told that in pointing out these sources of weakness that it is easy to find fault but not so easy to find remedies. I admit it, I agree with Robert Hale[13] that it requires more talent to build a decent pig stye [*sic*] than to tear down a considerable palace, and yet when the ship is to be repaired, it is of some consequence to find out where the unsound timbers are, when the opening seam is where the corroded bolt is, that we put in sounder, and I have been indicating where these points of unsoundness are. And I think I can leave this matter of reconstruction to the high constructive

---

12. Zachary Taylor (1784–1850) was an American military officer and politician. He was the twelfth president of the United States.
13. Robert Hale (1822–1881) was an American politician who served in the House of Representatives.

talent of this Anglo-Saxon race. The Negro has done his part if he succeeds in pointing out the source of danger to the republic. You will have done your part when you have corrected or removed these sources of danger. We have already grappled with very dangerous elements in our government, and we have performed a manly part, we have removed errors, but there are some errors to be removed, not so dangerous, not so shocking, perhaps, as those with which we have grappled; but nevertheless dangers requiring removal. Happy will it be for us, happy will it be for the land, happy for coming generations, if we shall discover these sources of danger, and grapple with them in time without the aid of a second rebellion—without the people being lashed and stung into another military necessity.

It is sad to think that half the glory, half the honor due to the great act of emancipation was lost in the tardiness of its performance. It has now gone irrevocably into history—not as an act of sacred choice by a great nation, of the right as against the wrong, of truth as against falsehood, of liberty as against slavery—but as a military necessity. We are called upon to be faithful to the American government, for our emancipation as black men. We do feel thankful, and we have the same reason to be thankful that the Israelites had to be thankful to Pharaoh for their emancipation, for their liberties. It was not until judgments terrible, wide-sweeping, far reaching and overwhelming, had smitten down this nation, that we were ready to part with our reverence for slavery, and ceased to quote Scripture in its defense. It was not until we felt the land trembling beneath our feet that we heard an accusing voice in the heart; the sky above was darkened, the wail came up from millions of hearth stones in our land. Our sons and brothers slain in battle, it was not until we saw our sons and brothers returning home mere stumps of men, armless, legless, it was not until we felt all crumbling beneath us and we saw the Star Spangled Banner clinging to the masthead heavy with blood.

It was not until agony was manifested from a million of hearthstones in our land, and the Southern sky was darkened, that we managed to part with our reverence for slavery, and to place a musket on the shoulders of the black man. We may now do from choice and from sacred choice what we did by military necessity.

29. "Our Composite Nationality," a speech delivered on December 7, 1869 in Boston, Massachusetts and published in *Boston Daily Advertiser*, December 8, 1869[14]

As nations are among the largest and the most complete divisions into which society is formed, the grandest aggregations of organized human power; as they raise to observation and distinction the world's greatest men, and call into requisition the highest order of talent and ability for their guidance, preservation and success, they are ever among the most attractive, instructive and useful subjects of thought, to those just entering upon the duties and activities of life.

The simple organization of a people into a national body, composite or otherwise, is of itself an impressive fact. As an original proceeding, it marks the point of departure of a people, from the darkness and chaos of unbridled barbarism, to the wholesome restraints of public law and society. It implies a willing surrender and subjection of individual aims and ends, often narrow and selfish, to the broader and better ones that arise out of society as a whole. It is both a sign and a result of civilization.

A knowledge of the character, resources and proceedings of other nations, affords us the means of comparison and criticism, without which progress would be feeble, tardy, and perhaps, impossible. It is by comparing one nation with another, and one learning from another, each competing with all, and all competing with each, that hurtful errors are exposed, great social truths discovered, and the wheels of civilization whirled onward.

I am especially to speak to you of the character and mission of the United States, with special reference to the question whether we are the better or the worse for being composed of different races of men. I propose to consider first, what we are, second, what we are likely to be, and, thirdly, what we ought to be.

---

14. During the course of the nineteenth century, there was an influx of immigrants to the United States from all over the globe. Some Americans reacted harshly to these new arrivals. During the time of this speech, the major source of nativist hostility was emerging in response to Chinese immigrants. In this speech, Douglass develops a sharp rebuke of nativism. One note should be made about the source of the speech. Although the version of this speech most commonly cited is this delivery in 1869, the best existing transcript of the speech is dated 1867 by Douglass, indicating that he may have written the speech (and possibly delivered it) prior to this 1869 delivery.

Without undue vanity or unjust depreciation of others, we may claim to be, in many respects, the most fortunate of nations. We stand in relations to all others, as youth to age. Other nations have had their day of greatness and glory; we are yet to have our day, and that day is coming. The dawn is already upon us. It is bright and full of promise. Other nations have reached their culminating point. We are at the beginning of our ascent. They have apparently exhausted the conditions essential to their further growth and extension, while we are abundant in all the material essential to further national growth and greatness.

The resources of European statesmanship are now sorely taxed to maintain their nationalities at their ancient height of greatness and power.

American statesmanship, worthy of the name, is now taxing its energies to frame measures to meet the demands of constantly increasing expansion of power, responsibility and duty.

Without fault or merit on either side, theirs or ours, the balance is largely in our favor. Like the grand old forests, renewed and enriched from decaying trunks once full of life and beauty, but now moss-covered, oozy and crumbling, we are destined to grow and flourish while they decline and fade.

This is one view of American position and destiny. It is proper to notice that it is not the only view. Different opinions and conflicting judgments meet us here, as elsewhere.

It is thought by many, and said by some, that this republic has already seen its best days; that the historian may now write the story of its decline and fall.

Two classes of men are just now especially afflicted with such forebodings. The first are those who are croakers by nature; the men who have a taste for funerals, and especially national funerals. They never see the bright side of anything, and probably never will. Like the raven in the lines of Edgar A. Poe,[15] they have learned two words, and those are, "never more." They usually begin by telling us what we never shall see. Their little speeches are about as follows: You will *never* see such statesmen in the councils of the nations as Clay, Calhoun and Webster. You will *never* see the South morally reconstructed and our once happy people again united. You will *never* see this government harmonious and successful while in the hands of different races. You will *never* make the Negro work without a master, or make him an intelligent voter, or a good and useful citizen. This last *never* is generally the parent of all the other little nevers that follow.

During the late contest for the Union, the air was full of nevers, every one of which was contradicted and put to shame by the result, and I doubt not that most of those we now hear in our troubled air will meet the same fate.

---

15. Edgar Allan Poe (1809–1849) was an American author.

It is probably well for us that some of our gloomy prophets are limited in their powers to prediction. Could they commend [*sic*] the destructive bolt, as readily as they commend the destructive word, it is hard to say what might happen to the country. They might fulfill their own gloomy prophecies. Of course it is easy to see why certain other classes of men speak hopelessly concerning us.

A government founded upon justice, and recognizing the equal rights of all men; claiming no higher authority for its existence, or sanction for its laws, than nature, reason and the regularly ascertained will of the people; steadily refusing to put its sword and purse in the service of any religious creed or family, is a standing offense to most of the governments of the world, and to some narrow and bigoted people among ourselves.

To those who doubt and deny the preponderance of good over evil in human nature; who think the few are made to rule, and the many to *serve*; who put rank above brotherhood, and race above humanity; who attach more importance to ancient forms than to the living realities of the present; who worship power in whatever hands it may be lodged and by whatever means it may have been obtained; our government is a mountain of sin, and, what is worse, it seems confirmed in its transgressions.

One of the latest and most potent European prophets, one who felt himself called upon for a special deliverance concerning us and our destiny as a nation, was the late Thomas Carlyle.[16] He described us as rushing to ruin, and when we may expect to reach the terrible end, our gloomy prophet, enveloped in the fogs of London, has not been pleased to tell us.

Warning and advice from any quarter are not to be despised, and especially not from one so eminent as Mr. Carlyle; and yet Americans will find it hard to heed even men like him, while the animus is so apparent, bitter and perverse.

A man to whom despotism is the savior and liberty the destroyer of society, who, during the last twenty years, in every contest between liberty and oppression, uniformly and promptly took sides with the oppressor; who regarded every extension of the right of suffrage, even to white men in his own country, as shooting Niagara; who gloated over deeds of cruelty, and talked of applying to the backs of men the beneficent whip, to the great delight of many of the slaveholders of America in particular, could have but little sympathy with our emancipated and progressive republic, or with the triumph of liberty anywhere.

But the American people can easily stand the utterances of such a man. They however have a right to be impatient and indignant at those among ourselves who turn the most hopeful portents into omens of disaster, and make themselves the ministers of despair, when they should be those of hope, and

---

16. Thomas Carlyle (1795–1881) was a Scottish writer.

help cheer on the country in the new grand career of justice upon which it has now so nobly and bravely entered.

Of errors and defects we certainly have not less than our full share, enough to keep the reformer awake, the statesman busy, and the country in a pretty lively state of agitation for some time to come.

Perfection is an object to be aimed at by all, but it is not an attribute of any form of government. Mutability is the law for all. Something different, something better, or something worse may come, but so far as respects our present system and form of government, and the altitude we occupy, we need not shrink from comparison with any nation of our times. We are today the best fed, the best clothed, the best sheltered and the best instructed people in the world.

There was a time when even brave men might look fearfully upon the destiny of the republic; when our country was involved in a tangled network of contradictions; when vast and irreconcilable social forces fiercely disputed for ascendency and control; when a heavy curse rested upon our very soil, defying alike the wisdom and the virtue of the people to remove it; when our professions were loudly mocked by our practice, and our name was a reproach and a byword to a mocking; when our good ship of state, freighted with the best hopes of the oppressed of all nations, was furiously hurled against the hard and flinty rocks of derision, and every cord, bolt, beam and bend in her body quivered beneath the shock, there was some apology for doubt and despair. But that day has happily passed away. The storm has been weathered, and the portents are nearly all in our favor.

There are clouds, wind, smoke and dust and noise, over head and around, and there always will be; but no genuine thunder, with destructive bolt, menaces from any quarter of the sky.

The real trouble with us was never our system or form of government, or the principles underlying it, but the peculiar composition of our people; the relations existing between them and the compromising spirit which controlled the ruling power of the country.

We have for a long time hesitated to adopt and carry out the only principle which can solve that difficulty and give peace, strength and security to the republic, *and that is* the principle of absolute *equality*.

We are a country of all extremes, ends and opposites; the most conspicuous example of composite nationality in the world. Our people defy all the ethnological and logical classifications. In races we range all the way from black to white, with intermediate shades which, as in the apocalyptic vision, no man can name or number.

In regard to creeds and faiths, the condition is no better, and no worse. Differences both as to race and to religion are evidently more likely to increase than to diminish.

We stand between the populous shores of two great oceans. Our land is capable of supporting one-fifth of all the globe. Here, labor is abundant and better remunerated than anywhere else. All moral, social and geographical causes conspire to bring to us the peoples of all other over populated countries.

Europe and Africa are already here, and the Indian was here before either. He stands today between the two extremes of black and white, too proud to claim fraternity with either, and yet too weak to withstand the power of either. Heretofore, the policy of our government has been governed by race pride, rather than by wisdom.

Until recently, neither the Indian nor the Negro has been treated as a part of the body politic. No attempt has been made to inspire either with a sentiment of patriotism, but the hearts of both races have been diligently sown with the dangerous seeds of discontent and hatred.

The policy of keeping the Indians to themselves, has kept the tomahawk and scalping knife busy upon our borders, and has cost us largely in blood and treasure.

Our treatment of the Negro has lacked humanity and filled the country with agitation and ill-feeling, and brought the nation to the verge of ruin.

Before the relations of those two races are satisfactorily settled, and in spite of all opposition, a new race is making its appearance within our borders, and claiming attention.

It is estimated that not less than one hundred thousand Chinamen are now within the limits of the United States. Several years ago every vessel, large or small, of steam or of sail, bound to our Pacific coast and hailing from the flowery kingdom, added to the number and strength of this new element of our population.

Men differ widely as to the magnitude of this potential Chinese immigration. The fact that by the late treaty with China we bind ourselves to receive immigrants from that country only as the subjects of the emperor, and by the construction at least are bound not to naturalize them, and the further fact that Chinamen themselves have a superstitious devotion to their country and an aversion to permanent location in any other, contracting even to have their bones carried back, should they die abroad, and from the fact that many have returned to China, and the still more stubborn fact that resistance to their coming has increased rather than diminished, it is inferred that we shall never have a large Chinese population in America. This, however, is not my opinion.

It may be admitted that these reasons, and others, may check and moderate the tide of immigration; but it is absurd to think that they will do more than this. Counting their number now by the thousands, the time is not remote when they will count them by the millions. The emperor'[s] hold upon the Chinamen may be strong, but the Chinaman's hold upon himself is stronger.

Treaties against naturalization, like all other treaties, are limited by circumstances. As to the superstitious attachment of the Chinese to China, that, like all other superstitions, will dissolve in the light and heat of truth and experience. The Chinaman may be a bigot, but it does not follow that he will continue to be one tomorrow. He is a man, and will be very likely to act like a man. He will not be long in finding out that a country that is good enough to live in is good enough to die in, and that a soil that was good enough to hold his body while alive, will be good enough to hold his bones when he is dead.

Those who doubt a large immigration should remember that the past furnishes no criterion as a basis of calculation. We live under new and improved conditions of migration, and these conditions are constantly improving.

America is no longer an obscure and inaccessible country. Our ships are in every sea, our commerce is in every port, our language is heard all around the globe, steam and lightning have revolutionized the whole domain of human thought, changed all geographical relations, make a day of the present seem equal to a thousand years of the past, and the continent that Columbus only conjectured four centuries ago is now the center of the world.

I believe Chinese immigration on a large scale will yet be an irrepressible fact. The spirit of race pride will not always prevail.

The reasons for this opinion are obvious; China is a vastly overcrowded country. Her people press against each other like cattle in a rail car. Many live upon the water and have laid out streets upon the waves.

Men, like bees, want room. When the hive is overflowing, the bees will swarm, and will be likely to take up their abode where they find the best prospect for honey. In matters of this sort, men are very much like bees. Hunger will not be quietly endured, even in the Celestial Empire, when it is once generally known that there is bread enough and to spare in America. What Satan said of Job[17] is true of the Chinaman, as well as of other men, "All that a man hath will he give for his life." They will come here to live, where they know the means of living are in abundance.

The same mighty forces which have swept to our shores the overflowing population of Europe; which have reduced the people of Ireland three millions below its normal standard; will operate in a similar manner upon the hungry population of China and other parts of Asia. Home has its charms, and native land has its charms, but hunger, oppression and destitution will dissolve these charms and send men in search of new countries and new homes.

Not only is there a Chinese motive behind this probable immigration, but there is also an American motive which will play its part, and which will be all the more active and energetic because there is in it an element of pride, of bitterness and revenge.

---

17. Job 2:4.

Southern gentlemen who led in the late rebellion have not parted with their convictions at this point, any more than at any other. They want to be independent of the Negro. They believed in slavery and they believe in it still. They believed in an aristocratic class, and they believe in it still, and though they have lost slavery, one element essential to such a class, they still have two important conditions to the reconstruction of that class. They have intelligence, and they have land. Of these, the land is the more important. They cling to it with all the tenacity of a cherished superstition. They will neither sell to the Negro, nor let the carpet-bagger[18] have it in peace, but are determined to hold it for themselves and their children forever.

They have not yet learned that when a principle is gone, the incident must go also; that what was wise and proper under slavery is foolish and mischievous in a state of general liberty; that the old bottles are worthless when the new wine has come; but they have found that land is a doubtful benefit, where there are no hands to till it.

Hence these gentlemen have turned their attention to the Celestial Empire. They would rather have laborers who would work for nothing; but as they cannot get the Negro on these terms, they want Chinamen, who, they hope, will work for next to nothing.

Companies and associations may yet be formed to promote this Mongolian invasion. The loss of the Negro is to gain them the Chinese, and if the thing works well, abolition, in their opinion, will have proved itself to be another blessing in disguise. To the statesman it will mean Southern independence. To the pulpit, it will be the hand of Providence, and bring about the time of the universal dominion of the Christian religion. To all but the Chinaman and the Negro it will mean wealth, ease and luxury.

But alas, for all the selfish invention and dreams of men! The Chinaman will not long be willing to wear the cast off shoes of the Negro, and, if he refuses, there will be trouble again. The Negro worked and took his pay in religion and the lash. The Chinaman is a different article and will want the cash. He may, like the Negro, accept Christianity, but, unlike the Negro, he will not care to pay for it in labor. He had the Golden Rule in substance five hundred years before the coming of Christ, and has notions of justice that are not to be confused by any of our *"Cursed be Canaan"* religion.

Nevertheless, the experiment will be tried. So far as getting the Chinese into our country is concerned, it will yet be a success. This elephant will be drawn by our Southern brethren, though they will hardly know in the end what to do with him.

Appreciation of the value of Chinamen as laborers will, I apprehend, become general in this country. The North was never indifferent to the Southern influence and example, and it will not be so in this instance.

---

18. This term was used to describe Northerners who migrated to the South after the Civil War.

The Chinese in themselves have first rate recommendations. They are industrious, docile, cleanly, frugal; they are dexterous of hand, patient in toil, marvelously gifted in the power of imitation, and have but few wants. Those who have carefully observed their habits in California say that they subsist upon what would be almost starvation to others.

The conclusion of the whole will be that they will want to come to us, and, as we become more liberal, we shall want them to come, and what we want done will naturally be done.

They will no longer halt upon the shores of California. They will burrow no longer in her exhausted and deserted gold mines, where they have gathered wealth from barrenness, taking what others left. They will turn their backs not only upon the Celestial Empire but upon the golden shores of the Pacific, and the wide waste of waters whose majestic waves spoke to them of home and country. They will withdraw their eyes from the glowing West and fix them upon the rising sun. They will cross the mountains, cross the plains, descend our rivers, penetrate to the heart of the country and fix their home with us forever.

Assuming then that immigration already has a foothold and will combine for many years to come, we have a new element in our national composition which is likely to exercise a large influence upon the thought and the action of the whole nation.

The old question as to what shall be done with the Negro will have to give place to the greater question "What shall be done with the Mongolian," and perhaps we shall see raised one still greater, namely, "What will the Mongolian do with both the Negro and the white?"

Already has the matter taken shape in California and on the Pacific coast generally. Already has California assumed a bitterly unfriendly attitude toward the Chinaman. Already has she driven them from her altars of justice. Already has she stamped them as outcasts and handed them over to popular contempts and vulgar jest. Already are they the constant victims of cruel harshness and brutal violence. Already have our Celtic brothers, never slow to execute the behests of popular prejudice against the weak and defenseless, recognized in the heads of these people, fit targets for their shilalahs [*sic*]. Already, too, are their associations formed in avowed hostility to the Chinese.

In all this there is, of course, nothing strange. Repugnance to the presence and influence of foreigners is an ancient feeling among men. It is peculiar to no particular race or nation. It is met with, not only in the conduct of one nation toward another, but in the conduct of the inhabitants of the different parts of the same country, some times of the same city, and even of the same village. "Lands intersected by a narrow frith abhor each other. Mountains interposed, make enemies of nations." To the Greek, every man not speaking Greek is a barbarian. To the Jew, every one not circumcised is a gentile. To the Mohametan, every one not believing in the prophet is a kaffer.

I need not repeat here the multitude of reproachful epithets expressive of the same sentiment among ourselves. All who are not to the manor born have been made to feel the lash and sting of these reproachful names.

For this feeling there are many apologies, for there was never yet an error, however flagrant and hurtful, for which some plausible defense could not be framed. Chattel slavery, king craft, priest craft, pious frauds, intolerance, persecution, suicide, assassination, repudiation, and a thousand other errors and crimes have all had their defenses and apologies.

Prejudice of race and color has been equally upheld.

The two best arguments in the defense are, first, the worthlessness of the class against which it is directed; and, second, that the feeling itself is entirely natural.

The way to overcome the first argument is to work for the elevation of those deemed worthless, and thus make them worthy of regard, and they will soon become worthy and not worthless. As to the natural argument, it may be said that nature has many sides. Many things are in a certain sense natural, which are neither wise nor best. It is natural to walk, but shall men therefore refuse to ride? It is natural to ride on horseback, shall men therefore refuse stream and rail? Civilization is itself a constant war upon some forces in nature, shall we therefore abandon civilization and go back to savage life?

Nature has two voices, the one high, the other low; one is in sweet accord with reason and justice, and the other apparently at war with both. The more men know of the essential nature of things, and of the true relation of mankind, the freer they are from prejudice of every kind. The child is afraid of the giant form of his own shadow. This is natural, but he will part with his fears when he is older and wiser. So ignorance is full of prejudice, but it will disappear with enlightenment. But I pass on.

I have said that the Chinese will come, and have given some reasons why we may expect them in very large numbers in no very distant future. Do you ask if I would favor such immigrations? I answer, *I would*. Would you admit them as witnesses in our courts of law? *I would*. Would you have them naturalized, and have them invested with all the rights of American citizenship? *I would*. Would you allow them to vote? *I would*. Would you allow them to hold office? *I would*.

But are there not reasons against all this? Is there not such a law or principle as that of self-preservation? Does not every race owe something to itself? Should it not attend to the dictates of common sense? Should not a superior race protect itself from contact with inferior ones? Are not the white people the owners of this continent? Have they not the right to say what kind of people shall be allowed to come here and settle? Is there not such a thing as being more generous than wise? In the effort to promote civilization may we not corrupt and destroy what we have? Is it best to take on board more passengers than the ship will carry?

To all this and more I have one among many answers, altogether satisfactory to me, though I cannot promise it will be entirely so to you.

I submit that this question of Chinese immigration should be settled upon higher principles than those of a cold and selfish expediency. There are such things in the world as human rights. They rest upon no conventional foundation, but are eternal, universal and indestructible.

Among these is the right of locomotion; the right of migration; the right which belongs to no particular race, but belongs alike to all and to all alike. It is the right you assert by staying here, and your fathers asserted by coming here. It is this great right that I assert for the Chinese and the Japanese, and for all other varieties of men equally with yourselves, now and forever. I know of no rights of race superior to the rights of humanity, and when there is a supposed conflict between human and national rights, it is safe to go to the side of humanity. I have great respect for the blue-eyed and light-haired races of America. They are a mighty people. In any struggle for the good things of this world, they need have no fear, they have no need to doubt that they will get their full share.

But I reject the arrogant and scornful theory by which they would limit migratory rights, or any other essential human rights, to themselves, and which would make them the owners of this great continent to the exclusion of all other races of men.

I want a home here not only for the Negro, the mulatto and the Latin races, but I want the Asiatic to find a home here in the United States, and feel at home here, both for his sake and for ours. Right wrongs no man. If respect is had to majorities, the fact that only one-fifth of the population of the globe is white and the other four-fifths are colored, ought to have some weight and influence in disposing of this and similar questions. It would be a sad reflection upon the laws of nature and upon the idea of justice, to say nothing of a common Creator, if four-fifths of mankind were deprived of the rights of migration to make room for the one-fifth. If the white race may exclude all other races from this continent, it may rightfully do the same in respect to all other lands, islands, capes and continents, and thus have all the world to itself, and thus what would seem to belong to the whole would become the property of only a part. So much for what is right, now let us see what is wise.

And here I hold that a liberal and brotherly welcome to all who are likely to come to the United States is the only wise policy which this nation can adopt.

It has been thoughtfully observed that every nation, owing to its peculiar character and composition, has a definite mission in the world. What that mission is, and what policy is best adapted to assist in its fulfillment, is the business of its people and its statesmen to know, and knowing, to make a noble use of this knowledge.

I need not stop here to name or describe the missions of other or more ancient nationalities. Ours seems plain and unmistakable. Our geographical position, our relation to the outside world, our fundamental principles of government, world-embracing in their scope and character, our vast resources, requiring all manner of labor to develop them, and our already existing composite population, all conspire to one grand end, and that is, to make us the perfect national illustration of the unity and dignity of the human family that the world has ever seen.

In whatever else other nations may have been great and grand, our greatness and grandeur will be found in the faithful application of the principle of perfect civil equality to the people of all races and of all creeds. We are not only bound to this position by our organic structure and by our revolutionary antecedents, but by the genius of our people. Gathered here from all quarters of the globe, by a common aspiration for national liberty as against caste, divine right govern and privileged classes, it would be unwise to be found fighting against ourselves and among ourselves, it would be unadvised to attempt to set up any one race above another, or one religion above another, or prescribe any on account of race, color or creed.

The apprehension that we shall be swamped or swallowed up by Mongolian civilization; that the Caucasian race may not be able to hold their own against that vast incoming population, does not seem entitled to much respect. Though they come as the waves come, we shall be all the stronger if we receive them as friends and give them a reason for loving our country and our institutions. They will find here a deeply rooted, indigenous, growing civilization, augmented by an ever-increasing stream of immigration from Europe, and possession is nine points of the law in this case, as well as in others. They will come as strangers. We are at home. They will come to us, not we to them. They will come in their weakness, we shall meet them in our strength. They will come as individuals, we will meet them in multitudes, and with all the advantages of organization. Chinese children are in American schools in San Francisco. None of our children are in Chinese schools, and probably never will be, though in some things they might well teach us valuable lessons. Contact with these yellow children of the Celestial Empire would convince us that the points of human difference, great as they, upon first sight, seem, are as nothing compared with the points of human agreement. Such contact would remove mountains of prejudice.

It is said that it is not good for man to be alone.[19] This is true, not only in the sense in which our women's rights friends so zealously and wisely teach, but it is true as to nations.

---

19. Genesis 2:18.

The voice of civilization speaks an unmistakable language against the isolation of families, nations and races, and pleads for composite nationality as essential to her triumphs.

Those races of men who have maintained the most distinct and separate existence for the longest periods of time; which have had the least intercourse with other races of men are standing confirmation of the folly of isolation. The very soil of the national mind becomes in such cases barren, and can only be resuscitated by assistance from without.

Look at England, whose mighty power is now felt, and for centuries has been felt, all around the world. It is worthy of special remark, that precisely those parts of that proud island which have received the largest and most diversified .populations, are to day the parts most distinguished for industry, enterprise, invention and general enlightenment. In Wales, and in the Highlands of Scotland the boast is made of their pure blood, and that they were never conquered, but no man can contemplate them without wishing they had been conquered. They are far in the rear of every other part of the English realm in all the comforts and conveniences of life, as well as in mental and physical development. Neither law nor learning descends to us from the mountains of Wales or from the Highlands of Scotland. The ancient Briton, whom Julius Caesar[20] would not have as a slave, is not to be compared with the round, burly, amplitudinous [*sic*] Englishman in many of his qualities of desirable manhood.

The theory that each race of men has some special faculty, some peculiar gift or quality of mind or heart, needed to the perfection and happiness of the whole is a broad and beneficent theory, and, besides its beneficence, has, in its support, the voice of experience. Nobody doubts this theory when applied to animals or plants, and no one can show that it is not equally true when applied to races.

All great qualities are never found in any one man or in any one race. The whole of humanity, like the whole of everything else, is ever greater than a part. Men only know themselves by knowing others, and contact is essential to this knowledge. In one race we perceive the predominance of imagination; in another, like the Chinese, we remark its almost total absence. In one people we have the reasoning faculty; in another the genius for music; in another exists courage, in another great physical vigor, and so on through the whole list of human qualities. All are needed to temper, modify, round and complete the whole man and the whole nation.

Not the least among the arguments whose consideration should dispose us to welcome among us the peoples of all countries, nationalities and colors, is the fact that all races and varieties of men are improvable. This is the grand distinguishing attribute of humanity, and separates man from all other animals.

---

20. Julius Caesar (100–44 BC) was a Roman political leader and writer.

If it could be shown that any particular race of men are literally incapable of improvement, we might hesitate to welcome them here. But no such men are any where to be found, and if they were, it is not likely that they would ever trouble us with their presence. The fact that the Chinese and other nations desire to come and do come is a proof of their capacity for improvement and of their fitness to come.

We should take counsel of both nature and art in the consideration of this question. When the architect intends a grand structure, he makes the foundation broad and strong. We should imitate this prudence in laying the foundations of the future republic. There is a law of harmony in all departments of nature. The oak is in the acorn. The career and destiny of individual men are enfolded in the elements of which they are composed. The same is true of a nation. It will be something or it will be nothing. It will be great, or it will be small, according to its own essential qualities. As these are rich and varied, or pure and simple, slender and feeble, broad and strong, so will be the life and destiny of the nation itself. The stream cannot rise higher than its source. The ship cannot sail faster than the wind. The flight of the arrow depends upon the strength and elasticity of the bow, and as with these, so with a nation.

If we would reach a degree of civilization higher and grander than any yet attained, we should welcome to our ample continent all the nations, kindreds, tongues and peoples, and as fast as they learn our language and comprehend the duties of citizenship, we should incorporate them into the American body politic. The outspread wings of the American eagle are broad enough to shelter all who are likely to come.

As a matter of selfish policy, leaving right and humanity out of the question, we cannot wisely pursue any other course. Other governments mainly depend for security upon the sword; ours depends mainly upon the friendship of the people. In all matters, in time of peace, in time of war, and at all times, it makes its appeal to the people, and to all classes of the people. Its strength lies in their friendship and cheerful support in every time of need, and that policy is a mad one which would reduce the number of its friends by excluding those who would come, or by alienating those who are already here.

Our republic is itself a strong argument in favor of composite nationality. It is no disparagement to the Americans of English descent to affirm that much of the wealth, leisure, culture, refinement and civilization of the country are due to the arm of the Negro and the muscle of the Irishman. Without these, and the wealth created by their sturdy toil, English civilization had still lingered this side of the Alleghenies, and the wolf still be howling on their summits.

To no class of our population are we more indebted for valuable qualities of head, heart, and hand, than to the German. Say what we will of their lager, their smoke, and their metaphysics, they have brought to us a fresh, vigorous and child-like nature; a boundless facility in the acquisition of knowledge; a subtle and far-reaching intellect, and a fearless love of truth. Though remarkable for patient and laborious thought, the true German is a joyous child of freedom, fond of manly sports, a lover of music, and a happy man generally. Though he never forgets that he is a German, he never fails to remember that he is an American.

A Frenchman comes here to make money, and that is about all that need be said of him. He is only a Frenchman. He neither learns our language nor loves our country. His hand is on our pocket and his eye on Paris. He gets what he wants and, like a sensible Frenchman, returns to France to spend it.

Now let us answer briefly some objections to the general scope of my arguments. I am [told] that science is against me; that races are not all of the same origin and that the unity theory of human origin has been exploded. I admit that this is a question that has two sides. It is impossible to trace the threads of human history sufficiently near their starting point to know much about the origin of races.

In disposing of this question whether we shall welcome or repel immigration from China, Japan, or elsewhere, we may leave the differences among the theological doctors to be settled by themselves.

Whether man originated at one time and one place; whether there was one Adam or five, or five hundred, does not affect the question.

The great right of migration and the great wisdom of incorporating foreign elements into our body politic, are founded not upon any genealogical or ethnological theory, however learned, but upon the broad fact of a common nature.

Man is man the world over. This fact is affirmed and admitted in any effort to deny it. The sentiments we exhibit, whether love or hate, confidence or fear, respect or contempt, will always imply a like humanity. A smile or a tear has no nationality. Joy and sorrow speak alike in all nations, and they above all the confusion of tongues proclaim the brotherhood of man.

It is objected to the Chinaman that he is secretive and treacherous, and will not tell the truth when he thinks it for his interest to tell a lie. There may be truth in all this; it sounds very much like the account of man's heart given in the creeds. If he will not tell the truth, except when it is for his interest to do so, let us make it for his interest to tell the truth. We can do it by applying to him the same principle of justice that we apply to ourselves.

But I doubt if the Chinese are more untruthful than other people. At this point I have one certain test. —Mankind are not held together by lies. Trust is the foundation of society. Where there is no truth, there can be no trust, and where there is no trust, there can be no society. Where there is society, there is trust, and where there is trust, there is something upon which it is supported. Now a people who have confided in each other for five thousand years; who have extended their empire in all directions until it embraces one-fifth of the population of the globe; who hold important commercial relations with all nations; who are now entering into treaty stipulations with ourselves, and with all the great European powers, cannot be a nation of cheats and liars, but must have some respect for veracity. The very existence of China for so long a period, and her progress in civilization, are proofs of her truthfulness. This is the last objection which should come from those who profess the all-conquering power of the Christian religion. If that religion cannot stand contact with the Chinese, religion or no religion, so much the worse for those who have adopted it. It is the Chinaman, not the Christian, who should be alarmed for his faith. He exposes that faith to great dangers by exposing it to the freer air of America. But shall we send missionaries to the heathen and yet deny the heathen the right to come to us? I think a few honest believers in the teachings of Confucius would be well employed in expounding his doctrines among us.

The next objection to the Chinese is that he cannot be induced to swear by the Bible. This is to me one of his best recommendations. The American people will swear by any thing in the heaven above or the earth beneath. We are a nation of swearers. We swear by a book whose most authoritative command is to swear not at all.

It is not of so much importance what a man swears by, as what he swears to, and if the Chinaman is so true to his convictions that he cannot be tempted or even coerced into so popular a custom as swearing by the Bible, he gives good evidence of his integrity and of his veracity.

Let the Chinaman come; he will help to augment the national wealth; he will help to develop our boundless resources; he will help to pay off our national debt; he will help to lighten the burden of our national taxation; he will give us the benefit of his skill as manufacturer and as a tiller of the soil, in which he is unsurpassed.

Even the matter of religious liberty, which has cost the world more tears, more blood and more agony, than any other interest, will be helped by his presence. I know of no church, however tolerant; of no priesthood, however enlightened, which could be safely trusted with the tremendous power which universal conformity would confer. We should welcome all men of every shade of religious opinion, as among the best means of checking the arrogance and intolerance which are the almost inevitable concomitants of general conformity. Religious liberty always flourishes best amid the clash of competition of rival religious creeds.

To the mind of superficial men the future of different races has already brought disaster and ruin upon the country. The poor Negro has been charged with all our woes. In the haste of these men they forget that our trouble was not ethnological, but moral, that it was not difference of complexion, but difference of conviction. It was not the Ethiopian as a man, but the Ethiopian as a slave and a coveted article of merchandise, that gave us trouble.

I close these remarks as I began. If our action shall be in accordance with the principles of justice, liberty, and perfect human equality, no eloquence can adequately portray the greatness and grandeur of the future of the republic.

We shall spread the network of our science and our civilization over all who seek their shelter, whether from Asia, Africa, or the isles of the sea. We shall mold them all, each after his kind, into Americans; Indian and Celt, Negro and Saxon, Latin and Teuton, Mongolian and Caucasian, Jew and gentile, all shall here bow to the same law, speak the same language, support the same government, enjoy the same liberty, vibrate with the same national enthusiasm, and seek the same national ends.

30. "Politics an Evil to the Negro," an essay published in *The New National Era*, August 24, 1871[21]

It is often alleged of late, and sometimes by those who are by no means unfriendly in their feelings toward the Negro, that he takes an interest in politics, far more lively and active, than is consistent with his welfare; that his interests would be more wisely consulted if he would consent to leave the direction of public affairs, and especially the holding of office, entirely to the white race—since the latter have the wealth, the experience, and the leisure, which a faithful discharge of public duties require for their proper performance. There may be something in this idea—and precisely what that something is, it may be well enough for colored men to know and consider, and guide their conduct accordingly. That the pursuit of politics is an evil to men generally, without distinction of race or color, is an old doctrine has long been the law and the practice. The common people are not supposed to be qualified for public affairs, and in some countries are not allowed to engage in public political discussion. The crowned heads and privileged classes in the Old World take political affairs under their exclusive jurisdiction—and such men as Mr. THOMAS CARLYLE magnify the wisdom of this arrangement. The common people are diverted with shows and amusements, and leave the weighty matter of government to the noble and great. Without referring to the revolutions which have from time to time occurred in the countries thus governed, or to the scenes of horror recently enacted in the streets of the splendid metropolis of France, and surveying only the general social condition of the peoples of Europe, we shall find but little in the results of the arrangement in question to strengthen our confidence or kindle our admiration. The standing objection to American institutions, and to free institutions generally, is that they tend to retard industry and endanger public order and safety by drawing the laboring classes away from quiet and useful occupations to mingle in the whirl and excitement of political agitations, where their passions are enflamed and their respect for the majesty of law is undermined. According to the views of these old time people, the policy of government, like war once in Rome, is considered the work of gentlemen, and not the work of the laboring classes. Thus, it will be seen that the substantial ground of objection to the active participation of colored men in American politics has ancient authority and example for its

---

21. Some political leaders opposed to granting freed slaves equal political rights attempted to buttress their arguments by downplaying the importance of political participation. In this essay, Douglass offers a series of responses to this line of argument.

origin and support. Those who urge it here against the black man, only take up the worn out lament of the fading aristocracy of the Old World.

For ourselves, it is scarcely necessary to say that we are opposed to all aristocracy, whether of wealth, power, or learning. The beauty and perfection of government in our eyes will be attained when all the people under it, men and women, black and white, shall be conceded the right of equal participation in wielding its power and enjoying its benefits. Equality is even a more important word with us than liberty. Equality before the law (a phrase introduced into American political discussions for the first time by CHARLES SUMNER) is to the colored man the crowing point of political wisdom.

In other and darker days than those which now shed their light and hope upon the American republic, while pursuing our anti-slavery labors, we were often tauntingly asked what we would have done with the Negro—as if nothing better than slavery could possibly be devised for him, and as if no satisfactory answer could possibly be returned to the inquiry. Now that slavery is abolished and the Negro is free, the same class of persons recur to the old question. Our standing answer in the old time was, "Do nothing with the Negro. Give him fair play, and let him alone. If he lives, well. If he dies, equally well." If a man cannot live and flourish where the conditions of life and prosperity are just and equal, his case furnishes the best reason in the world why he ought to die. Of course, the lame, the halt, and the blind, and persons of a like description are excepted from this philosophy. Aside from this, we have absolutely no retraction or modification to make of that answer. The principle that each member of the human family is bound to support and perpetuate his own existence, cannot be suspended in the interest of any class of men, black or white. All that any man has a right to expect, ask, give, or receive in this world, is fair play. When society has secured this to its members, and the humblest citizen of the republic is put into the undisturbed possession of the natural fruits of his own exertions, there is really very little left for society and government to do. What remains for enlightenment and civilization may be safely left to individual exertion, outside of governmental machinery. We accept that political faith universally believed in, but nowhere practiced, that that government is best which governs least— and altogether regret that other theory which assumes that, because governments are good for something, they are, therefore, good for everything. But this may seem somewhat remote from the question we have undertaken to discuss.

It is alleged that the Negro has already had done for him about all that government can properly do—that the fourteenth and fifteenth amendments of the Constitution place him upon a footing of perfect civil and political equality with other citizens—and hence the Negro, as a Negro, has no special reason to engage in the pursuit of politics, and that he will best consult his interests by devoting himself to the acquisition of money, education, and other means for rising in the social scale.

From this view of the Negro's situation, and from this idea of his proper vocation we dissent entirely. Both have their main support in the popular error, the existence of which, they constructively deny; they deny the Negro all specialty in order to assign him to a special sphere. They say he is already on a footing of equality, the better to deny the wisdom of his equal participation in politics. No truly patriotic man, with any brains, can wish to see the four or five millions of colored people of this country looking to politics as their proper vocation, or to government as the only means of their advancement in social well being; but scarcely less deplorable would be the condition of this people, if among them there should be found no disposition, no aspiration, and no talents for political activity. That man who would advise the black man to make no effort to distinguish himself in politics, will advise him to omit one of the most important levers that can be employed to elevate his race.

This will be very generally admitted when the nature of our government is duly considered. It is not a despotism nor a limited monarchy that we have to deal with. In countries where the masses are excluded from political privileges, to be one of the mass implies no special degradation. The disability being common it fixes no stigma. A burden great in itself becomes light when shared by everybody. Now, in a country where all other varieties of the human family join in the race and participate in the rewards of politics, it would imply the absence of manly qualities in that race if they made themselves or allowed themselves to be made an exception to the general rule. According to our views, there is nothing which is in itself, lawful and honorable for any race or people to do in this country, which colored may not do with equal freedom and equal honor. We fully concur with the sentiment of PETER H. CLARK,[22] (himself a colored man, one of the truest and most thoughtful among us) uttered by him in a recent speech, published in our columns last week, and we go further than he did. Knowing Mr. Clark as we do, knowing his learning, his eloquence, ability, and high moral worth, we say to the Republican Party of Ohio, they could in no way that we know of honor their republican principles, nor give that state a more capable public servant, than by placing this man CLARK, in the Congress of the United States. The speech printed in our columns last week is not an exceptional utterance of Mr. Clark. He is one whose brain expands to the measure of wise statesmanship and one whose elevation even to the Senate of the United States would do no discredit to that august body. His writings and speeches, though never deficient in rhetorical excellence, are always timely, able, and brim full of good sense. The elevation of a few such men as PETER H. CLARK to the high places of the nation would do more than cart-loads of noble resolutions asserting the equality of men, in breaking down the mean and hateful prejudice with which the colored race has been and continues to be assailed.

---

22. Peter H. Clark (1829–1925) was an American politician and activist.

31. "The Labor Question," an essay published in *The New National Era*, October 12, 1871[23]

Our caption has all the vagueness great issues, yet nebulous and dim, assume to the conservative mind. Logicians may justly complain of this indefiniteness, if they see no further than the surface. Whatever there is embodied in the movement thus rudely designated—and there is much of good and some of evil in it—must be frankly met and considered. Change from one amelioration or modification of conditions to some other, whose form is only indistinctly perceived, brings with its processes no unmixed benefit. Evil, or what seems to be such to our finite and limited vision, is as necessary a part of progress as the reverse. It is the law of existence, and accompanies all movement. The labor question—of which in this country the abolition of slavery, of property in man, was the first grand step—is not free from the evils of ignorance, passion, ambition, selfishness, and demagogism. It is to be feared that too many of those who have undertaken to lead in the portentous discussion it inaugurates, have no higher motive than that of obtaining a "new deal" for themselves and theirs. Very little of the spirit which seeks to reach the fundamental conditions of life is found in their mental make-up. At the best it is but amelioration they seek. The real object must necessarily be to arrive at the principles that affect society in its relations to production, and, especially to comprehend those laws which govern the distribution of labor's results, and which, it must be apparent to the most superficial thinker, now operate so unequally. The profound truth conveyed in the apparently paradoxical utterance of Jesus, when he said, "That unto every one which hath shall be given; and from him that hath not, even that he hath shall be taken away from him,"[24] receives daily and literal illustration in all the operations of our industrial civilization. The nonproducers now receive the larger share of what those who labor produce. The result is natural. Discontent culminates in exactly the same ratio that intelligence sustains aspiration. The laborer of today cannot by any possibility remain satisfied with the same surroundings and the same personal results that were sufficient to his father. The Chinese laborer, who, at home, thinks himself a rich man, with earnings averaging two dollars per month, will not in this country long be satisfied with twenty. The Irishman, eating his potatoes and porridge under

---

23. In this essay, Douglass considers a series of questions related to working conditions and material inequality in the United States.

24. Matthew 25:29.

his cabin's hatched roof at home; must by the very force of example when he migrates into other surroundings, demand better food and clothing; and, as a natural consequence, ideas follow and larger mental considerations brood in his vision and stir his brain to unwonted vigor. The freedman, once content as a slave with his weekly peck of corn meal, piece of rusty bacon, and one or two tow suits per year, now requires food, lodgings, and clothing, and, thank God! a higher class of mental conditions and attractions.

Good people, who are appalled with the startling evidences of widespread discontent at conditions which are everywhere visible in this as well as other countries among the laboring people—or, as they may be for the argument's sake termed, the wages class—fail to see that their own improved circumstances have not extended in any like equal proportions to those who are materially considered a grade or two below. The aspiration for the results of this improved condition is equally as marked among them, though it may not be as intelligently expressed, or, in general, as wisely directed. One fact must be apparent, that in all older communities, governed by the high-pressure principle of competition—the idea which is most tersely expressed in the common saying of "each for himself and the devil take the hindmost"—pauperism is on the increase, penury has become a fixed institution, and the "poverty of the masses the rule, not the exception." The question, whether civilization is designed primarily for man or for property, can have but one direct answer, whatever may be the methods each may think desirable by which to attain that end. The happiness of man must be the primal condition on which any form of society alone can found a title to existence. The civilization, then, looked at in its material aspect alone, which on the one hand constantly increases its wealth-creating capacities and on other as steadily leaves out the direct benefits thereof at least seven-tenths of all who live within its influence, cannot have realized the fundamental condition of its continuance. That society is a failure in which the large majority of its members, without any direct fault of their own, would, if any accidental circumstances deprived them for a month of the opportunity of earning regular wages, be dependent on private or public charity for daily bread. Yet such is the actual condition of even favored American labor. It is an appreciation of this dependence that gives such formidable impulse to the discontent of labor. It is the general ignorance of equitable remedies which makes that discontent so dangerous. The movement is fundamental. It grows with great rapidity. It will compel a hearing by the very force of numbers if nothing else. It is the duty of those who have been lifted up by this general movement, this attrition of classes, of which the coming struggle of the "proletariat" (to use a word common in European discussions, though hardly yet generally applicable to our condition) is the final and natural consequence. We say it is the duty of those first benefited to examine closely and consider fairly the grounds for this prevailing discontent, with a view to finding just remedies, conserving by their operations what is good and destroying what is wrong in present social and economic conditions. No movement which involves vast numbers as this does can be safely denounced or ignored. It must be met, treated fairly, and examined into, or the whole fabric will be wrenched by violent convulsions. There is always justice in the general demand. Ignorance may warp, prejudice contract, but the guiding impulse is one that seeks to right some wrong.

Inquiry into the condition of labor is the first step. Let the good people know how much truth there is in the reiterated charges that are made, "that the rich grow richer, the poor poorer"; that in all our manufacturing and industrial centers the gulf between classes is steadily widening, and that all the conditions under which the United States has hitherto been the paradise of labor are rapidly changing and steadily deviating; that, in fact, we are taking on the degrading conditions of European society. Somewhat of this is true. Enough, we believe, to warrant full examination into its causes and investigation into the remedies, if there be any.

Believing, then, such inquiry to be necessary, we urge upon the attention of the country, of all bodies interested in the questions embraced in the agitation, and of Congress, the important bill presented by the Hon. George F. Hoar,[25] representing the ninth congressional district in Massachusetts, to the forty-second Congress. . . :

Be it enacted, &c., "That there shall be appointed by the president, by and with the advice and consent of the Senate, a commission of three persons, who shall hold office for the period of two years from the date of their appointment, unless their duties shall have been sooner accomplished, who shall investigate the subject of the wages and hours of labor, and of the division of the joint profits of labor and capital between the laborer and the capitalist, and the social, educational, and sanitary condition of the laboring classes of the United States, and how the same are affected by existing laws regulating commerce, finance, and currency.

"Section 2. Said commissioners shall receive a salary of five thousand dollars each, shall be authorized to employ a clerk, and shall report the result of their investigation to the president, to be by him transmitted to Congress."

[. . . .]

We urge this measure upon the consideration of the two important national colored conventions about to assemble at Columbia, S.C. The National Labor Union will undoubtedly endorse this proposition. We have no doubt the other body will also do so. The Republican Party falls naturally into the consideration of such issues. Having begun the fight, by freeing the slave, it will not weary of well doing. It is not the party of race or color, but of man and his

---

25. George F. Hoar (1826–1904) was an American politician who served in the House of Representatives and the Senate of the United States.

advancement. If there be reasons for criticizing its actions in this particular, it will be found that, in the main, the conditions have been misapprehended, and the results have been other than expected.

The inquiry called for by Mr. Hoar's bill will be of especial advantage to colored labor. The country generally does not understand the degrading conditions in which it too largely remains, and therefore fails to see the means which might legitimately be enacted and set in motion to effect the changes so imperatively demanded.

32. "Oration of Frederick Douglass Delivered on the Occasion of the Unveiling of the Freedmen's Monument in Memory of Abraham Lincoln," a speech delivered in Washington, DC, on April 14, 1876 and published as a pamphlet (Washington, DC: Gibson Brothers Printers, 1876)[26]

FRIENDS AND FELLOW CITIZENS:

I warmly congratulate you upon the highly interesting object which has caused you to assemble in such numbers and spirit as you have today. This occasion is in some respects remarkable. Wise and thoughtful men of our race, who shall come after us, and study the lesson of our history in the United States; who shall survey the long and dreary spaces over which we have traveled; who shall count the links in the great chain of events by which we have reached our present position, will make a note of this occasion; they will think of it and speak of it with a sense of manly pride and complacency.

I congratulate you, also, upon the very favorable circumstances in which we meet today. They are high, inspiring, and uncommon. They lend grace, glory, and significance to the object for which we have met. Nowhere else in this great country, with its uncounted towns and cities, unlimited wealth, and immeasurable territory extending from sea to sea, could conditions be found more favorable to the success of this occasion than here.

We stand today at the national center to perform something like a national act—an act which is to go into history; and we are here where every pulsation of the national heart can be heard, felt, and reciprocated. A thousand wires, fed with thought and winged with lightning, put us in instantaneous communication with the loyal and true men all over this country.

Few facts could better illustrate the vast and wonderful change which has taken place in our condition as a people than the fact of our assembling here for the purpose we have today. Harmless, beautiful, proper, and praiseworthy as this demonstration is, I cannot forget that no such demonstration would have been tolerated here twenty years ago. The spirit of slavery and barbarism,

---

26. As noted in the introduction, Douglass delivered this speech before a crowd that included several prominent members of the Grant administration as well as justices of the US Supreme Court. Douglass thought the speech important enough to include as an appendix to his third autobiography, *The Life and Times of Frederick Douglass*.

which still lingers to blight and destroy in some dark and distant parts of our country, would have made our assembling here the signal and excuse for opening upon us all the floodgates of wrath and violence. That we are here in peace today is a compliment and a credit to American civilization, and a prophecy of still greater national enlightenment and progress in the future. I refer to the past not in malice, for this is no day for malice; but simply to place more distinctly in front the gratifying and glorious change which has come both to our white fellow-citizens and ourselves, and to congratulate all upon the contrast between now and then; the new dispensation of freedom with its thousand blessings to both races, and the old dispensation of slavery with its ten thousand evils to both races—white and black. In view, then, of the past, the present, and the future, with the long and dark history of our bondage behind us, and with liberty, progress, and enlightenment before us, I again congratulate you upon this auspicious day and hour.

Friends and fellow-citizens, the story of our presence here is soon and easily told. We are here in the District of Columbia, here in the city of Washington, the most luminous point of American territory; a city recently transformed and made beautiful in its body and in its spirit; we are here in the place where the ablest and best men of the country are sent to devise the policy, enact the laws, and shape the destiny of the republic; we are here, with the stately pillars and majestic dome of the Capitol of the nation looking down upon us; we are here, with the broad earth freshly adorned with the foliage and flowers of spring for our church, and all races, colors, and conditions of men for our congregation—in a word, we are here to express, as best we may, by appropriate forms and ceremonies, our grateful sense of the vast, high, and preeminent services rendered to ourselves, to our race, to our country, and to the whole world by Abraham Lincoln.

The sentiment that brings us here today is one of the noblest that can stir and thrill the human heart. It has crowned and made glorious the high places of all civilized nations with the grandest and most enduring works of art, designed to illustrate the characters and perpetuate the memories of great public men. It is the sentiment which from year to year adorns with fragrant and beautiful flowers the graves of our loyal, brave, and patriotic soldiers who fell in defense of the Union and liberty. It is the sentiment of gratitude and appreciation, which often, in the presence of many who hear me, has filled yonder heights of Arlington with the eloquence of eulogy and the sublime enthusiasm of poetry and song; a sentiment which can never die while the republic lives.

For the first time in the history of our people, and in the history of the whole American people, we join in this high worship, and march conspicuously in the line of this time-honored custom. First things are always interesting, and this is one of our first things. It is the first time that, in this form and manner, we have sought to do honor to an American great man, however deserving and illustrious. I commend the fact to notice; let it be told in every part of the republic; let men of all parties and opinions hear it; let those who despise us, not less than those who respect us, know that now and here, in the spirit of liberty, loyalty, and gratitude, let it be known everywhere, and by everybody who takes an interest in human progress and in the amelioration of the condition of mankind, that, in the presence and with the approval of the members of the American House of Representatives, reflecting the general sentiment of the country; that in the presence of that august body, the American Senate, representing the highest intelligence and the calmest judgment of the country; in the presence of the Supreme Court and chief-justice of the United States, to whose decisions we all patriotically bow; in the presence and under the steady eye of the honored and trusted president of the United States, with the members of his wise and patriotic cabinet, we, the colored people, newly emancipated and rejoicing in our blood-bought freedom, near the close of the first century in the life of this republic, have now and here unveiled, set apart, and dedicated a monument of enduring granite and bronze, in every line, feature, and figure of which the men of this generation may read, and those of after-coming generations may read, something of the exalted character and great works of Abraham Lincoln, the first martyr president of the United States.

Fellow-citizens, in what we have said and done today, and in what we may say and do hereafter, we disclaim everything like arrogance and assumption. We claim for ourselves no superior devotion to the character, history, and memory of the illustrious name whose monument we have here dedicated today. We fully comprehend the relation of Abraham Lincoln both to ourselves and to the white people of the United States. Truth is proper and beautiful at all times and in all places, and it is never more proper and beautiful in any case than when speaking of a great public man whose example is likely to be commended for honor and imitation long after his departure to the solemn shades, the silent continents of eternity. It must be admitted, truth compels me to admit, even here in the presence of the monument we have erected to his memory, Abraham Lincoln was not, in the fullest sense of the word, either our man or our model. In his interests, in his associations, in his habits of thought, and in his prejudices, he was a white man.

He was preeminently the white man's president, entirely devoted to the welfare of white men. He was ready and willing at any time during the first years of his administration to deny, postpone, and sacrifice the rights of humanity in the colored people to promote the welfare of the white people of this country. In all his education and feeling he was an American of the Americans. He came into the presidential chair upon one principle alone, namely, opposition to the extension of slavery. His arguments in furtherance of this policy had their motive and mainspring in his patriotic devotion to the interests of his own race. To protect, defend, and perpetuate slavery in the states where it existed Abraham Lincoln was not less ready than any other president to draw the sword of the nation. He was ready to execute all the supposed guarantees of the United States Constitution in favor of the slave system anywhere inside the slave states. He was willing to pursue, recapture, and send back the fugitive slave to his master, and to suppress a slave rising for liberty, though his guilty master were already in arms against the government. The race to which we belong were not the special objects of his consideration. Knowing this, I concede to you, my white fellow-citizens, a preeminence in this worship at once full and supreme. First, midst, and last, you and yours were the objects of his deepest affection and his most earnest solicitude. You are the children of Abraham Lincoln. We are at best only his stepchildren; children by adoption, children by forces of circumstances and necessity. To you it especially belongs to sound his praises, to preserve and perpetuate his memory, to multiply his statues, to hang his pictures high upon your walls, and commend his example, for to you he was a great and glorious friend and benefactor. Instead of supplanting you at this altar, we would exhort you to build high his monuments; let them be of the most costly material, of the most cunning workmanship; let their forms be symmetrical, beautiful, and perfect; let their bases be upon solid rocks, and their summits lean against the unchanging blue, overhanging sky, and let them endure forever! But while in the abundance of your wealth, and in the fullness of your just and patriotic devotion, you do all this, we entreat you to despise not the humble offering we this day unveil to view; for while Abraham Lincoln saved for you a country, he delivered us from a bondage, according to Jefferson, one hour of which was worse than ages of the oppression your fathers rose in rebellion to oppose.

Fellow-citizens, ours is no new-born zeal and devotion—merely a thing of this moment. The name of Abraham Lincoln was near and dear to our hearts in the darkest and most perilous hours of the republic. We were no more ashamed of him when shrouded in clouds of darkness, of doubt, and defeat than when we saw him crowned with victory, honor, and glory. Our faith in him was often taxed and strained to the uttermost, but it never failed. When he tarried long in the mountain; when he strangely told us that we were the cause of the war; when he still more strangely told us that we were to leave the land in which we were born; when he refused to employ our arms in defense of the Union; when, after accepting our services as colored soldiers, he refused to retaliate our murder and torture as colored prisoners; when he told us he would save the Union if he could with slavery; when he revoked the proclamation of emancipation of General Fremont; when he refused to remove the popular commander of the Army of the Potomac, in the days of its inaction and defeat, who was more zealous in his efforts to protect slavery than to suppress rebellion; when we saw all this, and more, we were at times grieved, stunned, and greatly bewildered; but our hearts believed while they ached and bled. Nor was this, even at that time, a blind and unreasoning superstition. Despite the mist *who is we?* and haze that surrounded him; despite the tumult, the hurry, and confusion of the hour, we were able to take a comprehensive view of Abraham Lincoln, and to make reasonable allowance for the circumstances of his position. We saw him, measured him, and estimated him; not by stray utterances to injudicious and tedious delegations, who often tried his patience; not by isolated facts torn from their connection; not by any partial and imperfect glimpses, caught at inopportune moments; but by a broad survey, in the light of the stern logic of great events, and in view of that divinity which shapes our ends, rough hew them how we will, we came to the conclusion that the hour and the man of our redemption had somehow met in the person of Abraham Lincoln. It mattered little to us what language he might employ on special occasions; it mattered little to us, when we fully knew him, whether he was swift or slow in his movements; it was enough for us that Abraham Lincoln was at the head of a great movement, and was in living and earnest sympathy with that movement, which, in the nature of things, must go on until slavery should be utterly and forever abolished in the United States.

When, therefore, it shall be asked what we have to do with the memory of Abraham Lincoln, or what Abraham Lincoln had to do with us, the answer is ready, full, and complete. Though he loved Caesar less than Rome,[27] though the Union was more to him than our freedom or our future, under his wise and beneficent rule we saw ourselves gradually lifted from the depths of slavery to the heights of liberty and manhood; under his wise and beneficent rule, and by measures approved and vigorously pressed by him, we saw that the handwriting of ages, in the form of prejudice and proscription, was rapidly fading away from the face of our whole country; under his rule, and in due time, about as soon after all as the country could tolerate the strange spectacle, we saw our brave sons and brothers laying off the rags of bondage, and being clothed all over in the blue uniforms of the soldiers of the United States; under his rule we saw two hundred thousand of our dark and dusky people responding to the call of Abraham Lincoln, and with muskets on their shoulders, and eagles on their buttons, timing their high footsteps to liberty and union under the national flag; under his rule we saw the independence of the black republic of Haiti, the special object of slaveholding aversion and horror, fully recognized, and her minister, a colored gentleman, duly received here in the city of Washington; under his rule we saw the internal slave-trade, which so long disgraced the nation, abolished, and slavery abolished in the District of Columbia; under his rule we saw for the first time the law enforced against the foreign slave trade, and the first slave-trader hanged like any other pirate or murderer; under his rule, assisted by the greatest captain of our age, and his inspiration, we saw the

27. William Shakespeare, *Julius Caesar*, act 3, sc. 2.

Confederate states, based upon the idea that our race must be slaves, and slaves forever, battered to pieces and scattered to the four winds; under his rule, and in the fullness of time, we saw Abraham Lincoln, after giving the slaveholders three months' grace in which to save their hateful slave system, penning the immortal paper, which, though special in its language, was general in its principles and effect, making slavery forever impossible in the United States. Though we waited long, we saw all this and more.

Can any colored man, or any white man friendly to the freedom of all men, ever forget the night which followed the first day of January, 1863, when the world was to see if Abraham Lincoln would prove to be as good as his word? I shall never forget that memorable night, when in a distant city I waited and watched at a public meeting, with three thousand others not less anxious than myself, for the word of deliverance which we have heard read today. Nor shall I ever forget the outburst of joy and thanksgiving that rent the air when the lightning brought to us the emancipation proclamation. In that happy hour we forgot all delay, and forgot all tardiness, forgot that the president had bribed the rebels to lay down their arms by a promise to withhold the bolt which would smite the slave-system with destruction; and we were thenceforward willing to allow the president all the latitude of time, phraseology, and every honorable device that statesmanship might require for the achievement of a great and beneficent measure of liberty and progress.

Fellow-citizens, there is little necessity on this occasion to speak at length and critically of this great and good man, and of his high mission in the world. That ground has been fully occupied and completely covered both here and elsewhere. The whole field of fact and fancy has been gleaned and garnered. Any man can say things that are true of Abraham Lincoln, but no man can say anything that is new of Abraham Lincoln. His personal traits and public acts are better known to the American people than are those of any other man of his age. He was a mystery to no man who saw him and heard him. Though high in position, the humblest could approach him and feel at home in his presence. Though deep, he was transparent; though strong, he was gentle; though decided and pronounced in his convictions, he was tolerant toward those who differed from him, and patient under reproaches. Even those who only knew him through his public utterance obtained a tolerably clear idea of his character and personality. The image of the man went out with his words, and those who read them knew him.

I have said that President Lincoln was a white man, and shared the prejudices common to his countrymen toward the colored race. Looking back to his times and to the condition of his country, we are compelled to admit that this unfriendly feeling on his part may be safely set down as one element of his wonderful success in organizing the loyal American people for the tremendous conflict before them, and bringing them safely through that conflict. His

great mission was to accomplish two things: first, to save his country from dismemberment and ruin; and, second, to free his country from the great crime
of slavery. To do one or the other, or both, he must have the earnest sympathy
and the powerful cooperation of his loyal fellow-countrymen. Without this
primary and essential condition to success his efforts must have been vain
and utterly fruitless. Had he put the abolition of slavery before the salvation
of the Union, he would have inevitably driven from him a powerful class of
the American people and rendered resistance to rebellion impossible. Viewed
from the genuine abolition ground, Mr. Lincoln seemed tardy, cold, dull, and
indifferent; but measuring him by the sentiment of his country, a sentiment
he was bound as a statesman to consult, he was swift, zealous, radical, and
determined.

Though Mr. Lincoln shared the prejudices of his white fellow-countrymen
against the Negro, it is hardly necessary to say that in his heart of hearts he
loathed and hated slavery. [At this point in the text, there is a footnote that
directs the reader to the following quotation in Lincoln's April 4, 1864 letter
to Albert G. Hodges: "I am naturally anti-slavery. I cannot remember when I
did not so think and feel. If slavery is not wrong, nothing is wrong."] The man
who could say, "Fondly do we hope, fervently do we pray, that this mighty
scourge of war shall soon pass away, yet if God wills it continue till all the
wealth piled by two hundred years of bondage shall have been wasted, and
each drop of blood drawn by the lash shall have been paid for by one drawn
by the sword, the judgments of the Lord are true and righteous altogether,"[28]
gives all needed proof of his feeling on the subject of slavery. He was willing,
while the South was loyal, that it should have its pound of flesh, because he
thought that it was so nominated in the bond; but farther than this no earthly
power could make him go.

Fellow-citizens, whatever else in this world may be partial, unjust, and
uncertain, time, time! is impartial, just, and certain in its action. In the realm
of mind, as well as in the realm of matter, it is a great worker, and often works
wonders. The honest and comprehensive statesman, clearly discerning the
needs of his country, and earnestly endeavoring to do his whole duty, though
covered and blistered with reproaches, may safely leave his course to the silent
judgment of time. Few great public men have ever been the victims of fiercer
denunciation than Abraham Lincoln was during his administration. He was
often wounded in the house of his friends. Reproaches came thick and fast
upon him from within and from without, and from opposite quarters. He was
assailed by abolitionists; he was assailed by slaveholders; he was assailed by the
men who were for peace at any price; he was assailed, by those who were for a
more vigorous prosecution of the war; he was assailed for not making the war

---

28. Douglass quotes Abraham Lincoln's second inaugural address.

an abolition war; and he was bitterly assailed for making the war an abolition war.

But now behold the change: the judgment of the present hour is, that taking him for all in all, measuring the tremendous magnitude of the work before him, considering the necessary means to ends, and surveying the end from the beginning, infinite wisdom has seldom sent any man into the world better fitted for his mission than Abraham Lincoln. His birth, his training, and his natural endowments, both mental and physical, were strongly in his favor. Born and reared among the lowly, a stranger to wealth and luxury, compelled to grapple single-handed with the flintiest hardships of life, from tender youth to sturdy manhood, he grew strong in the manly and heroic qualities demanded by the great mission to which he was called by the votes of his countrymen. The hard condition of his early life, which would have depressed and broken down weaker men, only gave greater life, vigor, and buoyancy to the heroic spirit of Abraham Lincoln. He was ready for any kind and any quality of work. What other young men dreaded in the shape of toil, he took hold of with the utmost cheerfulness.

> "A spade, a rake, a hoe,
> A pick-axe, or a bill;
> A hook to reap, a scythe to mow,
> A flail, or what you will."

All day long he could split heavy rails in the woods, and half the night long he could study his English grammar by the uncertain flare and glare of the light made by a pine-knot. He was at home on the land with his axe, with his maul, with gluts, and his wedges; and he was equally at home on water, with his oars, with his poles, with his planks, and with his boat-hooks. And whether in his flatboat on the Mississippi River, or at the fireside of his frontier cabin, he was a man of work. A son of toil himself, he was linked in brotherly sympathy with the sons of toil in every loyal part of the republic. This very fact gave him tremendous power with the American people, and materially contributed not only to selecting him to the presidency, but in sustaining his administration of the government.

Upon his inauguration as president of the United States, an office, even when assumed under the most favorable conditions, fitted to tax and strain the largest abilities, Abraham Lincoln was met by a tremendous crisis. He was called upon not merely to administer the government, but to decide, in the face of terrible odds, the fate of the republic.

A formidable rebellion rose in his path before him; the Union was already practically dissolved; his country was torn and rent asunder at the center. Hostile armies were already organized against the republic, armed with the munitions of war which the republic had provided for its own defense. The tremendous question for him to decide was whether his country should survive the crisis and flourish, or be dismembered and perish. His predecessor in office had already decided the question in favor of national dismemberment, by denying to it the right of self-defense and self-preservation—a right which belongs to the meanest insect.

Happily for the country, happily for you and for me, the judgment of James Buchanan, the patrician, was not the judgment of Abraham Lincoln, the plebeian. He brought his strong common sense, sharpened in the school of adversity, to bear upon the question. He did not hesitate, he did not doubt, he did not falter; but at once resolved that at whatever peril, at whatever cost, the union of the states should be preserved. A patriot himself, his faith was strong and unwavering in the patriotism of his countrymen. Timid men said before Mr. Lincoln's inauguration, that we had seen the last president of the United States. A voice in influential quarters said, "Let the Union slide." Some said that a Union maintained by the sword was worthless. Others said a rebellion of 8,000,000 cannot be suppressed; but in the midst of all this tumult and timidity, and against all this, Abraham Lincoln was clear in his duty, and had an oath in heaven. He calmly and bravely heard the voice of doubt and fear all around him; but he had an oath in heaven, and there was not power enough on earth to make this honest boatman, backwoodsman, and broad-handed splitter of rails evade or violate that sacred oath. He had not been schooled in the ethics of slavery; his plain life had favored his love of truth. He had not been taught that treason and perjury were the proof of honor and honesty. His moral training was against his saying one thing when he meant another. The trust that Abraham Lincoln had in himself and in the people was surprising and grand, but it was also enlightened and well founded. He knew the American people better than they knew themselves, and his truth was based upon this knowledge.

Fellow-citizens, the fourteenth day of April, 1865, of which this is the eleventh anniversary, is now and will ever remain a memorable day in the annals of this republic. It was on the evening of this day, while a fierce and sanguinary rebellion was in the last stages of its desolating power; while its armies were broken and scattered before the invincible armies of Grant and Sherman; while a great nation, torn and rent by war, was already beginning to raise to the skies loud anthems of joy at the dawn of peace, it was startled, amazed, and overwhelmed by the crowning crime of slavery—the assassination of Abraham Lincoln. It was a new crime, a pure act of malice. No purpose of the rebellion was to be served by it. It was the simple gratification of a hell-black spirit of revenge. But it has done good after all. It has filled the country with a deeper abhorrence of slavery and a deeper love for the great liberator.

Had Abraham Lincoln died from any of the numerous ills to which flesh is heir; had he reached that good old age of which his vigorous constitution and his temperate habits gave promise; had he been permitted to see the end of his great work; had the solemn curtain of death come down but gradually—we should still have been smitten with a heavy grief, and treasured his name lovingly. But dying as he did die, by the red hand of violence, killed, assassinated, taken off without warning, not because of personal hate—for no man who knew Abraham Lincoln could hate him—but because of his fidelity to union and liberty, he is doubly dear to us, and his memory will be precious forever.

Fellow-citizens, I end, as I began, with congratulations. We have done a good work for our race today. In doing honor to the memory of our friend and liberator, we have been doing highest honors to ourselves and those who come after us; we have been fastening ourselves to a name and fame imperishable and immortal; we have also been defending ourselves from a blighting scandal. When now it shall be said that the colored man is soulless, that he has no appreciation of benefits or benefactors; when the foul reproach of ingratitude is hurled at us, and it is attempted to scourge us beyond the range of human brotherhood, we may calmly point to the monument we have this day erected to the memory of Abraham Lincoln.

Stereotype / trope placed on BLM protesters today.

33. "Extract from a speech on the West India Emancipation," delivered in Elmira, New York on August 1, 1880 and published as an Appendix in *The Life and Times of Frederick Douglass* (Hartford, CT: Park Publishing Company, 1881)[29]

M R. PRESIDENT:

I thank you very sincerely for this cordial greeting. I hear in your speech something like a welcome home after a long absence. More years of my life and labors have been spent in this than in any other state of the Union. Anywhere within a hundred miles of the goodly city of Rochester, I feel myself at home and among friends. Within that circumference, there resides a people which have no superiors in points of enlightenment, liberality, and civilization. Allow me to thank you also, for your generous words of sympathy and approval. In respect to this important support of a public man, I have been unusually fortunate. My forty years of work in the cause of the oppressed and enslaved, have been well noted, well appreciated, and well rewarded. All classes and colors of men, at home and abroad, have in this way assisted in holding up my hands. Looking back through these long years of toil and conflict, during which I have had blows to take as well as blows to give, and have sometimes received wounds and bruises, both in body and in mind; my only regret is that I have been enabled to do so little to lift up and strengthen our long enslaved and still oppressed people. My apology for these remarks personal to myself, is in the fact that I am now standing mainly in the presence of a new generation. Most of the men with whom I lived and labored in the early years of the abolition movement, have passed beyond the borders of this life. Scarcely any of the colored men who advocated our cause, and who started when I did, are now numbered among the living, and I begin to feel somewhat lonely. But while I have the sympathy and approval of men and women like these before me, I shall give with joy my latest breath in support of your claim to justice, liberty, and equality among men. The day we celebrate is preeminently the colored man's day. The great event by which it is distinguished, and by which it will for ever be distinguished from all other days of the year, has justly claimed

---

29. In this speech, Douglass provides useful reflections on the course of Reconstruction policy after the Civil War. He thought this speech was important enough to include as an appendix in his third autobiography, *The Life and Times of Frederick Douglass*. Thanks to Jack Turner for reminding me of the importance of this speech in Douglass' political thought.

thoughtful attention among statesmen and social reformers throughout the world. While to them it is a luminous point in human history, and worthy of thought in the colored man, it addresses not merely the intelligence, but the feeling. The emancipation of our brothers in the West Indies comes home to us, stirs our hearts, and fills our souls with those grateful sentiments which link mankind in a common brotherhood.

In the history of the American conflict with slavery, the day we celebrate has played an important part. Emancipation in the West Indies was the first bright star in a stormy sky; the first smile after a long providential frown; the first ray of hope; the first tangible fact demonstrating the possibility of a peaceful transition from slavery to freedom of the Negro race. Whoever else may forget or slight the claims of this day, it can never be to us other than memorable and glorious. The story of it shall be brief and soon told. Six-and-forty years ago, on the day we now celebrate, there went forth over the blue waters of the Caribbean Sea a great message from the British throne, hailed with startling shouts of joy, and thrilling songs of praise. That message liberated, set free, and brought within the pale of civilization eight hundred thousand people, who, till then, had been esteemed as beasts of burden. How vast, sudden, and startling was this transformation! In one moment, a mere tick of a watch, the twinkle of an eye, the glance of the morning sun, saw a bondage which had resisted the humanity of ages, defied earth and heaven, instantly ended; saw the slave-whip burned to ashes; saw the slave's chains melted; saw his fetters broken, and the irresponsible power of the slave master over his victim for ever destroyed.

I have been told by eyewitnesses of the scene, that, in the first moment of it, the emancipated hesitated to accept it for what it was. They did not know whether to receive it as a reality, a dream, or a vision of the fancy.

No wonder they were thus amazed, and doubtful, after their terrible years of darkness and sorrow, which seemed to have no end. Like much other good news, it was thought too good to be true. But the silence and hesitation they observed was only momentary. When fully assured the good tidings which had come across the sea to them were not only good, but true; that they were indeed no longer slaves, but free; that the lash of the slave-driver was no longer in the air, but buried in the earth; that their limbs were no longer chained, but subject to their own will, the manifestations of their joy and gratitude knew no bounds, and sought expression in the loudest and wildest possible forms. They ran about, they danced, they sang, they gazed into the blue sky, bounded into the air, kneeled, prayed, shouted, rolled upon the ground, and embraced each other. They laughed and wept for joy. Those who witnessed the scene say they never saw anything like it before.

We are sometimes asked why we American citizens annually celebrate West India emancipation when we might celebrate American emancipation. Why go abroad, say they, when we might as well stay at home?

The answer is easily given. Human liberty excludes all idea of home and abroad. It is universal and spurns localization.

"When the deed is done for freedom,
Through the broad earth's aching breast
Runs a thrill of joy prophetic,
Trembling on from East to West."

It is bounded by no geographical lines, and knows no national limitations. Like the glorious sun of the heavens, its light shines for all. But besides this general consideration, this boundless power and glory of liberty, West India emancipation has claims upon us as an event in this nineteenth century in which we live, for rich as this century is in moral and material achievements, in progress and civilization, it can claim nothing for itself greater and grander than this act of West India emancipation.

Whether we consider the matter or the manner of it, the tree or its fruit, it is noteworthy, memorable, and sublime. Especially is the manner of its accomplishment worthy of consideration. Its best lesson to the world, its most encouraging word to all who toil and trust in the cause of justice and liberty, to all who oppose oppression and slavery, is a word of sublime faith and courage—faith in the truth and courage in the expression.

Great and valuable concessions have in different ages been made to the liberties of mankind. They have, however, come not at the command of reason and persuasion, but by the sharp and terrible edge of the sword. To this rule West India emancipation is a splendid exception. It came not by the sword, but by the word; not by the brute force of numbers, but by the still small voice of truth; not by barricades, bayonets, and bloody revolution, but by peaceful agitation; not by divine interference, but by the exercise of simple human reason and feeling. I repeat that, in this peculiarity, we have what is most valuable to the human race generally.

It is a revelation of a power inherent in human society. It shows what can be done against wrong in the world, without the aid of armies on the earth or of angels in the sky. It shows that men have in their own hands the peaceful means of putting all their moral and political enemies under their feet, and of making this world a healthy and happy dwelling-place, if they will but faithfully and courageously use them.

The world needed just such a revelation of the power of conscience and of human brotherhood, one that overleaped the accident of color and of race, and set at naught the whisperings of prejudice. The friends of freedom in England saw in the Negro a man, a moral and responsible being. Having settled this in their own minds, they, in the name of humanity, denounced the crime of his enslavement. It was the faithful, persistent, and enduring enthusiasm of Thomas Clarkson, William Wilberforce, Granville Sharp, William Knibb, Henry Brougham, Thomas Fowell Buxton, Daniel O'Connell, George Thompson,[30] and their noble co-workers, that finally thawed the British heart into sympathy for the slave, and moved the strong arm of that government in mercy to put an end to his bondage.

Let no American, especially no colored American, withhold a generous recognition of this stupendous achievement. What though it was not American, but British; what though it was not republican, but monarchical; what though it was not from the American Congress, but from the British Parliament; what though it was not from the chair of a president, but from the throne of a queen, it was none the less a triumph of right over wrong, of good over evil, and a victory for the whole human race.

Besides: We may properly celebrate this day because of its special relation to our American emancipation. In doing this we do not sacrifice the general to the special, the universal to the local. The cause of human liberty is one the whole world over. The downfall of slavery under British power meant the downfall of slavery, ultimately, under American power, and the downfall of Negro slavery everywhere. But the effect of this great and philanthropic measure, naturally enough, was greater here than elsewhere. Outside the British empire no other nation was in a position to feel it so much as we. The stimulus it gave to the American anti-slavery movement was immediate, pronounced, and powerful. British example became a tremendous lever in the hands of American abolitionists. It did much to shame and discourage the spirit of caste and the advocacy of slavery in church and state. It could not well have been otherwise. No man liveth unto himself.[31]

What is true in this respect of individual men, is equally true of nations. Both impart good or ill to their age and generation. But putting aside this consideration, so worthy of thought, we have special reasons for claiming the first of August as the birthday of Negro emancipation, not only in the West Indies, but in the United States. Spite of our national independence, a common language, a common literature, a common history, a common civilization makes us and keeps us still a part of the British nation, if not a part of the British Empire. England can take no step forward in the pathway of a higher civilization without drawing us in the same direction, She is still the mother country, and the mother, too, of our abolition movement. Though her emancipation came in peace, and ours in war; though hers cost treasure, and ours blood; though hers was the result of a sacred preference, and ours resulted in part from necessity, the motive and mainspring of the respective measures were the same in both.

---

30. Douglass identifies a number of abolitionist leaders and politicians from England and Ireland.
31. Romans 14:7.

The abolitionists of this country have been charged with bringing on the war between the North and South, and in one sense this is true. Had there been no anti-slavery agitation at the North, there would have been no anti-slavery anywhere to resist the demands of the slave-power at the South, and where there is no resistance there can be no war. Slavery would then have been nationalized, and the whole country would then have been subjected to its power. Resistance to slavery and the extension of slavery invited and provoked secession and war to perpetuate and extend the slave system. Thus, in the same sense, England is responsible for our civil war. The abolition of slavery in the West Indies gave life and vigor to the abolition movement in America. Clarkson of England gave us Garrison of America; Granville Sharpe of England gave us our Wendell Phillips; and Wilberforce of England gave us our peerless Charles Sumner.

These grand men and their brave co-workers here, took up the moral thunder-bolts which had struck down slavery in the West Indies, and hurled them with increased zeal and power against the gigantic system of slavery here, till, goaded to madness, the traffickers in the souls and bodies of men flew to arms, rent asunder the Union at the center, and filled the land with hostile armies and the ten thousand horrors of war. Out of this tempest, out of this whirlwind and earthquake of war, came the abolition of slavery, came the employment of colored troops, came colored citizens, came colored jurymen, came colored congressmen, came colored schools in the South, and came the great amendments of our national Constitution.

[. . . .]

How stands the case with the recently emancipated millions of colored people in our own country? What is their condition today? What is their relation to the people who formerly held them as slaves? These are important questions, and they are such as trouble the minds of thoughtful men of all colors, at home and abroad. By law, by the Constitution of the United States, slavery has no existence in our country. The legal form has been abolished. By the law of the Constitution, the Negro is a man and a citizen, and has all the rights and liberties guaranteed to any other variety of the human family, residing in the United States.

He has a country, a flag, and a government, and may legally claim full and complete protection under the laws. It was the ruling wish, intention, and purpose of the loyal people, after rebellion was suppressed, to have an end to the entire cause of that calamity by forever putting away the system of slavery and all its incidents. In pursuance of this idea, the Negro was made free, made a citizen, made eligible to hold office, to be a juryman, a legislator, and a magistrate. To this end, several amendments to the Constitution were proposed, recommended, and adopted. They are now a part of the supreme law of the land, binding alike upon every state and territory of the United States,

North and South. Briefly, this is our legal and theoretical condition. This is our condition on paper and parchment. If only from the national statute book we were left to learn the true condition of the colored race, the result would be altogether creditable to the American people. It would give them a clear title to a place among the most enlightened and liberal nations of the world. We could say of our country, as [John Philpot] Curran[32] once said of England, "The spirit of British law makes liberty commensurate with, and inseparable from, the British soil." Now I say that this eloquent tribute to England, if only we looked into our Constitution, might apply to us. In that instrument we have laid down the law, now and forever, and there shall be no slavery or involuntary servitude in this republic, except for crime.

We have gone still further. We have laid the heavy hand of the Constitution upon the matchless meanness of caste, as well as the hell-black crime of slavery, we have declared before all the world that there shall be no denial of rights on account of race, color, or previous condition of servitude. The advantage gained in this respect is immense.

It is a great thing to have the supreme law of the land on the side of justice and liberty. It is the line up to which the nation is destined to march—the law to which the nation's life must ultimately conform. It is a great principle, up to which we may educate the people, and to this extent its value exceeds all speech.

But today, in most of the Southern states, the fourteenth and fifteenth amendments are virtually nullified.

The rights which they were intended to guarantee are denied and held in contempt. The citizenship granted in the fourteenth amendment is practically a mockery, and the right to vote, provided for in the fifteenth amendment, is literally stamped out in face of government. The old master class is today triumphant, and the newly-enfranchised class in a condition but little above that in which they were found before the rebellion.

Do you ask me how, after all that has been done, this state of things has been made possible? I will tell you. Our reconstruction measures were radically defective. They left the former slave completely in the power of the old master, the loyal citizen in the hands of the disloyal rebel against the government. Wise, grand, and comprehensive in scope and design, as were the reconstruction measures, high and honorable as were the intentions of the statesmen by whom they were framed and adopted, time and experience, which try all things, have demonstrated that they did not successfully meet the case.

In the hurry and confusion of the hour, and the eager desire to have the Union restored, there was more care for sublime super-structure of the

---

32. John Philpot Curran (1750–1817) was an Irish politician and writer.

republic than for the solid foundation upon which it could alone be upheld. They gave freedmen the machinery of liberty, but denied them the steam to put it in motion. They gave them the uniform of soldiers, but no arms; they called them citizens, but left [them] subjects; they called them free, and almost left them slaves. They did not deprive the old master class of the power of life and death which was the soul of the relation of master and slave. They could not, of course, sell them, but they retained the power to starve them to death, and wherever this power is held, there is the power of slavery. He who can say to his fellow-man, "You shall serve me or starve," is a master, and his subject is a slave. This was seen and felt by Thaddeus Stevens,[33] Charles Sumner, and leading stalwart Republicans, and had their counsels prevailed the terrible evils from which we now suffer would have been averted. The Negro today would not be on his knees, as he is, abjectly supplicating the old master class to give him leave to toil. Nor would he now be leaving the South, as from a doomed city, and seeking a home in the uncongenial North, but tilling his native soil in comparative independence. Though no longer a slave, he is in a thralldom grievous and intolerable, compelled to work for whatever his employer is pleased to pay him, swindled out of his hard earnings by money orders redeemed in stores, compelled to pay the price of an acre of ground for its use during a single year, to pay four times more than a fair price for a pound of bacon, and be kept upon the narrowest margin between life and starvation. Much complaint has been made that the freedmen have shown so little ability to take care of themselves since their emancipation. Men have marveled that they have made so little progress. I question the justice of this complaint. It is neither reasonable, nor in any sense just. To me, the wonder is, not that the freedmen have made so little progress, but, rather, that they have made so much; not that they have been standing still, but that they have been able to stand at all.

We have only to reflect for a moment upon the situation in which these people found themselves when liberated: consider their ignorance, their poverty, their destitution, and their absolute dependence upon the very class by whom they had been held in bondage for centuries, a class whose every sentiment was averse to their freedom, and we shall be prepared to marvel that they have under the circumstances done so well.

History does not furnish an example of emancipation under conditions less friendly to the emancipated class, than this American example. Liberty came to the freedmen of the United States, not in mercy but in wrath; not by moral choice, but by military necessity; not by the generous action of the people among whom they were to live, and whose good will was essential to the success of the measure, but by strangers, foreigners, invaders,

---

33. Thaddeus Stevens (1792–1868) was an American politician who served in the House of Representatives.

trespassers, aliens, and enemies. The very manner of their emancipation invited to the heads of the freedmen the bitterest hostility of race and class. They were hated because they had been slaves, hated because they were now free, and hated because of those who had freed them. Nothing was to have been expected other than what has happened; and he is a poor student of the human heart who does not see that the old master class would naturally employ every power and means in their reach to make the great measure of emancipation unsuccessful and utterly odious. It was born in the tempest and whirlwind of war, and has lived in a storm of violence and blood. When the Hebrews were emancipated, they were told to take spoil from the Egyptians. When the serfs of Russia were emancipated, they were given three acres of ground upon which they could live and make a living. But not so when our slaves were emancipated. They were sent away empty-handed, without money, without friends, and without a foot of land upon which to stand. Old and young, sick and well, were turned loose to the naked sky, naked to their enemies. The old slave quarter that had before sheltered them, and the fields that had yielded them corn, were now denied them. The old master class in its wrath said, "Clear out! The Yankees have freed you, now let them feed and shelter you!"

Inhuman as was this treatment, it was the natural result of the bitter resentment felt by the old master class, and in view of it the wonder is, not that the colored people of the South have done so little in the way of acquiring a comfortable living, but that they live at all.

Taking all the circumstances into consideration, the colored people have no reason to despair. We still live, and while there is life there is hope. The fact that we have endured wrongs and hardships, which would have destroyed any other race, and have increased in numbers and public consideration, ought to strengthen our faith in ourselves and our future. Let us then, wherever we are, whether at the North or at the South, resolutely struggle on, in the belief that there is a better day coming, and that we by patience, industry, uprightness, and economy may hasten that better day. I will not listen, myself, and I would not have you listen, to the nonsense, that no people can succeed in life among a people by whom they have been despised and oppressed.

The statement is erroneous, and contradicted by the whole history of human progress. A few centuries ago, all Europe was cursed with serfdom, or slavery. Traces of this bondage still remain but are not easily discernible.

The Jews, only a century ago, were despised, hated, and oppressed, but they have defied, met, and vanquished the hard conditions imposed upon them, and are now opulent and powerful, and compel respect in all countries.

Take courage from the example of all religious denominations that have sprung up since Martin Luther. Each in its turn has been oppressed and persecuted. Methodists, Baptists, and Quakers, have all been compelled to feel the lash and sting of popular disfavor—yet all in turn have conquered the prejudice and hate of their surroundings.

Greatness does not come to any people on flowery beds of ease. We must fight to win the prize. No people to whom liberty is given can hold it as firmly and wear it as grandly as those who wrench their liberty from the iron hand of the tyrant. The hardships and dangers involved in the struggle give strength and toughness to the character, and enable it to stand firm in storm as well as in sunshine.

One thought more before I leave this subject, and it is a thought I wish you all to lay to heart. Practice it yourselves and teach it to your children. It is this, neither we, nor any other people, will ever be respected till we respect ourselves, and we will never respect ourselves till we have the means to live respectfully. An exceptionally poor and dependent people will be despised by the opulent, and despise themselves.

You cannot make an empty sack stand on end. A race which cannot save its earnings, which spends all it makes and goes in debt when it is sick, can never rise in the scale of civilization, no matter under what laws it may chance to be. Put us in Kansas or in Africa, and until we learn to save more than we spend, we are sure to sink and perish. It is not in the nature of things that we should be equally rich in this world's goods. Some will be more successful than others, and poverty, in many cases, is the result of misfortune rather than of crime; but no race can afford to have all its members the victims of this misfortune, without being considered a worthless race. Pardon me, therefore, for urging upon you, my people, the importance of saving your earnings; of denying yourselves in the present, that you may have something in the future, of consuming less for yourselves that your children may have a start in life when you are gone.

With money and property comes the means of knowledge and power. A poverty-stricken class will be an ignorant and despised class, and no amount of sentiment can make it otherwise. This part of our destiny is in our own hands. Every dollar you lay up, represents one day's independence, one day of rest and security in the future. If the time shall ever come when we shall possess, in the colored people of the United States, a class of men noted for enterprise, industry, economy, and success, we shall no longer have any trouble in the matter of civil and political rights. The battle against popular prejudice will have been fought and won, and in common with all other races and colors, we shall have an equal chance in the race of life.

34. "John Brown," a speech delivered in Harpers Ferry, West Virginia at the Fourteenth Anniversary of Storer College on May 30, 1881 and published as *John Brown: An Address by Frederick Douglass at the Fourteenth Anniversary of Storer College, Harpers Ferry, West Virginia, May 30, 1881* (Dover, NH: Morningstar Job Printing House, 1881)[34]

Not to fan the flame of sectional animosity now happily in the process of rapid and I hope permanent extinction; not to revive and keep alive a sense of shame and remorse for a great national crime, which has brought its own punishment, in loss of treasure, tears and blood; not to recount the long list of wrongs, inflicted on my race during more than two hundred years of merciless bondage; nor yet to draw, from the labyrinths of far-off centuries, incidents and achievements wherewith to rouse your passions, and enkindle your enthusiasm, but to pay a just debt long due, to vindicate in some degree a great historical character, of our own time and country, one with whom I was myself well acquainted, and whose friendship and confidence it was my good fortune to share, and to give you such recollections, impressions and facts, as I can, of a grand, brave and good old man, and especially to promote a better understanding of the raid upon Harper's Ferry of which he was the chief, is the object of this address.

In all the thirty years' conflict with slavery, if we except the late tremendous war, there is no subject which in its interest and importance will be remembered longer, or will form a more thrilling chapter in American history than this strange, wild, bloody and mournful drama. The story of it is still fresh in the minds of many who now hear me, but for the sake of those who may have forgotten its details, and in order to have our subject in its entire range more fully and clearly before us at the outset, I will briefly state the facts in that extraordinary transaction.

On the night of the 16th of October, 1859, there appeared near the confluence of the Potomac and Shenandoah rivers, a party of nineteen men—

---

34. As noted in the introduction, John Brown was a radical abolitionist who participated in guerilla warfare over slavery in Kansas and, in 1859, led a raid on the federal arsenal at Harpers Ferry, Virginia. Brown was captured and executed after the raid, and there was a great deal of debate about how we ought to think about Brown's legacy. Douglass was, from the start, one of Brown's most eloquent defenders, and this speech provides some of his most sophisticated reflections on Brown's significance in American history. Douglass included an apostrophe in his references to Harpers Ferry. This original punctuation is maintained in references here.

fourteen white and five colored. They were not only armed themselves, but had brought with them a large supply of arms for such persons as might join them. These men invaded Harper's Ferry, disarmed the watchman, took possession of the arsenal, rifle-factory, armory and other government property at that place, arrested and made prisoners nearly all the prominent citizens of the neighborhood, collected about fifty slaves, put bayonets into the hands of such as were able and willing to fight for their liberty, killed three men, proclaimed general emancipation, held the ground more than thirty hours, were subsequently overpowered and nearly all killed, wounded or captured, by a body of United States troops, under command of Colonel Robert E. Lee, since famous as the rebel Gen. Lee. Three out of the nineteen invaders were captured while fighting, and one of these was Captain John Brown, the man who originated, planned and commanded the expedition. At the time of his capture Capt. Brown was supposed to be mortally wounded, as he had several ugly gashes and bayonet wounds on his head and body; and apprehending that he might speedily die, or that he might be rescued by his friends, and thus the opportunity of making him a signal example of slave-holding vengeance would be lost, his captors hurried him to Charlestown two miles further within the border of Virginia, placed him in prison strongly guarded by troops, and before his wounds were healed, he was brought into court, subjected to a nominal trial, convicted of high treason and inciting slaves to insurrection, and was executed. His corpse was given to his woe-stricken widow, and she, assisted by anti-slavery friends, caused it to be borne to North Elba, Essex County, N.Y., and there his dust now reposes, amid the silent, solemn and snowy grandeur of the Adirondacks.

Such is the story; with no lines softened or hardened to my inclining. It is certainly not a story to please, but to pain. It is not a story to increase our sense of social safety and security, but to fill the imagination with wild and troubled fancies of doubt and danger. It was a sudden and startling surprise to the people of Harper's Ferry, and it is not easy to conceive of a situation more abundant in all the elements of horror and consternation. They had retired as usual to rest, with no suspicion that an enemy lurked in the surrounding darkness. They had quietly and trustingly given themselves up to "tired nature's sweet restorer, balmy sleep,"[35] and while thus all unconscious of danger, they were roused from their peaceful slumbers by the sharp crack of the invader's rifle, and felt the keen-edged sword of war at their throats, three of their number being already slain.

Every feeling of the human heart was naturally outraged at this occurrence, and hence at the moment the air was full of denunciation and execration. So intense was this feeling, that few ventured to whisper a word of apology. But

---

35. Edward Young, *Night Thoughts*, "Night I."

happily reason has her voice as well as feeling, and though slower in deciding, her judgments are broader, deeper, clearer and more enduring. It is not easy to reconcile human feeling to the shedding of blood for any purpose, unless indeed in the excitement which the shedding of blood itself occasions. The knife is to feeling always an offense. Even when in the hands of a skillful surgeon, it refuses consent to the operation long after reason has demonstrated its necessity. It even pleads the cause of the known murderer on the day of his execution, and calls society half criminal when, in cold blood, it takes life as a protection of itself from crime. Let no word be said against this holy feeling; more than to law and government are we indebted to this tender sentiment of regard for human life for the safety with which we walk the streets by day and sleep secure in our beds at night. It is nature's grand police, vigilant and faithful, sentineled in the soul, guarding against violence to peace and life. But while so much is freely accorded to feeling in the economy of human welfare, something more than feeling is necessary to grapple with a fact so grim and significant as was this raid. Viewed apart and alone, as a transaction separate and distinct from its antecedents and bearings, it takes rank with the most cold blooded and atrocious wrongs ever perpetrated; but just here is the trouble—this raid on Harper's Ferry, no more than Sherman's march to the sea[36] can consent to be thus viewed alone.

There is, in the world's government, a force which has in all ages been recognized, sometimes as nemesis, sometimes as the judgment of God and sometimes as retributive justice; but under whatever name, all history attests the wisdom and beneficence of its chastisements, and men become reconciled to the agents through whom it operates, and have extolled them as heroes, benefactors and demigods.

To the broad vision of a true philosophy, nothing in this world stands alone. Everything is a necessary part of everything else. The margin of chance is narrowed by every extension of reason and knowledge, and nothing comes unbidden to the feast of human experience. The universe, of which we are part, is continually proving itself a stupendous whole, a system of law and order, eternal and perfect. Every seed bears fruit after its kind, and nothing is reaped which was not sowed. The distance between seed time and harvest, in the moral world, may not be quite so well defined or as clearly intelligible as in the physical, but there is a seed time, and there is a harvest time, and though ages may intervene, and neither he who plowed nor he who sowed may reap in person, yet the harvest nevertheless will surely come; and as in the physical world there are century plants, so it may be in the moral world, and their fruitage is as certain in the one as in the other. The bloody harvest of Harper's Ferry was

---

36. Douglass refers to the Union Army's Savannah campaign, which proved to be pivotal to Union victory in the Civil War.

ripened by the heat and moisture of merciless bondage of more than two hundred years. That startling cry of alarm on the banks of the Potomac was but the answering back of the avenging angel to the midnight invasions of Christian slave-traders on the sleeping hamlets of Africa. The history of the African slave-trade furnishes many illustrations far more cruel and bloody.

Viewed thus broadly our subject is worthy of thoughtful and dispassionate consideration. It invites the study of the poet, scholar, philosopher and statesman. What the masters in natural science have done for man in the physical world, the masters of social science may yet do for him in the moral world. Science now tells us when storms are in the sky, and when and where their violence will be most felt. Why may we not yet know with equal certainty when storms are in the moral sky, and how to avoid their desolating force? But I can invite you to no such profound discussions. I am not the man, nor is this the occasion for such philosophical enquiry. Mine is the word of grateful memory to an old friend; to tell you what I knew of him—what I knew of his inner life—of what he did and what he attempted, and thus if possible to make the mainspring of his actions manifest and thereby give you a clearer view of his character and services.

It is said that next in value to the performance of great deeds ourselves, is the capacity to appreciate such when performed by others; to more than this I do not presume. Allow me one other personal word before I proceed. In the minds of some of the American people I was myself credited with an important agency in the John Brown raid. Governor Henry A. Wise was manifestly of that opinion. He was at the pains of having Mr. Buchanan send his marshals to Rochester to invite me to accompany them to Virginia. Fortunately I left town several hours previous to their arrival.

What ground there was for this distinguished consideration shall duly appear in the natural course of this lecture. I wish however to say just here that there was no foundation whatever for the charge that I in any wise urged or instigated John Brown to his dangerous work. I rejoice that it is my good fortune to have seen, not only the end of slavery, but to see the day when the whole truth can be told about this matter without prejudice to either the living or the dead. I shall however allow myself little prominence in these disclosures. Your interests, like mine, are in the all-commanding figure of the story, and to him I consecrate the hour. His zeal in the cause of my race was far greater than mine—it was as the burning sun to my taper light—mine was bounded by time, his stretched away to the boundless shores of eternity. I could live for the slave, but he could die for him. The crown of martyrdom is high, far beyond the reach of ordinary mortals, and yet happily no special greatness or superior moral excellence is necessary to discern and in some measure appreciate a truly great soul. Cold, calculating and unspiritual as most of us are, we are not wholly insensible to real greatness; and when we are brought in contact with a man of commanding mold, towering high and alone above the millions, free from all conventional fetters, true to his own moral convictions, a "law unto himself," ready to suffer misconstruction, ignoring torture and death for what he believes to be right, we are compelled to do him homage.

In the stately shadow, in the sublime presence of such a soul I find myself standing tonight; and how to do it reverence, how to do it justice, how to honor the dead with due regard to the living, has been a matter of most anxious solicitude.

Much has been said of John Brown, much that is wise and beautiful, but in looking over what may be called the John Brown literature, I have been little assisted with material, and even less encouraged with any hope of success in treating the subject. Scholarship, genius and devotion have hastened with poetry and eloquence, story and song to this simple altar of human virtue, and have retired dissatisfied and distressed with the thinness and poverty of their offerings, as I shall with mine.

The difficulty in doing justice to the life and character of such a man is not altogether due to the quality of the zeal, or of the ability brought to the work, nor yet to any imperfections in the qualities of the man himself; the state of the moral atmosphere about us has much to do with it. The fault is not in our eyes, nor yet in the object, if under a murky sky we fail to discover the object. Wonderfully tenacious is the taint of a great wrong. The evil, as well as "the good that men do, lives after them." Slavery is indeed gone, but its long, black shadow yet falls broad and large over the face of the whole country. It is the old truth oft repeated, and never more fitly than now, "a prophet is without honor in his own country and among his own people."[37] Though more than twenty years have rolled between us and the Harper's Ferry raid, though since then the armies of the nation have found it necessary to do on a large scale what John Brown attempted to do on a small one, and the great captain who fought his way through slavery has filled with honor the presidential chair, we yet stand too near the days of slavery, and the life and times of John Brown, to see clearly the true martyr and hero that he was and rightly to estimate the value of the man and his works. Like the great and good of all ages—the men born in advance of their times, the men whose bleeding footprints attest the immense cost of reform, and show us the long and dreary spaces, between the luminous points in the progress of mankind, —this our noblest American hero must wait the polishing wheels of after-coming centuries to make his glory more manifest, and his worth more generally acknowledged. Such instances are abundant and familiar. If we go back four and twenty centuries, to the stately city of Athens, and search among her architectural splendor and her miracles of art for the Socrates of today, and as he stands in history, we shall find ourselves perplexed

---

37. Matthew 13:57.

and disappointed. In Jerusalem Jesus himself was only the "carpenter's son"—
a young man wonderfully destitute of worldly prudence—a pestilent fellow,
"inexcusably and perpetually interfering in the world's business"—"upsetting
the tables of the money-changers"—preaching sedition, opposing the good
old religion—"making himself greater than Abraham," and at the same time
"keeping company" with very low people; but behold the change! He was a
great miracle-worker, in his day, but time has worked for him a greater miracle
than all his miracles, for now his name stands for all that is desirable in government, noble in life, orderly and beautiful in society. That which time has
done for other great men of his class, that will time certainly do for John
Brown. The brightest gems shine at first with subdued light, and the strongest
characters are subject to the same limitations. Under the influence of adverse
education and hereditary bias, few things are more difficult than to render
impartial justice. Men hold up their hands to heaven, and swear they will do
justice, but what are oaths against prejudice and against inclination! In the face
of high-sounding professions and affirmations we know well how hard it is for
a Turk to do justice to a Christian, or for a Christian to do justice to a Jew.
How hard for an Englishman to do justice to an Irishman, for an Irishman to
do justice to an Englishman, harder still for an American tainted by slavery to
do justice to the Negro or the Negro's friends. "John Brown," said the late Wm.
H. Seward, "was justly hanged." "John Brown," said the late John A. Andrew,[38]
"was right." It is easy to perceive the sources of these two opposite judgments:
the one was the verdict of slave-holding and panic-stricken Virginia, the other
was the verdict of the best heart and brain of free old Massachusetts. One was
the heated judgment of the passing and passionate hour, and the other was the
calm, clear, unimpeachable judgment of the broad, illimitable future.

There is, however, one aspect of the present subject quite worthy of notice,
for it makes the hero of Harper's Ferry in some degree an exception to the
general rules to which I have just now adverted. Despite the hold which slavery had at that time on the country, despite the popular prejudice against the
Negro, despite the shock which the first alarm occasioned, almost from the
first John Brown received a large measure of sympathy and appreciation. New
England recognized in him the spirit which brought the pilgrims to Plymouth
Rock and hailed him as a martyr and saint. True he had broken the law, true
he had struck for a despised people, true he had crept upon his foe stealthily,
like a wolf upon the fold, and had dealt his blow in the dark while his enemy
slept, but with all this and more to disturb the moral sense, men discerned in
him the greatest and best qualities known to human nature, and pronounced
him "good." Many consented to his death, and then went home and taught

---

38. John A. Andrew (1818–1867) was an American lawyer and politician who served as governor of Massachusetts during the Civil War.

their children to sing his praise as one whose "soul is marching on" through the realms of endless bliss. One element in explanation of this somewhat anomalous circumstance will probably be found in the troubled times which immediately succeeded, for "when judgments are abroad in the world, men learn righteousness."[39]

The country had before this learned the value of Brown's heroic character. He had shown boundless courage and skill in dealing with the enemies of liberty in Kansas. With men so few, and means so small, and odds against him so great, no captain ever surpassed him in achievements, some of which seem almost beyond belief. With only eight men in that bitter war, he met, fought and captured Henry Clay Pate,[40] with twenty-five well-armed and mounted men. In this memorable encounter, he selected his ground so wisely, handled his men so skillfully, and attacked the enemy so vigorously, that they could neither run nor fight, and were therefore compelled to surrender to a force less than one-third their own. . . . Before leaving Kansas, he went into the border of Missouri, and liberated a dozen slaves in a single night, and, in spite of slave laws and marshals, he brought these people through a half dozen states, and landed them safely in Canada. With eighteen men this man shook the whole social fabric of Virginia. With eighteen men he overpowered a town of nearly three thousand souls. With these eighteen men he held that large community firmly in his grasp for thirty long hours. With these eighteen men he rallied in a single night fifty slaves to his standard, and made prisoners of an equal number of the slave-holding class. With these eighteen men he defied the power and bravery of a dozen of the best militia companies that Virginia could send against him. Now, when slavery struck, as it certainly did strike, at the life of the country, it was not the fault of John Brown that our rulers did not at first know how to deal with it. He had already shown us the weak side of the rebellion, had shown us where to strike and how. It was not from lack of native courage that Virginia submitted for thirty long hours and at last was relieved only by federal troops; but because the attack was made on the side of her conscience and thus armed her against herself. She beheld at her side the sullen brow of a black Ireland. When John Brown proclaimed emancipation to the slaves of Maryland and Virginia he added to his war power the force of a moral earthquake. Virginia felt all her strong-ribbed mountains to shake under the heavy tread of armed insurgents. Of his army of nineteen her conscience made an army of nineteen hundred.

Another feature of the times, worthy of notice, was the effect of this blow upon the country at large. At the first moment we were stunned and

---

39. Isaiah 26:9.
40. Henry Clay Pate (1832–1864) was a proslavery journalist and guerilla fighter in the dispute over slavery in Kansas territory.

bewildered. Slavery had so benumbed the moral sense of the nation, that it never suspected the possibility of an explosion like this, and it was difficult for Captain Brown to get himself taken for what he really was. Few could seem to comprehend that freedom to the slaves was his only object. If you will go back with me to that time you will find that the most curious and contradictory versions of the affair were industriously circulated, and those which were the least rational and true seemed to command the readiest belief. In the view of some, it assumed tremendous proportions. To such it was nothing less than a wide-sweeping rebellion to overthrow the existing government, and construct another upon its ruins, with Brown for its president and commander-in-chief; the proof of this was found in the old man's carpet-bag in the shape of a constitution for a new republic, an instrument which in reality had been executed to govern the conduct of his men in the mountains. Smaller and meaner natures saw in it nothing higher than a purpose to plunder. To them John Brown and his men were a gang of desperate robbers, who had learned by some means that the government had sent a large sum of money to Harper's Ferry to pay off the workmen in its employ there, and they had gone thence to fill their pockets from this money. The fact is, that outside of a few friends, scattered in different parts of the country, and the slave-holders of Virginia, few persons understood the significance of the hour. That a man might do something very audacious and desperate for money, power or fame, was to the general apprehension quite possible; but, in face of plainly-written law, in face of constitutional guarantees protecting each state against domestic violence, in face of a nation of forty million of people, that nineteen men could invade a great state to liberate a despised and hated race, was to the average intellect and conscience, too monstrous for belief. In this respect the vision of Virginia was clearer than that of the nation. Conscious of her guilt and therefore full of suspicion, sleeping on pistols for pillows, startled at every unusual sound, constantly fearing and expecting a repetition of the Nat Turner insurrection,[41] she at once understood the meaning, if not the magnitude of the affair. It was this understanding which caused her to raise the lusty and imploring cry to the federal government for help, and it was not till he who struck the blow had fully explained his motives and object, that the incredulous nation in any wise comprehended the true spirit of the raid, or of its commander. Fortunate for his memory, fortunate for the brave men associated with him, fortunate for the truth of history, John Brown survived the saber gashes, bayonet wounds and bullet holes, and was able, though covered with blood, to tell his own story and make his own defense. Had he with all his men, as might have been the case, gone down in the shock of battle, the world would have had no true basis for its judgment, and one of the most heroic efforts ever witnessed in behalf

---

41. In 1831, a slave named Nat Turner led a revolt in Virginia.

of liberty would have been confounded with base and selfish purposes. When, like savages, the Wises, the Vallandinghams, the Washingtons, the Stuarts and others stood around the fallen and bleeding hero, and sought by torturing questions to wring from his supposed dying lips some word by which to soil the sublime undertaking, by implicating Gerrit Smith, Joshua R. Giddings, Dr. S. G. Howe, G. L. Stearns, Edwin Morton, Frank Sanborn,[42] and other prominent anti-slavery men, the brave old man, not only avowed his object to be the emancipation of the slaves, but serenely and proudly announced himself as solely responsible for all that had happened. Though some thought of his own life might at such a moment have seemed natural and excusable, he showed none, and scornfully rejected the idea that he acted as the agent or instrument of any man or set of men. He admitted that he had friends and sympathizers, but to his own head he invited all the bolts of slave-holding wrath and fury, and welcomed them to do their worst. His manly courage and self-forgetful nobleness were not lost upon the crowd about him, nor upon the country. They drew applause from his bitterest enemies. Said Henry A. Wise, "He is the gamest man I ever met." "He was kind and humane to his prisoners," said Col. Lewis Washington.[43]

To the outward eye of men, John Brown was a criminal, but to their inward eye he was a just man and true. His deeds might be disowned, but the spirit which made those deeds possible was worthy of the highest honor. It has been often asked, why did not Virginia spare the life of this man? why did she not avail herself of this grand opportunity to add to her other glory that of a lofty magnanimity? Had they spared the good old man's life—had they said to him, "You see we have you in our power, and could easily take your life, but we have no desire to hurt you in any way; you have committed a terrible crime against society; you have invaded us at midnight and attacked a sleeping community, but we recognize you as a fanatic, and in some sense instigated by others; and on this ground and others, we release you. Go about your business, and tell those who sent you that we can afford to be magnanimous to our enemies." I say, had Virginia held some such language as this to John Brown, she would have inflicted a heavy blow on the whole Northern abolition movement, one which only the omnipotence of truth and the force of truth would have overcome. I have no doubt Gov. Wise would have done so gladly, but, alas, he was the executive of a state which thought she could not afford such magnanimity. She had that within her bosom which could more safely tolerate the presence of a criminal than a saint, a highway robber than a moral hero. All her hills and valleys were studded with material for a disastrous conflagration, and one spark

----

42. Douglass identifies several prominent antislavery politicians and activists.
43. Colonel Lewis Washington was among the hostages taken by Brown and his men during the raid on the federal arsenal at Harpers Ferry.

of the dauntless spirit of Brown might set the whole state in flames. A sense of this appalling liability put an end to every noble consideration. His death was a foregone conclusion, and his trial was simply one of form.

Honor to the brave young Col. [George] Hoyt[44] who hastened from Massachusetts to defend his friend's life at the peril of his own; but there would have been no hope of success had he been allowed to plead the case. He might have surpassed [Rufus] Choate or [Daniel] Webster in power—a thousand physicians might have sworn that Capt. Brown was insane, it would have been all to no purpose; neither eloquence nor testimony could have prevailed. Slavery was the idol of Virginia, and pardon and life to Brown meant condemnation and death to slavery. He had practically illustrated a truth stranger than fiction—a truth higher than Virginia had ever known, —a truth more noble and beautiful than Jefferson ever wrote. He had evinced a conception of the sacredness and value of liberty which transcended in sublimity that of her own Patrick Henry[45] and made even his fire flashing sentiment of "liberty or death" seem dark and tame and selfish. Henry loved liberty for himself, but this man loved liberty for all men, and for those most despised and scorned, as well as for those most esteemed and honored. Just here was the true glory of John Brown's mission. It was not for his own freedom that he was thus ready to lay down his life, for with Paul he could say, "I was born free."[46] No chain had bound his ankle, no yoke had galled his neck. History has no better illustration of pure, disinterested benevolence. It was not Caucasian for Caucasian—white man for white man; not rich man for rich man, but Caucasian for Ethiopian—white man for black man—rich man for poor man—the man admitted and respected, for the man despised and rejected. "I want you to understand, gentlemen," he said to his persecutors, "that I respect the rights of the poorest and weakest of the colored people, oppressed by the slave system, as I do those of the most wealthy and powerful." In this we have the key to the whole life and career of the man. Than in this sentiment humanity has nothing more touching, reason nothing more noble, imagination nothing more sublime; and if we could reduce all the religions of the world to one essence we could find in it nothing more divine. It is much to be regretted that some great artist, in sympathy with the spirit of the occasion, had not been present when these and similar words were spoken. The situation was thrilling. An old man in the center of an excited and angry crowd, far away from home, in an enemy's country—with no friend near— overpowered, defeated, wounded, bleeding—covered with reproaches—his brave companions nearly all dead—his two faithful sons stark and cold by his

44. George Hoyt (1837–1877) was an abolitionist who served as John Brown's lawyer.
45. Patrick Henry (1736–1799) was an American politician and a prominent figure in the American Revolution.
46. Acts 22:28.

side—reading his death-warrant in his fast-oozing blood and increasing weakness as in the faces of all around him—yet calm, collected, brave, with a heart for any fate—using his supposed dying moments to explain his course and vindicate his cause: such a subject would have been at once an inspiration and a power for one of the grandest historical pictures ever painted.

With John Brown, as with every other man fit to die for a cause, the hour of his physical weakness was the hour of his moral strength—the hour of his defeat was the hour of his triumph—the moment of his capture was the crowning victory of his life. With the Alleghany Mountains for his pulpit, the country for his church and the whole civilized world for his audience, he was a thousand times more effective as a preacher than as a warrior, and the consciousness of this fact was the secret of his amazing complacency. Mighty with the sword of steel, he was mightier with the sword of the truth, and with this sword he literally swept the horizon. He was more than a match for all the Wises, Masons, Vallandinghams and Washingtons, who could rise against him. They could kill him, but they could not answer him.

In studying the character and works of a great man, it is always desirable to learn in what he is distinguished from others, and what have been the causes of this difference. Such men as he whom we are now considering, come on to the theater of life only at long intervals. It is not always easy to explain the exact and logical causes that produce them, or the subtle influences which sustain them, at the immense heights where we sometimes find them; but we know that the hour and the man are seldom far apart, and that here, as elsewhere, the demand may, in some mysterious way, regulate the supply. A great iniquity, hoary with age, proud and defiant, tainting the whole moral atmosphere of the country, subjecting both church and state to its control, demanded the startling shock which John Brown seemed especially inspired to give it.

Apart from this mission there was nothing very remarkable about him. He was a wool-dealer, and a good judge of wool, as a wool-dealer ought to be. In all visible respects he was a man like unto other men. No outward sign of Kansas or Harper's Ferry was about him. As I knew him, he was an even-tempered man, neither morose, malicious nor misanthropic, but kind, amiable, courteous, and gentle in his intercourse with men. His words were very few, well chosen and forcible. He was a good business man, and a good neighbor. A good friend, a good citizen, a good husband and father: a man apparently in every way calculated to make a smooth and pleasant path for himself through the world. He loved society, he loved little children, he liked music, and was fond of animals. To no one was the world more beautiful or life more sweet. How then as I have said shall we explain his apparent indifference to life? I can find but one answer, and that is, his intense hatred to oppression. I have talked with many men, but I remember none, who seemed so deeply excited upon the subject of slavery as he. He would walk the room in agitation at mention of the word. He saw the evil through no mist or haze, but in a light of infinite brightness, which left no line of its ten thousand horrors out of sight. Law, religion, learning, were interposed in its behalf in vain. His law in regard to it was that which Lord Brougham described, as "the law above all the enactments of human codes, the same in all time, the same throughout the world—the law unchangeable and eternal—the law written by the finger of God on the human heart—that law by which property in man is, and ever must remain, a wild and guilty phantasy."

Against truth and right, legislative enactments were to his mind mere cobwebs—the pompous emptiness of human pride—the pitiful outbreathings [*sic*] of human nothingness. He used to say "whenever there is a right thing to be done, there is a 'thus saith the Lord' that it shall be done."

It must be admitted that Brown assumed tremendous responsibility in making war upon the peaceful people of Harper's Ferry, but it must be remembered also that in his eye a slave-holding community could not be peaceable, but was, in the nature of the case, in one incessant state of war. To him such a community was not more sacred than a band of robbers: it was the right of any one to assault it by day or night. He saw no hope that slavery would ever be abolished by moral or political means: "he knew," he said, "the proud and hard hearts of the slave-holders, and that they never would consent to give up their slaves, till they felt a big stick about their heads."

It was five years before this event at Harper's Ferry, while the conflict between freedom and slavery was waxing hotter and hotter with every hour, that the blundering statesmanship of the national government repealed the Missouri Compromise, and thus launched the territory of Kansas as a prize to be battled for between the North and the South. The remarkable part taken in this contest by Brown has been already referred to, and it doubtless helped to prepare him for the final tragedy, and though it did not by any means originate the plan, it confirmed him in it and hastened its execution.

During his four years' service in Kansas it was my good fortune to see him often. On his trips to and from the territory he sometimes stopped several days at my house, and at one time several weeks. It was on this last occasion that liberty had been victorious in Kansas, and he felt that he must hereafter devote himself to what he considered his larger work. It was the theme of all his conversation, filling his nights with dreams and his days with visions. An incident of his boyhood may explain, in some measure, the intense abhorrence he felt to slavery. He had for some reason been sent into the State of Kentucky, where he made the acquaintance of a slave boy, about his own age, of whom he became very fond. For some petty offense this boy was one day subjected to a brutal beating. The blows were dealt with an iron shovel and fell fast and furiously upon his slender body. Born in a free state and unaccustomed to such scenes of cruelty, young Brown's pure and sensitive soul revolted at the shocking spectacle and at that early age he swore eternal hatred to slavery. After years never obliterated the impression, and he found in this early experience an argument against contempt for small things. It is true that the boy is the father of the man. From the acorn comes the oak. The impression of a horse's foot in the sand suggested that art of printing. The fall of an apple intimated the law of gravitation. A word dropped in the woods of Vincennes, by royal hunters, gave Europe and the world a "William the Silent,"[47] and a thirty years' war. The beating of a Hebrew bondsman, by an Egyptian, created a Moses, and the infliction of a similar outrage on a helpless slave boy in our own land may have caused, forty years afterward, a John Brown and a Harper's Ferry raid.

Most of us can remember some event or incident which has at some time come to us, and made itself a permanent part of our lives. Such an incident came to me in the year 1847. I had then the honor of spending a day and a night under the roof of a man, whose character and conversation made a very deep impression on my mind and heart; and as the circumstance does not lie entirely out of the range of our present observations, you will pardon for a moment a seeming digression. The name of the person alluded to had been several times mentioned to me, in a tone that made me curious to see him and to make his acquaintance. He was a merchant, and our first meeting was at his store—a substantial brick building, giving evidence of a flourishing business. After a few minutes' detention here, long enough for me to observe the neatness and order of the place, I was conducted by him to his residence where I was kindly received by his family as an expected guest. I was a little disappointed at the appearance of this man's house, for after seeing his fine store, I was prepared to see a fine residence; but this logic was entirely contradicted by the facts. The house was a small, wooden one, on a black street in a neighborhood of laboring men and mechanics, respectable enough, but not just the spot where one would expect to find the home of a successful merchant. Plain as was the outside, the inside was plainer. Its furniture might have pleased a Spartan. It would take longer to tell what was not in it, than what was; no sofas, no cushions, no curtains, no carpets, no easy rocking chairs inviting to enervation or rest or repose. My first meal passed under the misnomer of tea. It was none of your tea and toast sort, but potatoes and cabbage, and beef soup; such a meal as a man might relish after following the plow all day, or after performing a forced march of a dozen miles over rough ground in frosty weather. Innocent of paint, veneering, varnish or tablecloth, the table announced itself unmistakably and honestly pine and of the plainest workmanship. No hired help passed from kitchen to dining room, staring in amazement at the colored man at the white man's table. The mother, daughters and sons did the serving, and did it well. I heard no apology for doing their own work; they went through it as if used

---

47. William the Silent (1533–1584) was a military and political leader in Holland.

to it, untouched by any thought of degradation or impropriety. Supper over, the boys helped to clear the table and wash the dishes. This style of housekeeping struck me as a little odd. I mention it because household management is worthy of thought. A house is more than brick and mortar, wood or paint; this to me at least was. In its plainness it was a truthful reflection of its inmates; no disguises, no illusions, no make-believes here, but stern truth and solid purpose breathed in all its arrangements. I was not long in company with the master of this house before I discovered that he was indeed the master of it, and likely to become mine too, if I stayed long with him. He fulfilled St. Paul's idea of the head of the family—his wife believed in him, and his children observed him with reverence. Whenever he spoke, his words commanded earnest attention. His arguments which I ventured at some points to oppose, seemed to convince all, his appeals touched all, and his will impressed all. Certainly I never felt myself in the presence of a stronger religious influence than while in this house. "God and duty, God and duty," run like a thread of gold through all his utterances, and his family supplied a ready "Amen." In person he was lean and sinewy, of the best New England mold, built for times of trouble, fitted to grapple with the flintiest hardships. Clad in plain American woolen, shod in boots of cowhide leather, and wearing a cravat of the same substantial material, under six feet high, less than one hundred and fifty lbs. in weight, aged about fifty, he presented a figure straight and symmetrical as a mountain pine. His bearing was singularly impressive. His head was not large, but compact and high. His hair was coarse, strong, slightly gray and closely trimmed and grew close to his forehead. His face was smoothly shaved and revealed a strong square mouth, supported by a broad and prominent chin. His eyes were clear and gray, and in conversation they alternated with tears and fire. When on the street, he moved with a long springing, race-horse step, absorbed by his own reflections, neither seeking nor shunning observation. Such was the man whose name I heard uttered in whispers—such was the house in which he lived—such were his family and household management—and such was Captain John Brown.

He said to me at this meeting, that he had invited me to his house for the especial purpose of laying before me his plan for the speedy emancipation of my race. He seemed to apprehend opposition on my part as he opened the subject and touched my vanity by saying, that he had observed my course at home and abroad, and wanted my cooperation. He said he had been for the last thirty years looking for colored men to whom he could safely reveal his secret, and had almost despaired, at times, of finding such, but that now he was encouraged for he saw heads rising up in all directions, to whom he thought he could with safety impart his plan. As this plan then lay in his mind it was very simple, and had much to commend it. It did not, as was supposed by many, contemplate a general rising among the slaves, and a general slaughter of the slave masters (an insurrection he thought would only defeat the object), but it did contemplate the creating of an armed force which should act in the very heart of the South. He was not averse to the shedding of blood, and thought the practice of carrying arms would be a good one for the colored people to adopt, as it would give them a sense of manhood. No people he said could have self-respect or be respected who would not fight for their freedom. He called my attention to a large map of the United States, and pointed out to me the far-reaching Alleghenies, stretching away from the borders of New York into the Southern states. "These mountains," he said, "are the basis of my plan. God has given the strength of these hills to freedom; they were placed here to aid the emancipation of your race; they are full of natural forts, where one man for defense would be equal to a hundred for attack; they are also full of good hiding places where a large number of men could be concealed and baffle and elude pursuit for a long time. I know these mountains well and could take a body of men into them and keep them there in spite of all the efforts of Virginia to dislodge me, and drive me out. I would take at first about twenty-five picked men and begin on a small scale, supply them arms and ammunition, post them in squads of fives on a line of twenty-five miles, these squads to bust themselves for a time in gathering recruits from the surrounding farms, seeking and selecting the most restless and daring." He saw that in this part of the work the utmost care must be used to guard against treachery and disclosure; only the most conscientious and skillful should be sent on this perilous duty. With care and enterprise he thought he could soon gather a force of one hundred hardy men, men who would be content to lead the free and adventurous life to which he proposed to train them. When once properly drilled, and each had found the place for which he was best suited, they would begin work in earnest; they would run off the slaves in large numbers, retain the strong and brave ones in the mountains, and send the weak and timid ones to the North by the Underground Railroad; his operations would be enlarged with increasing numbers and would not be confined to one locality. Slaveholders should in some cases be approached at midnight and told to give up their slaves and to let them have their best horses to ride away upon. Slavery was a state of war, he said, to which the slaves were unwilling parties and consequently they had a right to anything necessary to their peace and freedom. He would shed no blood and would avoid a fight except in self-defense, when he would of course do his best. He believed this movement would weaken slavery in two ways—first by making slave property insecure, it would become undesirable; and secondly it would keep the anti-slavery agitation alive and public attention fixed upon it, and thus lead to the adoption of measures to abolish the evil altogether. He held that there was need of something startling to prevent the agitation of the question from dying out; that slavery had come near being abolished in Virginia by the Nat. Turner insurrection, and he thought his method would speedily put an end to it, both in Maryland and Virginia.

The trouble was to get the right men to start with and money enough to equip them. He had adopted the simple and economical mode of living to which I have referred with a view to save money for this purpose. This was said in no boastful tone, for he felt that he had delayed already too long and had no room to boast either his zeal or his self denial.

From 8 o'clock in the evening till 3 in the morning, Capt. Brown and I sat face to face, he arguing in favor of his plan, and I finding all the objections I could against it. Now mark! this meeting of ours was full twelve years before the strike at Harper's Ferry. He had been watching and waiting all that time for suitable heads to rise or "pop up" as he said among the sable millions in whom he could confide; hence forty years had passed between his thought and his act. Forty years, though not a long time in the life of a nation, is a long time in the life of a man; and here forty long years, this man was struggling with this one idea; like Moses he was forty years in the wilderness. Youth, manhood, middle age had come and gone; two marriages had been consummated, twenty children had called him father; and through all the storms and vicissitudes of busy life, this one thought, like the angel in the burning bush, had confronted him with its blazing light, bidding him on to his work. Like Moses he had made excuses, and as with Moses his excuses were overruled. Nothing should postpone further what was to him a divine command, the performance of which seemed to him his only apology for existence. He often said to me, though life was sweet to him, he would willingly lay it down for the freedom of my people; and on one occasion he added, that he had already lived about as long as most men, since he had slept less, and if he should now lay down his life the loss would not be great, for in fact he knew no better use for it. During his last visit to us in Rochester there appeared in the newspapers a touching story connected with the horrors of the Sepoy War in British India.[48] A Scotch missionary and his family were in the hands of the enemy, and were to be massacred the next morning. During the night, when they had given up every hope of rescue, suddenly the wife insisted that relief would come. Placing her ear close to the ground she declared she heard the "Slogan"—the Scotch war song. For long hours in the night no member of the family could hear the advancing music but herself. "Dinna ye hear it? Dinna ye hear it?" she would say, but they could not hear it. As the morning slowly dawned a Scotch regiment was found encamped indeed about them, and they were saved from the threatened slaughter. This circumstance, coming at such a time, gave Capt. Brown a new word of cheer. He would come to the table in the morning his countenance fairly illuminated, saying that he had heard the "Slogan," and he would add, "Dinna ye hear it? *Dinna* ye hear it?" Alas! like the Scotch missionary I was obliged to say "No." Two weeks prior to the meditated attack, Capt.

---

48. This is a reference to the Indian Rebellion against the British in 1857.

Brown summoned me to meet him in an old stone quarry on the Coneco-chequi River, near the town of Chambersburgh, Pennsylvania. His arms and ammunition were stored in that town and were to be moved on to Harper's Ferry. In company with Shields Green I obeyed the summons, and prompt to the hour we met the dear old man, with Kagi, his secretary, at the appointed place. Our meeting was in some sense a council of war. We spent the Saturday and succeeding Sunday in conference on the question, whether the desperate step should then be taken, or the old plan as already described should be car-ried out. He was for boldly striking at Harper's Ferry at once and running the risk of getting into the mountains afterward. I was for avoiding Harper's Ferry altogether. Shields Green and Mr. Kagi remained silent listeners throughout. It is needless to repeat here what was said, after what has happened. Suffice it, that after all I could say, I saw that my old friend had resolved on his own course and that it was idle to parley. I told him finally that it was impossible for me to join him. I could see Harper's Ferry only as a trap of steel, and ourselves in the wrong side of it. He regretted my decision and we parted.

Thus far, I have spoken exclusively of Capt. Brown. Let me say a word or two of his brave and devoted men, and first of Shields Green. He was a fugitive slave from Charleston, South Carolina, and had attested his love of liberty by escaping from slavery and making his way through many dangers to Rochester, where he had lived in my family, and where he met the man with whom he went to the scaffold. I said to him, as I was about to leave, "Now Shields, you have heard our discussion. If in view of it, you do not wish to stay, you have but to say so, and you can go back with me." He answered, "I b'l'eve I'll go down wid de old man"; and go with him he did, into the fight, and to the gallows, and bore himself as grandly as any of the number. At the moment when Capt. Brown was surrounded, and all chance of escape was cut off, Green was in the mountains and could have made his escape as Osborne Anderson[49] did, but when asked to do so, he made the same answer he did at Chambersburg, "I b'l'eve I'll go down wid de ole man." When in prison at Charlestown, and he was not allowed to see his old friend, his fidelity to him was in no wise weakened, and no complaint against Brown could be extorted from him by those who talked with him.

If a monument should be erected to the memory of John Brown, as there ought to be, the form and name of Shields Green should have a conspicuous place upon it. . . .

For the disastrous termination of this invasion, several causes have been assigned. It has been said that Capt. Brown found it necessary to strike before he was ready; that men had promised to join him from the North who failed to arrive; that the cowardly Negroes did not rally to his support as he expected, but the true

---

49. Osborne Anderson (1830–1872) was among the men who joined John Brown in the raid on the federal arsenal at Harpers Ferry.

cause as stated by himself, contradicts all these theories, and from his statement there is no appeal. Among the questions put to him by Mr. Vallandingham after his capture were the following: "Did you expect a general uprising of the slaves in case of your success?" To this he answered, "No, sir, nor did I wish it. I expected to gather strength from time to time and then to set them free." "Did you expect to hold possession here until then?" Answer, "Well, probably I had quite a different idea. I do not know as I ought to reveal my plans. I am here wounded and a prisoner because I foolishly permitted myself to be so. You overstate your strength when you suppose I could have been taken if I had not allowed it. I was too tardy after commencing the open attack in delaying my movements through Monday night and up to the time of the arrival of government troops. It was all because of my desire to spare the feelings of my prisoners and their families."

But the question is, Did John Brown fail? He certainly did fail to get out of Harper's Ferry before being beaten down by United States soldiers; he did fail to save his own life, and to lead a liberating army into the mountains of Virginia. But he did not go to Harper's Ferry to save his life. The true question is, Did John Brown draw his sword against slavery and thereby lose his life in vain? and to this I answer ten thousand times, No! No man fails, or can fail who so grandly gives himself and all he has to a righteous cause. No man, who in his hour of extremest [sic] need, when on his way to meet an ignominious death, could so forget himself as to stop and kiss a little child, one of the hated race for whom he was about to die, could by any possibility fail. Did John Brown fail? Ask Henry A. Wise in whose house less than two years after, a school for the emancipated slaves was taught. Did John Brown fail? Ask James M. Mason, the author of the inhuman fugitive slave bill, who was cooped up in Fort Warren, as a traitor less than two years from the time that he stood over the prostrate body of John Brown. Did John Brown fail? Ask Clement C. Vallandingham, one other of the inquisitorial party; for he too went down in the tremendous whirlpool created by the powerful hand of this bold invader. If John Brown did not end the war that ended slavery, he did at least begin the war that ended slavery. If we look over the dates, places and men, for which this honor is claimed, we shall find that not Carolina, but Virginia—not Fort Sumter, but Harper's Ferry and the arsenal—not Col. Anderson, but John Brown, began the war that ended American slavery and made this a free republic. Until this blow was struck, the prospect for freedom was dim, shadowy and uncertain. The irrepressible conflict was one of words, votes and compromises. When John Brown stretched forth his arm the sky was cleared. The time for compromises was gone—the armed hosts of freedom stood face to face over the chasm of a broken Union—and the clash of arms was at hand. The South staked all upon getting possession of the federal government, and failing to do that, drew the sword of rebellion and thus made her own, and not Brown's, the lost cause of the century.

35. "Decoration Day," a speech delivered at Franklin Square in Rochester, New York on May 30, 1882 and published in the *Rochester Daily Union and Advertiser*, May 30, 1882[50]

FRIENDS AND FELLOW CITIZENS:

If anything like pride or self-gratulation [*sic*] were permissible or pardonable in any man, on an occasion like this, I might be excused for entertaining some such feeling in view of the invitation to appear here as your orator today. In your estimation and in mine, and in the estimation of loyal men generally, especially in the loyal North, the annual memorial occasions have a deep and sacred significance. They stand as a sign of something real, valuable and important. He who is deemed worthy to participate in them, be he ever so humble and his part ever so limited, may well enough feel himself exalted. It is more than ribbons, or stars, or garters. It makes a man as one of the American people, a man among men, a full partaker in the rights, duties, privileges and immunities of American citizenship—a citizenship having a grander future than any bestowed by any other country in the world.

[. . . .]

Fellow-citizens—Though I have not participated with you personally, upon occasions like this, my peculiar experience, together with that common interest and common memory which makes this day sacred to all of us, I have in spirit united with you in its observance.

No people in the United States, so far as I know, perform the rites and ceremonies which belong to this day, more scrupulously, appropriately, and impressively, than do the people of Rochester; and from my recollection of your experience of the clouds, darkness and blood attending the war, when gloom filled your homes, and sorrow sat at your hearthstones, no people have better reason so to perform these rites and ceremonies.

The patriotism this day honors found not its birth but its expression in that momentous struggle. It was seen that the accumulation of wealth, and the ease and luxury, which such accumulation brought, had not destroyed the heroic spirit of the days that tried men's souls. I seem even now to feel the effects of the sights and the sounds of that dreadful period. I see the flags from windows and housetops fluttering in the breeze. I see and hear the steady tramp

---

50. As Douglass explains in this speech, Decoration Day originated after the Civil War as a holiday to honor Union soldiers killed during the Civil War. In this speech, Douglass defends the propriety of the observance of the holiday.

of armed men in blue uniforms through all your streets. I see the recruiting sergeant with drum and fife, with banner and badge, calling for men, young men and strong, to go to the front and fill up the gaps made by rebel powder and by pestilence. I hear the piercing sound of trumpets that told us plainly that peace had taken its flight from our borders; that our country was divided and involved in the turmoil of a terrible war.

Fellow citizens, I am not here to flatter, unless truth itself be flattery, but I do like to say pleasant things when I can say them truthfully, and this I can say of you, your patriotism during all that great trial was, according to my observation, equal to the occasion. Though you felt the common gloom you were not cowed by defeat nor made careless or overconfident by victory. Your zeal and your courage burned with steady flame alike amid the gusts and calms of the war.

What Rochester was at the beginning of the war that Rochester was during the war and at the end of the war. As an eyewitness I am here to say that though there were croakers here as elsewhere during all that momentous struggle her courage never quailed, her mind never doubted, her enthusiasm never cooled, her purse never closed, her arm never wearied.

Fellow citizens: In the name of your country, and in behalf of emancipated millions, and in my own behalf, I am here to thank you, and to thank your brave soldiers, and to thank your able statesmen, to thank the living and the dead, for their fidelity to principle, their patriotic fervor, and for what they attempted, suffered and accomplished.

The fact, to which we today invite the attention of loyal and patriotic men, in every part of our common country, is that we are still upon duty, and that we do not forget our patriotic dead.

We call attention to the fact that within the sacred enclosure of Mt. Hope, a place well named, and well suited to the solemn purpose to which it is devoted, a ground hallowed by affection, adorned by art, beautified by wealth, skill and industry, coupled with holiest memories, where strong men go to meditate and widows and orphans go to weep, we have met to strew choice flowers, with lavish, loyal, loving hands, upon the green graves of our brave young men, who, in the hour of national peril, went forth and nobly gave their lives, all that men can give, to save their country from dismemberment and ruin.

Does any man question the right or the propriety of this annual ceremony? Can any man who loves his country advise its discontinuance? Is there anywhere another altar better than this, around which the nation can meet one day in each year to renew its national vows and manifest its loyal devotion to the principles of our free government? Is there any eminence from which we can better survey the past, the present, the future? For my part I know of no other such day. There is none other so abundant in suggestions and themes of immediate national interests as this day.

In saying this I am not unaware that the world is full of anachronisms, empty form and superstitions, kept above ground and upon exhibition by hollow, heartless and unthinking custom; things that wear the appearance of life while destitute of its power and have little or no relation to the generations now living.

I am not only aware of this fact, but I am also aware that the time may come when this national Decoration Day, which means so much to us, shall share the fate of other great days. Having answered the end of its ordination it will fade and vanish, and it will be given to some other day more nearly allied with the wants and events of another age. So let it be. Everything is beautiful in its season. Let not the smoke survive the candle.

When an institution has answered the end for which it was created it should follow the order of nature and disappear. Here as elsewhere there is no pause, no stopping place. There have been many plans and policies proposed in the interests of what is called conservation, but the combined wisdom of all the ages has not yet devised any means to guard and guarantee the world against mutations in human society, or revolutions in the structure of human government.

The law of change is everywhere vindicated. What has happened once may happen again. Sufficient unto the day is the evil thereof, and we may console ourselves in the thought that whatever may be the immediate or distant future, whatever may hallow another day, and make it great in the eyes of the American people, for the present at least, there is no national holiday which contains so much for the head and heart of our day and generation as this Decoration Day. We may say of it, as Daniel Webster once said of Bunker Hill Monument: "It looks, it speaks, it acts." It recalls to us with the emphasis—of the roar of a thousand cannons, the scenes and incidents of a tremendous war. It is full of lessons of wisdom, courage, and patriotism. It may, as I have said, lose its hold on the attention of the people and cease to be observed, but the broad and manly sentiment of which it is born, and by which it is sustained, will live, flourish and bear similar fruit forever.

While good and evil, loyalty and treason, liberty and slavery remain opposites and irreconcilable, while they retain their fighting qualities, and shall contend, as they must contend, for ascendency in the world, their respective forces will adopt opposite emblems and tokens.

Fellow-citizens: Two very conflicting sentiments and policies have been expressed and espoused in respect to our duty toward the people lately in rebellion.

One of these would regard and treat the Southern people precisely as they would regard and treat them had they been always loyal and true to the government. It is said that this cruel war is over, that the late rebels have repented their folly and have accepted in good faith the results of the late war, and that now, we should forget and forgive the past, and turn our attention entirely to the future. Even that moral and intellectual giant in the councils of the nation, the late Charles Sumner, would have had all our battle flags banished from view, and nothing left to tell that there had ever been trouble to our national family. Much in the same line were the views and sentiments of the late Horace Greeley, Gerrit Smith, Chief Justice Chase[51] and other eminent men.

Opposed to this view of our national duty it is held that the rebellion is suppressed but not conquered: that its spirit is still abroad and only waits to reassert itself in flagrant disloyalty.

Though the doctrine of forgiveness and forgetfulness has been adopted by many of the noblest and most intelligent men of our country, men for whom I have the highest respect, I am wholly unable to accept it, to the extent to which it is asserted. I certainly cannot accept it to the extent of abandoning the observance of Decoration Day. If rebellion was wrong and loyalty right, if slavery was wrong and emancipation right, we are rightfully here today.

We are not here to fan the flames of sectional animosity, not to revive the malign sentiments, which naturally sprung up in the heat and fire of a bloody conflict. We are not here to visit upon the children the sins of the fathers, but we are here to remember the causes, the incidents, and the results of the late rebellion. We come around this national family altar, one day in each year, to pay our grateful homage to the memory of brave men—to express and emphasize by speech and pageantry our reverence for those great qualities of enlightened and exalted human nature, which in every land are the stay and salvation of the race; the qualities without which states would perish, society dissolve, progress become impossible and mankind sink back into a howling wilderness of barbarism.

In a word, we are here to reassert and re-proclaim our admiration for the patriotic zeal, the stern fortitude, the noble self-sacrifice, the unflinching determination, the quenchless enthusiasm, the high and measureless courage with which loyal men, true to the republic in the hour of supreme peril, dashed themselves against a wanton, wicked and gigantic rebellion, and suppressed it beyond the power to rise again.

I base my views of the propriety of this occasion not upon partisan, partial and temporary considerations, but upon the broad foundations of human nature itself. Man is neither wood nor stone. He is described by the great poet, as a being looking before and after.[52] He has a past, present and future. To eliminate either is a violation of his nature and an infringement upon his

---

51. Douglass identifies several prominent antislavery figures in order to demonstrate that not all of those committed to the abolition of slavery shared his view of Decoration Day.
52. "The great poet" is a reference to William Shakespeare, and Douglass cites *Hamlet*, act 4, sc. 4.

dignity. He is a progressive being, and memory, reason, and reflection are the resources of his improvement. With these perfections everything in the world, every great event has an alphabet, a picture, and a voice to instruct. He

> *"Finds tongues in trees, books in the running brooks,*
> *Sermons in stones and good in everything."*[53]

For him every foot of bird or beast leaves its imprint upon the earth, every wheel of cart or carriage leaves its track upon the road, every keel of ship or schooner leaves its wake in the seamless ocean, to tell the mariner where he has deviated from his true course. If these may be consulted for the purposes of knowledge and wisdom, how much more the course of our rebellion-tossed ship of state, freighted with all that is precious in human hope and human existence.

I am, then, for remembering the past, for only out of the mists and shadows of the past may the thoughtful statesman read, with some degree of certainty, the probable events of the future.

But even here in this broad domain of memory, reason, experience and reflection, upon which man moves so grandly and so like a god, he is still a circumscribed and limited being. He can only travel so far. The ocean is large, but it has its bounds beyond which it may not pass. The same is the case with man. The strongest memory gives him at last only a vague, confused, and imperfect impression of the facts and experiences of the past. He at last sees men in that direction only as trees walking.

In the fierce battle for existence, little time is left to most of us for events long gone by. We live and must live in the hurry and tumult of the passing hour.

Now when, to these considerations, we add the natural weakness of all human powers, the dullness of observation, the imperfection of memory, the fading effect produced by time and distance, upon all that happens in the world, it is easily seen that man is followed and must be followed by a cloud of oblivion almost as dark and impenetrable as to the things of the past as that dark curtain or cloud which conceals from the present the mighty events which are awaiting the world in the distant future.

Hence, from natural causes, we are likely to take along with us, too little, rather than too much of the past, and may forget too soon, rather than remember too long, the tremendous facts of the late war. At any rate no special effort is needed to efface from memory the record of the past, or to conceal from our children the bitter experiences of their fathers. They are a part of our national history and worthy of special observation, thought and study.

---

53. William Shakespeare, *As You Like It*, act 2, sc. 1.

The motto that tells us not to speak naught but good of the dead, does not apply here. Death has no power to change moral qualities. What was bad before the war and during the war, has not been made good since the war. Besides, though the rebellion is dead, though slavery is dead, both the rebellion and slavery have left behind influences, which will remain with us, it may be, for generations to come.

Rapid indeed is the march of time. We are already fast getting far away from the days of rebellion and slavery. Men are already losing adequate comprehension of the stupendous wickedness of both. The generations coming after us who shall look only into our Declaration of Independence and our Constitution for a knowledge of our character as a nation, will find it hard to believe that a part of the people professing to believe in the principles of those great charters of liberty could fall from their high estate, reject the creed of their fathers, become traitors to their country and wage cruel and unrelenting war upon their loyal brothers during four long years, for no other purpose in the world than to propagate, maintain and perpetuate a system of slavery the most cruel and savage and debasing upon which the sun ever looked down.

Many disguises have been assumed by the South in regard to that war. It has been said that it was fighting for independence, but the South was already a sharer in the national independence. It has been said that the South was fighting for liberty, but the South was already a sharer in the national liberty. It has been said that the South was fighting for the right to govern itself, but the South had already the ballot and the right to govern itself. What more could it want? What more did it want?

If we would know the answer to these inquiries we have only to read the utterances of Alexander H. Stephens, the vice-president of the Southern Confederacy, the clearest headed statesman on that side of the question.

From him we shall learn that the great and all-commanding object for which the South withdrew from the Senate to the field, appealed from the deliberations of reason to the arbitrament [*sic*] of the sword, from debate to bayonets, from the ballot to the battlefield, was to found and erect a government based upon the idea of a privileged class, of inequality of natural rights, and of the rightfulness of slavery.

Most of the rebellions and uprisings in the history of nations have been for freedom, and not for slavery. They have found their mainspring and power among the lowly. But here was a rebellion, not for freedom, but for slavery, not to break fetters, but to forge them, not to secure the blessings of liberty, but to bind with chains millions of the human race. It was not from the low, but from the high, not from the plebeian, but from the patrician, not from the oppressed, but from the oppressor.

For this, and only for this, we lost millions of treasure and rivers of blood. For this, and only for this, the beautiful South was made desolate; the nation weighed down under a debt heavier than a mountain of gold, and half a million of our sons and brothers swept into bloody graves.

Fellow citizens: I am not indifferent to the claims of a generous forgetfulness, but whatever else I may forget, I shall never forget the difference between those who fought for liberty and those who fought for slavery; those who fought to save the republic and those who fought to destroy it.

We are sometimes asked, "What was gained by the suppression of this slave-holding rebellion?" and whether it is worth what it cost? It had perhaps better be asked, what we should have lost had we failed to suppress the rebellion? In what condition would this country be with the lower half of the Mississippi in the hands of a foreign and hostile power? Who can paint the horrors of wars and incursions which would have reddened the line running east and west, separating two governments, one based upon liberty and equality, and the other upon slavery and race inferiority? Would not the raw edges of such a line be always chafing and bleeding? Heavy as has been the cost of the war would not a heavier one have fallen upon the country had the war failed?

Fellow citizens: You lament, I lament, and we all lament the war forced upon us by the propagandists of slavery and caste. Your hearts ache in the contemplation of its dreadful hardships and horrors, for war here, as elsewhere, was a vast and terrible calamity.

But to estimate properly what was lost and what was gained, a more comprehensive generalization than present space will permit is required.

If the existence of society is more than the lives of individual men; if all history proves that no great addition has ever been made to the liberties of mankind, except through war; if the progress of the human race has been disputed by force and it has only succeeded by opposing force with force; if nations are most effectively taught righteousness by affliction and suffering; if the eternal laws of rectitude are essential to the preservation, happiness and perfection of the human race; if there is anything in the world worth living for, fighting for and dying for, the suppression of our rebellion by force was not only a thing right and proper in itself but an immense and immeasurable gain to our country and the world. Had that rebellion succeeded with all its malign purposes, what then would have become of our grand example of free institutions, of what value then would have been our government of the people by the people and for the people? What ray of light would have been left above the horizon, to kindle the first hope of the toiling millions in Europe? Every despot in the Old World would have seen in our manifest instability of government, a new and powerful argument in favor of despotic power.

A failure to suppress this rebellion would not only have lost us prestige abroad, but it would have entailed upon us innumerable and intolerable troubles at home. Successful wickedness is contagious and repeats itself. Jefferson Davis and his rebellion successful, would have prepared the way for other rebels and traitors. Instead of our rival and hostile confederacy, in that case, this great country would have in time become divided, torn and rent into numerous petty states, each warring upon and devouring the substance of the other. So this great war of ours may have saved us many wars.

It is said that we might have lived in peace with the so-called Confederate States of America.

To my mind such peace would have been impossible. If we could have lived in peace in separation, as contended, separation itself would have been impossible. If we could not live in peace when we were citizens of the same country, under the same flag, participating in the same government, with the same powerful national motives for cultivating friendly and fraternal relations, it is not reasonable to suppose that peace and amity would spring up between us under separate governments, based upon diametrically opposite principles.

To us the suppression of the rebellion means peace, nationality, liberty, and progress. It means the everlasting exclusion from the entire borders of the republic of that system of barbarism, which gave birth to the rebellion, a system that branded our Declaration of Independence as a lie, our civilization as a sham, our religion as a mockery, and made our name a byword and a hissing among all the nations of the earth.

In a speech delivered recently in the city of New Orleans Mr. Jefferson Davis made the following statement:

"As for me—I speak only for myself—our course was so just, so sacred, that, had I known all that has come to pass, had I known what was to be inflicted upon me, all that my country was to suffer, all that our posterity was to endure, I would do it over and over again." [Great applause].

When we see sentiments like these emanating from Southern men and rapturously applauded by admiring assemblies of the people we may well enough keep in mind the principles and benefits which we sought to sustain, and did sustain, in our contest with that slaveholding rebellion.

But what of the emancipated class? How stands the case with them today? Has liberty been a blessing or a curse? Has their freedom been a credit or a calamity to them? I admit that on the surface there are some reasons for asking these questions; but plainly enough they are superficial reasons and are derived from shallow and imperfect reflection.

Unquestionably the condition of the freedman is not what it ought to be, but the cause of their affliction is not to be found in their present freedom, but in their former slavery. It does not belong to the present, but to the past. They were emancipated under unfavorable conditions, they were literally turned loose, hungry and naked, to the open sky. They had neither home, nor friends, nor money. Such was their destitution at the start that their enemies consoled themselves with the thought that hunger and exposure would soon thin them out, and possibly destroy them all together. Those who now carp

284   *The Essential Douglass*

at their destitution, and speak of them with contempt, should judge them leniently, and measure their progress, not from the heights to which they may in time attain, but from the depths from which they have come. They have perished neither from cold nor hunger, and from the last United States census we learn that their increase is ten percent; greater than that of the native white population of the South.

Twenty-five years ago no child of these people was permitted to attend school and learn to read; now there are two hundred thousand of these children attending school. The time would fail me to tell of the various efforts now being made to improve the condition of the emancipated class, and to place them within the range of an equal chance in the race of life, and to tell you how the opportunities now afforded them are embraced, appreciated and improved.

While, as most of you know, my whole life has been devoted to the work of abolishing slavery and to the further work of making a favorable impression for the colored race, on the minds of the American people, when freedom came to the enslaved in the sudden and striking manner in which it did come, I was oppressed with serious doubts and fears that they might in some way in the intoxication of their new freedom, damage their cause and invite destruction. The transition from slavery to freedom, from political degradation to political equality, from abject dependence to personal responsibility and self reliance, is seldom made without suffering. What has happened in the West Indies, what has happened in Russia was naturally expected to happen here. But happily for us, the trouble here has not been so great as in either of the countries named.

For one, I am not so much surprised by the shortcomings of the emancipated race, as by their successes; I do not despair, no man should despair of a people whom neither slavery nor freedom can kill. No man should despair of a race that, in the face of a prejudiced and a hate, more active, intense and bitter, than ever assailed California Chinamen, border Indians, or Russian Jews, has risen from the ashes of utter destruction, and increased the numbers ten percent; beyond that of people in the most favored conditions.

On an occasion like this, it should not be forgotten that these emancipated people, who are often so harshly criticized were the only friends the loyal nation had in the South during the war.

They were eyes to our blind, legs to our lame, guides to our wounded and escaping prisoners, and often supplied information to our generals. Which prevented the slaughter of thousands. It should also not be forgotten that, when permitted to do so, they enrolled themselves as soldiers of the republic, and they did help you to suppress it.

Fellow citizens: my sympathies are not limited by my relation to any race. I can take no part in oppressing and persecuting any variety of the human family. Whether in Russia, Germany, or California, my sympathy is with the oppressed, be he Chinaman or Hebrew.

I have no sympathy with the narrow, selfish, notion of economy, which assumes that every crumb of bread, which goes into the mouths of one class, is so much taken from the mouths of another class; and hence, I cannot join with those who would drive the Chinaman from our borders.

Fellow citizens, in conclusion, I would bring you back to what I consider grand and sacred local duty, and that is, the erection here in Rochester of some monument of bronze, marble, or granite, which shall commemorate to after-coming generations, the unfaltering courage, the unswerving fidelity, the heroic self-sacrifice of your sons and brothers, during the late war. Rochester is a luminous point in Western New York, and is seen alike by the lakes and by the ocean. It is fit and proper that she should have a monument to the virtues developed in her in the momentous crisis wherein was involved the life and death, the salvation and destruction of the republic. This monument, symmetrical and beautiful, would be a just tribute to the dead, and a noble inspiration to the living. It would stand before your people mute but eloquent—a sacred object around which your children and your children's children could rally, and draw high inspiration of patriotism and self-sacrifice by studying the deeds of their fathers, which saved their country to peace, to union and to liberty.

36. "It Moves, or the Philosophy of Reform," a speech delivered to the Bethel Literary and Historical Association in Washington, DC, on November 20, 1883 and published as a pamphlet (Washington, DC: Bethel Literary and Historical Association, 1883)[54]

IT MOVES.

Such was the half suppressed and therefore cowardly and yet confident, affirmation of Galileo,[55] the great Italian mathematician.

He had solved a vast problem and had done more than any man of his day and generation to dispel the intellectual darkness of ages, and reform the astronomical thought of the world; yet here he was virtually upon his knees before the power of ignorance and superstition; selling his soul to save his life.

The circumstances under which the above words were spoken or whispered, for they were not spoken aloud, were critical, as, indeed, circumstances always are, when a new truth is born into the world. For there is ever at such times some Herod ready to seek the young child's life, and a multitude to cry out, "Crucify him!"

The courage and integrity of this apostle of a new truth was put to the severest test. He had been solemnly arraigned, fiercely accused, and sternly condemned to death for teaching a new doctrine at war with the prevailing theology of the period.

Theology in those days endured no contradiction. The voice of the Church was all powerful. It was able not only to punish the soul, and shut the gates of heaven against whom it would, but to kill the body as well. The case of Galileo was therefore one of life and death. He must either affirm the truth and die, or deny the truth and live. Skin for skin, as was said of Job, all that a man hath will he give for his life. Under this terrible pressure the courage of the great man quailed. Hence he, in open court denied and repudiated the grand and luminous truth which he had demonstrated, and with which his name was to be forever associated. His denial was probably not less hearty and vehement

---

54. "It Moves" is among Douglass' many reflections on "the philosophy of reform" after the Civil War. In the speech, he offers his thoughts on the meaning of reform and the moral responsibility each human being has to make the world a better place.
55. Galileo Galilei (1564–1642) was an Italian scientist and philosopher.

than was that of Peter when he denied his Lord.[56] There was not only likeness in their denial, but likeness in their repentance.

The words I have quoted were the tremulous reaffirmation to himself of the truth that he had denied in the hall of his rigorous judges. They were no doubt forced from his quivering lips to silence the upbraiding of an accusing conscience. There is generally a great tumult in the human soul when guilty of any meanness, especially to such a soul as has not become hardened by persistent violation of its moral nature. Peter and Galileo were great-hearted men. The one sought relief in bitter tears, the other in reaffirming to himself the truth he had denied to the world.

Is there no apology for these examples of human weakness? If there is much that is humiliating in the attitude of these two great men, for great men they were, spite of their weakness, there is also something to commend. He should step lightly who sits in judgment upon the weakness of those who pioneer an unpopular cause. Heroic courage is a noble quality; but it is not always the possession of great minds. "Stand by your principles!" shouts the crowd, but, if put to such a test as that of our two worthies, how many of all the crowd could be found to practice what they preach?

If only the truly brave were allowed to throw stones at the cowards, few stones would be thrown, and few wounds would be inflicted. Any man can be brave where there is no danger. If those only are true believers who can face peril, torture and death for their faith, the true church is small, and true believers are few. Men are easily heroes to heaven while they are cowards to earth. They can brave the unknown terrors of eternity, while they quail before the known terrors of time. Erasmus[57] expressed much of genuine human nature, when he declared that he would rather trust God with his soul than the inquisition with his body. Even the mercy of the law allows something for the deviation from the straight line of truth, when a man swears under duress.

It should never be forgotten that the instruments of reform are not necessarily perfect at all points of possible human character. Men may be very good and useful and yet far from being the stuff out of which martyrs are made.

Though Peter denied his Lord, and Galileo science, though both quailed before the terrors of martyrdom, and though neither was as strong as the truth they had denied, the world is vastly better off for their lives, their words and their works. It required a larger measure of courage for Galileo to whisper truth in his day than for us to proclaim the same truth now upon the house-top.

The greatest coward can now shout that he has been with Jesus, but only the grandly heroic could do so when menaced by the spears and swords of Roman

---

56. Matthew 26:69–75.
57. Desidirius Erasmus (1466–1536) was a Dutch philosopher and theologian.

soldiers, in the judgment hall of Pilate, with death upon the cross the probable penalty for being in such company.

I am to speak to you of the philosophy of reform. According to the dictionary, and we are bound to adhere to the truth of words, the word reform is defined, "to put in a new and improved condition; to bring from bad to good; to change from worse to better." This is true, apply it as we may; whether it be self reform, social reform, national reform, or reform in any direction whatever.

We are nevertheless met at the outset of this discussion with the question as to whether there is any such thing as reform in the sense defined in the dictionary. It is contended by some very respectable writers and thinkers, that reform is a delusion, a deceitful appearance; that there is no such thing as making the world better; that the phenomenon of change every where observable, brings no substantial improvement; that mankind are like the sea, whose waves rise and fall, advance and retreat, while the general level remains forever the same.

It is contended that the balance between good and evil remains, like the sea, fixed, unchangeable, and eternally the same. In support of this disheartening theory, these turn our eyes toward the East and lead us about among its decayed and wasted civilizations, its ancient cities, its broken monuments, its moldering temples, its ruined altars, its buried treasures, its shattered walls and fallen pillars, and picture to us in brilliant colors their former greatness and glory, and with the gloomy Byron, they inquire, "Where are their greatness and glory now?"

I shall not stop to combat this skepticism till I have mentioned another and a worse form of unbelief, not the denial that the world is growing better, but the assertion that it is growing worse. Improvement is not only denied, but deterioration is affirmed. According to the advocates of this theory, mankind are on the descending grade; physically, morally and intellectually, the men and women of our age are in no respect equal to the ancients, and art, science and philosophy have gained nothing. This misanthropic view of the world may, I think, be easily answered. It has about it show of truth and learning, but they are only seeming, not real.

One cause of the error may be for want of a proper knowledge of the remote past. Here, as elsewhere, 'tis distance lends enchantment to the view. We fail to make due allowance for the refractive nature of the medium through which we are compelled to view the past. We naturally magnify the greatness of that which is remote. By this the imagination is addressed rather than the understanding. The dim and shadowing figures of the past are clothed in glorious light, and pigmies appear as giants.

Grand and sublime, however, as is the glorious faculty of imagination as a reflector and creator, and while it is the explanation of all religion, and, perhaps, the source of all progress, it is nevertheless the least safe of all our faculties for the discernment of what is truth. There are two sufficient modes of answering theories in denial of progress and reform. One is an appeal to the essential nature of man; the other is to historical facts and experience. A denial of progress and the assumption of retrogression is a point-blank contradiction to the ascertained and essential nature of man. It opposes the known natural desire for change, and denies the instinctive hope and aspiration of humanity for something better.

A theory involving such results may well enough be rejected, even without further reason. It is just as natural for man to seek and discover improved conditions of existence, as it is for birds to fly in the air or to fill the morning with melody or to build their nests in the spring. The very conditions of helplessness in which men are born suggest reform and progress as the necessity of their nature. He literally brings nothing into the world to meet his multitudinous necessities. He is, upon first blush, less fortunate than all other animals.

Nature has prepared nothing for him. He must find his own needed food, raiment and shelter, or the iron hand of nature will smite him with death. But he has a dignity which belongs to himself alone. He is an object, not only to himself, but to his species, and his species an object to him. Every well formed man finds no rest to his soul while any portion of his species suffers from a recognized evil. The deepest wish of a true man's heart is that good may be augmented and evil, moral and physical, be diminished, and that each generation shall be an improvement on its predecessor.

I do not know that I am an evolutionist, but to this extent I am one. I certainly have more patience with those who trace mankind upward from a low condition, even from the lower animals, than with those that start him at a high point of perfection and conduct him to a level with the brutes. I have no sympathy with a theory that starts man in heaven and stops him in hell.

To this complexion it must come at last, if no progress is made, and the only movement of mankind is a downward or retrograde movement. Happily for us the world does move, and better still, its movement is an upward movement. Kingdoms, empires, powers, principalities and dominions, may appear and disappear; may flourish and decay; but mankind as a whole must ever move onward, and increase in the perfection of character and in the grandeur of achievement.

That the world moves, as affirmed and demonstrated by the Italian mathematician, was long since admitted; but movement is not less true of the moral, intellectual and social universe than of the physical. Here, as elsewhere, there are centripetal and centrifugal forces forever at work. Those of the physical world are not more active, certain and effective, than those of the moral world.

An irrepressible conflict, grander than that described by the late William H. Seward, is perpetually going on. Two hostile and irreconcilable tendencies, broad as the world of man, are in the open field; good and evil, truth and error, enlightenment and superstition. Progress and reaction, the ideal and the actual, the spiritual and material, the old and the new, are in perpetual conflict, and the battle must go on till the ideal, the spiritual side of humanity shall gain perfect victory over all that is low and vile in the world. This must be so unless we concede that what is divine is less potent than what is animal; that truth is less powerful than error; that ignorance is mightier than enlightenment, and that progress is less to be desired than reaction, darkness and stagnation. It is worthy of remark that, in the battle of reform, all the powers on both sides are not usually engaged. The grosser forms of wrong are, as they appear, first confronted. One truth is discovered in the moral sky, and lo! another illumines the horizon. One error is vanquished, and lo! another, clad in complete steel, invites demolition, and thus the conflict goes on and will go on forever.

But we are still met with the question: "Is there any substantial gain to the right?" "Is only one evil suppressed to give rise to another?" "Does one error disappear only to make room for another?" It is impossible to keep questions like these out of the minds of thoughtful men. The facts in answer to them are abundant, familiar, and, as I think, conclusive. First, let us look at the science of astronomy. How grand and magnificent have been the discoveries in that field of knowledge. What victories over error have been achieved by the telescope. That instrument did not bring down what the great poet calls "the brave over-hanging sky,"[58] nor the shining stars in it; but it did bring down and dispel vast clouds of error, both in respect of the sky and of our planet. It must be confessed, too, that it took something from the importance of our planet. The idea that all the hosts of heaven are mere appendages to this earth is no longer entertained by average men, and no man, except our good brother Hampton of England and brother Jasper of Richmond, now stand by the old theory for which the church proposed to murder Galileo. Men are compelled to admit that the Genesis by Moses is less trustworthy as to the time of creating the heavens and the earth than are the rocks and the stars.

Espy unfolded the science of storms, and forthwith thunder and lightning parted with their ancient predicates of wrath and were no longer visitations of divine vengeance.

Experience and observation in the science of government gave us clearer views of justice, and the means of ascertaining it, and jury trial speedily took the trial by ordeal, poison and combat.

Vaccination was discovered, and, like all new discoveries, had at the first to maintain a vigorous battle for existence. It was condemned by the church as a cunning device of the devil to defeat the judgments of God. Nevertheless, it has triumphed, and is now adopted by the best instructed of all nations.

---

58. William Shakespeare, *Hamlet*, act 2, sc. 2.

The history of the world shows that mankind have been gradually getting the victory over famine, plagues and pestilence, and that diseases of all kinds are parting with their repulsive grossness.

When we look in the direction of religion, we see Luther, Melancthon, Erasmus and Zwingle,[59] and other stalwart reformers, confronting and defying the Vatican and repudiating pontifical authority. What is the result? Why, this: men are no longer, as formerly, tortured, burned, strangled and starved to death, on account of their religious opinions. Learning has unlocked to us the mysteries of Egypt. It has deciphered the hieroglyphics, and shown us that the slaughter of animals and the slaughter of men as sacrifices was a rude device of the religious sentiment to propitiate the favor of imaginary gods.

The Christian religion dawned upon Western Europe and a thousand men were no longer slain to make a Roman holiday. A little common sense took the place of unreasoning faith in the Puritan, and old women in New England were no longer hanged as witches.

Science tells us what storms are in the sky and when and where they will descend upon our continent, and nobody now thinks of praying for rain or fair weather.

Only a few centuries ago women were not allowed to learn the letters of the alphabet, now she takes her place among the intellectual forces of the day and ranks with our finest scholars, best teachers and most successful authors. Lundy, Walker and Garrison,[60] shocked by the enormities of slavery, branded the system as a crime against human nature; and, after thirty years of fierce and fiery conflict against press and pulpit, church and state, men have ceased to quote the Scriptures to prove slavery a divine institution.

The fathers of the American Revolution took a vast step in the direction of political knowledge when they discovered and announced humanity as the source and authority for human government. To them we are indebted today for a government of the people. Even Europe itself is gradually parting with its notion of the divine right of kings.

The conception of deity in the younger days of the world was, as all know, wild, fantastic and grotesque. It fashioned its idea into huge, repulsive and monstrous images, with a worship of corresponding grossness, abounding in bloody sacrifices of animals and men. Who will tell us today that there has been no real progress in this phase of human thought and practice, or that the change in the religious conceptions of the world is no improvement? "Even more marked and emphatic" are the evidences of progress when we turn from the religious to the material interests of man. Art, science, discovery and

---

59. Douglass identifies several important religious reformers.
60. Douglass identifies several prominent American abolitionists who emerged early in the movement's history.

invention, startle and bewilder us at every turn, by their rapid, vast and wonderful achievements.

These forces have made men lords where they were vassals; masters where they were slaves, and kings where they were subjects. They have abolished the limitations of time and space and have brought the ends of the earth together.

It is nothing in favor of misanthropy to which the foregoing is in some sense a reply, that evils, hardships and sufferings still remain, and that the fact of life is still far in the rear of our best conceptions of what life should be; for, so long as the most desponding of the present cannot point us to any period in the history of the world for which we would exchange the present, our argument for progress will remain conclusive.

It should be remembered that the so-called splendid civilizations of the East were all coupled with conditions wholly impossible at the present day; and which the masses of mankind must now contemplate with a shudder. We have traveled far beyond Egyptian, Grecian and Roman civilizations, and have largely transcended their religious conceptions.

In view of the fact that reform always contemplates the destruction of evil, it is strange that nearly all efforts of reform meet with more determined and bitter resistance from the recognized good, than from those that make no pretensions to unusual sanctity. It would, upon first blush seem, that, since all reform is an effort to bring man more and more into harmony with the laws of his own being and with those of the universe, the church should be the first to hail it with approval at its inception; but this is a superficial view of the subject.

Of course the message of reform is, in itself an impeachment of the existing order of things. It is a call to those who think themselves already high, to come up higher, and, naturally enough, they resent the implied censure. It is also worthy of remark that, in every struggle between the worse and the better, the old and the new, the advantage at the commencement is, in all cases, with the former. It is the few against the mass. The old and long established has the advantage of organization and respectability. It has possession. It occupies the ground, which is said to be nine points of the law.

Besides, every thing which is of long standing in this world has power to beget a character and condition in the men and things around it, favorable to its own continuance. Even a thing so shocking and hateful as slavery had power to entrench and fortify itself behind the ramparts of church and state, and to make the pulpit defend it as a divine institution.

Another reason why ancient wrong is able to defend itself, is that the wrong of the present, though enormous and flagrant, has taken the place of some greater wrong which has been overthrown. Slavery, for instance, was better than killing captives in war. Dueling is better than private assassination. Gambling better than highway robbery. War, as waged by civilized nations, is better than the indiscriminate massacre practiced in the olden time.

The advocates of slavery could argue with some plausibility that the slaves were better off here than in Africa; that here they could hear the gospel preached, and learn the way to heaven. But deeper down than this plausible view of existing wrong, ancient evil finds advantage in the contest with reform.

Human nature itself has a warm and friendly side for what is old; for what has withstood the tide of time and become venerable by age. Men will long travel the old road, though you show them a shorter and better one, simply because they have always traveled that road. They will live in the old house long after they see the need of a new one. Sweet and precious associations bind us to the dear old home. We cling to it though the midnight stars shine through its shingles; though the North winds from snow-clad mountains whistle their icy songs through its ragged rents and crumbling walls; and though, in shape and size, it may be an architectural anachronism, old fashioned, outlandish and dilapidated. The thought that father and mother lived here in peace, happiness and serene content, makes the old house, with all its defects, still dear to the hearts of their children, from generation to generation. As with the old house, so with the old custom, the old church and the old creed, men love them, stand by them, fight for them, refuse to see their defects, because of the comfort they have given to innumerable souls in sickness and health, in sorrow and death.

It is this love and veneration which today revolts at the revision of the Scriptures. Better that a thousand errors should remain, it insists, than that the faith of the multitude shall be shocked and unsettled by the discovery of error in what was believed infallible and perfect.

Thus there are silent forces always at work, riveting men's hearts to the old, and rendering them distrustful of all innovation upon the long-established order of things, whatever may be the errors and imperfections of that order. Evils, multitudinous and powerful, avail themselves of routine, custom and habit, and manage to live on, long after their baleful influence is well-known and felt.

The reformer, therefore, has, at the outset, a difficult and disagreeable task before him. He has to part with old friends; break away from the beaten paths of society, and advance against the vehement protests of the most sacred sentiments of the human heart.

No wonder that prophets were stoned, apostles imprisoned, and Protestants burned at the stake. No wonder that Garrison was mobbed and haltered; Lovejoy shot down like a felon; Torrey wasted in prison;[61] John Brown hanged, and Lincoln murdered.

It may not be a useless speculation to inquire whence comes the disposition or suggestion of reform; whence that irresistible power that impels men to brave all the hardships and dangers involved in pioneering an unpopular cause?

---

61. Douglass identifies several examples of violence used against abolitionists.

Has it a natural or a celestial origin? Is it human or is it divine, or is it both? I have no hesitation in stating where I stand in respect of these questions. It seems to me that the true philosophy of reform is not found in the clouds, or in the stars, or anywhere else outside of humanity itself.

So far as the laws of the universe have been discovered and understood, they seem to teach that the mission of man's improvement and perfection has been wholly committed to man himself. So is he to be his own savior or his own destroyer. He has neither angels to help him nor devils to hinder him.

It does not appear from the operation of these laws, or from any trustworthy data, that divine power is ever exerted to remove any evil from the world, how great so ever it may be. Especially does it never appear to protect the weak against the strong, the simple against the cunning, the oppressed against the oppressor, the slave against his master, the subject against his king, or one hostile army against another, although it is usual to pray for such interference, and usual also for the conquerors to thank God for the victory, though such thanksgiving assumes that the Heavenly Father is always with the strong and against the weak, and with the victors against the vanquished. No power in nature asserts itself to save even innocence from the consequences of violated law.

The babe and the lunatic perish alike when they throw themselves down or by accident fall from a sufficient altitude upon sharp and flinty rocks beneath; for this is the fixed and unalterable penalty for the transgression of the law of gravitation.

The law in all directions is imperative and inexorable, but beneficial withal. Though it accepts no excuses, grants no prayers, heeds no tears, but visits all transgressors with cold and iron-hearted impartiality, its lessons, on this very account, are all the more easily and certainly learned. If it were not thus fixed, inflexible and immutable, it would always be a trumpet of uncertain sound, and men could never depend upon it, or hope to attain complete and perfect adjustment to its requirements; because what might be in harmony with it at one time, would be discordant at another. Or, if it could be propitiated by prayers or other religious offerings, the ever shifting sands of piety or impiety would take the place of law, and men would be destitute of any standard of right, any test of obedience, or any stability of moral government.

The angry ocean engulfs its hundreds of ships and thousands of lives annually. There is something horrible, appalling and stunning in the contemplation of the remorseless, pitiless indifference with which it rolls on after swallowing its weeping, shivering, shrinking, imploring victims; but reflection vindicates the wisdom of law here, as elsewhere. It is the one limb cut off, the better to save the whole body. What may seem cruel and remorseless in its treatment of the few, is, nevertheless, mercy and compassion to the many; and the wisdom of the law is manifested, not alone by its violation, but by its due observance, as well.

Every calamity arising from human ignorance and negligence upon the sea, tends to the perfection of naval architecture, to increase the knowledge of ocean navigation, and thereby to fashion the minds of men more and more in the likeness of the divine mind.

Men easily comprehend the wisdom of inflexible and unchangeable law, when it is thought to apply only to the government of matter, though for the purpose of miracle, they sometimes seem to deny even this. They contend that these laws may be suspended or evaded by the power of faith. They hold that fire will not burn, that water will not drown, and that poison will not destroy life in particular cases where faith intervenes.

But such views may be dismissed as the outpourings of enthusiasm. Some things are true to faith, which are false to fact; and miraculous things address themselves to faith rather than to science. The more thoughtful among orthodox believers concede that the laws appertaining to matter are unchangeable and eternal.

They have ceased to pray for rain, or for clear weather; but to save something from the wreck which this admission must make in their theological system they except the spiritual nature of man from the operation of fixed and unchangeable laws. Plainly enough, they gain nothing by this distinction. If the smallest particle of matter in any part of the universe is subject to law, it seems to me that a thing so important as the moral nature of man cannot be less so.

It may be further objected to the orthodox view of this question, that, in effect, it does away with moral and spiritual law altogether, and leaves man without any rule of moral and spiritual life. For where there is no law, there can be no transgression, and hence, no penalty. This is not the only difficulty in the way of our acceptance of the common theology, and where it manifestly stands in contradiction to sound reason.

If it is admitted that there are moral laws, but affirmed that the consequence of their violation may all be removed by a prayer, a sigh or a tear, the result is about the same as if there were no law. Faith, in that case, takes the place of law, and belief, the place of life. On this theory a man has only to believe himself pure and right, a subject of special divine favor, and he is so. Absurd as this position is, to some of us, it is, in some vague way, held by the whole Christian world about us, and Christians must cling to it, or give up the entire significance of their prayers and worship.

I discard this office of faith, for many reasons. It seems to me that it strikes at the fundamental principles of all real progress, and ought, by some means or other, to be removed from the minds of men.

I think it will be found that all genuine reform must rest on the assumption that man is a creature of absolute, inflexible law, moral and spiritual, and that his happiness and well-being can only be secured by perfect obedience to such law.

All thought of evasion, by faith or penance, or by any means, must be discarded. "Whatsoever a man soweth, that shall he also reap,"[62] and from this there is no appeal.

It is given to man to first discover the law and to enforce compliance by all his power of precept and example. The great and all commanding means to this end is not remote. It is the truth. This only is the "light of the world."

"All the space between man's mind and God's mind," says Theodore Parker, "is crowded with truth that waits to be discovered and organized into law, for the government and happiness of mankind."

It would be pleasant to dwell here upon the transcendent achievements of truth, in proof of its reforming power. No advancement or improvement has been effected in human character or in human institutions, except through the agency and power of truth. It is the pillar of cloud by day and the pillar of fire by night, to lead the human race through the wilderness of ignorance and out of the thraldom of error.

I am not ashamed of the gospel, says an apostle,[63] for it is the power of God unto salvation. In this we have only a glowing theological statement of a grand philosophical truth.

A gospel which is simply good news, for that is the meaning of the word, has no saving power in it whatever. The only saving power there is in any good news depends entirely upon the truth of such news. Without that quality, good news is an aggravation, a contradiction, and a disappointment; a Dead Sea apple, fair without and foul within.

To a shipwrecked mariner clinging to a spar or a plank or a life preserver, amid the towering billows of a storm-tossed ocean, near the point of despair, the news that a ship in the distance is coming to his relief would be good news indeed, but there would be no salvation in it, unless the news itself were true.

The soul of the apostle's utterance therefore, is, that he is not ashamed of the truth, because it is the power of God unto salvation. Like all grand reformers, this great apostle, filled with a holy enthusiasm, was not ashamed of the message in which, to him, was the power to save the world from sin, and the consequences of sin, though all the world were against him.

Having said thus much of truth and its power, it may be asked, as Pilate in his judgment hall, asked the Savior, "What is Truth?"[64] It is now, as it was then, easier to ask than to answer questions.

For the purpose of this discourse, and the thought it aims to inculcate, it is enough to say that any expression, communication or suggestion, whether it be objective or subjective, intuitive or acquired, which conveys to the human

---

62. Galatians 6:7.
63. Romans 1:16.
64. John 18:38.

understanding a knowledge of things as they exist in all their relations and bearings, without admixture of error, is the truth in respect of all the particular things comprehended in the said expression, communication or suggestion.

A broad distinction, however, must always be observed between the expression and the thing expressed, and also between the expression and the understanding of the expression.

The expression is but the body; the thing expressed is the soul. It is not too metaphysical to say that truth has a distinct and independent existence, both from any expression of it, and any individual understanding of it; and that it is always the same however diverse the creeds of men may be concerning it.

Contemplated as a whole, it is too great for human conception or expression, whether in books or creeds. It is the illimitable thought of the universe, upholding all things, governing all things, superior to all things. Reigning in eternity, it is sublimely patient with our slow approximation to it, and our imperfect understanding of it, even where its lessons are clearly taught and easily understood. It has a life of its own, and will live on, as the light of a star will shine on, whether our dull eyes shall see it or not.

But, as already intimated no definite idea of absolute truth can be perfectly conveyed to the human understanding by any form of speech. Prophets, apostles, philosophers and poets alike fail here.

Impressed with this impossibility of the human mind to comprehend the divine, the sacred writers exclaim, "God is love!" "God is truth!" It is the best of which the case admits, and with it the world must be content. Yet there is consolation here; for, though subject to limitations, man is not absolutely helpless.

While truth, when contemplated as a totality, is so vast as to transcend man's ability to grasp it in all its fullness and glory, there are, nevertheless, individual truths, sparks from the great All-Truth, quite within the range of his mental vision, which, if discovered and obeyed, will light his pathway through the world and make his life successful and happy.

He may not approach the resplendent sun in the sky and gaze into its fathomless depths, into its tempests of fire, or withstand its thunderous flame, storming away into space, thousands of miles beyond its own immeasurable circumference, but he may be warmed and enlivened by the heat, and walk in safety by its light.

All truth to be valuable must be wisely applied. Each class of facts conducts us to its own peculiar truth or principle, obedience or disobedience to which, brings its own special and appropriate results, and each after its kind.

A man may conform himself to one important truth and reap the advantage of his conformity and at the same time be utterly at fault in respect to another truth and suffer the bitterest consequences. He may go through life like a bird with one wing, right on one side, wrong on the other, and confined to earth when he might otherwise soar to heaven. He may be well versed in sanitary truth, and secure to himself sound bodily health, but at the same time violate all the great principles of truth which tend to elevate and improve the mind and purify the heart. On the other hand he may be well versed in all the great truths of morality, but totally ignorant of the laws of mechanics.

An immoral man, well instructed in the science of naval architecture, may build a ship which will easily survive the ten thousand perils of the ocean; while a perfect saint who is ignorant of the laws of navigation and disregards them, will see his ship go to the bottom in the first storm though her deck be crowded with missionaries to the heathen.

Among the common errors of the world, none is more conspicuous than the error of seeking desirable ends by inappropriate and illogical means. An uncivil word is resented by a blow, as if a blow on the body could cure an affront to the mind or change the mind of the offender. A reflection upon personal honor provokes a duel, as if putting your body up to be shot at were proof that you were an honest man. A difference of religious opinion sends you to another store to buy goods, as if a man's principles and not his goods were for sale.

If, as a man can go into a store and purchase a garment, he could go into a church and select a creed to his liking, he might be properly praised or blamed for the wisdom or folly of his choice. But this thing which we call belief does not come by choice, but by necessity; not by taste, but by evidence brought home to the understanding and the heart.

All reform, whether moral or physical, whether individual or social, is the result of some new truth or of a logical inference from an old and admitted truth.

Strictly speaking, however, it is a misnomer to prefix the word truth with the words new and old. Such qualifying prefixes have no proper application to any truth. Error may be old, or it may be new, for it has a beginning and must have an end. It is a departure from truth and a contradiction to the truth, and must pass away with the progressive enlightenment of the race; but truth knows no beginning and has no end, and can therefore be neither old nor new, but is unchangeable, indestructible and eternal.

Hence all genuine and lasting reforms must involve a renunciation of error which is transient, and a return to truth which is eternal.

The mission of the reformer is to discover truth, or the settled and eternal order of the universe. This word discover is an important word. It has a deeper meaning than the merely becoming cognizant of truth, or of any other subject previously unknown. It is not simply the opening of our eyes and seeing what was not seen before, but it seems to uncover, the removal of whatever may obstruct, hinder or prevent the understanding from grasping any object of which it may properly be cognizant. It involves effort, work, either of body or mind, or both.

To the outward eye this work may seem opposed to nature, but to the eye of thought it is found to be in accordance with the higher laws of nature. The men you see yonder, armed with picks, shovels, spades, drills, powder and fire, blasting rocks, tunneling mountains, breaking through the virgin soil, digging down the ancient hills, filling up the deep ravines and valleys, are simply uncovering the great truth of the level, one of nature's best helps to man in promoting civilization, bearing our burdens, and enabling us to keep pace with the birds in travel and commerce.

Yonder block of solid marble contains within its rough, unseemly form the fine symmetrical proportions of a stately Corinthian pillar, one upon which the eyes of unborn generations may look with pleasure; or there may sleep in its cold embrace the entrancing form of woman, or the statue of a scholar, statesman, or poet. Genius and skill only are needed to uncover and reveal it as a thing of beauty and a joy forever.

It is not a war with nature, this hammer and chisel business, but only a loving embracement of her deeper, wiser, and more glorious truths and perfections. It is, as all reform is a kind of Jacob wrestling with the angel[65] for larger blessings.

What is true of external nature is also true of that strange, mysterious, and indescribable, which earnestly endeavors in some degree to measure and grasp the deepest thought and to get at the soul of things; to make our subjective consciousness, objective, in thought, form and speech.

In the necessary conflict between the old and the new, the outward and inward essence of things, men naturally range themselves into two great classes; the one radical, the other conservative. There are many shades of difference between these two extremes. Positive and perfect neutrality is only possible to the absolutely ignorant and stupid. This class of men see only results; but know nothing as to the method or the labor of bringing them about. The most they can say when the work of the reformer is accomplished is, "Thank Providence!"

Antislavery men, against a storm of violence and persecution which would have appalled most men, educated the people of the North to believe that slavery was a crime; educated them up to the point of resistance to the slave power, and thus brought about the abolition of slavery. Yet the ignorant and stupid will still ask, "What have Garrison, Gerrit Smith and others done for the colored people?" They see the colored man free; they see him riding on railways and steamboats, where they were never allowed to ride before; they see him going to school and crowding his way into the high places of the land, which twenty years ago would have been thought impossible to him, but they do not see by whose intelligence, courage and heroic endeavor these results have been accomplished. They are neutral from ignorance and stupidity. They have no part or lot in the work of reform, except to share its fruits.

---

65. Genesis 22:32.

Besides this stupid class, there is another, which may be called intermediates. They stand between the two extremes; men who compliment themselves for their moderation, because they are neither hot nor cold; men who sometimes help a good cause a little in order to hinder it a good deal. They are, however, of little account in the conflict with evil. They are mere drift wood; what sailors call dead water. They follow in the wake of their respective forces, being themselves destitute of motive power.

It is the extreme men on either side who constitute the real forces. All others move as they are moved upon. By their timidity and dead weight, they do much to retard a good cause; but when the conflict is over and the victory won, they are usually found at the front, shouting more loudly than any of those who shared in the conflict.

It is ever the first step in any great cause that costs, and the fate of pioneers is to suffer reproach and persecution.

> *"Then to side with Truth is noble,*
> *When we share her wretched crust,*
> *Ere her cause bring fame or profit,*
> *And 'tis prosperous to be just;*
> *Then it is the brave man chooses,*
> *While the coward stands aside,*
> *Doubting in his abject spirit,*
> *Till his Lord is crucified;*
> *And the multitude make virtue*
> *Of the faith they had denied.*
> *For Humanity sweeps onward;*
> *Where today the martyr stands,*
> *On the morrow crouches Judas,*
> *With the silver in his hands;*
> *Far in front the cross stands ready*
> *And the crackling fagots burn,*
> *While the hooting mob of yesterday,*
> *With silent awe return*
> *To glean up the scattered ashes*
> *Into History's golden urn."*[66]

---

66. James Russell Lowell, "The Present Crisis."

37. "Address to the Annual Meeting of the New England Woman Suffrage Association," a speech delivered in Boston, Massachusetts, May 24, 1886 and published as "Frederick Douglass on Woman Suffrage" in the *Boston Women's Journal*, June 5, 1886[67]

LADIES AND GENTLEMEN:

It is a long time since it was my privilege to address a convention of reformers in Boston. In my more youthful days, when slavery was the great evil of the land, and demanded the voice and vote of the humblest for its removal, it was often my lot to be a speaker upon such occasions. But since the abolition of slavery and the enfranchisement of the freedman, both my occupation and my facility as a speaker have been considerably diminished.

Yet I can truly say that it gives me very great pleasure to be again in Boston, and to stand upon this platform, and to say my word, however humbly and unskillfully it may be, for the cause of woman.

When invited to be here, I was impelled to comply by three reasons: First, because I believe in the justice of the cause of woman; second, because I believe in agitation; and third, because I gratefully appreciate the services rendered by woman to the cause of emancipation.

When I consider what was done for the slave by such women as Lucretia Mott, Lydia Maria Child, Elizabeth Cady Stanton, Maria W. Chapman, Thankful Southwick, Lucy Stone, Abby Kelley Foster, Angelina Grimke, Elizabeth B. Chace,[68] and other noble women, I not only feel it a grateful duty, but a high privilege, to give my voice and vote in favor of a larger sphere, and a broader liberty for the activities of woman.

I, however, come before you with little confidence in my ability to assist your cause. I can add nothing to the force and very little to the volume of argument in favor of the claims you make. The most I can hope to do is to give back to you, in some humble measure, the thought and feeling common to all the friends of this movement.

As in the days of the anti-slavery conflict, so in respect of this cause, our mission is the *reiteration* of truths familiar to all, for here, as elsewhere, there

---

67. In this speech, Douglass responds to several common arguments against the extension of suffrage to women. It is among his most detailed defenses of gender equality.
68. Douglass identifies several women who contributed significantly to the movement to abolish slavery in the United States.

is nothing new under the sun. The terms new and old do not properly apply to any great truth or principle. Error may be new or it may be old. It has a beginning and must have an end; but truth is neither new nor old. It is the fundamental law of the universe. It is from everlasting to everlasting, and can never pass away.

It is upon this broad, unchangeable and eternal foundation that I base every right of man or woman, and I know of no cause which rests more squarely upon this foundation than the cause which this convention has assembled to promote.

I congratulate you, my friends, upon the progress already made in fixing this fundamental idea in the public mind and heart. I think a glance at the history of your movement is full of encouragement. Though small and apparently insignificant in its origin, though limited in its resources, though met at the beginning by a storm of derision, and threatened with extinction, though the powers that be, in church and state, opposed it, though the heathen raged and the people imagined a vain thing, its growth has been strong, steady, and irrepressible. Those who doubt the ultimate success of this cause will do well to remember, not merely what remains to be done, but what has already been accomplished.

Fifty years ago, woman was but feebly recognized as a factor in the political civilization of our country. She was almost unknown to the world as a platform and public teacher. Her silence in this field was akin to the silence of the grave. When she attempted to speak she started at the sound of her own voice; her mission was to be seen, but not heard. We have no better evidence of her progress today than is found in her complete triumph over this childlike timidity. I live in Washington, and often listen to speeches in Congress, but the most eloquent and able speakers in Congress do not speak with more self-possession or assurance of fitness than such women as Mrs. Livermore, Mrs. Stone, Mrs. Stanton, Miss Eastman and others.[69] I am wrong, however, in asserting that woman was entirely silent in public forty years ago. She in fact made a good deal of noise more than twice forty years ago, and that fact illustrates the inconsistency of the opposition still felt to her speaking in public. Her voice was then louder in song than it is now in speech. Even the disciples of Paul would permit her to sing in church, and would applaud her in the concert-room, and on the boards of the theater. Her voice was never dreadful or shocking until it was made to express her own convictions of truth and duty. A vast and wonderful change has taken place in the public mind as to what is proper for woman in this respect. In her right of speech her victory is complete. There is literally no language nor speech in which her voice is not heard. In Europe as well as in America, thousands listen to her eloquence and applaud her wisdom. She is

---

69. Douglass identifies several prominent advocates of women's suffrage.

hailed today not only as an angel of beauty, but as an angel of peace, temperance, and social order.

Of course this victory has not come all at once, without effort, without labor and suffering. No victory that is worth anything to the world ever comes in that way. It is a part of the settled order of Providence that the cross must ever precede the crown, and that battle must precede victory. In bearing this cross and maintaining this conflict, woman has risen in grandeur and glory, like the rainbow above the storm.

In securing the right to think and to speak, the right to use her voice and her pen, she has secured the means of victory in all other right directions. For speech is the lever that moves the world. In her ability to speak, write, and publish, organize and agitate, she has a weapon superior to swords, guns, and dynamite; a weapon before which powers and principalities and all forms of oppression may well fear and tremble.

A word of the wisdom of the movement.

Whether intentional or accidental, this movement for the rights of woman has been conducted with remarkable wisdom. It has observed the expediency of doing one thing at a time, and everything in its order. "Without haste, without rest," woman has shown that patience and persistence which has never yet failed of success in a good cause. Her first demand was not for suffrage, but for the right to think and speak for herself. Her next was a demand for a higher education and an enlargement of her opportunities for making an honest living.

She has measurably compelled compliance with all these demands. She has unbarred the gates to nearly all the schools, colleges, and universities; she has made her way into all the learned professions; she has become both a discoverer and an inventor, and has greatly enlarged the boundaries of her industrial avocations.

Forty years ago there were not thirty occupations open to woman. Now there are more than three hundred open to her.

Wisely and well in the earlier years, woman demanded bread for her hungry sisters, and urged it with wonderful skill and effect. This was an appeal which went straight home to the heart of humanity. The advocates of woman suffrage listened to the reports from all the miserable abodes of their sex; from dark cellars; from dilapidated garrets; and told the story of glassy eyed hunger, of shriveled forms, of famished hands, with heart-melting eloquence, for none could tell the story of woman like woman herself.

[. . . .]

To man there are a thousand ways of escape, but only a few to women. If this movement in behalf of woman had accomplished nothing more than the enlargement of woman's industrial pursuits, it would have fully vindicated its right to be gratefully recognized as one of the most beneficent movements of the age. It has increased the number and variety of woman's works in the world, and these results will continue and will increase.

The progress of society is in the direction of refinement and spirituality. Some form of grossness is eliminated with every step upward of the race. It is in accordance with the divine order. Not that which is spiritual is first, but that which is natural; after that, that which is spiritual. The heavier kinds of labor, which require toughness of fiber and great strength of muscle, will be done by machinery; and mind, rather than muscle, will be increasingly demanded, as the wheels of progress roll on. In this labor of the mind, woman's quickness of perception, delicacy of touch, and agility of movement, will give her superior facility in doing most of the needed work of the world. But whether this shall be so or not, it is evident that blindness and prejudice will yet have to admit that woman has a right to do anything and everything which tends to the perfection of the human soul and of human well-being.

But now I come to the point, the one insisted upon by this convention, and which constitutes the all-commanding claim set up by woman, namely: The equal right to participate with man in the government under which she lives. In this demand, she, more than all others, shocks the nerves and develops the greatest opposition of her fellow-citizens. It is the great right which includes all others, and puts woman on an equal plane with man in all that concerns the safety and welfare of the state and the nation. In that single right is contained the right not only to vote, but to be voted for; not only to appoint others to office, but to hold office equally with others. In a word, it implies all that is contained in the idea of complete and perfect citizenship. It means the ballot-box, the jury-box, the cartridge-box, and all the boxes connected with the safety, progress, and welfare of society.

Considering the long and universal subjection of woman to the legal and political power of man, it is not strange that men for the moment stand aghast at the magnitude of this demand. It falls upon their ears like a trumpet-call from the barricade of domestic rebellion, to surrender. Naturally enough, the first feeling among men is one of surprise, the next resentment, and the last a stubborn determination to hold the fort at all hazards.

In order that woman should not give up the contest too soon, she should fully comprehend the difficulty of sudden compliance with her demand for suffrage. Large bodies move slowly, but they move. "The sun do move." The world has been going so long and with such force and steadiness in the wrong direction that it cannot turn all at once in a new and untried way. It is not altogether owing to man's disposition to trample upon the weak and play the tyrant that he refuses to accede to woman's demand for suffrage. He is not, as the wise Mrs. Howe has well said, "Satan behind the scene." He must be reasoned with a little as well as scolded a good deal—and in what I have to say I shall try to do both. It is not enough to assert that the right of woman to suffrage is self-evident, for against prejudice, custom, and superstition, nothing is self-evident. The longest wars and the fiercest battles that the world has ever seen have been waged where self-evident rights were involved. The late tremendous war between the North and the South was over the question whether a man is the rightful owner of his own body. The war for American independence was a war for the self-evident rights of the American people, as against the pretensions of a British king. The great political fight now progressing in England is over the self-evident rights of Ireland. The eighty years' war in the Netherlands was over the self-evident right of the people to worship God according to the dictates of their own conscience.

Indeed, it would seem in many cases that the plainer and simpler the proposition, the more widely and bitterly will men differ about it. Suffrage for woman—self-evident to us—upon first blush, to the average man, seems absurd, monstrous, and shocking. But when he stops to consider and to ask his reason a few pertinent questions, the case will appear in a different light.

In advocating the claim of the slave to freedom, the fundamental and unanswerable argument was, that the slave is a man. In that one assertion was a whole encyclopedia of argument, and so I reason in regard to suffrage for woman. The question which should be put to every man and which every man should put to himself is, Who and what is woman? Is there really anything in her nature and constitution which necessarily unfits her for the exercise of suffrage? Is she a rational being? Has she a knowledge of right and wrong? Can she discern between good and evil? Is she a legitimate subject of government? Is she capable of forming an intelligent opinion of public men and public measures? Has she a will as well as well as a mind? Is she able to express her thoughts and opinions by words and acts? As a member of society and a citizen of the state, has she interests like those of men, which may be promoted or hindered, created or destroyed, by the legislative and judicial action of the government?

When these questions are answered according to truth, the right of woman to participate in the government under which she lives, and which she is taxed to support, does not seem absurd.

I hold that there is not one reason, not one consideration of justice and expediency, upon which man can claim the right to vote which does not apply equally to woman. If he knows right from wrong, so does she; if he is a subject of government, so is she; if he has a natural right to vote, so has she; if she has no right to exclude him, he has no right to exclude her.

If we turn to the constructive elements of the American government, we are conducted to the same conclusion. The American doctrine of liberty is that governments derive their right to govern from the just consent of the governed, that taxation without representation is tyranny, and the founders of the republic went so far as to say that resistance to tyrants is obedience to God. On these principles, woman not less than man has a right to vote. She has all the attributes that fit her for citizenship. Equally with man she is a subject of the law. Equally with man she is bound to honor the law. Equally with man she is bound to obey the law. There is no more escape from its penalties for her than for him. When she violates the law in any way, or commits crime, she is arrested, arraigned, tried, condemned, and punished, like any other criminal. She then finds in her womanhood neither excuse nor protection. If the law takes no thought of sex when it accuses her of crime, why should it take thought of sex when it bestows its privileges?

Plainly enough, woman has a heavy grievance in being denied the exercise of the elective franchise. She is taxed without representation, tried without a jury of her peers, governed without her consent, and punished for violating laws she has had no hand in making.

If it be contended that government has a right to high intelligence for its direction, and I think it has, woman possesses the required qualification. There is no branch of knowledge which man has mastered that she may not master. She is seen in all the learned professions. She is teacher, preacher, doctor, lawyer; why, then, may she not be a voter and a statesman? When the colored man was denied the right to vote because he did not know enough, I used to say, "If he knows enough to know the law, he knows enough to vote. If he knows enough to pay taxes, he knows enough to vote. If he knows enough to be punished for crime, he knows enough to vote. If he knows as much when sober as an Irishman knows when drunk, he knows enough to vote." And so I can now say of woman. Now, after all, what argument can be brought against the conclusion thus reached? Is there anything in nature, reason, justice, or expediency, against the right or propriety of extending suffrage to woman?

The first and most plausible objection to what I have now been saying is in the assertion that woman is already represented in the government, that she is so represented by her husband, her sons, and her brothers.

On first sight this objection seems valid; but, in point of fact, it is sophistical and delusive. No man can be said to represent another, who has not been chosen by that other to represent him. In the old times it was said that the rich represented the poor, that the whites represented the blacks, that the masters represented the slaves, that the educated represented the ignorant. But the vice of all the pretended representations as the fact that they represented themselves, and, in the nature of things, could only represent themselves. The Germans have a proverb that "those who have the cross, will bless themselves." And this is as true of the ballot as of the cross. If man could represent woman it follows that woman could represent man, but no opponent of women's suffrage would admit that woman could represent him in the government, and in taking that position he would be right; since neither can, in the nature of things, represent the other, for the obvious reason that neither can be the other.

The great fact underlying the claim for universal suffrage is that every man is himself and belongs to himself, and represents his own individuality, not only in form and feature, but in thought and feeling. And the same is true of woman. She is herself, and can be nobody else than herself. Her selfhood is as perfect as perfect and as absolute as is the selfhood of man. She can no more part with her personality than she can part with her shadow.

This fundamental, unchangeable, and everlasting condition or law of nature is, to some extent, recognized both by the government of the state and of the nation. Even in the relation of husband and wife, the individuality of woman is preserved. However united in feeling and in interests they may be, the law wisely recognizes and treats them as two separate, individuals, and as possessing two minds, two wills, and each mind and will equally-entitled to be consulted independently of the other. Where the sale or transfer of property is concerned, the wife is consulted, in the language of the law, "separate and apart from her husband." With this fundamental principle supported by reason and by law, there stands another quite as familiar and quite as self-evident, namely, "The whole of a thing is more than a part"; a proposition as true of humanity and of human qualities as of anything else. All the men and women together are more than the women by themselves, or all the men by themselves. And if governments are strong or weak in proportion to the amount of wisdom and virtue by which they are guided, it follows that that government is wisest and strongest which is guided and controlled by the combined wisdom of all the men and all the women.

A government by man alone is only half supplied with the sum of human excellence within its reach. It is a boat with one oar, a bird with one wing, a fish with one fin, and is crippled by its halfness. It is divested of woman's intuitive nature, her quick sense of right and wrong, her tender solicitude for childhood, her abhorrence of war, her love of peace and temperance. It deprives itself of her delicacy and refinement, and her conservative tendencies, and makes possible coarse, drunken, dissolute, and turbulent rulers.

Believing, as I firmly do believe, that human nature, as a whole, contains more good than evil, I am willing to trust the whole, rather than a part, in the conduct of human affairs.

But I come to another and far more popular objection to the enfranchisement of woman. It is this: Suffrage will degrade her. It will drag her down from her present elevated position. It will plunge her into the muddy waters of politics. In this statement we have two objections chained together, and the one is about as unsound as the other, and yet both are echoed over and over again with the utmost confidence in their soundness. What could be more absurd on the face of it than to pretend that to put woman on a plane of political equality with man is to degrade her, when the whole argument for making man the exclusive possessor of the ballot is based upon his superiority to woman? Does the possession of suffrage degrade man? If not, it will not degrade woman. By means of suffrage he shares the honor, power, and dignity of the government under which he lives. And what suffrage does in this respect for man that it will do for woman. To be made the political equal of her husband will invest her with a new consequence, a new responsibility, and a new honor. She will be consulted as to kind and the quality of the men who shall make and administer the laws, who shall frame the policy, and control the destiny, of the nation. If this is to degrade woman, I should like to know by what means she can be elevated and honored.

But this is only one-half of the objection. We are told she will be *plunged*— she will not step into, not to fall into, but to be plunged into the muddy waters of politics. Plainly enough, the force of this objection lies in the plunging part of it. There is something dreadful about being plunged. It makes one think of those dreadful lines, "plunged in a gulf of dark despair!" But woman is not only to be plunged, but she is to be plunged into the muddy waters of politics! But how came politics [to be] muddy? Politics is the science of government, and to the eye of science as well as religion, "to the pure all things are pure," and there is no more reason for mud in politics than in any other branch of science.

If there is mud there, it is there as an importation, not as an original element. You might as well describe your boots as mud, because you have stepped into the mud, or a man a horse, because you have seen him in a stable. A man's politics ought to be as pure as his religion, and there is no defilement in politics apart from the personal defilement and character of the men who exercise the right of suffrage.

Besides, it is something more than an opinion, for it accords with all experience that woman's presence, at the polls and everywhere else, is a conservator of manner, morals, and decency. But admitting this fact, says the objector, it cannot be denied that politics will bring woman into uncomfortable contact with low, vulgar, and coarse men. Well, granting that it will, what then? Shall we violate a great principle of justice and fair play because of such a liability? Shall a necessary principle be disregarded because of an unnecessary incident connected with its application? Will you banish woman from the polls because of the vulgarity? Will you not rather banish the vulgarity and admit the woman? But women have a complete answer to this objection in a separate ballot-box, where their votes can be deposited entirely apart from the dreaded contact with vulgar men.

But men are over nice in this matter; more nice than wise. The danger does not justify the alarm. Woman is not entirely a stranger to the vulgar crowd. She meets it on the sidewalk, at the depot, in the market-place, in the street-car, in the theater. She meets it on highways, byways, and railways, and everywhere knows how to preserve her dignity and to command respect. If this be true, —and no one can well deny it, —why may she not do the same thing at the polls, where all she has to do is to drop a piece of paper precisely as she drops a letter into a box at the post office?

No matter who, what, or how many may be represented at the ballotbox, she represents herself and only herself, and order, decency, and politeness, and is as far apart from the vulgar characters who may be there as are the poles of the moral universe.

Again, if seclusion and absence from contact with the outside world were the best protection to womanly dignity, the harem would surpass the home. The caged, veiled, and cushioned women of the East, never allowed to be seen by the vulgar crowd, watched over by eyes as vigilant as the suspicions of despotism, would furnish the highest example of refinement and virtue. But such is not the case. Enforced morality is artificial morality. It is the safety that never drowns because it never goes into the water, the virtue that never falls because never tempted.

But there is another objection which a full and faithful discussion of this subject compels me to notice. It is this: it is alleged that woman herself [is] opposed to the woman suffrage movement; that she is contented and happy, and is entirely satisfied with her condition, and would not have the ballot if it were given her by a change in the Constitution. There is doubtless some truth in this statement, but it is manifestly not "the whole truth and nothing but the truth." If the opponents of woman suffrage really believed what they say on this point, they would not be at pains and expense of writing long arguments, making long speeches, and preaching long sermons against the woman suffrage movement. They would allow it to fall by its own weight and weakness. But is it true that woman is contented with her present condition, and would not have the ballot if it were given to her? It is a statement which may be fairly questioned.

Years ago, I heard the same arguments employed against the abolition movement. The slaves were then contented and happy people, who would not have their liberty if it were given them; just as we are now told that women are contented and happy, and would not have the ballot if it were given them. It was not true of the slaves then, and it is not true of woman now. The same men who told us of the contentment and happiness of the slaves were, at the same time, busy framing laws to prevent their escape from slavery. The same is being done now in Congress and in state legislatures against woman suffrage. It must be admitted that my argument at this point does not dispose of this objection conclusively. It does not follow that because the slave was not contented and happy in slavery, that women are not contented in their condition. Nor does it follow that because the slave wanted his freedom, women want to vote. What I have said simply proves the probability of what is true.

But what, after all, if it could be shown that women generally do not want to vote. That fact would not affect the right of others. It would not affect the rights of those who do want to vote. That one man does not want freedom is no reason why another man should be made a slave.

It is for men to recognize the right of woman to vote, and leave to her, as they leave to man, the option whether or not she shall vote. It will be time enough when they do that for them to announce that women will or will not vote. Should the right be once acknowledged, I venture to say that no president could ever be elected to that high office without the votes of women. The most persuasive eloquence of both parties would be employed in gaining their support. Men who oppose granting suffrage would not be much behind those who favor it in soliciting such support. But here is another objection and one very much relied upon in opposing the extension of suffrage to woman, "She cannot perform military service. She is physically incapable of bearing arms, and cannot therefore fight the battles of the country." This objection, which seems so strong to those who bring it, has been answered a thousand times; it contains a vice and a weakness even more fatal to its validity than the objection just disposed of. It founds one of the grandest intellectual and moral rights of human nature upon a purely physical basis.

According to it, the basis of civil government is not mind, but muscle; not reason, but force; not rightful might; it is not human, but bestial. It belongs to man rather as a savage, than to man as a civilized being. Were this theory of government sound, Sullivan, the slugger,[70] should have more political power than Sherman, the senator.[71] The burly prize-fighter should stand higher than the intelligent president of a college.

Besides, this doctrine rules out nearly all the great men of the world, for the profoundest thinkers and students are generally more distinguished for mind than for muscle. If those only who are strong enough to defend the country on the battlefield should be allowed to vote, one-third of all the men of this country would be disfranchised.

All men over forty-five years of age and all who have bodily ailments are exempted from military service, yet all such men have the right to vote. The denial of woman's right to vote on the ground of physical disability appears not only wrong but mean, since it is a discrimination against her which is not applied to others, and by the strong against the weak. But it is not true that women cannot perform military duty. History affirms the contrary. There is no more thrilling chapter in the history of the war in the Netherlands than that which describes the defense of Leyden, where wives fought beside their husbands, and sisters beside their brothers, and where the women were as brave and enduring as the men. In our late war she did exceptional military service

---

70. John L. Sullivan (1858–1918) was an American boxer.
71. John Sherman (1823–1900) was an American politician and diplomat who served as secretary of state and in the House of Representatives and the US senate.

in their care for the sick and wounded, in their administrative capacity, in the gathering and distributing of supplies, in the establishment and support of hospitals, and even in the planning of campaigns.

But granting all that is claimed as to woman's unfitness to perform military duty, is not war exceptional, and peace the normal condition of society? Shall we base a right upon an exception, and disregard a right based upon principle? Is that logical and reasonable? What right have we to measure the rights of a human being under civil government by a condition of things that excludes civil government? War sets aside civil government, and brings us under martial law. Under it, vice becomes virtue; stealing, lying, and robbing excusable; and murder meritorious. Surely, ability to do those things should not be made the basis of political rights.

But perhaps a more serious objection to woman's participation in civil government than either of the preceding ones, relates to its supposed effect upon the home. It is alleged that woman suffrage will introduce strife and division into the family. It is said that woman will be ranged upon one side and man upon the other, and that home will no longer be "sweet home," and that peace and tranquility will no longer dwell under the family roof.

Now, such consequences would be alarming if they were necessary and inevitable, but they do not appear to the eye of sober reason in any such light, and may, therefore, be rejected. It is assumed that difference of opinion in the state may be more safely tolerated than difference of opinion in the family, bound together by respect, tenderness, and love, and therefore more able to sustain such difference. It holds that in order to have peace and tranquility in the family, the woman, the wife, the daughter, and the sister, must have no opinion of their own, or must not be allowed to express such opinion if they have them; that they must deny their intellect and conscience, and become moral, social, and intellectual monstrosities, bodies without souls; in fact, like the gods of the heathen, have ears, and hear not, have eyes and see not; and have tongues, and speak not. Certainly, a principle which requires such self-abnegation, such stultification and self-abasement, cannot be sound, or other than absurd and vicious.

But, happily for the enfranchisement of woman, we have no right to predicate any such dire consequences. Husbands and wives differ in opinion every day, about a variety of subjects, and yet dwell together in love and harmony. How insufferably flat, stale, and unprofitable is that family in which no difference of opinion enters. Who on earth can want to spend his or her days as a simple echo? A body without a soul, a mind without an opinion, a mere bundle of thoughtless concessions, a light under a bushel, a talent buried in silence, a piece of intellectual emptiness and social nothingness?

A difference of opinion, like a discord in music, sometimes gives the highest effects of harmony. A thousand times better is it to have a brave, outspoken woman by one's side, than a piece of mincing nothingness that is ashamed to have an opinion. For myself, from what I know of the nature of the human understanding, I at once suspect the sincerity of the man or the woman who never has an opinion in opposition to mine. Differing, as all human minds do, in all their processes and operations, such uniform agreement is unnatural, and must be false, assumed, and dishonest. The fact is, no family or state can rest upon any foundation less solid than trust and honesty.

But here comes another objection, which is in point-blank contradiction to the one just answered. It is a positive denial that anything will be either gained or lost in the final result of any election, by the enfranchisement of woman, because, as it is affirmed, woman's vote will only express the views and wishes of her husband and brothers. In the former objection, the home was to be broken up by disagreement. In the latter objection, there is to be no disagreement, and woman is to vote according to the political preferences of her husband, and, hence, there will be no difference except in the additional number of the votes cast and counted.

We have only to array one of these objections against the other, to neutralize and destroy the effect of both. Both may be wrong, but both cannot be right. But suppose, however, that the latter objection is true: That is, that the vote of the wife shall simply duplicate that of her husband. Certainly no harm could come of such a result. It would simply be two votes on the same side of whatever question might be involved in the election from this the state could receive no detriment, unless, indeed both votes should be on the wrong side, a circumstance not nearly so likely to occur where two heads are consulted as when one alone shall do all the voting. So this objection, like all the rest, is, in the light of reason, entirely groundless.

But while no evil could come to the state from woman's suffrage, and admitting that no special good would come to the state, which I do not admit except for the sake of the argument, a vast advantage would come to woman herself. Her dignity and importance, as a member of society would be greatly augmented. She would be brought into responsible and honorable relations to the government, her citizenship would be full and complete, and instead of being merely a subject, and she would be sovereign.

And now I ask, What right have I, what right have you, what right has anybody who believes in a government of the people, by the people, and for the people,[72] to deny to woman this full and complete citizenship? What right have I, what right have you, what right has anybody, thus to humiliate one-half of the human family? There is no such right outside of the right of the robber and the usurper!

---

72. Douglass refers to Abraham Lincoln's 1863 Gettysburg Address.

Nothing is clearer in my mind than this, that no person, man or woman, living in this country, can be excluded from participation in its governing power, without positive injury. If woman shall be enfranchised, her views and wishes will be consulted, both as to the men and measures of government. She will be recognized as a power which all men are bound to respect.

No matter upon what pretext, upon what ground of assurance, woman is deprived of the right of suffrage, she is in the condition of a proscribed person. The mark of Cain[73] is set upon her. The thoughtless may not see it. The giddy may not feel it. The masses of women may deny it; but the thoughtful, sober, and intelligent women of the country do see and feel this deprivation to be a useless and bitter proscription. What business has man to inflict this hardship upon sensitive woman? In one breath he praises her as the mother of manners, the model of refinement, the mainstay of virtue, the joy of life, and, in the next breath, he degrades her, and classes her with paupers, idiots, and criminals.

This hardship, for it truly is a hardship, is more painful and crushing in a free government like ours, than under governments where the few are born to rule, and the many to serve. Where a disability is imposed upon all and is borne by all, the burden is divided and the weight for each is light. But here the case is different. Universal suffrage is the rule. Everybody, gentle and simple, good and bad, may vote, except paupers, criminals, idiots, and women. Heaven grant that the day be not distant, when, like the system of chattel slavery, this handwriting of baseness and barbarism shall be blotted out, and when woman before the law, and at the ballot-box, shall stand by the side of man, equal in all that pertains to American citizenship.

---

73. Genesis 4:15.

38. "The Nation's Problem," a speech delivered before the Bethel Literary and Historical Society in Washington, DC, on April 16, 1889 and published as a pamphlet titled, *The Nation's Problem: A Speech Delivered by Frederick Douglass, Before the Bethel Literary and Historical Society, in Washington, D.C.* (Washington, DC: Bethel Literary and Historical Society, 1889)[74]

FRIENDS AND FELLOW CITIZENS:

I congratulate you upon this the twenty-seventh anniversary of the abolition of slavery in the District of Columbia, and I gratefully acknowledge the compliment implied in calling upon me to assist in expressing the thoughts and sentiments natural to this and other similar occasions.

[. . . .]

For reasons which will become apparent in the course of my address, I respond to your call with more than my usual diffidence.

It has been our custom to hail the anniversary of our emancipation as a joyous event. We have observed it with every manifestation of gratitude. During the years immediately succeeding the abolition of slavery, our speeches and addresses on such occasions naturally overflowed with joy, gratitude and praise. We remembered with veneration and love the great men by whose moral testimonies, statesmanship, and philanthropy was brought about the long delayed and long prayed for deliverance of our people.

The great names of Garrison, Whittier, Sumner, Phillips, Stevens, Lincoln and others were gratefully and lovingly repeated. We shouted the praises of these great men as God inspired benefactors. At that time, too, it was well enough and easy to blow aloud our brazen trumpets, call out the crowd, throng the streets with gay processions, and to shout aloud and make a joyful noise over the event, for since the great exodus of the Hebrews from Egyptian bondage no people had had greater cause for such joyful demonstrations. But the time for such demonstrations is over. It is not the past, but the present and the

---

74. This speech is one of many delivered by Douglass late in his life in which he reflects on the national political scene, with particular attention paid to the status of African Americans. It is a wide-ranging speech in which he comments not only on the successes and failures in the realm of policy but also on the moral atmosphere in the country as a whole and in the African American community.

future that most concern us today. Our past was slavery. We cannot recur to it with any sense of complacency or composure. The history of it is a record of stripes, a revelation of agony. It is written in characters of blood. Its breath is a sigh, its voice a groan, and we turn from it with a shudder. The duty of today is to meet the questions that confront us with intelligence and courage.

Without the least desire to awaken undue alarm, I declare to you that, in my judgment, at no period since the abolition of slavery in the District of Columbia, have the moral, social, and political surroundings of the colored people of this country been more solemn and foreboding than they are this day. If this statement is startling it is only because the facts are startling. I speak only the things I have seen. Nature has given me a buoyant disposition. I like to look upon the bright and hopeful side of affairs. No man can see the silver lining of a black cloud more joyfully than I. But he is a more hopeful man than I am who will tell you that the rights and liberties of the colored people in this country

HAVE PASSED BEYOND THE DANGER LINE.

Mark, if you please, the fact, for it is a fact, an ominous fact, that at no time in the history of the conflict between slavery and freedom has the character of the Negro as a man been made the subject of a fiercer and more serious discussion in all the avenues of debate than during the past and present year. Against him have been marshaled the whole artillery of science, philosophy, and history. We are not only confronted by open foes, but we are assailed in the guise of sympathy and friendship and presented as objects of pity.

The strong point made against the Negro and his cause is the statement widely circulated and greatly relied upon that no two people so different in race and color can live together in the same country on a level of equal civil and political rights and powers; that nature herself has ordained that the relations of two such races must be that of domination and subjugation. This old slaveholding Calhoun . . . doctrine, which we long ago thought dead and buried, is revived in unexpected quarters, and confronts us today as sternly as it did forty years ago. Then it was employed as the sure defense of slavery. Now it is employed as a justification of the fraud and violence by which colored men are divested of their citizenship, and robbed of their constitutional rights in the solid South.

To those who are hopefully assuming that there is no cause of apprehension, that we are secure in the possession of all that has been gained by the war and by reconstruction, I ask, what means the universal and palpable concern manifested through all the avenues of debate as to the future of the Negro in this country? For this question meets us now at every turn. Letters fairly pour upon me burdened with this inquiry. Whence this solicitude, or apparent solicitude? To me the question has a sinister meaning. It is prompted not so much by concern for the welfare of the Negro as by consideration of how his relation to the American government may affect the welfare and happiness of the American people. The Negro is now a member of the body politic. This talk about him implies that he is regarded as a diseased member. It is wisely said by physicians that any member of the human body is in a healthy condition when it gives no occasion to think of it. The fact that the American people of the Caucasian race are continually thinking of the Negro, and never cease to call attention to him, shows that his relation to them is felt to be abnormal and unhealthy.

I want the colored people of this country to understand the true character of the great race which rules, and must rule and determine the destiny of this republic. Justice and magnanimity are elements of American character. They may do much for us. But we are in no condition to depend upon these qualities exclusively. Depend upon it, whenever the American people shall become convinced that they have gone too far in recognizing the rights of the Negro, they will find some way to abridge those rights. The Negro is great, but the welfare of the nation will be considered greater. They will forget the Negro's service in the late war. They will forget his loyalty to the republic. They will forget the enmity of the old slaveholding class to the government. They will forget their solemn obligations of friendship to the Negro, and press to their bosoms the white enemies of the nation while they give the cold shoulder to the black friends of the nation. Be not deceived. History repeats itself. The black man fought for American independence. The Negro's blood mingled with the white man's blood at Bunker Hill, and in State St., Boston. But this sacrifice on his part won for him only temporary applause. He was returned to his former condition. He fought bravely with Gen. Jackson at New Orleans, but his reward was only slavery and chains. These facts speak, trumpet-tongued, of the kind of people with whom we have to deal, and through them we contemplate the sternest

POSSIBILITIES OF THE FUTURE.

I have said that at no time has the character of the Negro been so generally, seriously and unfavorably discussed as now. I do not regard discussion as an evil in itself. On the contrary I regard it not as an enemy, but as a friend. It has served us well at other times in our history, and I hope it may serve us well hereafter. Controversy, whether of words or blows, whether in the forum or on the battlefield, may help us, if we but make the right use of it. We are not, however, to be like dumb driven cattle in this discussion, in this war of words and conflicting theories. Our business is to answer back wisely, modestly, and yet grandly.

While I do not regard discussion as an enemy in itself, I cannot but deem it in this instance as out of place and unfortunate. It comes to us as a surprise and a bitter disappointment. It implies a deplorable unrest and unsoundness in the public mind. It shows that the reconstruction of our national institutions upon a basis of liberty, justice and equality is not yet honestly accepted as a final and irrevocable settlement of the Negro's relation to the government, and of his membership in the body politic. There seems to be in it a lurking disposition, a looking around for some plausible excuse for dispossessing the Negro of some part of his inheritance conceded to him in the generous spirit of the new departure of our government. We seem to be trying how not to do it.

Going back to the early days of the anti-slavery movement, I cannot but remark, and I call upon you to remark, the striking contrast between the disposition which then existed to utterly ignore the Negro and the present disposition to make him a topic of universal interest and the deepest concern. When the Negro was a slave and stood outside the government, nobody but a few so-called abolition fanatics thought him worthy of the smallest attention. He was almost as completely outside of the nation's thought as he was outside of the nation's law and the nation's religion. But now all is changed. His freedom makes him discussed on every hand. The platform, the pulpit, the press and the legislative hall regard him and struggle with him as a great and difficult problem, one that requires almost divine wisdom to solve. Men are praying over it. It is always a dangerous symptom when men pray to know what their duty is.

Now it is to this gigantic representation to which I object. I deny that the Negro is correctly represented by it. The statement of it is a prejudice to the Negro's cause. It denotes the presence of the death-dealing shadow of an ancient curse. We had fondly hoped, and had reason to hope, that when the Negro ceased to be a thing and became a man, when he ceased to be an alien and became a citizen, when the Constitution of the United States ceased to be the charter of slavery and became the charter of liberty, the Negro problem was solved and settled forever. The whole contention now raised over him is an anachronism, a misnomer, a false pretense, a delusion and a sham, a crafty substitution of a false issue for the true one.

I deny and utterly scout the idea that there is now, properly speaking, any such thing as a Negro problem now before the American people. It is not the Negro, educated or illiterate, intelligent or ignorant, who is on trial or whose qualities are giving trouble to the nation. The real problem lies in the other direction. It is not so much what the Negro is, what he has been, or what he may be that constitutes the problem. Here, as elsewhere, the lesser is included in the greater. The Negro's significance is dwarfed by a factor vastly larger than himself. The real question, the all-commanding question is whether American justice, American liberty, American civilization, American law and American Christianity can be made to include and protect alike and forever all American citizens in the rights which, in a generous moment in the nation's life, have been guaranteed to them by the organic and fundamental law of the land. It is whether this great nation shall conquer its prejudices, rise to the dignity of its professions, and proceed in the sublime course of truth and liberty marked out for itself since the late war, or shall swing back to its ancient moorings of slavery and barbarism. The Negro is of inferior activity and power in the solution of this problem. He is the clay, the nation is the potter. He is the subject, the nation is the sovereign. It is not what he shall be or do, but what the nation shall be and do, which is

TO SOLVE THIS GREAT NATIONAL PROBLEM.

Speaking for him, I can commend him upon every ground. He is loyal and patriotic; service is the badge of all his tribe. He has proved it before, and will prove it again. The country has never called upon him in vain. What he has been in the past in this respect that he will be in the future. All he asks now, all he has ever asked, all he will ever ask, is that the nation shall fulfill toward him its own recognized and self-imposed obligations. When he asks for bread he will not accept a stone. When he asks for fish he will not accept a serpent. His protest now is against being cheated by cunningly-devised judicial decisions, by frauds upon the ballot box, or by brutal violence of red-shirted rebels. He only asks the American people to adjust the practice to the justice and the wisdom of their laws, and he holds that this is first, midst, and last, and the only problem to be solved.

While, however, the Negro may very properly protest against the popular statement of the question, and while he may insist that the only one; while he may hold that primarily and fundamentally it is an American problem and not a Negro problem, he may materially assist in its solution. He can assume an attitude, develop a character, improve his condition, and, in a measure, compel the respect and esteem of his fellow-men.

In order to do this we have, first of all, to learn and to understand thoroughly the nature of the social, moral, and political forces that surround us. And how to shape our ends and wisely determine our destiny. We should endeavor to discover the true sources or our danger—whether they be within ourselves or in circumstances external to ourselves. If I am here for any useful purpose, it is in some measure to answer the question, "What of the night?"

For the present I have seemed to forget that this is an occasion of joy. I have thus far spoken mainly in sorrow rather than in gladness; in grief rather than in gratitude. Like the resolution of Hamlet, my outlook has been sicklied [*sic*] o'er with that pale cast of thought. I must go on in the same line.

Now, what of the night?[75] What of the night? Is it cheered by the beams of celestial light and hope, or is it saddened by ominous clouds, darkness and

---

75. Isaiah 21:11.

distant thunder? The latter, and not the former, is the true answer. You and I should be brave enough to look the facts fairly and firmly in the face.

I profoundly wish I could make a different response to this inquiry. But the omens are against me. I am compelled to say that while we have no longer to contend with the physical wrongs and abominations of slavery; while we have no longer to chill the blood of our hearers by talking of whips, chains, branding irons and blood-hounds; we have, as already intimated, to contend with a foe, which, though less palpable, is still a fierce and formidable foe. It is the ghost of a by-gone, dead and buried institution. It loads the very air with a malignant prejudice of race. It has poisoned the fountains of justice, and defiled the altars of religion. It acts upon the body politic as the leprous distilment acted upon the blood and body of the murdered king of Denmark.[76] In antebellum times it was the standing defense of slavery. In our own times it is employed in defense of oppression and proscription. Until this foe is conquered and driven from the breasts of the American people, our relations will be unhappy, our progress slow, our lives embittered, our freedom a mockery, and

OUR CITIZENSHIP A DELUSION.

The work before us is to meet and combat this prejudice by lives and acquirements which contradict and put to shame this narrow and malignant feeling. We have errors of our own to abandon, habits to reform, manners to improve, ignorance to dispel, and character to build up. This is something which no power on earth can do for us, and which no power on earth can prevent our doing for ourselves, if we will.

In pointing out errors and mistakes common among ourselves, I shall run the risk of incurring displeasure; for no people with whom I am acquainted are less tolerant of criticism than ourselves, especially from one of our own number. We have been so long in the habit of tracing our failures and misfortunes to the views and acts of others that we seem, in some measure, to have lost talent and disposition of seeing our own faults, or of "seeing ourselves as other see us." And yet no man can do better service to another man than to correct his mistakes, point out his hurtful errors, show him the path of truth, duty, and safety.

One of the few errors to which we are clinging most persistently and, as I think, mischievously, has come into great prominence of late. It is the cultivation and simulation among us of a sentiment which we are pleased to call race pride. I find it in all our books, papers, and speeches. For my part I see no superiority or inferiority in race or color. Neither the one nor the other is a proper source of pride or complacency. Our race and color are not of our own choosing. We have no volition in the case one way or another. The only

---

76. William Shakespeare, *Hamlet*, act 1, sc. 5.

excuse for pride in individuals or races is the fact of their own achievements. Our color is the gift of the Almighty. We should neither be proud of it or ashamed of it. But we may well enough be proud or ashamed when we ourselves achieved success or have failed of success. If the sun has curled our hair and tanned our skin let the sun be proud of its achievement, for we have done nothing for it one way or the other. I see no benefit to be derived from this everlasting exhortation by speakers and writers among us to the cultivation of race pride. On the contrary, I see in it a positive evil. It is building on a false foundation. Besides, what is the thing we are fighting against, and what are we fighting for in this country? What is the mountain, the lion in the way of our progress? What is it, but American race pride; an assumption of superiority upon the ground of race and color? Do we not know that every argument we make, and every pretension we set up in favor of race pride is giving the enemy a stick to break our own heads?

But it may be said that we shall put down race pride in the white people by cultivating race pride among ourselves. The answer to this is that devils are cast out not by Beelzebub, the prince of devils. The poorest and meanest white man, drunk or sober, when he has nothing else to commend him says: "I am a white man, I am." We can all see the low extremity reached by that sort of race pride, and yet we encourage it when we pride ourselves upon the fact of our color. I heard a Negro say, "I am a Negro, I am." Let us do away with this supercilious nonsense. If we are proud let it be because we have had some agency in producing that of which to be proud. Do not let us be proud of what we can neither help nor hinder. The Bible puts us in the condition in this respect of the leopard, and says that we can no more change our skin color than the leopard his spots.[77] If we are unfortunate in being placed among a people with whom our color is a badge of inferiority, there is no need of making ourselves ridiculous but forever, in words, affecting to be proud of a circumstance due to no virtue in us, and over which we have no control.

You will, perhaps, think this criticism uncalled for. My answer is that truth is never uncalled for. Right thinking is essential to right acting, and I hope that we shall hereafter see the wisdom of basing our pride and complacency upon substantial

RESULTS ACCOMPLISHED BY THE RACE.

The question here raised is not merely theoretical, but is of practical significance. In some of our colored public journals, with a view to crippling my humble influence with the colored race, I have seen myself charged with a lack of race pride. I am not ashamed of that charge. I have no apology or vindication to offer. If fifty years of uncompromising devotion to the cause of

---

77. Jeremiah 13:23.

the colored man in this country does not vindicate me, I am content to live without vindication.

While I have no more reason to be proud of one race than another, I dare say, and I fear no contradiction, that there is no other man in the United States prouder than myself of any great achievement, mental or mechanical, of which any colored man or woman is the author. This is not because I am a colored man, but because I am a man, and because color is a misfortune and is treated as a crime by the American people. My sentiments at this point originate not in my color, but in a sense of justice common to all right-minded men. It is not because I am a Negro, but because I am a man. It is that which gives sympathy of the crowd to the underdog, no matter what may be his color. When a colored man is charged with a want of race pride, he may well ask, What race? for a large percentage of the colored race are related in some degree to more than one race. But the whole assumption of race pride is ridiculous. Let us have done with complexional superiorities or inferiorities, complexional pride or shame. I want no better basis for my activities and affinities than the broad foundation laid by the Bible itself, that God has made of one blood[78] all nations of men to dwell on all, the face of the earth. This comprehends the Fatherhood of God and the brotherhood of man.

I have another criticism to make of a position which, I think, often invites unfavorable comparison and positive disparagement. It is our noisy assertion of equality with the Caucasian race. There are two kinds of equality, the potential and the other actual, one theoretical and the other practical. We should not be satisfied by merely quoting the doctrine of potential equality as laid down in the Declaration of Independence, but we should give it practical illustration. We have to do as well as to be. If we had built great ships, sailed around the world, taught the science of navigation, discovered far-off islands, capes, and continents, enlarged the boundaries of human knowledge, improved the conditions of man's existence, brought valuable contributions of art, science, and literature, revealed great truths, organized great states, administered great governments, defined the laws of the universe, formulated systems of mental and moral philosophy, invented railroads, steam engines, mowing machines, sewing machines, taught the sun to take pictures, the lightning to carry messages, we then might claim, not only potential and theoretical equality, but actual and practical equality. Nothing is gained to our cause by claiming for ourselves more than of right we can establish belongs to us. Manly self-assertion, I know, is a power, and I would have that power employed within the bounds of truth and sobriety. We should never forget, in our relations with our fellows, that

---

78. Acts 17:26.

MODESTY IS ALSO A POWER.

When it is manifested without any touch of servility it is as sure to win respect as unfounded pretension is sure to provoke and receive contempt. We should give our critics no advantage at this point, either by word or conduct. Our battle with popular prejudice requires on our part the utmost circumspection in word and in deed. Our men should be gentlemen and our women ladies, and we can be neither without a modest reserve in mind and in manners.

Were I not speaking to the most cultivated class of our people, for the Bethel Literary Society comprises that class, I might hesitate to employ this course of remark. You, I am quite sure, will not misapprehend my statements or my motives.

There is one other point worthy of animadversion—it is the error that union among ourselves is an essential element of success in our relations to the white race. This, in my judgment, is a very serious mistake. I can hardly point out one more pregnant with peril. It is contended that we are now eight millions, that we hold the balance of power between the two great political parties of the country, and that, if we were only united in one body, under wise and powerful leaders, we could shape the policy of both political parties, make and unmake parties, control the destiny of the republic, and secure for ourselves a desirable and happy future. They say that in union there is strength; that united we stand and divided we fall, and much else of the same sort.

My position is the reverse of all this. I hold that our union is our weakness. In quoting these wise sayings colored men seem to forget that there are exceptions to all general rules, and that our position in this country is an exceptional position.

The rule for us is the exception. There are times and places when separation and division are better than union, when to stand apart is wiser than standing together. There are buildings which will hold a few, but which will break down under the weight of a crowd; the ice of the river may be strong enough to bear a man, but would break through under the weight of an elephant. The ice under us in this country is very thin, and is made very weak by the warm fogs of prejudice. A few colored people scattered among large white communities are easily accepted by such communities, and a larger measure of liberty is accorded to the few than would be to the many. The trouble is that when we assemble in great numbers anywhere we are apt to form communities by ourselves, and our occupation of any part of a town or city, apart from the people surrounding us, brings us into separate schools, separate churches, separate benevolent and literary societies, and the result is the adoption of a scale of manners, morals, and customs peculiar to our condition and to our antecedents as an oppressed people. When we thus isolate ourselves we say to those around us, "We have nothing in common with you," and, very naturally, the reply of our neighbors is in the same tone and to the same effect; for when a people care for nobody, nobody will care for them. When we isolate ourselves we lose, in large measure, the common benefit of association with those whose advantages have been superior to ours.

The foundation upon which we stand in this country is not strong enough to make it safe to stand together. A nation within a nation is an anomaly. There can be but one American nation under the American government, and we are Americans. The Constitution of the country makes us such, and our lines of activity should accord with our citizenship. Our circumstances now compel us in certain directions to maintain separate neighborhoods and separate institutions. But these circumstances should only be yielded to when they are irresistible. A Negro neighborhood depreciates market value of property. We should distribute ourselves among the people, build our houses, where if they take fire other houses will be in danger. Common dangers will create common safeguards.

OUR POLICY SHOULD BE

to unite with the great mass of the American people in all their activities and resolve to fall or flourish with our common country. We cannot afford draw the color line in politics, trade, education, manners, religion, fashion or civilization. Especially, we cannot afford to draw the color line in politics. No folly could be greater. A party acting upon that basis would be not merely a misfortune, but a dire calamity to our people. The rule of the majority is the fundamental principle of the American government, and it may be safely affirmed that the American people will never permit, tolerate, or submit to the success of any political device or strategy calculated to circumvent and defeat the just application and operation of this fundamental principle of our government.

It is also fair to state that no part of the American people—Irish, Scotch, Italian, or German—could attempt any such political jugglery with less success than us.

[. . . .]

But I leave this aspect of our relations and duties to make a few remarks upon the changed condition of our country.

Four years ago we assembled to celebrate the abolition of slavery in the District of Columbia

UNDER A DARK AND PORTENTOUS CLOUD.

The honorable Grover Cleveland,[79] the approved leader and representative of the Democratic Party, had, only a few weeks before, been duly inaugurated president of the United States. The fact of his election had carried alarm and consternation into every black man's cabin in the Southern states. For the

---

79. Grover Cleveland (1837–1908) was an American politician who served as governor of New York and served two (nonconsecutive) terms as president of the United States.

moment it must have seemed to them that the sun of freedom had gone down, and the night of slavery had succeeded. The terror was dismal and heartbreaking enough, and although it turned out to be groundless, it was not altogether unnatural. The Democratic Party had, in its day, done much well calculated to create a dread of its return to power.

In the old time it was the ever-faithful ally of the slaveholders, and the inflexible defenders of slavery. In the new time, it has been distinguished as the party of the shotgun, the cart whip, and the solid South.

While Mr. Cleveland's election brought dreadful forebodings to the cabins of the South, it brought pleasing anticipations to the mansions of the South. The joy of the oppressor was the sorrow of the oppressed. It required very positive assurances from President Cleveland and his friends to allay the apprehensions of the freedmen. The impression made by the election of General Harrison was in striking contrast. It had precisely the opposite effect to that of Mr. Cleveland. The alarm was transferred from the cabin to the mansion— from the former slave to the former master. In the freedmen's breasts confidence took the place of doubt, hope the place of fear, and a sense of relief the place of anxiety. Without the utterance of a single word, without the performance of a single act, the simple fact of the election of a Republican president carried with it the assurance of protection from the power of the oppressor. No higher eulogium could be bestowed upon the Republican Party than this faith in the justice and beneficence by the simple, uneducated, and oppressed laborers of the South. Great, too, will the sorrow and disappointment if some measure shall not be devised under this Republican administration to arrest the arm of lawless violence and prove to these simple people that there is a difference between the Republican Party and the Democratic Party.

Some of you may remember that in my celebration address four years ago I took occasion to express my satisfaction with the inaugural utterances of Hon. Grover Cleveland, and, although I have been much criticized for what I then said, I have no word of that commendation to retract or qualify. I thought well of Mr. Cleveland's words then and think well of them now. What I said was this, "No better words have dropped from the east portico of the Capitol since the days of Abraham Lincoln and Ulysses S. Grant." I did not say, as some of my lying critics found it necessary to allege, that Mr. Cleveland had uttered better words than either Lincoln or Grant. You will also remember that, while I commended the language of Mr. Cleveland, I strongly doubted his ability to live up to the sentiments he then and there expressed, and that doubt has been fully and sadly justified. During all the four years of his administration, after having solemnly sworn to support and enforce the Constitution of the United States, he said no word and did not act, expressed no desire to arrest the hand of violence, to stay the effusion of innocent blood, or vindicate in any manner the Negro's constitutional right to vote. He could almost hazard a war with

England to protect our fishermen; he could send two ships of war to Haiti to protect an American filibuster, but not one word or blow to protect colored citizens against

SOUTHERN ASSASSINS AND MURDERERS.

While I commended the words of Mr. Cleveland, I knew the party and not Mr. Cleveland would determine the character of his administration.

Well, now the American people have returned the Republican Party to power, and the question is, what it will do? It has a great prestige, a glorious record. It is the party that carried on the war against treason and rebellion. It is the party that saved the Union, abolished slavery, amended the Constitution, and made the colored man a soldier, a citizen, and a legal voter. In view of this splendid record there ought to be no doubt or fear as to the course of this present administration. But past experiences make us thoughtful. For a dozen years or more the Republican Party has seemed in a measure paralyzed in the presence of high-handed fraud and brutal violence toward its newly-made citizens. The question now is, will it regain its former health, activity and power? Will it be as true to its friends in the South as the Democratic Party has been to its friends in that section, or will it sacrifice its friends to conciliate its enemies? I have seen this last alternative suggested as the possible outcome of this administration, but I stamp with unmitigated scorn and contempt all such intimations. I know General [Benjamin] Harrison,[80] and believe in General Harrison. I know his cabinet and believe in its members, and no power can make me believe that this administration will not step to the verge of its constitutional power to protect the rights guaranteed by the Constitution. Not only the Negro, but all honest men, North and South, must hold the Republican Party in contempt, if it fails to do its whole duty at this point. The Republican Party has made the colored man free, and the Republican Party must make him secure in his freedom, or abandon its pretensions.

[. . . .]

It was once said by Abraham Lincoln that this republic, could not long endure half slave and half free, and the same may be said with even more truth of the black citizens of this country. They cannot remain half slave and half free. They must be one thing or the other.

And this brings me to consider the alternative now presented between slavery and freedom in this country. From my outlook I am free to affirm that I see nothing for the Negro of the South but a condition of absolute freedom or of absolute slavery. I see no half-way place for him. One or the other of these conditions is to solve the so-called Negro problem. There are forces at work in each

---

80. Benjamin Harrison was an American politician and military commander. He served in the US senate and he was the twenty-third president of the United States.

of these directions, and for the present, that which aims at the re-enslavement of the Negro seems to have the advantage. Let it be remembered that the labor of the Negro is his only capital. Take this from him and he dies from starvation. The present mode of obtaining his labor in the South gives the old master-class a complete mastery over him. I showed this in my last annual celebration address, and I need not go into it here. The payment of the Negro by orders on stores, where the storekeeper controls price, quality, and quantity, and is subject to no competition, so that the Negro must buy there and nowhere else—an arrangement by which the Negro never has a dollar to lay by, and can be kept in debt to his employer year in and year out, puts him completely at the mercy of the old master class. He who could say to the Negro, when a slave, you shall work for me or be whipped to death, can now say to him with equal emphasis, you shall work for me or I will starve you to death. This is the plain, matter-of-fact, and unexaggerated condition of the plantation Negro in the Southern states today.

Do you ask me,

WHY THE NEGRO DOES NOT EMIGRATE?

Why does he not seek a home where he would fare better? I will tell you. He has not a cent of money to emigrate with and if he had, and desired to exercise that right, he would be arrested for debt, for non-fulfillment of contract, or be shot down like a dog in his tracks. When Southern senators tell you that they want to be rid of the Negro, and would be glad to have them all clear out, you know, and I know, and they know that they are speaking falsely, and simply with a view to mislead the North. Only a few days ago armed resistance was made in North Carolina to colored emigration from that state, and the first exodus to Kansas was arrested by the old master class with shotguns and Winchester rifles. The desire to get rid of the Negro is a hollow sham. His labor is wanted today in the South just as it was wanted in the old times when he was hunted by two-legged and four-legged bloodhounds.

Now, when a man is in one place, and held there by the force of many or few, and cannot get out of it, he is not far from a condition of slavery. But these old slave-holders have their allies and one is strong drink. Whisky makes the Negro drunk, and drunkenness makes him a criminal as well as a pauper, and when he is made both a pauper and criminal the law steps in for satisfaction. It does not send him to prison to work for the state, but, as in the old times, puts him on the auction block and sells him to the highest bidder to work for a planter, where all the manhood he ever had is worked or whipped out of him. What is all this but slavery in another form?

I know that it will be said, that I am here exaggerating the danger that impends over the Negro. It will be said that slavery can never exist by law in the South, and that without legislation slavery cannot be revived in the South. This is a stupendous error.

My answer to this argument is, that slavery can as really exist without law as with it, and in some instances more securely, because less likely to be interfered with in the absence of law than in its presence. No man can point to any law in the United States by which slavery was originally established. The fact of slavery always precedes enactments making it legal. Men first make slaves and then make laws affirming the right of slavery.

What they have done in the past they may also do in the future. We must not forget that there is nothing in Southern morals, manners, or religion against the reestablishment of slavery. A genuine Southern man looks at a Negro simply as an article of property, capable of being exchanged for rice, cotton, sugar, and tobacco.

Now, with such a conscience, armed with whisky, armed with ignorance, and the payment of labor with orders on stores, the old master-class has the landless colored laborer literally by the throat, and is naturally ragging him back to the house of bondage.

Another and still more important step already taken in the direction of slavery is the precaution to deprive the Negro of all means of defense and protection. In the exercise of their power, acquired by long mastery over the Negro, they have forced him to surrender all arms and ammunition found in his log cabin. No lamb was ever more completely within the power of the wolf than the plantation Negro of today is within the hands of the old master class. The old masters know it, and the Negroes know it, and the fact makes the one haughty, domineering, and defiant, and the other spiritless, servile, and submissive. One is armed and the other defenseless. It is nothing against the courage of the Negro that he does not fight his way to the ballot box, instead of waiting for the government to protect him as it is its duty to do, for even a brave man, unarmed, will stand and deliver at the mouth of a Winchester rifle or

THE BLADE OF A BOWIE KNIFE.

To the mass of mankind life is more than liberty, for with it there ever remains the hope of liberty.

Now, when you remember that the Negro is taught to believe that the government may be against him; when it is remembered that he is denied the power to keep and bear arms; that he has not recovered from his enforced ignorance of two hundred years; that no adequate means of education has been provided for him; that his vote avails him nothing; that emigration is impossible; that there is neither religion nor conscience in the South to take his part, that he, of all men, is easiest convicted of crime that he does not see or receive a dollar in payment of wages; that labor as he will, he is brought in debt to the landed proprietor at the end of the year; that he can lay up nothing for a rainy day; that by the opinion of the Supreme Court of the United States the fourteenth amendment affords him no protection against individuals of a state. —I say, when you remember all this, you may realize something of the perilous condition of the Negro citizens—of the South.

Then, again, the fate of John M. Clayton and of Mr. Phillips, of Arkansas,[81] one of them shot down while peaceably seeking the proofs of his election to Congress, brutally assassinated, and the other kicked and shot to death in open daylight, and neither the murderers in the one case nor the assassinators in the other have been made to answer for their crimes admonish us that neither the Negro nor the friends of the Negro have yet any standing before the law or in the public opinion of the old slave states.

Now I point to these facts tending toward the re-establishment of Negro slavery in the South, not because I believe slavery will finally be established there, but because they are features of the situation and should be exposed in order that the end at which they aim may not be realized—forewarned, forearmed. The price of liberty is eternal vigilance. I bring this aspect before you upon the principle that an illustrious lawyer adopted, namely, always to try a cause first against his client.

It is easy to indulge in the illusions of hope, and to rejoice over what we have gained, and it is always more or less painful to contemplate the possibility of misfortune and disaster. But a brave man will not shrink from looking truth squarely in the face, no matter what may be the consequences, and you and I, and all of us know that if slavery is not reestablished in the Southern states, it will not be because there is any power inside those states, at present, to prevent this practice and return to barbarism.

From every view I have been able to take of the present situation in relation to the colored people of the United States I am forced to the conclusion that the irrepressible conflict, of which we heard so much before the war of the rebellion and during the war, is still in progress, is still the battle between two opposite civilizations—the one created and sustained by slavery, and the other framed and fashioned in the spirit of liberty and humanity, and this conflict will not be ended until one or the other shall be completely adopted in every section of our common country.

THE SOUTH IS STILL THE SOUTH

and under the doctrine of local self-government, it shelters the vicious idea that it can defy the Constitution and the laws of the United States, especially those laws which respect the enfranchisement of colored citizens. The idea of local self-government destroyed the freedman's bureau, drove United States soldiers out of the South, expelled Northern immigrants, excluded Negro citizens from state legislatures, and gave all power to the Southern slave masters. Such is the

81. Douglass refers to two acts of violence against supporters of African American civil rights.

situation today, and it remains to be seen whether it is to be permanent or transient. In my opinion this state of things cannot be permanent.

While revolutions may for a time seem to roll backward; while reactionary tendencies and forces may arrest the wheels of progress, and while the colored man of the South may still have to suffer the lash and sting of a by-gone condition, there are forces and influences silently and yet powerfully working out his deliverance. The individual Southern states are great, but the nation is greater. Justice, honor, liberty, and fidelity to the Constitution and laws may seem to sleep, but they are not dead. They are alive and had more to do with bringing our Republican president into the presidential chair than is sometimes supposed. The red-shirted rifle companies of Carolina and Mississippi[82] may rule for a time, but only for a time. They may rob the Negro of his vote today, but the Negro will have his vote tomorrow. The spirit of the age is with him. Slavery is vanishing from even the darkest corners of the earth. The schoolmaster is abroad—even in the South. The Negro of the plantation may be ignorant, but the Negro of the town and the city will be intelligent. The light of education which has illuminated the one will in time, illuminate the other.

But there is another force to be relied upon. It is the fact that the representatives of the best civilization of our times are compelled, in self-defense, to extirpate the illegal, unconstitutional barbarism of the late slave-holding states.

There is yet good reason to believe in the virtue of the loyal American people. They hate fraud, loathe rapine and despise meanness. It was no reckless freak or madness that made them pour out their blood and their treasure in the late war and there was a deep moral and patriotic purpose at the bottom of that sacrifice, a purpose that is not extinct, and will not be easily abandoned. If the Republican Party shall fail to carry out this purpose, God will raise up another party which will be faithful. They resented secession, and fought to make a free, strong, and united nation. It was the aim of good men then, and it is the aim of good men now, and the effort to gain it will continue till that end shall be obtained. They may be patient and long-suffering. They have been patient and long-suffering. But patience itself will cease to be a virtue.

Do you ask me what can be done? I answer, we can at least purify the ballot box by requiring that no man shall hold a seat, in Congress, who reaches it by fraud, violence, and intimidation; by requiring that every man from the South, and from the North, and from everywhere else, shall come into that body by means uncorrupted by fraud, and unstained by blood. They will yet see to it that murder and assassination shall not be the passport to a seat in the councils of the nation. There is today a man in that body who holds his place because

---

82. The "Red Shirts" were a white supremacist group that committed acts of racist terror in the South during the late nineteenth and early twentieth centuries.

assassination has stepped between him and an honest contestant. White men may make light

THE MURDER OF A SCORE OF NEGROES,

they may shut their eyes and ridicule all denunciation of murder, when committed against defenseless Negroes, but they will not be deaf to the white man's blood, when it cries from the ground for vengeance. The advantage of the black man's cause is that the white man cannot help himself without helping him. Law and order for the one will ultimately be law and order for the other.

There is still another ground of hope for the freemen of the Southern states. It is that the good citizens of these states cannot afford, and will not consent always to lag far behind the old free states in all the elements of civilization. They want population, capital, invention, and enterprise. They have rich resources to be developed, and they want both men and money to develop them and enhance their prosperity. The wise and loyal people in these states know very well that they can never be prosperous; that they can never have their share of immigration from at home or abroad, while they are known and distinguished for intolerance, fraud, violence, and lynch law. They know that while this character attaches to them, capital will hold aloof from them, and population shun them as it would shun a land blasted by pestilence and death. They know that their rich mines and fertile soil will fail to attract immigrants from any country unblasted by slavery. They know that industrious and enterprising men, searching for homes will turn their backs upon the South and make their way to the West and North, where they can hold and express their opinions without fear of the bowie knife and shotgun of the assassin.

Thus the self-interest of the people of these states will yet teach them justice, humanity, and civilization. For the present, the better element at the South is terror stricken and silent, but encouraged by the trend of the nation to higher and better conditions of existence, it will not ,always remain dumb and inactive, but will assert itself as Missouri is already doing, and as Arkansas will yet do. I was in this latter state only a few days after the assassination of John M. Clayton. I saw the wholesome horror manifested by the intelligent and worthy citizens of that state at this dastardly political murder. They were anxious for the good name of Arkansas, and asked me how the people of the North would regard them. I had to tell them in sadness that the outside world would look at them through the warm red blood of John M. Clayton and that the state of Arkansas would be held rigidly responsible till the arrest, trial, conviction, and punishment of

THE ASSASSIN AND HIS INSTIGATORS.

In conclusion, while I have plainly portrayed the sources of danger to our people, while I have described the reactionary forces with which we have to contend, I have no fears as to the character of the final result. The American people are governed, not only by laws and selfish interests, but by large ideas of moral and material civilization. The spirit of justice, liberty, and fair play is abroad in the land. It is in the air. It animates men of all stations, of all professions and callings and can neither be silenced nor extirpated. It has an agent in every bar of railroad iron; a servant in every electric wire, a missionary in every traveler. It not only tunnels the mountains, fills up the valleys, and sheds upon us the light of science, but it will ultimately destroy the unnumbered wrongs inherited by both races from the system of slavery and barbarism. In this direction is the trend of the nation. States may lag, parties may hesitate, leaders may halt, but to this complexion it must come at last. States, parties, and leaders must, and will in the end, adjust themselves to this overwhelming and irresistible tendency. It will make parties, and unmake parties, it will make rulers, and unmake rulers, until it shall become the fixed, universal and irreversible law of the land. For fifty years it has made progress against all contradictions. It stemmed the current of opposition in church and state. It has removed many proscriptions. It has opened the gates of knowledge. It was abolished slavery. It has saved the Union. It has reconstructed the government upon a basis of justice and liberty, and it will see to it that the last vestige of fraud and violence on the ballot box shall disappear, and there shall be one country, one law, one liberty, for all the people of the United States.

39. "Self-Made Men," a speech delivered at the Indian Industrial School, Carlisle, Pennsylvania, March of 1893 and published as a pamphlet (Carlisle: Indian Print, 1893)[83]

The subject announced for this evening's entertainment is not new. Man in one form or another, has been a frequent and fruitful subject for the press, the pulpit and the platform. This subject has come up for consideration under a variety of attractive titles, such as "Great Men," "Representative Men," "Peculiar Men," "Scientific Men," "Literary Men," "Successful Men," "Men of Genius," and "Men of the World"; but under whatever name or designation, the vital point of interest in the discussion has ever been the same, and that is, manhood itself, and this in its broadest and most comprehensive sense.

This tendency to the universal, in such discussion, is altogether natural and all controlling; for when we consider what man, as whole, is; what he has been; what he aspires to be, and what, by a wise and vigorous cultivation of his faculties, he may yet become, we see that it leads irresistibly to this broad view of him as a subject of thought and inquiry.

The saying of the poet that "The proper study of mankind is man,"[84] and which has been the starting point of so many lectures, essays and speeches, holds its place, like all other great utterances, because it contains a great truth and a truth alike for every age and generation of men. It is always new and can never grow old. It is neither dimmed by time nor tarnished by repetition; for man, both in respect of himself and of his species, is now, and evermore will be, the center of unsatisfied human curiosity.

The pleasure we derive from any department of knowledge is largely due to the glimpse which it gives to us of our own nature. We may travel far over land and sea, brave all climates, dare all dangers, endure all hardships, try all latitudes and longitudes; we may penetrate the earth, sound the ocean's depths and sweep the hollow sky with our glasses, in the pursuit of other knowledge; we may contemplate the glorious landscape gemmed by forest, lake and river and dotted with peaceful homes and quiet herds; we may whirl away to the

---

83. Historian John W. Blassingame has identified "Self-Made Men" as the speech Douglass delivered more than any other (between the years of 1859 and 1893). See John W. Blassingame, *The Frederick Douglass Papers, Series One*, vol. 5 (New Haven, CT: Yale University Press, 1992), 545–46. The speech is an implicitly autobiographical defense of the idea that each individual has it within his or her power to "make" (and remake) him- or herself in significant ways.
84. Alexander Pope, "Essay on Man."

great cities, all aglow with life and enterprise; we may mingle with the imposing assemblages of wealth and power; we may visit the halls where art works
her miracles in music, speech and color, and where science unbars the gates
to higher planes of civilization; but no matter how radiant the colors, how
enchanting the melody, how gorgeous and splendid the pageant; man himself, with eyes turned inward upon his own wondrous attributes and powers
surpasses them all. A single human soul standing here upon the margin we
call TIME, overlooking, in the vastness of its range, the solemn past which
can neither be recalled nor remodeled, ever chafing against finite limitations,
entangled with interminable contradictions, eagerly seeking to scan the invisible past and to pierce the clouds and darkness of the ever mysterious future,
has attractions for thought and study, more numerous and powerful than all
other objects beneath the sky. To human thought and inquiry he is broader
than all visible worlds, loftier than all heights and deeper than all depths.
Were I called upon to point out the broadest and most permanent distinction
between mankind and other animals, it would be this; their earnest desire for
the fullest knowledge of human nature on all its many sides. The importance
of this knowledge is immeasurable, and by no other is human life so affected
and colored. Nothing can bring to man so much of happiness or so much of
misery as man himself. Today he exalts himself to heaven by his virtues and
achievements; tomorrow he smites with sadness and pain, by his crimes and
follies. But whether exalted or debased, charitable or wicked; whether saint or
villain, priest or prize fighter; if only he be great in his line, he is an unfailing
source of interest, as one of a common brotherhood; for the best man finds in
his breast the evidence of kinship with the worst, and the worst with the best.
Confront us with either extreme and you will rivet our attention and fix us in
earnest contemplation, for our chief desire is to know what there is in man and
to know him at all extremes and ends and opposites, and for this knowledge,
or for the want of it, we will follow him from the gates of life to the gates of
death, and beyond them.

As this subject can never become old, so it can never be exhausted. Man
is too closely related to the Infinite to be divided, weighed, measured and
reduced to fixed standards, and thus adjusted to finite comprehension. No two
of anything are exactly alike, and what is true of man in one generation may
lack some degree of truth in another, but his distinctive qualities as man, are
inherent and remain forever. Progressive in his nature, he defies the power of
progress to overtake him to make known, definitely, the limits of his marvelous
powers and possibilities.

From man comes all that we know or can imagine of heaven and earth, of
time and eternity. He is the prolific constituter of manners, morals, religions
and governments. He spins them out as the spider spins his web, and they are
coarse or fine, kind or cruel, according to the degree of intelligence reached by

him at the period of their establishment. He compels us to contemplate his past with wonder and to survey his future with much the same feelings as those with which Columbus is supposed to have gazed westward over the sea. It is the faith of the race that in man there exists far outlying continents of power, thought and feeling, which remain to be discovered, explored, cultivated, made practical and glorified.

Mr. [Ralph Waldo] Emerson has declared that it is natural to believe in great men. Whether this is a fact, or not, we do believe in them and worship them. The Visible God of the New Testament is revealed to us as a man of like passions with ourselves. We seek out our wisest and best man, the man who, by eloquence or the sword compels us to believe him such, and make him our leader, prophet, preacher and law giver. We do this, not because he is essentially different from us, but because of his identity with us. He is our best representative and reflects, on a colossal scale, the scale to which we would aspire, our highest aims, objects, powers and possibilities.

This natural reverence for all that is great in man, and this tendency to deify and worship him, though natural and the source of man's elevation, has not always shown itself wise but has often shown itself far otherwise than wise. It has often given us a wicked ruler for a righteous one, a false prophet for a true one, a corrupt preacher for a pure one, a man of war for a man of peace, and a distorted and vengeful image of God for an image of justice and mercy.

But it is not my purpose to attempt here any comprehensive and exhaustive theory or philosophy of the nature of manhood in all the range I have indicated. I am here to speak to you of a peculiar type of manhood under the title of

SELF-MADE MEN.

That there is, in more respects than one, something like a solecism in this title, I freely admit. Properly speaking, there are in the world no such men as self-made men. That term implies an individual independence of the past and present which can never exist.

Our best and most valued acquisitions have been obtained either from our contemporaries or from those who have preceded us in the field of thought and discovery. We have all either begged, borrowed or stolen. We have reaped where others have sown, and that which others have strown [*sic*], we have gathered. It must in truth be said though it may not accord well with self-conscious individuality and self-conceit, that no possible native force of character, and no depth or wealth of originality, can lift a man into absolute independence of his fellow-men, and no generation of men can be independent of the preceding generation. The brotherhood and inter-dependence of mankind are guarded and defended at all points. I believe in individuality, but individuals are, to the mass, like waves to the ocean. The highest order of genius is as dependent as is the lowest. It, like the loftiest waves of the sea, derives its power and greatness from the grandeur and vastness of the ocean of which it forms a part. We differ as the waves, but are one as the sea. To do something well does not necessarily imply the ability to do everything else equally well. If you can do in one direction that which I cannot do, I may in another direction, be able to do that which you cannot do. Thus the balance of power is kept comparatively even, and a self-acting brotherhood and inter-dependence is maintained.

Nevertheless, the title of my lecture is eminently descriptive of a class and is, moreover, a fit and convenient one for my purpose, in illustrating the idea which I have in view. In the order of discussion I shall adopt the style of an old-fashioned preacher and have a "firstly," a "secondly," a "thirdly," a "fourthly" and, possibly, a "conclusion."

My first is, "Who are self-made men?" My second is, "What is the true theory of their success?" My third is, "The advantages which self-made men derive from the manners and institutions of their surroundings," and my fourth is, "The grounds of the criticism to which they are, as a class, especially exposed."

On the first point I may say that, by the term "self-made men," I mean especially what, to the popular mind, the term itself imports. Self-made men are the men who, under peculiar difficulties and without the ordinary helps of favoring circumstances, have attained knowledge, usefulness, power and position and have learned from themselves the best uses to which life can be put in this world, and in the exercises of these uses to build up worthy character. They are the men who owe little or nothing to birth, relationship, friendly surroundings; to wealth inherited or to early approved means of education; who are what they are, without the aid of any of the favoring conditions by which other men usually rise in the world and achieve great results. In fact they are the men who are not brought up but who are obliged to come up, not only without the voluntary assistance of friendly cooperation of society, but often in open and derisive defiance of all the efforts of society and the tendency of circumstances to repress, retard and keep them down. They are the men who, in a world of schools, academies, colleges and other institutions of learning, are often compelled by unfriendly circumstances to acquire their education elsewhere and, amid unfavorable conditions, to hew out for themselves a way to success, and thus to become the architects of their own good fortunes. They are in a peculiar sense, indebted to themselves for themselves. If they have traveled far, they have made the road on which they traveled. If they have ascended high, they have built their own ladder. From the depths of poverty such as these have often come. From the heartless pavements of large and crowded cities; barefooted, homeless, and friendless, they have come. From hunger, rags and destitution, they have come; motherless and fatherless, they have come, and may come. Flung overboard in the midnight storm on the broad and tempest-tossed ocean of life; left without ropes, planks, oars or life-preservers, they have bravely buffeted the frowning billows and have risen in safety and life where others, supplied with the best appliances for safety and success, have fainted, despaired and gone down forever.

Such men as these, whether found in one position or another, whether in the college or in the factory; whether professors or plowmen; whether Caucasian or Indian; whether Anglo-Saxon or Anglo-African, are self-made men and are entitled to a certain measure of respect for their success and for proving to the world the grandest possibilities of human nature, of whatever variety of race or color.

Though a man of this class need not claim to be a hero or to be worshiped as such, there is genuine heroism in his struggle and something of sublimity and glory in his triumph. Every instance of such success is an example and a help to humanity. It, better than any mere assertion, gives us assurance of the latent powers and resources of simple and unaided manhood. It dignifies labor, honors application, lessens pain and depression, dispels gloom from the brow of the destitute and weariness from the heart of him about to faint, and enables man to take hold of the roughest and flintiest hardships incident to the battle of life, with a lighter heart, with higher hopes and a larger courage.

But I come at once to the second part of my subject, which respects the

THEORY OF SELF-MADE MEN.

"Upon what meat doth this, our CAESAR, feed, he hath grown so great?"[85] How happens it that the cottager is often found equal to the Lord, and that, in the race of life, the sons of the poor often get even with, and surpass even, the sons of the rich? How happens it from the field often come statesmen equal to those from the college? I am sorry to say that, upon this interesting point, I can promise nothing absolute nor anything which will be entirely satisfactory and conclusive. [Robert] Burns says:

> *"I see how folks live that hae riches,*
> *But surely poor folks maun be witches."*

The various conditions of men and the different uses they make of their powers and opportunities in life, are full of puzzling contrasts and contradictions. Here, as elsewhere, it is easy to dogmatize, but it is not so easy to define, explain and demonstrate. The natural laws for the government, well-being and progress of mankind, seem to be equal and are equal; but the subjects of these laws everywhere abound in inequalities, discords and contrasts. We cannot have fruit without flowers, but we often have flowers without fruit. The

---

85. William Shakespeare, *Julius Caesar*, act 1, sc. 2.

promise of youth often breaks down in manhood, and real excellence often comes unheralded and from unexpected quarters.

The scene presented from this view is as a thousand arrows shot from the same point and aimed at the same object. United in aim, they are divided in flight. Some fly too high, others too low. Some go to the right, others to the left. Some fly too far and others, not far enough, and only a few hit the mark. Such is life. United in the quiver, they are divided in the air. Matched when dormant, they are unmatched in action.

When we attempt to account for greatness we never get nearer to the truth than did the greatest of poets and philosophers when he classified the conditions of greatness: "Some are born great, some achieve greatness and some have greatness thrust upon them."[86] We may take our choice of these three separate explanations and make which of them we please, most prominent in our discussion. Much can certainly be said of superior mental endowments, and I should on some accounts, lean strongly to that theory, but for numerous examples which seem to, and do, contradict it, and but for the depressing tendency such a theory must have upon humanity generally.

This theory has truth in it, but it is not the whole truth. Men of very ordinary faculties have, nevertheless, made a very respectable way in the world and have sometimes presented even brilliant examples of success. On the other hand, what is called genius is often found by the wayside, a miserable wreck; the more deplorable and shocking because from the height from which it has fallen and the loss and ruin involved in the fall. There is, perhaps, a compensation in disappointment and in the contradiction of means to ends and promise to performance. These imply a constant effort on the part of nature to hold the balance evenly between all her children and to bring success within the reach of the humblest as well as of the most exalted.

From apparently the basest metals we have the finest toned bells, and we are taught respect from simple manhood when we see how, from the various dregs of society, there come men who may well be regarded as the pride and as the watch towers of the race.

Steel is improved by laying on damp ground, and the rusty razor gets a keener edge after giving its dross to the dirt in which it has been allowed to lie neglected and forgotten. In like manner, too, humanity, though it lay among the pots, covered with the dust of neglect and poverty, may still retain the divine impulse and the element of improvement and progress. It is natural to revolt at squalor, but we may well relax our lip of scorn and contempt when we stand among the lowly and despised, for out of the rags of the meanest cradle there may come a great man and this is a treasure richer than all the wealth of the Orient.

---

86. William Shakespeare, *Twelfth Night* act 2, sc. 5.

I do not think much of the accident or good luck theory of self-made men. It is worth but little attention and has no practical value. An apple carelessly flung into a crowd may hit one person, or it may hit another, or it may hit nobody. The probabilities are precisely the same in this accident theory of self-made men. It divorces a man from his own achievements, contemplates him as a being of chance and leaves him without will, motive, ambition and aspiration. Yet the accident theory is among the most popular theories of individual success. It has about it the air of mystery which the multitude so well like, and withal, it does something to mar the complacency of the successful.

It is one of the easiest and commonest things in the world for a successful man to be followed in his career through life and to have constantly pointed out this or that particular stroke of good fortune which fixed his destiny and made him successful. If not ourselves great, we like to explain why others are so. We are stingy in our praise to merit, but generous in our praise to chance. Besides, a man feels himself measurably great when he can point out the precise moment and circumstance which made his neighbor great. He easily fancies that the slight difference between himself and his friend is simply one of luck. It was his friend who was lucky but it might easily have been himself. Then too, the next best thing to success is a valid apology for non-success. Detraction is, to many, a delicious morsel. The excellence which it loudly denies to others it silently claims for itself. It possesses the means of covering the small with the glory of the great. It adds to failure that which it takes from success and shortens the distance between those in front and those in the rear. Even here there is an upward tendency worthy of notice and respect. The kitchen is ever the critic of the parlor. The talk of those below is of those above. We imitate those we revere and admire.

But the main objection to this very comfortable theory is that, like most other theories, it is made to explain too much. While it ascribes success to chance and friendly circumstances, it is apt to take no cognizance of the very different uses to which different men put their circumstances and their chances.

Fortune may crowd a man's life with favorable circumstances and happy opportunities, but they will, as all know, avail him nothing unless he makes a wise and vigorous use of them. It does not matter that the wind is fair and the tide at its flood, if the mariner refuses to weigh his anchor and spread his canvas to the breeze. The golden harvest is ripe in vain if the farmer refuses to reap. Opportunity is important but exertion is indispensable. "There is a tide in the affairs of men which, taken at its flood, leads on to fortune"[87]; but it must be taken at its flood.

Within this realm of man's being, as elsewhere, science is diffusing its broad, beneficent light. As this light increases, dependence upon chance or luck is

---

87. William Shakespeare, *Julius Caesar* act 4, sc. 3.

destined to vanish and the wisdom of adapting means to ends, to become more manifest.

It was once more common than it is now, to hear men religiously ascribing their good or ill fortune directly to supernatural intervention. Success and failure, wealth and poverty, intelligence and ignorance, liberty and slavery, happiness and misery, were all bestowed or inflicted upon individual men by a divine hand and for All-Wise purposes. Man was, by such reasoners [*sic*], made a very insignificant agent in his own affairs. It was all the Lord's doings and marvelous to human eyes. Of course along with this superstition came the fortune teller, the pretender to divination and the miracle working priest who could save from famine by praying easier than by under-draining and deep plowing.

In such matter a wise man has little use for altars or oracle. He knows that the laws of God are perfect and unchangeable. He knows that health is maintained by right living; that disease is cured by the right use of remedies; that bread is produced by tilling the soil; that knowledge is obtained by study; that wealth is secured by saving and that battles are won by fighting. To him, the lazy man is the unlucky man and the man of luck is the man of work.

> *"The fault, dear Brutus, is not in our stars,*
> *But in ourselves, that we are underlings."*[88]

When we find a man who has ascended heights beyond ourselves; who has a broader range of vision than we and a sky with more stars in it than we have in ours, we may know that he has worked harder, better and more wisely than we. He was awake while we slept. He was busy while we were idle and he was wisely improving his time and talents while we were wasting ours.

[. . . .]

I am certain that there is nothing good, great or desirable which man can possess in this world, that does not come by some kind of labor, either physical or mental, moral or spiritual. A man may, at times, get something for nothing, but it will, in his hands, amount to nothing. What is true in the world of matter, is equally true in the world of mind. Without culture there can be no growth; without exertion, no acquisition; without friction, no polish; without labor, no knowledge; without action, no progress and without conflict, no victory. The man who lies down a fool at night, hoping that he will waken wise in the morning, will rise up in the morning as he laid down in the evening.

Faith, in the absence of work, seems to be worth little, if anything. The preacher who finds it easier to pray for knowledge than to tax his brain with study and application will find his congregation growing beautifully less and his flock looking elsewhere for their spiritual and mental food. In the old slave

---

88. William Shakespeare, *Julius Caesar*, act 1, sc. 2.

times colored ministers were somewhat remarkable for the fervor with which they prayed for knowledge, but it did not appear that they were remarkable for any wonderful success. In fact, they who prayed loudest seemed to get least. They thought if they opened their mouths they would be filled. The result was an abundance of sound with a great destitution of sense.

Not only in man's experience, but also in nature do we find exemplified the truth upon which I have been insisting. My Father worketh, said the Savior,[89] and I also work. In every view which we obtain of the perfections of the universe; whether we look to the bright stars in the peaceful blue dome above us, or to the long shore line of the ocean, where land and water maintain eternal conflict; the lesson taught is the same; that of endless action and reaction. Those beautifully rounded pebbles which you gather on the sand and which you hold in your hand and marvel at their exceeding smoothness, were chiseled into their varied and graceful forms by the ceaseless action of countless waves. Nature is herself a great worker and never tolerates, without certain rebuke, any contradiction to her wise example. Inaction is followed by stagnation. Stagnation is followed by pestilence and pestilence is followed by death. . . .

From these remarks it will be evident that, allowing only ordinary ability and opportunity, we may explain success mainly by one word and that word is WORK! WORK!! WORK!!! WORK!!!! Not transient and fitful effort, but patient, enduring, honest, unremitting and indefatigable work, into which the whole heart is put, and which, in both temporal and spiritual affairs, is the true miracle worker. Every one may avail himself of this marvelous power, if he will. There is no royal road to perfection. Certainly no one must wait for some kind of friend to put a springing board under his feet, upon which he may easily bound from the first round of the ladder onward and upward to its highest round. If he waits for this, he may wait long and perhaps forever. He who does not think himself worth saving from poverty and ignorance, by his own efforts, will hardly be thought worth the efforts of anybody else.

The lesson taught at this point by human experience is simply this, that the man who will get up will be helped up; and that the man who will not get up will be allowed to stay down. This rule may appear somewhat harsh, but in its general application and operation it is wise, just and beneficent. I know of no other rule which can be substituted for it without bringing social chaos. Personal independence is a virtue and it is the soul out of which comes the sturdiest manhood. But there can be no independence without a large share of self-dependence, and this virtue cannot be bestowed. It must be developed from within.

I have been asked "How will this theory affect the Negro?" and "What shall be done in his case?" My general answer is "Give the Negro fair play and let

---

89. John 5:17.

him alone. If he lives, well. If he dies, equally well. If he cannot stand up, let him fall down."

The apple must have strength and vitality enough in itself to hold on, or it will fall to the ground where it belongs. The strongest influence prevails and should prevail. If the vital relation of the fruit is severed, it is folly to tie the stem to the branch or the branch to the tree or to shelter the fruit from the wind. So, too, there is no wisdom in lifting from the earth a head which must only fall the more heavily when the help is withdrawn. Do right though the heavens fall; but they will not fall.

I have said "Give the Negro fair play and let him alone." I meant all that I said and a good deal more than some understand by fair play. It is not fair play to start the Negro out in life, from nothing and with nothing, while others start with the advantage of a thousand years behind them. He should be measured, not by the heights others have obtained, but from the depths from which he has come. For any adjustment of the scale of comparison, fair play demands that to the barbarism from which the Negro started shall be added two hundred years heavy with human bondage. Should the American people put a school house in every valley of the South and a church on every hill side and supply the one with teachers and the other with preachers, for a hundred years to come, they would not then have given fair play to the Negro.

The nearest approach to justice to the Negro for the past is to do him justice in the present. Throw open to him the doors of the schools, the factories, the workshops, and of all mechanical industries. For his own welfare, give him a chance to do whatever he can do well. If he fails then, let him fail! I can, however, assure you that he will not fail. Already has he proven it. As a soldier he proved it. He has since proved it by industry and sobriety and by the acquisition of knowledge and property. He is almost the only successful tiller of the soil of the South, and is fast becoming the owner of land formerly owned by his old master and by the old master class. In a thousand instances has he verified my theory of self-made men. He well performed the task of making bricks without straw[90]; now give him straw. Give him all the facilities for honest and successful livelihood, and in all honorable avocations receive him as a man among men.

I have by implication admitted that work alone is not the only explanation of self-made men, or of the secret of success. Industry, to be sure, is the superficial and visible cause of success, but what is the cause of industry? In the answer to this question one element is easily pointed out, and that element is necessity. [William Makepeace] Thackeray[91] very wisely remarks that "All men are about as lazy as they can afford to be." Men cannot be depended upon

---

90. Exodus 5:6–18.
91. William Makepeace Thackeray (1811–1863) was an English writer.

to work when they are asked to work for nothing. They are not only as lazy as they can afford to be, but I have found many who were a great deal more so. We all hate the task master, but all men, however industrious, are either lured or lashed through the world, and we should be a lazy, good-for-nothing set, if we were not so lured and lashed.

Necessity is not only the mother of invention, but the mainspring of exertion. The presence of some urgent, pinching, imperious necessity, will often not only sting a man into marvelous exertion, but into a sense of the possession, within himself, of powers and resources which else had slumbered on through a long life, unknown to himself and never suspected by others. A man never knows the strength of his grip till life and limb depend upon it. Something is likely to be done when something must be done.

If you wish to make your son helpless, you need not cripple him with bullet or bludgeon, but simply place him beyond the reach of necessity and surround him with ease and luxury. This experiment has often been tried and has seldom failed. As a general rule, where circumstances do most for men, there man will do least for himself; and where man does least, he himself is least. His doing or not doing makes or unmakes him.

Under the palm trees of Africa man finds, without effort, food, raiment and shelter. For him, there, nature has done all and he has done nothing. The result is that the glory of Africa is in her palms, —and not in her men.

In your search after manhood go not to those delightful latitudes where "summer is blossoming all the year long," but rather to the hardy North, to Maine, New Hampshire and Vermont, to the coldest and flintiest parts of New England, where men work gardens with gunpowder, blast rocks to find places to plant potatoes; where, for six months of the year, the earth covered with snow and ice. Go to the states which Daniel Webster thought good enough to emigrate from, and there you will find the highest type of American physical and intellectual manhood.

Happily for mankind, labor not only supplies the good things for which it is exerted, but it increases its own resources and improves, sharpens and strengthens its own instruments.

The primary condition upon which men have and retain power and skill is exertion. Nature has no use for unused power. She abhors a vacuum. She permits no preemption without occupation. Every organ of body and mind has its use and improves by use. "Better to wear out than to rust out," is sound philosophy as well as common sense. The eye of the watch-maker is severely taxed by the intense light and effort necessary in order to see minute objects, yet it remains clear and keen long after those of other men have failed. I was told at the Remington Rifle Works, by the workmen there employed who have to straighten the rifle barrels by flashing intense light through them, that, by this practice, severe as it seems, their eyes were made stronger.

But what the hands find to do must be done in earnest. Nature tolerates no halfness. He who wants hard hands must not, at sight of the first blister, fling away the spade, the rake, the broad axe or the hoe; for the blister is a primary condition to the needed hardness. To abandon work is not only to throw away the means of success, but it is also to part with the ability to work. To be able to walk well, one must walk on, and to work with ease and effect, one must work on.

Thus the law of labor is self-acting, beneficent and perfect; increasing skill and ability according to exertion. Faithful, earnest and protracted industry gives strength to the mind and facility to the hand. Within certain limits, the more that a man does, the more he can do.

Few men ever reach, in any one direction, the limits of their possibilities. As in commerce, so here, the relation of supply to demand rules. Our mechanical and intellectual forces increase or decrease according to the demands made upon them. He who uses most will have most to use. . . .

Exertion of muscle or mind, for pleasure and amusement alone, cannot bring anything like the good results of earnest labor. Such exertion lacks the element attached to duty. To play perfectly upon any complicated instrument, one must play long, laboriously and with earnest purpose. Though it be an amusement at first, it must be labor at the end, if any proficiency is reached. If one plays for one's own pleasure alone, the performance will give little pleasure to any one else and will finally become a rather hard and dry pleasure to one's self.

In this respect one cannot receive much more than one gives. Men may cheat their neighbors and may cheat themselves but they cannot cheat nature. She will only pay the wages one honestly earns.

In the idea of exertion, of course fortitude and perseverance are included. We have all met a class of men, very remarkable for their activity, and who yet make but little headway in life; men who, in their noisy and impulsive pursuit of knowledge, never get beyond the outer bark of an idea, from a lack of patience and perseverance to dig to the core; men who begin everything and complete nothing; who see, but do not perceive; who read, but forget what they read, and are as if they had not read; who travel, but go nowhere in particular, and have nothing of value to impart when they return. Such men may have greatness thrust upon them but they never achieve greatness.

As the gold in the mountain is concealed in huge and flinty rocks, so the most valuable ideas and inventions are often enveloped in doubt and uncertainty. The printing press, the sewing machine, the railroad, the telegraph and the locomotive, are all simple enough now, but who can measure the patience, the persistence, the fortitude, the wearing labor and the brain sweat, which produced these wonderful and indispensable additions to our modern civilization.

My theory of self-made men is, then, simply this; that they are men of work. Whether or not such men have acquired material, moral or intellectual excellence, honest labor faithfully, steadily and persistently pursued, is the best, if not the only, explanation of their success. But in thus awarding praise to industry, as the main agency in the production and culture of self-made men, I do not exclude other factors of the problem. I only make them subordinate. Other agencies cooperate, but this is the principal one and the one without which all others would fail.

Indolence and failure can give a thousand excuses for themselves. How often do we hear men say, "If I had the head of this one, or the hands of that one; the health of this one, or the strength of that one; the chances of this or of that one, I might have been this, that, or the other"; and much more the same sort.

Sound bodily health and mental faculties unimpaired are very desirable, if not absolutely indispensable. But a man need not be a physical giant or an intellectual prodigy, in order to make a tolerable way in the world. The health and strength of the soul is of far more importance than is that of the body, even when viewed as a means of mundane results. The soul is the main thing. Man can do a great many things; some easily and some with difficulty, but he cannot build a sound ship with rotten timber. Her model may be faultless; her spars may be the finest and her canvas the whitest and the flags of all nations may be displayed at her masthead, but she will go down in the first storm. And when the soul is lost, all is lost. All human experience proves over and over again, that any success which comes through meanness, trickery, fraud and dishonor, is but emptiness and will only be a torment to its possessor.

Let not the morally strong, though the physically weak abandon the struggle of life. For such happily, there is both place and chance in the world. The highest services to man and the richest rewards to the worker are not conditioned entirely upon physical power. The higher the plane of civilization, the more abundant the opportunities of the weak and infirm. Society and civilization move according to celestial order. "Not that which is spiritual is first, but that which is natural. After that, that which is spiritual."[92] The order of progress, is, first, barbarism; afterward, civilization. Barbarism represents physical force. Civilization represents spiritual power. The primary condition, that of barbarism, knows no other law than that of force; not right, but might. In this condition of society, or rather of no society, the man of mind is pushed aside by the man of muscle. . . .

Where ferocious beasts and savage inhabitants have been dispersed and the rudeness of nature has been subdued, we welcome milder methods and gentler instrumentalities for the service of mankind. Here the race is not to the swift nor the battle to the strong, but the prize is brought within the reach of those

---

92. I Corinthians 15:46.

who are neither swift nor strong. None need despair. There is room and work for all: for the weak as well as the strong. Activity is the law for all and its rewards are open to all. Vast acquirements and splendid achievements stand to the credit of men and feeble frames and slender constitutions. Channing was physically weak. Milton was blind. Montgomery was small and effeminate. But these men were more to the world than a thousand Sampsons. Mrs. Stowe would be nothing among the grizzly bears of the Rocky Mountains. We should not be likely to ask for her help at a barn raising, or ship launch; but when a great national evil was to be removed; when a nation's heart was to be touched; when a whole country was to be redeemed and regenerated and millions of slaves converted into free men, the civilized world knew no earthly power equal to hers.

But another element of the secret of success demands a word. That element is order, systematic endeavor. We succeed, not alone by the laborious exertion of our faculties, be they small or great, but by the regular, thoughtful and systematic exercise of them. Order, the first law of heaven, is itself a power. The battle is nearly lost when your lines are in disorder. Regular, orderly and systematic effort which moves without friction and needless loss of time or power; which has a place for everything and everything in its place; which knows just where to begin, how to proceed and where to end, though marked by no extraordinary outlay of energy or activity, will work wonders, not only in the matter of accomplishment, but also in the increase of the ability of the individual. It will make the weak man strong and the strong man stronger; the simple man wise and the wise man, wiser, and will insure success by the power and influence that belong to habit.

On the other hand, no matter what gifts and what aptitudes a man may possess; no matter though his mind be of the highest order and fitted for the noblest achievements; yet, without this systematic effort, his genius will only serve as a fire of shavings, soon in blaze and soon out.

Spontaneity has a special charm, and the fitful outcroppings of genius are, in speech or action, delightful; but the success attained by these is neither solid nor lasting. A man who, for nearly forty years, was the foremost orator in New England, was asked by me, if his speeches were extemporaneous? They flowed so smoothly that I had my doubts about it. He answered, "No, I carefully think out and write my speeches, before I utter them." When such a man rises to speak, he knows what he is going to say. When he speaks, he knows what he is saying. When he retires from the platform, he knows what he *has* said.

There is still another element essential to success, and that is, a commanding object and a sense of its importance. The vigor of the action depends upon the power of the motive. The wheels of the locomotive lie idle upon the rail until they feel the impelling force of the steam; but when that is applied, the whole ponderous train is set in motion. But energy ought not to be wasted. A man may dispose of his life as Paddy did of his powder, —aim at nothing, and hit it every time.

If each man in the world did his share of honest work, we should have no need of a millennium. The world would teem with abundance, and the temptation to evil in a thousand directions, would disappear. But work is not often undertaken for its own sake. The worker is conscious of an object worthy of effort, and works for that object; not for what he is to it, but for what it is to him. All are not moved by the same objects. Happiness is the object of some. Wealth and fame are the objects of others. But wealth and fame are beyond the reach of the majority of men, and thus, to them, these are not motive-impelling objects. Happily, however, personal, family and neighborhood well-being stand near to us all and are full of lofty inspirations to earnest endeavor, if we would but respond to their influence.

I do not desire my lecture to become a sermon; but, were this allowable, I would rebuke the growing tendency to sport and pleasure. The time, money and strength devoted to these phantoms, would banish darkness and hunger from every hearthstone in our land. Multitudes, unconscious of any controlling object in life, flit, like birds, from point to point; now here, now there; and so accomplish nothing, either here or there.

[. . . .]

But the industrious man does find real pleasure. He finds it in qualities and quantities to which the baffled pleasure seeker is a perpetual stranger. He finds it in the house well built, in the farm well tilled, in the books well kept, in the page well written, in the thought well expressed, in all the improved conditions of life around him and in whatsoever useful work may, for the moment, engage his time and energies.

I will give you, in one simple statement, my idea, my observation and my experience of the chief agent in the success of self-made men. It is not luck, nor is it great mental endowments, but it is well directed, honest toil. "Toil and trust!" was the motto of John Quincy Adams,[93] and his presidency of the republic proved its wisdom as well as its truth. Great in his opportunities, great in his mental endowments and great in his relationships, he was still greater in persevering and indefatigable industry.

Examples of successful self-culture and self-help under great difficulties and discouragements, are abundant, and they vindicate the theory of success thus feebly and with homely common sense, presented. [At this point in the speech, Douglass provides descriptions of the lives of several "self-made men," including Hugh Miller, Louis Kossuth, Abraham Lincoln, Benjamin Banneker,

---

93. John Quincy Adams (1767–1848) was an American politician and diplomat. He served as secretary of state, in the House of Representatives, and in the US senate, and he was the sixth president of the United States.

William Dietz, and Toussaint L'Overture before proceeding back to the main line of his argument.]

[. . . .]

The testimony of these and a thousand others who have come up from the depths of society, confirms the theory that industry is the most potent factor in the success of self-made men, and thus raises the dignity of labor; for whatever may be one's natural gifts, success, as I have said, is due mainly to this great means, open and free to all.

A word now upon the third point suggested at the beginning of this paper; namely, the friendly relation and influence of American ideas and institutions to this class of men.

America is said, and not without reason, to be preeminently the home and patron of self-made men. Here, all doors fly open to them. They may aspire to any position. Courts, senates and cabinets, spread rich carpets for their feet, and they stand among our foremost men in every honorable service. Many causes have made it easy, here, for this class to rise and flourish, and first among these causes is the general respectability of labor. Search where you will, there is no country on the globe where labor is so respected and the laborer so honored, as in this country. The conditions in which American society originated; the free spirit which framed its independence and created its government based upon the will of the people, exalted both labor and laborer. The strife between capital and labor is, here, comparatively equal. The one is not the haughty and powerful master and the other the weak and abject slave as is the case in some parts of Europe. Here, the man of toil is not bowed, but erect and strong. He feels that capital is not more indispensable than labor, and he can therefore meet the capitalist as the representative of an equal power.

Of course these remarks are not intended to apply to the states where slavery has but recently existed. That system was the extreme degradation of labor, and though happily now abolished its consequences still linger and may not disappear for a century. Today, in the presence of the capitalist, the Southern black laborer stands abashed, confused and intimidated. He is compelled to beg his fellow worm to give him leave to toil. Labor can never be respected where the laborer is despised. This is today, the great trouble at the South. The land owners still resent emancipation and oppose the elevation of labor. They have yet to learn that a condition of affairs well suited to a time of slavery may not be well suited to a time of freedom. They will one day learn that large farms and ignorant laborers are as little suited to the South as to the North.

But the respectability of labor is not, as already intimated, the only or the most powerful cause of the facility with which men rise from humble conditions to affluence and importance in the United States. A more subtle and powerful influence is exerted by the fact that the principle of measuring and valuing men according to their respective merits and without regard to their antecedents, is better established and more generally enforced here than in any other country. In Europe, greatness is often thrust upon men. They are made legislators by birth.

> *"A king can make a belted knight,*
> *A marquis, duke and a' that."*[94]

But here, wealth and greatness are forced by no such capricious and arbitrary power. Equality of rights brings equality of positions and dignities. Here society very properly saves itself the trouble of looking up a man's kinsfolks in order to determine his grade in life and the measure of respect due him. It cares very little who was his father or grandfather. The boast of the Jews, "We have Abraham for our father," has no practical significance here. He who demands consideration on the strength of a reputation of a dead father, is, properly enough, rewarded with derision. We have no reverence to throw away in this wise.

As a people, we have only a decent respect for our seniors. We cannot be beguiled into accepting empty-headed sons for full-headed fathers. As some one has said, we dispense with the smoke when the candle is out. In popular phrase we exhort every man as he comes upon the stage of active life, "Now do your level best!" "Help yourself!" "Put your shoulder to the wheel!" "Make your own record!" "Paddle your own canoe!" "Be the architect of your own fortune!"

The sons of illustrious men are put upon trial like the sons of common people. They must prove themselves real CLAYS, WEBSTERS and LINCOLNS, if they would attract to themselves the cordial respect and admiration generally awarded to their brilliant fathers. There is, here, no law of entail or primogeniture.

Our great men drop out from their various groups and circles of greatness as bright meteors vanish from the blue overhanging sky bearing away their own silvery light and leaving the places where they once shone so brightly, robed in darkness till relighted in turn by the glory of succeeding ones.

I would not assume that we are entirely devoid of affection for families and for great names. We have this feeling, but it is a feeling qualified and limited by the popular thought; a thought which springs from the heart of free institutions and is destined to grow stronger the longer these institutions shall endure. George Washington, Jr., or Andrew Jackson, Jr., stand no better chance of being future presidents than do the sons of Smith or Jones, or the sons of anybody else.

[. . . .]

---

94. Robert Burns, "A Man's a Man for A' That."

We have as a people no past and very little present, but a boundless and glorious future. With us, it is not so much what has been, or what is now, but what is to be in the good time coming. Our mottoes are "Look ahead!" and "Go ahead!", and especially the latter. Our moral atmosphere is full of the inspiration of hope and courage. Every man has his chance. If he cannot be president he can, at least, be prosperous. In this respect, America is not only the exception to the general rule, but the social wonder of the world. . . .

[. . . .]

Ladies and gentlemen: Accept my thanks for your patient attention. I will detain you no longer. If, by statement, argument, sentiment or example, I have awakened in any, a sense of the dignity of labor or the value of manhood, or have stirred in any mind, a courageous resolution to make one more effort toward self-improvement and higher usefulness, I have not spoken altogether in vain, and your patience is justified.

40. "The Blessings of Liberty and Education," a speech delivered at Manassas Industrial School in Manassas, Virginia, September 3, 1894 and published in the *Richmond Dispatch*, September 4, 1894[95]

LADIES, GENTLEMEN AND FRIENDS:

As I am a stranger among you and a sojourner,[96] you will, I hope, allow me a word about myself, by way of introduction. I want to say something about the day upon which we met. Coincidents [*sic*] are always more or less, interesting and here is one such of a somewhat striking character. This day has for me a special interest. It happens to be the anniversary of my escape from bondage. Fifty-six years ago today, it was my good fortune to cease to be a slave, a chattel personal, and to become a man. It was upon the third day of September, 1838, that I started upon my little life work in the world. It was a great day for me. With slavery behind me and all the great untried world before me, my heart throbbed with many anxious thoughts as to what the future might have in store for me. I will not attempt here any description of what were my emotions in this crisis. I leave you to imagine the difference between what they were and what they are on this happy occasion. I then found myself in a strange land, unknown, friendless, and pursued as if I were a fugitive from justice. I was a stranger to every one I met in the streets of the great city of New York, for that city was the first place in which I felt at liberty to halt in my flight farther North. New York, at that day was by no means a city of refuge. On the contrary, it was a city in which slave-hunters and slave-catchers delighted to congregate. It was one of the best fields for that sport this side of Africa. The game once started was easily taken. If they had caught me, I should have been elsewhere than here to assist in founding an industrial school for colored youth in Virginia. . . .

My second thought germane to this occasion, and which must have some interest for us all, very naturally relates to the noted place where we now happen to be assembled. Since the great and terrible battle with which its name is associated and which has now passed into history as the birth of many battles,

---

95. As an elder statesman, Douglass was invited to give this speech at the dedication of a school in Manassas, Virginia. He used the opportunity to deliver an eloquent oration on the relationship between education and liberty. A few months later, on February 20, 1895, Douglass would die of natural causes.

96. Douglass paraphrases Genesis 23:4.

no event has occurred here so important in its character and influence and so every way significant, as the event which we have this day met to inaugurate and celebrate. To found an educational institution for any people is worthy of note; but to found a school in which to instruct, improve and develop all that is noblest and best in the souls of a deeply wronged and long neglected people, is especially noteworthy. This spot, once the scene of fratricidal war,[97] and the witness of its innumerable and indescribable horrors, is, we hope to be hereafter the scene of brotherly kindness, charity and peace. We are to witness here a display of the best elements of advanced civilization and good citizenship. It is to be the place where the children of a once enslaved people may realize the blessings of liberty and education, and learn how to make for themselves and for all others the best of both worlds.

No spot on the soil of Virginia could have been more fitly chosen for planting this school, than on this historic battlefield. It has not only the high advantage of forming an instructive contrast and illustrating the compensation possible to mankind, by patiently awaiting the quiet operation of time and events, but suggests the battle to be waged here against ignorance and vice. Thirty years ago, when federal and Confederate armies met here in deadly conflict over the question of the perpetual enslavement of the Negro, who would or could have dreamed, that, in a single generation, such changes would be wrought in the minds of men that a school would be founded here, for the mental, moral and industrial education of the children of this same people whose enslavement was sought even with the sword? Who would have imagined that Virginia, after the agony of war and in a time so short, would become so enlightened and so liberal as to be willing and even pleased to welcome here, upon her "sacred soil," a school for the children of her former slaves? Thirty years ago neither poet, priest nor prophet, could have foretold the vast and wonderful changes which have taken place in the opinions of the American people on this subject since the war. The North has changed, and the South has changed, and we have all changed, and all changed for the better. Otherwise, we should not be here today engaged in the business of establishing this institution.

The liberality on the part of the people of Virginia, a typical state of the South, which has encouraged and justified the founding of this industrial school, not only within her borders, but here on the very first great battlefield between the two great sections of our Union, is as much a cause of amazement, satisfaction and joy, as is the readiness with which the good people of the North have responded to the call for pecuniary aid and thus made this enterprise successful. Both circumstances are today causes of joy and congratulation. They show that the colored man need not despair; that he has friends in both sections of the republic. In view of this school and of the changes in public

---

97. Douglass refers to the battle at Manassas that occurred during the Civil War.

sentiment which it indicates, we may well exclaim with [John] Milton, "Peace hath her victories no less renowned than war!"

When first invited to speak a few words in celebration of the founding of this industrial school, I was disposed to decline the honor, in favor of some of my younger and better educated brothers. But I am glad that I did not decline the honor. The duty devolved upon me, but which I then hesitated to assume, involves, in every respect, an agreeable duty. I am glad that, at my time of life, the opportunity is afforded me to connect my name with a school so meritorious and which I can reasonably hope will be of so great and permanent service to a people so greatly needing it. It is in line with my relations to the Negro. I have pleaded the cause of the oppressed against all comers, during more than fifty years of conflict. Were a period put to my career today, I could hardly wish for a time or place, or an occasion, better suited for a desired ending, than here and now. The founding of this and similar schools on the soil of Virginia, —a state formerly the breeder, buyer and seller of slaves; a state so averse in the past to the education of colored people, as to make it a crime to teach a Negro to read, —is one of the best fruits of the agitation of a half a century, and a firm foundation of hope for the future.

The idea at the bottom of this institution is rapidly gaining ground everywhere. Industrial education is, with me, however, no new idea. Nearly forty years ago I was its advocate, and at that time I held it to be the chief want of the free colored people of the North. I was then editor of the *North Star*, a newspaper printed in Rochester, New York. I saw even then, that the free Negro of the North, with everything great expected of him, but with no means at hand to meet such expectations, could not hope to rise while he was excluded from all profitable employments. He was free by law, but denied the chief advantages of freedom; he was indeed but nominally free; he was not compelled to call any man his master, and no one could call him slave, but he was still in fact a slave, a slave to society, and could only be a hewer of wood and a drawer of water. It was easier at that day to get a black boy into a lawyer's office to study law, or into a doctor's office to study medicine, than it was to get him into a carpenter's shop to push a plane, or into a blacksmith's shop to hammer iron.

While I have no sympathy whatever with those who affect to despise labor, even the humblest forms of it, and hold that whatever is needful to be done it is honorable to do, it is, nevertheless, plain that no people, white or black, can, in any country, continue long respected who are confined exclusively to mere menial service for which but little intelligence or skill are required, and for which but the smallest wages are paid or received; especially if the laborer does not make an effort to rise above that condition. While the employment as waiters at hotels and on steamboats and railroads, is perfectly proper and entirely honorable, in the circumstances which now surround the colored people, no one variety of the American people can afford to be known only as waiters and domestic servants. While I say this, I fully believe in the dignity of all needful labor. All honest effort to better human conditions is entitled to respect. I have met at Poland Springs, in the State of Maine, and at the White Mountains in New Hampshire, and at other places, as well as at the late World's Columbian Exposition at Chicago, many young white ladies and gentlemen, who were truly such, students and teachers in high schools and seminaries, gladly serving as waiters during their vacation, and doing so with no sense of being in any degree degraded, or embarrassed by such service. This would not have been the case with them, if society, by any law or custom, had decided that this service should be, for such persons, their only calling and vocation in life. Daniel Webster used to say that New Hampshire was a good state to emigrate from. So I say of menial service—it is a good condition to separate from, just as soon as one can find any other calling, which is more remunerative and more elevating in its tendency. It is not the labor that degrades, but the want of spirit to rise above it.

Exclusive service, or exclusive mastery, is not good for the moral or mental health of any class. Pride and insolence will certainly be developed in the one class, and weakness and servility in the other. The colored people, to be respected, must furnish their due proportion to each class. They must not be all masters, or all servants. They must command, as well as be commanded. However much I may regret that it was my lot to have been a slave, I shall never regret that I was once a common laborer; a servant, if you please so to term it. But I felt myself as much a man then, as I feel myself a man now; for I had an ambition above my calling, and I was determined then, as I have been ever since, to use every means in my power to rise to a higher plane of service, just as soon and as fast as that could be possible.

My philosophy of work is, that a man is worked upon by that upon which he works. Some work requires more muscle than it does mind. That work which requires the most thought, skill and ingenuity, will receive the highest commendation, and will otherwise do most for the worker. Things which can be done simply with the exertion of muscle, and with little or no exertion of the intellect, will develop the muscle, but dwarf the mind.

Long ago it was asked, "How can he get wisdom, who holdeth the plow and whose talk is of oxen?"[98]

The school which we are about to establish here, is, if I understand its object, intended to teach the colored youth, who shall avail themselves of its privileges, the use of both mind and body. It is to educate the hand as well as the brain; to teach men to work as well as to think, and to think as well as to work. It is to teach them to join thought to work, and thus to get the very best result of thought and work. There is in my opinion, no useful thing that a man can do, that cannot be better done by an educated man than by an uneducated one.

---

98. Ecclesiastes 38:25.

In the old slave times, colored people were expected to work without thinking. They were commanded to do as they were told. They were to be hands—only hands, not heads. Thought was the prerogative of the master. Obedience was the duty of the slave. I, in my innocence, once told my old master I thought a certain way of doing some work I had in hand was the best way to do it. He promptly demanded, "Who gave you the right to think?" I might have answered in the language of Robert Burns,

> "Were I designed yon lordling's slave,
> By Nature's law designed,
> Why was an independent thought
> E'er placed in my mind?"

But I had not then read Robert Burns. Burns had high ideas of the dignity of simple manhood. In respect of the dignity of man we may well exclaim with the great Shakespeare concerning him: "What a piece of work is man! How noble in reason! How infinite in faculties! In form and moving, how express and admirable! In action, how like an angel! In apprehension how like a God! The beauty of the world, the paragon of animals!"[99] Yet, if man be benighted, this glowing description of his power and dignity is merely a "glittering generality," an empty tumult of words, without any support of facts.

In his natural condition, however, man is only potentially great. As a mere physical being, he does not take high rank, even among the beasts of the field. He is not so fleet as a horse or a hound, or so strong as an ox or a mule. His true dignity is not to be sought in his arm, or in his legs, but in his head. Here is the seat and source of all that is of especially great or practical importance in him. There is fire in the flint and steel, but it is friction that causes it to flash, flame and burn, and give light where all else may be darkness. There is music in the violin, but the touch of the master is needed to fill the air and the soul with the concord of sweet sounds. There is power in the human mind, but education is needed for its development. As man is the highest being on earth, it follows that the vocation of the scholar is among the highest known to man. It is to teach and induce man's potential and latent greatness, to discover and develop the noblest, highest and best that is in him. In view of this fact, no man whose business it is to teach should ever allow himself to feel that his mission is mean, inferior, or circumscribed. In my estimation, neither politics nor religion present to us a calling higher than this primary business of unfolding and strengthening the powers of the human soul. It is a permanent vocation. Some know the value of education, by having it. I know its value by not having it. It is a want that begins with the beginning of human existence, and

---

99. William Shakespeare, *Hamlet*, act 2, sc. 2.

continues through all the journey of human life. Of all the creatures that live and move and have their being on this green earth, man, at his birth, is the most helpless and the most in need of instruction. He does not know even how to seek his food. His little life is menaced on every hand. The very elements conspire against him. The cattle upon a thousand hills; the wolves and bears in the forest, all come into the world better equipped for life than does man. From first to last, his existence depends upon instruction.

Yet this little helpless weakling, whose life can be put out as we put out the flame of a candle, with a breath, is the Lord of creation. Though in his beginning, he is only potentially this Lord, with education he is the commander of armies; the builder of cities; the tamer of wild beasts; the navigator of unknown seas; the discoverer of unknown islands, capes and continents, and the founder of great empires, and capable of limitless civilization.

But if man is without education, although with all his latent possibility attaching to him, he is, as I have said, but a pitiable object; a giant in body, but a pigmy in intellect, and, at best, but half a man. Without education, he lives within the narrow, dark and grimy walls of ignorance. He is a poor prisoner without hope. The little light that he gets comes to him as through dark corridors and grated windows. The sights and sounds that reach him, so significant and full of meaning to the well-trained mind, are to him of dim and shadowy and uncertain importance. He sees, but does not perceive. He hears, but does not understand. The silent and majestic heavens, fretted with stars, so inspiring and uplifting, so sublime and glorious to the souls of other men, bear no message to him. They suggest to him no idea of the wonderful world in which we live, or of the harmony of this great universe, and hence impart to him no happiness.

Education, on the other hand, means emancipation. It means light and liberty. It means the uplifting of the soul of man into the glorious light of truth, the light by which men can only be made free. To deny education to any people is one of the greatest crimes against human nature. It is to deny them the means of freedom and the rightful pursuit of happiness, and to defeat the very end of their being. They can neither honor themselves nor their Creator. Than this, no greater wrong can be inflicted; and, on the other hand, no greater benefit can be bestowed upon a long benighted people than giving to them, as we are here this day endeavoring to do, the means of useful education. . . .

It is sometimes said that we have done enough for the Negro; that we have given him his liberty and we should now let him do for himself. This sounds well, but that is all. I do not undervalue freedom from chattel slavery. It was a great and glorious triumph of justice and humanity. It was the fruit of long years of labor, agitation and sacrifice. But let us look at his emancipation and see where it left the Negro, and we shall see how far it falls short of the plainest demands of justice and of what we owe the Negro.

To find an adequate measure of compensation for any wrong, we must first ascertain the nature and extent of the wrong itself. The mere act of enslaving the Negro was not the only wrong done him, nor were the labors and stripes imposed upon him, though heavy and grievous to bear, the sum of his wrongs. They were, indeed, terrible enough; but deeper down and more terrible still were the mental and moral wrongs which enter into his claim for a slight measure of compensation. For two hundred and forty years the light of letters was denied him, and the gates of knowledge were closed against him.

He was driven from time to eternity in the darkest ignorance. He was herded with the beasts of the field, was without marriage, without family, without schools and without any moral training, other than that which came by the slave driver's lash. People who live now and talk of doing too much for the Negro, think nothing of these things, and those who know them, seem to desire to forget them especially when they are made the basis of a claim for a larger measure of justice to the Negro. They forget that for these terrible wrongs there is, in truth, no redress and no adequate compensation. The enslaved and battered millions have come, suffered, died and gone with all their moral and physical wounds into eternity. To them no recompense can be made. If the American people could put a schoolhouse in every valley and a church on every hilltop of the South and supply them with a teacher and a preacher respectively, and welcome the descendants of the former slaves to all the moral and intellectual benefits of the one and the other, without money and without price, such a sacrifice would not compensate their children for the terrible wrong done to their fathers and mothers by their enslavement and enforced degradation.

I have another complaint. It is said that the people of the South have made but little progress since their emancipation. This complaint is not only groundless, but adds insult to injury. Under the whole heavens there never was a people liberated from bondage under conditions less favorable to the beginning of a new and free mode of life, than were the freedmen of the South. Criminals, guilty of heinous crimes against the state and society, are let go free on more generous conditions than were our slaves.

The despotic government of Russia was more liberal and humane to its emancipated slaves than our republic was to ours. Each head of a family of slaves in Russia was given three acres of land and necessary farming implements with which to begin life, but our slaves were turned loose without anything— naked to the elements.

As one of the number of enslaved, I am none the less disposed to observe and note with pleasure and gratitude every effort of our white friends and brothers to remedy the evils wrought by the long years of slavery and its concomitants. And in such wise I rejoice in the effort made here today.

I have a word now upon another subject, and what I have to say may be more useful than palatable. That subject is the talk now so generally prevailing about races and race lines. I have no hesitation in telling you that I think the colored people and their friends make a great mistake in saying so much of race and color. I know no such basis for the claims of justice. I know no such motive for efforts at self-improvement. In this race-way they put the emphasis in the wrong place. I do now and always have attached more importance to manhood than to mere kinship or identity with any variety of the human family. Race, in the popular sense, is narrow; humanity is broad. The one is special; the other is universal. The one is transient; the other permanent. In the essential dignity of man as man, I find all necessary incentives and aspirations to a useful and noble life. Manhood is broad enough and high enough as a platform for you and me and all of us. The colored people of this country should advance to the high position of the Constitution of the country. It makes no distinction on account of race or color, and they should make none.

Since emancipation, we hear much said by our modern colored leaders in commendation of race pride, race love, race effort, race superiority, race men, and the like. One man is praised for being a race man and another is condemned for not being a race man. In all this talk of race, the motive may be good, but the method is bad. It is an effort to cast out Satan by Beelzebub.[100] The evils which are now crushing the Negro to earth have their root and sap, their force or mainspring, in this narrow spirit of race and color, and the Negro has no more right to excuse and foster it than have men of any other race. I recognize and adopt no narrow basis for my thoughts, feelings, or modes of action. I would place myself, and I would place you, my young friends, upon grounds vastly higher and broader than any founded upon race or color. Neither law, learning, nor religion, is addressed to any man's color or race. Science, education, the Word of God, and all the virtues known among men, are recommended to us, not as races, but as men. We are not recommended to love or hate any particular variety of the human family more than any other. Not as Ethiopians; not as Caucasians; not as Mongolians; not as Afro-Americans, or Anglo-Americans, are we addressed, but as men. God and nature speak to our manhood, and to our manhood alone. Here all ideas of duty and moral obligation are predicated. We are accountable only as men. In the language of Scripture, we are called upon to "quit ourselves like men."[101] To those who are everlastingly prating about race men, I have to say: Gentlemen, you reflect upon your best friends. It was not the race or the color of the Negro that won for him the battle of liberty. That great battle was won, not because the victim of slavery was a Negro, mulatto, or an Afro-American, but because the victim

---

100. Matthew 12:24–27.
101. I Corinthians 16:13.

of slavery was a man and a brother to all other men, a child of God, and could claim with all mankind a common Father, and therefore should be recognized as an accountable being, a subject of government, and entitled to justice, liberty and equality before the law, and everywhere else. Man saw that he had a right to liberty, to education, and to equal education and to an equal chance with all other men in the common race of life and in the pursuit of happiness.

While slavery lasted, you know that we could seldom get ourselves recognized in any form of law or language, as men. Our old masters were remarkably shy of recognizing our manhood, even in words written or spoken. They called a man, with a head as white as mine, a boy. The old advertisements were carefully worded: "Run away, my boy Tom, Jim or Harry," never, "my man."

Hence, at the risk of being deemed deficient in the quality of love and loyalty to race and color, I confess that in my advocacy of the colored man's cause, whether in the name of education or freedom, I have had more to say of manhood and of what is comprehended in manhood and in womanhood, than of the mere accident of race and color; and, if this is disloyalty to race and color, I am guilty. I insist upon it that the lesson which colored people, not less than white people, ought now to learn, is, that there is no moral or intellectual quality in the color of a man's cuticle; that color, in itself, is neither good nor bad; that to be black or white is neither a proper source of pride or of shame. I go further, and declare that no man's devotion to the cause of justice, liberty, and humanity, is to be weighed, measured and determined by his color or race. We should never forget that the ablest and most eloquent voices ever raised in behalf of the black man's cause, were the voices of white men. Not for the race; not for color, but for man and manhood alone, they labored, fought and died. Neither Phillips, nor Sumner, nor Garrison, nor John Brown, nor Gerrit Smith was a black man. They were white men, and yet no black men were ever truer to the black man's cause than these and other men like them. They saw in the slave, manhood, brotherhood, and womanhood outraged, neglected and degraded, and their own noble manhood, not their racehood, revolted at the offense. They placed the emphasis where it belonged; not on the mint, anise and cumin of race and color, but upon manhood the weightier matters of the law.

Thus compassed about by so great a cloud of witnesses, I can easily afford to be reproached and denounced for standing, in defense of this principle, against all comers. My position is, that it is better to regard ourselves as a part of the whole than as the whole of a part. It is better to be a member of the great human family, than a member of any particular variety of the human family. In regard to men as in regard to things, the whole is more than a part. Away then with the nonsense that a man must be black to be true to the rights of black men. I put my foot upon the effort to draw lines between the white and the black, or between blacks and so-called Afro-Americans, or race line any where in the domain of liberty. Whoever is for equal rights, for equal education, for equal opportunities for all men, of whatever race or color, —I hail him as a "countryman, clansman, kinsman and brother beloved."

I must not further occupy your time, except to answer briefly the inquiry, "What of the night?" You young people have a right to ask me what the future has in store for you and the people with whom you are classed. I have been a watchman on your walls more than fifty years, so long that you think I ought to know what the future will bring to pass and to discern for you the signs of the times. You want to know whether the hour is one of hope or despair. I have no time to answer this solemn inquiry at length or as it deserves, and will content myself with giving you the assurance of my belief. I think the situation is serious, but it is not hopeless. On the contrary, there are many encouraging signs in the moral skies. I have seen many dark hours and yet have never despaired of the colored man's future. There is no time in our history that I would prefer to the present. Go back to the annexation of Texas, the fugitive slave law times, and the border war in Kansas. The existence of this Industrial School of Manassas is a triumphant rebuke to the cry of despair now heard in some quarters. Nor does it stand alone. It is a type of such institutions in nearly all of the Southern states. Schools and colleges for colored youth are multiplying all over the land. Hampton, Tuskeegee, Cappahoosic, are brilliant examples. The light of education is shedding its beams more brightly and more effectively upon the colored people in the South, than it ever did in the cause of any other emancipated people in the world. These efforts cannot fail in the end to bear fruit.

But it is said that we are now being greatly persecuted. I know it. I admit it. I deplore it. I denounce it. Attempts are being made to set aside the amendments of the Constitution; to wrest from us the elective franchise; to exclude us from respectable railroad cars; to draw against us the color line in religious organizations; to exclude us from hotels and to make us a proscribed class. I know it all, and yet I see in it all a convincing evidence of our progress and the promise of a brighter future. The resistance that we now meet is the proof of our progress. We are not the only people who have been persecuted.

The resistance is not to the colored man as a slave, a servant or a menial, or as a person. It is aimed at the Negro as a gentleman, as a successful man and a scholar. The Negro in ignorance and in rags meets no resistance. He is rather liked than otherwise. He is thought to be in his place. It is only when he acquires education, property, popularity and influence; only when he attempts to rise above his ancient level, when he was numbered with the beasts of the field, and aspires to be a man and a man among men, that he invites repression. Even in the laws of the South excluding him from railroad cars and other places, care is taken to allow him to ride as a servant, a valet or a porter. He may make a bed, but must not sleep in it. He may handle bread, but must not eat it. It is not the Negro, but the quality of the Negro that disturbs popular prejudice. It is his character, not his personality, which makes him an offense or otherwise. In one quality he is smiled upon as a very serviceable animal; in the other he is scorned as an upstart entirely out of his place, and is made to take a back seat. I am not much disturbed by this, for the same resistance in kind, though not in degree, has to be met by white men and white women who rise from lowly conditions. The successful and opulent esteem them as upstarts. A lady as elegant and splendid as Mrs. Potter Palmer,[102] of Chicago, had to submit to the test. She was compelled to hear herself talked about as a "shoddy" upstart; the "wife of a tavern-keeper," and the like, during the Columbian Exposition. But the upstart of today is the elite of tomorrow.

A ship at anchor, with halliards broken, sails mildewed, hull empty, her bottom covered with seaweed and barnacles, meets no resistance. She lies perfectly still; but when she spreads her canvas to the breeze, sets out on her voyage, turns her prow to the open sea, the higher shall be her speed, the greater shall be her resistance. So it is with the colored man. He meets with resistance now, because more than ever, he is fitting himself for a higher life. He is shedding the old rags of slavery and putting on the apparel of freedom.

In conclusion, my dear young friends, be not discouraged. Accept the inspiration of hope. Imitate the example of the brave mariner, who, amid clouds and darkness, amid hail, rain and storm bolts, battles his way against all that the sea opposes to his progress and you will reach the goal of your noble ambition in safety.

---

102. Douglass refers to the Bertha Palmer (1849–1918), the wife of Chicago real estate magnate Potter Palmer (1826–1902).

Index